Caspar F. Goodrich

Report of the British Naval and Military Operations in Egypt, 1882

Vol. 1

Caspar F. Goodrich

Report of the British Naval and Military Operations in Egypt, 1882
Vol. 1

ISBN/EAN: 9783337239916

Printed in Europe, USA, Canada, Australia, Japan

Cover: Foto ©ninafisch / pixelio.de

More available books at **www.hansebooks.com**

War Series, No. III.

INFORMATION FROM ABROAD.

REPORT

OF THE

BRITISH NAVAL AND MILITARY OPERATIONS

IN

EGYPT,

1882.

BY

LIEUTENANT-COMMANDER CASPAR F. GOODRICH,

UNITED STATES NAVY.

OFFICE OF NAVAL INTELLIGENCE,
BUREAU OF NAVIGATION,
NAVY DEPARTMENT,
1883.

WASHINGTON:
GOVERNMENT PRINTING OFFICE.
1883.

918 EG

CONTENTS.

	Page.
Letter of transmittal	7

PART I.

I.—PRELIMINARY	9
The negotiations immediately preceding hostilities.	
II.—GENERAL REVIEW OF THE DEFENSES OF ALEXANDRIA	13
III.—THE ATTACKING FLEET	25
Alexandra — Inflexible — Sultan — Superb — Temeraire—Invincible—Monarch—Penelope—Gun-vessels.	
IV.—THE BOMBARDMENT	31
Order of battle—The action—Report of the senior officer of the offshore squadron—Other details, &c.	
V.—THE EFFECT UPON THE SHIPS.	40
Alexandra—Inflexible—Invincible—Penelope—Sultan—Superb.	
VI.—THE FORTIFICATIONS AND THE DAMAGES SUSTAINED BY THEM	46
Silsileh—Pharos—Ada—The Ras-el-Tin Lines—The Hospital Battery—The Central Battery—The Tower Battery—The Light-House Fort—Sale Aga—Unnamed battery—Oom-el-Kabebe—Mex Lines—Mex Fort—Marsa-el-Khanat—Marabout—Adjemi.	
VII.—GENERAL CONCLUSIONS	69

PART II.

VIII.—OPERATIONS BY THE BRITISH NAVY AT ALEXANDRIA SUBSEQUENT TO THE BOMBARDMENT	79
The occupation—The landing party from the United States fleet—Arrival of troops—The destruction of Egyptian ammunition—The naval battery at Ramleh.	
IX.—OTHER OPERATIONS PRECEDING THE CHANGE OF BASE	87
The land defenses of Alexandria—The occupation of Ramleh—Defenses of Ramleh—The outpost at Antoniades Garden—The reconnaissance in force of August 5—Operations at other points.	
X.—THE COMPOSITION OF THE EXPEDITIONARY FORCE	97
XI.—THE SEIZURE OF THE SUEZ CANAL AND THE CHANGE OF BASE..	105
General report—Work at Port Said—In the canal—At Ismailia—South of Lake Timsah—At Chalouf—Action of M. de Lesseps—British proclamations.	
XII.—THE CAMPAIGN	125
Seizure of Nefiche—El Magfar—Tel-el-Mahuta and Mahsameh—Kassassin—Action of August 28, at Kassassin—Condition of the advanced troops—Action of September 9, at Kassassin—Disposition of Egyptian troops at this time.	

CONTENTS

	Page
XIII.—THE BATTLE OF TEL-EL-KEBIR AND THE CONCLUSION OF THE WAR..	146

The battle—Seizure of Zagazig—Of Cairo—The withdrawal of the British troops.

PART III.

XIV.—THE WORKING OF THE NAVAL TRANSPORT SERVICE	165
XV.—THE ARMED TRAINS	182

One employed at Alexandria—One employed on the Ismailia and Tel-el-Kebir line.

XVI.—THE BOAT TRANSPORT ON THE SWEET WATER CANAL	190
XVII.—THE NAVAL BRIGADE AT TEL-EL-KEBIR	196
XVIII.—THE MARINE BATTALIONS	214

The Royal Marine Light Infantry—The Royal Marine Artillery.

XIX.—THE LINES OF COMMUNICATION	208
XX.—THE COMMISSARIAT AND TRANSPORT CORPS	215
XXI.—THE TROOPS	221

The cavalry—The mounted infantry—The infantry.

XXII.—THE ROYAL ARTILLERY	230

16-pdr.—13-pdr.—Artillery work during the campaign—El Magfar—Tel-el-Mahuta and Mahsameh—Kassassin. (For Tel-el-Kebir see p. 146 *ante*.)

XXIII.—THE ROYAL ENGINEERS	249

The 8th Company—17th Company—18th Company—21st Company—24th Company—26th Company—Establishment of a field company—The pontoon troop—Field park.

XXIV.—THE RAILWAY COMPANY	258
XXV.—THE TELEGRAPH TROOP	266
XXVI.—THE CORPS OF SIGNALERS	277
XXVII.—THE MILITARY POLICE	286
XXVIII.—THE MEDICAL DEPARTMENT	288
XXIX.—THE ARMY POST-OFFICE	295
XXX.—THE INDIAN CONTINGENT	297

Peculiarity of organization in Indian regiments—Equipment, followers, &c. (Kabul scale)—Cavalry—Infantry—The 7-pdr. jointed-steel M. L. R. and the mule battery—Indian rations—Outfit, &c.—Indian transport—Medical arrangements—Veterinary department—Historical notes—Action at Chalouf-Serapeum. (For Tel-el-Kebir see p. — *ante.*)

XXXI.—MISCELLANEOUS	333

U. S. FLAGSHIP LANCASTER, 2D RATE,
Gravesend, England, May 30, 1883.

SIR: In obedience to the Department's order of August 29, 1882, I have the honor to forward a report upon the British naval and military operations in Egypt during the past year.

The report is based upon personal observation on the spot, upon the accounts of officers present at the several engagements, upon official reports, and other trustworthy documents. * * *

My aim has been to make the development and progress of the campaign as clear as possible. I have touched upon organization and equipment only in so far as they are of especial interest, as they serve to throw light upon the methods employed, or as they furnish matter deserving analysis and serious attention. * * *

It would give me pleasure if the State Department could be informed of the valuable assistance rendered me by C. Breed Eynaud, esq., our vice-consul at Malta.

During my stay in Egypt I experienced nothing but kindness wherever my duty called me. Were I to mention the names of those to whom I am indebted for professional and other courtesies, I should simply have to inclose a list of the British officers of both services with whom I was brought in contact. I should, however, be gratified if some acknowledgment other than my own personal thanks could be made to General Lord Wolseley of Cairo, G. C. B., G. C. M. G., &c., for his hospitable reception of me at his headquarters, and for his kindness in affording me all possible facilities for travel and for obtaining necessary data; to Admiral Lord Alcester, G. C. B., &c., for his many acts of politeness, which were only limited, in the direction of technical information, by the confidential nature of many of the official reports; and to Major G. B. N. Martin, R. A., and Captain George S. Clarke, R. E., for peculiarly valuable assistance at the cost of much trouble, and (in the last case) of great personal discomfort.

I am, with great respect, your obedient servant,

C. F. GOODRICH,
Lieutenant-Commander, United States Navy.

To Hon. WILLIAM E. CHANDLER,
Secretary of the Navy, Washington, D. C.

Forwarded.

C. H. BALDWIN,
Rear-Admiral,
Commanding United States Naval Force on European Station.

ABBREVIATIONS.

R. N	Royal Navy.
R. A	Royal Artillery.
R. E	Royal Engineers.
R. H. A	Royal Horse Artillery.
R. M. A	Royal Marine Artillery.
R. M. L. I	Royal Marine Light Infantry.
N. A	N Battery, A Brigade (Royal Horse Artillery).
N. 2	N Battery, Second Brigade (Mountain Artillery).
1. 3	First Battery, Third Brigade (Field Battery).
M. L. R	Muzzle-loading rifle.
B. L. R	Breech-loading rifle.
S. B	Smooth-bore.
Pdr	Pounder.
C^m	Centimetre.
A. D. C	Aide-de-camp.
V. C	Victoria Cross.
C. B	Commander of the Bath.
K. C. B	Knight Commander of the Bath.
G. C. B	Grand Commander of the Bath.
C. M. G	Commander Saint Michael and Saint George.
K. C. M. G	Knight Commander Saint Michael and Saint George.
C. S. I	Commander Star India.
B. W. G	British wire-gauge.
R. L. G	Rifle, large grain.
H. M. S	Her Majesty's Ship.

PART I.

THE BOMBARDMENT OF THE FORTIFICATIONS
AT
ALEXANDRIA.

BRITISH NAVAL AND MILITARY OPERATIONS IN EGYPT.

I.

PRELIMINARY.

The political events which brought about the bombardment of the fortifications at Alexandria, and the dispatch of a British army corps to Egypt, do not come within the province of this report. It will not, however, be out of place to refer briefly to a few of the principal features in the state of affairs immediately preceding hostilities.

It will be remembered that by a series of bold, insubordinate, and successful maneuvers, a group of men, for the most part officers in the Egyptian army, had gradually but surely wrested the power from the hands of the Khedive, their legitimate ruler, and had wielded it in such a manner as to paralyze trade, destroy confidence, and cause the foreign population to desert the country by thousands. The religious fanaticism of the Mohammedans, the vast majority of all the sects in Egypt, had been excited to a dangerous pitch. The presence of the French and British fleets, sent to Alexandria early in the year, in the hope that the mere display of their enormous preponderance of force would exert a calming influence, had only served to still further arouse the now practically universal hatred of the European. The country had already almost come to a standstill in all the arts of peace, when the massacre of June 11 completed the destruction of the hopes, yet entertained by a confiding few, that the excitement would pass away and matters return, of their own accord, to their original condition. The forbearance of the foreign residents was sorely tried; yet, officially and privately, everything possible was done to avoid a conflict with the natives. Ships-of-war of all nations collected at Alexandria to receive and shelter or else forward the refugees that were swarming out of the land at the sacrifice of all their possessions, protection from insult and injury on shore being simply out of the question

The military party openly conceded to be the sole rulers in Egypt now proceeded to take active steps, strengthening the fortifications of Alexandria, mounting new guns, &c. The British admiral, Sir Beauchamp Seymour, in view of the strained relations then existing, and of the formidable character of the unmounted guns at the disposition of the Egyptians, felt that he could not be justified in permitting such open acts of hostile preparation which would have for a result the infliction of increased injury upon the fleet he commanded, in the event of an engagement, now almost inevitable.

The action which Admiral Seymour proceeded to take is indicated by the following telegram, which he sent on the 5th of July to the Admiralty in London:

Shall demand from military governor, to-morrow, cessation of all work on the batteries. As French appear indisposed to act, shall detain Penelope here until result of demand is known.

On the following day he telegraphs again:

Military commander assures me, in reply to my note of to-day, no guns have been recently added to the forts or military preparations made. Dervish Pasha* confirms this statement. No signs of operations since yesterday afternoon, probably in obedience to Sultan's commands. Shall not hesitate acting if works be continued. * * *

This telegram is based upon the following letters of that date:

1. *From Admiral Sir Beauchamp Seymour to the Military Commandant of Alexandria.*

I have the honor to inform your Excellency that it has been officially reported to me that yesterday two or more additional guns were mounted on the sea defenses, and that other warlike preparations are being made on the northern face of Alexandria against the squadron under my command. Under the circumstances I have to notify your Excellency that unless such proceedings be discontinued, or if, having been discontinued, they should be renewed, it will become my duty to open fire on the works in course of construction.

2. *The reply.*

To the Admiral of the British Fleet:

MY FRIEND ENGLISH ADMIRAL: I had the honor to receive your letter of the 6th July, in which you state that you had been informed that two guns had been mounted and that other works are going on on the sea-shore, and in reply I beg to assure you that the said assertions are unfounded. * * *

TOULBA.

On July 9 Admiral Seymour telegraphs to the Admiralty:

With reference to my telegram of the 4th of July, no doubt about armament. Guns are now being mounted in Fort Silsileh. Shall give foreign consuls notice at daylight to-morrow morning, and commence action twenty-four hours after unless forts on the isthmus and those commanding the entrance to the harbor are surrendered.

The Admiralty replied directing the admiral to substitute for the word "surrendered" the words "temporarily surrendered for purposes of disarmament."

The information upon which Admiral Seymour purposed acting was in the shape of a declaration from a lieutenant of Her Majesty's flagship Invincible, quoted here at length:

I, Lieutenant Henry Theophilus Smith-Dorrien, do most solemnly declare that on the morning of the 9th day of July, 1882, at about 7.30 a. m., I drove through the Rosetta

---

*The Turkish commissioner sent to Egypt by His Majesty the Sultan.

gate, and passing the European cemeteries, reached the old quarantine station, where I left my carriage and proceeded on foot to the fort marked on admiralty chart "Tabia el Silsile," and when within 50 yards of the said fort I observed inside two working parties of Arabs, about 200 strong, under the superintendence of soldiers, parbuckling two smooth-bore guns, apparently 32-pounders, towards their respective carriages and slides, which were facing in the direction of the harbor, and which seemed to have been lately placed ready for their reception.

Dated at Alexandria this 9th day of July, 1882.

H. T. SMITH-DORRIEN,
Lieutenant R. N., H. M. S. Invincible.

On the 10th the admiral sent the following letter to Toulba Pasha, the military governor of Alexandria:

I have the honor to inform your Excellency that as hostile preparations, evidently directed against the squadron under my command, were in progress during yesterday at Forts Isali,* Pharos, and Silsili.† I shall carry out the intention expressed to you in my letter of the 6th instant, at sunrise to-morrow, the 11th instant, unless previous to that hour you shall have temporarily surrendered to me, for the purpose of disarming, the batteries on the isthmus of Ras-el-Tin and the southern shore of the harbor of Alexandria.

The answer to the foregoing was signed by Ragheb Pasha, President of the Council and Minister of Foreign Affairs. The translation from the original French is as follows:

ALEXANDRIA, *July* 10, 1882.

ADMIRAL: As I had the honor to promise in the conversation which I had with you this morning, I have submitted to His Highness the Khedive, in a meeting of the Ministers and principal dignitaries of the state, the conditions contained in the letter you were good enough to address this morning to the commandant of the place, according to the terms of which you will put into execution to-morrow, the 11th instant, at daybreak, the intentions, expressed in your letter of the 6th instant to the commandant of the place, if, before that time, the batteries on the isthmus of Ras-el-Tin and the southern shore of the port of Alexandria are not temporarily surrendered to you to be disarmed.

I regret to announce to you that the Government of His Highness does not consider this proposition as acceptable. It does not in the least desire to alter its good relations with Great Britain, but it cannot perceive that it has taken any measures which can be regarded as a menace to the English fleet by works, by the mounting of new guns, or by other military preparations.

Nevertheless as a proof of our spirit of conciliation and of our desire, to a certain extent, to accede to your demand, we are disposed to dismount three guns in the batteries you have mentioned, either separated or together.

If in spite of this offer you persist in opening fire, the Government reserves its freedom of action and leaves with you the responsibility of this act of aggression.

Receive, Admiral, the assurances, &c., &c.

The rejoinder was as brief and to the point as the letter itself was long and rambling. The latter was handed to the admiral during the night of July 10 and 11. The answer was returned at once. It ran thus:

I have the honor to acknowledge the receipt of your communication of yesterday's date, and regret that I am unable to accept the proposal contained therein.

---

* Saleh Aga. † Silsileh.

On July 10 the port was deserted by all the shipping that could get away except the Egyptian Government vessels, which were kept inside and brought close to the Ras-el-Tin palace, out of the reach of shot, and the inshore squadron of the British fleet, composed of the following ships, viz, the Invincible (flag), Monarch and Penelope, ironclads; the Beacon, Bittern, Condor, Cygnet, and Decoy, gun-vessels, and the Helicon, tender and dispatch-boat. Outside the bar were the five armored ships, the Sultan (senior officer's), Alexandra, Inflexible, Superb, and Temeraire, anchored to the eastward of the Corvette Pass, and a large fleet of merchant vessels and men of-war off the mouth of the Central or Boghaz Pass and placed out of the line of fire of the Egyptian batteries.

Pending the preliminary negotiations, and in anticipation of serious work in Egypt, the authorities in England had begun preparations of a warlike nature. The Channel fleet, which had rendezvoused at Malta, was ordered to leave that port on July 9 for Cyprus, within easy reach of Alexandria, having on board two regiments of infantry and some engineers belonging to the garrison of the former place. Two hired transports, the Nerissa and Rhosina, were to follow immediately with more troops. At home, the selection was made of the regiments it was determined to hold in readiness for foreign service; the details of the commissariat and transport companies were perfected and draught animals secured, and the various officers of all branches, likely to be needed, were warned to expect definite orders at any moment.

The Iris, steel dispatch-vessel, with ordnance and other stores, and the Humber, ammunition-ship, were sent to Alexandria from Malta, while an additional light iron-clad, the Penelope, drawing but 17 feet 6 inches of water, and manned by men of the coast-guard or reserve, sailed from the same port on July 3 to reinforce Sir Beauchamp's fleet. Two days later, the Tamar, troop-ship, with the Royal Marine Light Infantry and Royal Marine Artillery battalions, left Malta for Cyprus. Two small iron gun-boats for river service, the Don and the Dee, were sent out from England for contingent use in the Suez Canal, leaving Plymouth on July 9, in tow of the tug Samson. In all the dock-yards and arsenals unusual activity prevailed; extra bodies of workmen were taken on and no exertion spared to expedite the fitting out of ships and the equipment of men in both the army and the navy; while outside, the Naval Transport Department was busy in preparing lists of steamers available as hired transports, and in determining their capacity for troops, for stores, and for animals.

Before passing to the bombardment, and the damage sustained by the opposing forces, it is necessary to consider the nature and strength of the position defended and the resources of the attacking fleet.

II.

GENERAL REVIEW OF THE DEFENSES OF ALEXANDRIA.

A glance at Plate 1 will show that the main harbor of Alexandria is a long, narrow, natural basin of roughly rectangular shape, extending in a general northeasterly and southwesterly direction, between the mainland and an outlying limestone reef, bounded, at one extremity, by the shoulder of land terminating at Fort Adjemi, and at the other by the stem of a T-shaped peninsula upon which the city is built. The length of this harbor is between five and six nautical miles, and its average width one and a quarter.

The western branch of the T-shaped peninsula is the longer of the two. Upon its farther point is the principal light-house of Alexandria. Stretching beyond this, and separated from it by a small channel navigable by boats, is a handsome breakwater, completed in 1874, built upon the reef and inclosing a spacious and well sheltered port. Beyond the city, to the eastward, is a small circular harbor, termed the New Port, used only by small craft.

Through the reef referred to above are three passages. The eastern or Corvette Pass lies close to the breakwater, and affords an entrance for vessels drawing under 18 feet of water. It makes a wide angle with the general direction of the reef.

The Boghaz or Central Pass is the main ship-channel. It has a rather awkward turn at its shallowest part. With very smooth water it is navigable by vessels drawing as much as 22 feet. In general terms its direction is normal to the reef.

The western or Marabout Pass is seldom used, the leading-marks being very far inland and rather close together. A skillful pilot can keep a ship in not less than 23 feet, provided there is no swell on the bar.

The distance over which these approaches are distributed (Adjemi being more than 7 nautical miles from Silsileh) and the exposed situation of the town have necessitated the extension of the sea defenses of Alexandria along a line of inordinate length. The fortifications consist of nearly continuous series of open works, having closed works at the principal salients.

Referring to Plate 1, and beginning at the eastern extremity, it will be seen that the defenses are as follows:

East of the city:
1. Fort Silsileh.

North of the city:
2. Fort Pharos.
3. Fort Ada.
4. The Ras-el-Tin Lines.
5. The Light-House Fort.

South of the city:
6. Fort Saleh Aga.
7. Unnamed open battery.
8. Oom-el-Kabebe Fort.
9. Fort Kumaria.

Southwest of the city:
10. The Mex Lines.
11. Fort Mex.
12. Mex Citadel or Fort Namusia.

West of the city:
13. Fort Marsa-el-Khanat.
14. Fort Marabout.
15. Fort Adjemi.

The nomenclature adopted is that of Admiral Seymour's official report of the bombardment. It must, however, be remembered that several of these works bear other names as well.

The sites of the forts were, in the main, selected with good judgment. Silsileh defends the eastern approach, Pharos the eastern and northern, aided in the latter by Ada, the Ras-el-Tin Lines, and the Light-House Fort. The command of this last fort includes the Corvette and Boghaz Passes and the inner harbor.

Any vessel attempting the Corvette or the Boghaz Pass would also be exposed to the fire of Saleh Aga, Oom-el-Kabebe, Kumaria, the Mex Lines, and Mex, while Marsa-el-Khanat and Marabout were admirably placed to protect the Marabout Pass.

Saleh Aga, Oom-el-Kabebe, and Kumaria were furthermore intended to aid in the defense of the narrow neck of land lying between the Mediterranean on the north, or, strictly speaking, Alexandria Harbor, and Lake Marœotis on the south.

Fort Adjemi is the newest work of all. If ever completed, it will be the strongest point of the sea defense of Alexandria, but it commands a line along which no one would ever dream of approaching, and is, practically, as useless as if planted in the middle of the Sahara.

Besides these, an unimportant work on the southern shore of the eastern harbor, variously designated, may be mentioned as existing. This, with Forts Kumaria and Adjemi, took no part in the action of July 11.

The Pharillon, incorrectly marked as a fort on all charts, is an ancient square tower now in ruinous condition. It mounts no guns.

The land about Alexandria being extremely low, none of these works have any considerable elevation above the sea. They are of old design and construction in every case (except Adjemi), and they derive their value chiefly from the modern Armstrong muzzle-loading rifles with which the principal among them are armed. To adapt the old fortifications to the new guns, the parapets were sometimes heightened and thickened, embrasures cut, and traverses built.

The guns in these works are mounted in the open, none having overhead protection, except those in the casemates of Fort Pharos. In the majority of instances the parapet between the heavy rifles is provided with merlons, while the old-fashioned smooth-bores are mounted *en barbette*.

The rifled guns were generally in batteries apart from the more antiquated ordnance, although this rule was not observed in Forts Ada and Mex.

While guns of nearly every description in their possession were used during the bombardment, the Egyptians placed most reliance upon the Armstrong rifles.

The trace of the works was generally irregular, the irregularity sometimes, as in Fort Oom-el-Kabebe, reaching the grotesque. The form of the fort, both as to trace and profile, seems to have been governed by the configuration of the ground. The Light-House Fort was the only one with a complete bastioned front.

Without exception, in every fort there were buildings, such as shell-stores, barracks, and even magazines, showing well above the crest of the parapet and affording admirable targets to the attack.

Of the materials of which the fortifications are constructed it is impossible to speak in adequate terms. A limestone, quarried near Mex, so soft that it is simply cut out with sharp tools, bonded with coarse lime mortar overcharged with sand, formed the retaining walls, and these were backed with sand. The penetration of the British modern projectiles into this masonry could not be accurately determined. In the scarp of the Light-House Fort blind shell buried themselves more than ten feet, the *débris* behind them preventing the sounding rod from entering further. A similar experience was had at Fort Ada.

The parapets are usually formed of light sand, which, in this dry climate, will stand at a slope of about 30°. In the newer batteries the superior and exterior slopes are covered with a light plaster, which splits off freely when walked over.

The embrasures have 60° train, as a rule, and their soles a depression of from 3° to 5°. Their cheeks are revetted with concrete, and the sill is formed generally of a single piece of granite.

The interior slopes are vertical and of varying height. The actual crest is ordinarily 18 inches above the top of the retaining wall, which is either built of regular masonry or of rough rubble laid in mortar.

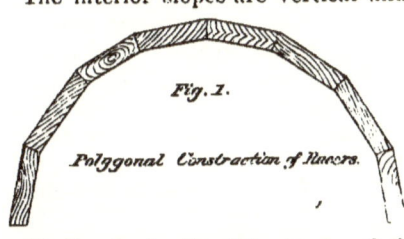

Fig. 1.
Polygonal Construction of Racers.

The sides of the ramps, the slopes in rear of the terreplein, &c., have vertical walls.

The tracks for the slide trucks of the rifled guns are of iron, laid on stone platforms; for those of the smooth-bores, of wood (usually rotten), arranged as shown in Fig. 1.

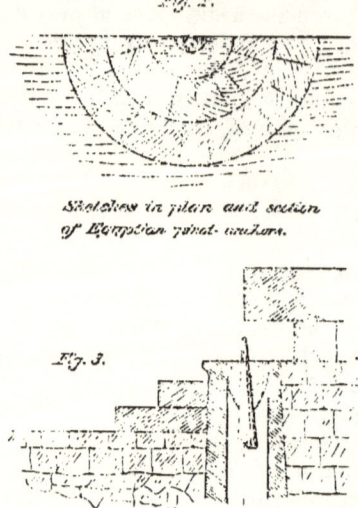

Fig. 2.

Sketches in plan and section of Egyptian pivot mounts.

Fig. 3.

The pivots are secured by wedges in the muzzles of old smoothbore guns sunk on end in the masonry, Figs. 2, 3. As a finish, two neatly-fashioned stone steps are laid up to the muzzle of the gun.

Great care has been taken to arrange the pieces of the steps radially. As a result they give absolutely no support at a place where support is sadly needed. In very few instances have the pivots thus secured stood the strain of the action without complaining, while in some the smooth bore gun has started from its bed. In all cases the pivot proved to be the weakest point in the mounting of the guns. The slide of the Armstrong gun is fitted with two bars or holdfasts (Plate 35), with eyes which slip over the pivot. A key through the pivot holds them in place. The recoil of the gun naturally tends to lift these holdfasts off the pivot. Occasionally the key has broken, or been sheared off, the holdfasts have left the pivot, the slide upended, and the gun been disabled (Plate 127).

The magazines in these forts are, as a general rule, from 5 to 8 feet below the surface. They lack sufficient overhead protection. But, no rule being without its exceptions in this interesting collection of old-fashioned defensive works, those at Forts Ada and Mex were found to be in dangerously-exposed buildings. The passages leading into the magazines are planned solely with reference to convenience, and seem frequently to have been devised with a deliberate view to ready combustion. Ventilation is secured by means of vertical chimneys of the rudest nature, while the lighting arrangements are almost *nil*, a large double horn lantern being employed. As if to invite attack, their lightning-conductors are tall and conspicuous. The floors are boarded and covered with copper or *iron !* The only wonder is how any of these ingeniously-designed man-traps could have escaped destruction during the bombardment, or accidental explosion at any other time.

The shell-houses are always in the open, and are without any pretense of protection. As a consequence, they suffered badly in the action. The shells seem to have been well cared for, but to have been kept unfilled. Traces were very generally visible of the filling of projectiles during the engagement.

The barracks connected with these forts are built in the simplest fashion. A passage-way runs through the middle of a long room, with an earthen platform on each side, 18 inches high and 7 feet broad. This platform serves as a bed. Along the wall is a shelf, and underneath the shelf a row of pegs. The windows are unglazed, but provided with shutters. There was evidently no lavish waste of funds on the accommodations of a private soldier in Egypt.

The ordnance mounted in these works was of the following types:

RIFLES.

10-inch Armstrong M. L. R., of 18 tons.
9-inch Armstrong M. L. R., of 12 tons.
8-inch Armstrong M. L. R., of 9 tons.
7-inch Armstrong M. L. R., of 7 tons.
40-pounder Armstrong B. L. R.

SMOOTH-BORES.	MORTARS.
XV-inch.	XX-inch.
X-inch, heavy.	XIII-inch, sea service.
X-inch, medium.	XIII inch, land service.
X-inch, light.	XI-inch.
6½-inch.	X-inch.
X-inch howitzer.	

The Armstrong guns bear dates ranging from 1869 to 1874. The guns of each caliber are not all of the same pattern.

The 10-inch guns were traversed by gearing, the smaller guns by tackles hooked to posts sunk in the ground. Their carriages were all fitted with plate compressors. Apparently in the heat of action the compressors were not always carefully attended to. Referring to Plate 27, it will be observed that the rear slide trucks are placed very far in towards the muzzle of the gun. The shock of the recoil, especially if the latter is not controlled by the compressor, and if the gun brings up violently against the rear buffers, would occasion a tremendous shearing strain upon the key through the pivot-bolt, and if this key were to yield, nothing would remain to prevent the gun, carriage and all, from assuming the position indicated in Plate 27.

Of the Armstrong guns, one, a 9-inch, was mounted on a Moncrieff carriage, behind the Khedive's palace in the Ras-el-Tin Lines. It would seem as though no one in authority among the Egyptians knew how to place this heavy and costly gun-carriage, for it was simply stuck up in an open space, towering high in air, and offering an admirable target. The gun was not fired during the action.

The use of the XV-inch S. B. is not clearly established; but the weight of evidence appears to be against their having been fired. They are believed to have been cast in France about forty years ago. In external appearance they resemble the other smooth-bores seen in many of the plates.

The 6½-inch guns throw a shot weighing about 36 pounds. In accounts of the engagement they are frequently spoken of as 32-pdrs. They date back to the time of Mehemet Ali.

One X-inch howitzer was mounted in Fort Pharos. The carriage is too rotten to have been used.

The mortars in the Ras-el-Tin Lines " were used pretty freely at first," and a X-inch mortar in Marabout was undoubtedly fired. They scored nothing but misses. One hit would have probably given a new turn to the present development of ordnance.

The B. L. R. 40-pdrs. were four in number. Two in the lower casement of Fort Pharos and one in Mex Citadel were mounted on wooden garrison carriages and were used during the action. The fourth was mounted at the western end of the Ras-el-Tin Lines, on the lift carriage designed by Beverly Kennon, but was not used during the action.

The mounting of the S. B. guns was simple in the extreme—a wooden slide and top carriage, as shown in Plate 33, generally too rotten for safe employment; wooden quoins for elevating and a quadrant for laying the gun. The tracks were even more rotten than the carriages.

The Egyptian supply of ammunition was enormous. There were two kinds of M. L. R. shell, common and battering, in lavish profusion. The store of shrapnel was not so great. There was a fair proportion of chilled shot.

There were hundreds of barrels of powder. The powder was compressed in disks, shown in Figs. 4 and 5, manufactured by Messrs. Curtis & Harvey. The cartridges appear to have been filled as needed during the engagement. The rudeness of the scales found in or near the magazines must have caused the charge to vary in weight, and may thus account for a portion of the great variation in range which was a characteristic of the Egyptian practice.  The disks described were for use with the rifled guns. For the smooth-bores a large-grained, finely-glazed powder, made by the same English firm, was provided. In addition some barrels of powder from the British Government factory at Waltham Abbey were found in the magazines. At Fort Marabout there was an ample supply of filled cartridges.

Their stock of fuzes included Armstrong's combined time and percussion fuze, and two simple percussion fuzes, besides other well-known forms.

The former, Figs. 6, 7, and 8, contain two independent trains. The first or percussion train is at the base of the fuze. X is a pellet of fulminate of mercury, and Y a quick-composition, both carried by a plunger, a, on the outside of which is turned a broad, shallow groove to receive a brass ring, b, resting between the lower shoulder of the groove and the cylindrical guard c. The shock of firing dislodges the ring and leaves the plunger free, on impact, to rush forward against the steel needle d, exploding the priming, and hence, in turn, the shell.

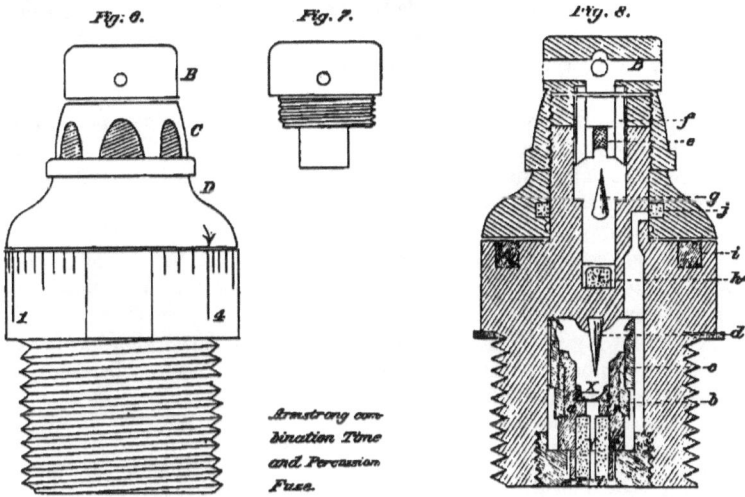

Armstrong combination Time and Percussion Fuze.

The time fuze is composed of the following parts: a primer ignited by concussion as the shot leaves its seat; a quick-match conveying the flame to a slow-composition; a mechanical device by which the amount of this slow-composition to be burned can be regulated; and, lastly, a channel admitting the flame, after the desired lapse of time, through the bottom of the fuze to the bursting-charge. The primer e is carried by a plunger, f, held in the thimble B by a fine copper wire (which breaks by the inertia of the plunger as the gun is fired). d is a steel needle,

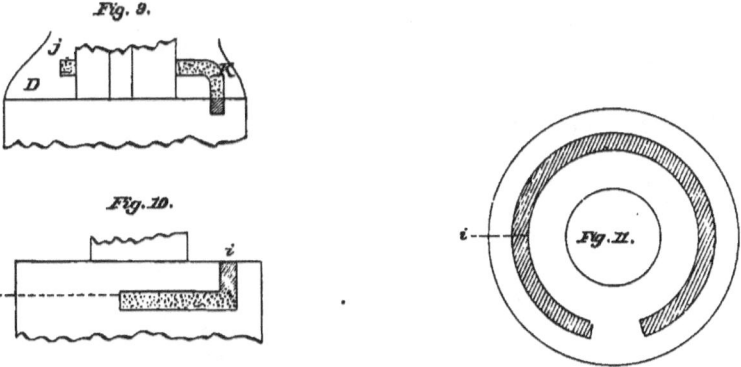

which ignites the primer. The flame communicates with a quick-match, h, extending radially across the fuze. The time-composition is pressed into a circular groove, i, Fig. 11, on the top of the shoulder. D, Fig. 9, is a cover turned at will and clamped by the nut C. On the inside of D is a groove, j, filled with quick-match. A fire-hole, k, Fig. 19, also containing quick-composition, leads to this groove from a point at the bottom of the cover D. This point on the base of d corresponds to the index mark on the outside of the fuze. From this groove j there is a free passage to the base of the fuze, interrupted only by the safety disk i, which is blown out in action by the flame on its way to the bursting-charge of the shell.

The safety appliance in the percussion train seems less trustworthy than that of our Schenkel fuze, and the time arrangement appears very complicated.

This fuze was employed later in the war by the battery of jointed mountain-gun accompanying the Indian Contingent. The officers of this battery spoke well of its action.

The following is a description of the percussion fuze which was found after the bombardment in the greatest numbers, and may be assumed to have been most employed.

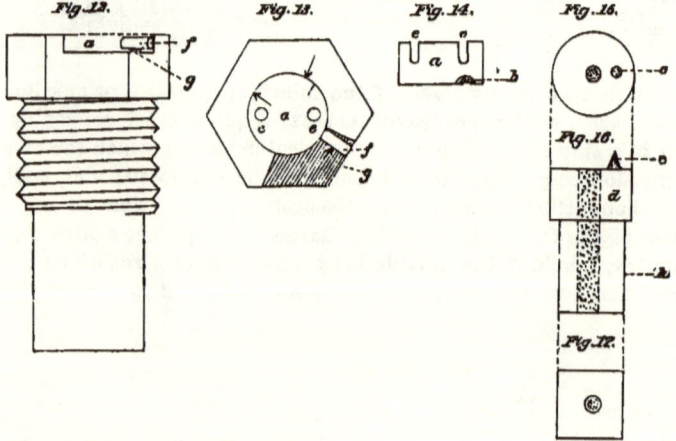

The disk a, Figs. 12, 13, 14, and 15, contains the fulminating composition in a chamber, b, placed eccentrically underneath. The needle c is in the plunger d, and is also placed eccentrically. When a is turned through 90° by means of a key fitting into the key-holes $e\ e$, the fulminate is brought opposite the needle and the fuze is rendered active. The plunger has a square tail working in a square hole in the stock, and hence cannot be turned. It is held near the bottom of the stock by a brittle wire. The stock is cut away on the face for an angular distance of 90°, Figs. 12 and 13. In this space a pin, f, inserted horizontally into the disk a, finds room to move. It is held, usually, in the safety position of the disk by a slight burr, g, cut into the stock with a sharp tool. The fuze is set by moving the plug *a* until two feather-marks, one on the plug and one on the fuze stock, coincide. The plunger, Figs. 16 and 17, contains a magazine of quick-composition, *h*.

A second type of percussion fuze was not examined, through lack of appliances for dealing with such dangerous articles. It is of brass, and very beautifully finished. Its external appearance is shown in Figs. 18 and 19.

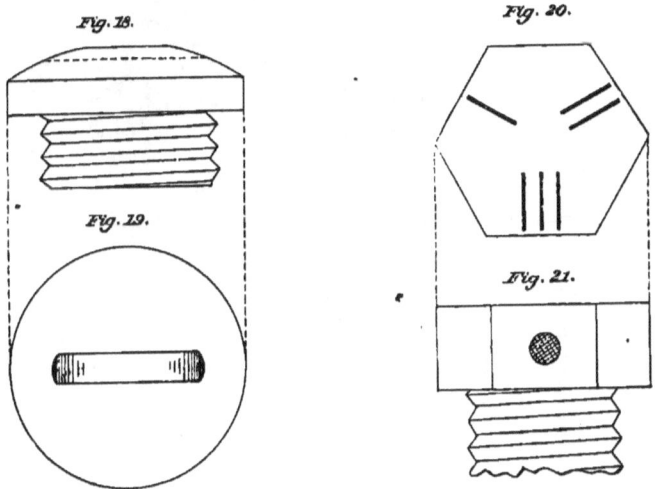

Fig. 18.   Fig. 20.

Fig. 19.   Fig. 21.

A metal time fuze was used having a hexagonal head, on three sides of which were chisel marks, Figs. 20 and 21. These sides had each a hole plugged with a soft resinous composition. It is supposed that the marks corresponded to three known times of burning, but the fuze could not be opened for investigation.

The other time fuzes were of the well-known Boxer type. In some cases they bore the British broad arrow, and were packed in boxes on which were pasted instructions for use from the British Royal Laboratory.

The mortar time fuzes were of the usual pattern. The longest of these fuzes burns for 60 seconds.

For primers, an ordinary friction tube of the cross pattern was employed, as well as another type in which the fulminate is packed in the main tube and is exploded by a fine twisted wire passing through it. In one smooth-bore gun a quick-match was found in the vent.

On the part of the Egyptians, at least, the manner of carrying on the action was that of the last century. An enemy of to-day would have planted torpedoes in front of the fortifications and in the entrances to the harbor to such an extent as to seriously embarrass the attack, but the Egyptians neglected this branch of the art of military defenses, although ample means were at hand. At Mex, after the bombardment, were found—

500-pound gun-cotton mines (Figs. 22, 23) 87
250-pound gun-cotton mines (Figs. 24, 25) 87
100-pound electro-contact mines (Fig. 27) 500
Circuit closers (Fig. 26) 400
Buoys, &c., in large numbers.

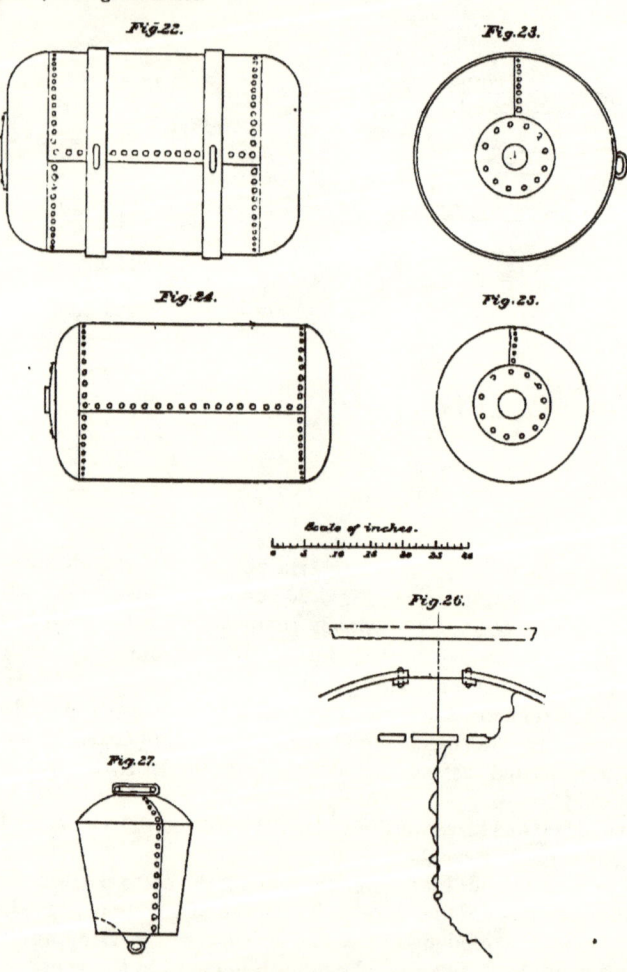

A large number of copper and zinc plates were found, and some sulphuric acid, but no complete electric batteries.

The mouth-pieces of the mines were found in a ravelin near Mex. Each contained two disks of gun-cotton fitted with a detonator. One wire led from the detonator through the mouth-piece, and the other was soldered to the inside of the envelope, making a terminal *earth*.

All the appliances necessary for torpedo operations except cable were present in sufficient quantities. Of cable only two knots could be found. It was 7-strand copper wire of the usual size (about 22 B. W. G.), and was insulated with gutta percha.

Besides the gun-cotton blown up by the Monarch during the engagement, other stores were discovered near Mex. The gun-cotton was stowed in five wooden sheds, constructed for the purpose, each containing about five tons. That found after the bombardment was burnt by men from H. M. S. Hecla. In a smith's shed were 166 cases holding 664 of Abel's mechanical primers. The circuit closer was on a well-known principle. A vertical rod, articulated at the lower extremity, carries near its upper extremity an insulated metal collar which is one pole of the circuit. The rod is kept centered in a watertight aperture in the head of the case by a flexible diaphragm. A heavy shock would bring the collar in contact with the metal case, put the pole to earth, and thus complete the circuit (see Fig. 26).

The failure to employ this torpedo apparatus must be regarded as due to the lack of experience and competent *personnel*. Professionally it is to be regretted that such a favorable opportunity of demonstrating the real value of this system of harbor defense was lost. The movements of the fleet would at least have been very greatly hampered by the moral effect, even if the ships themselves had entirely escaped injury.

The defenses of Alexandria may be divided into two distinct lines: the northern, or outer, with terminals at Pharos and the Light-House; and the southern, or inner, between Saleh Aga and Marsa-el-Khanat, with an advanced flank at Marabout.

Counting only those guns which could be trained upon the attacking fleet, the northern line was capable of bringing to bear the following pieces, viz:

10-inch Armstrong M. L. R	4
9-inch Armstrong M. L. R	*9
8-inch Armstrong M. L. R	5
7-inch Armstrong M. L. R	2
40-pdr. Armstrong B. L. R	3
XV-inch S. B	6
X-inch S. B	31
6½-inch S. B	25
XV-inch mortar	1
XIII-inch mortars	13
XI-inch mortars	2
X-inch mortars	2
In all	103

The twenty large modern rifled guns were all in good condition, and without exception were used during the bombardment. They formed

---

* That mounted on the Moncrieff carriage is not counted.

the main reliance of the Egyptians, and a fair proportion of the damage inflicted upon the ships was due to them.

It is difficult to ascertain the exact number of the S. B. guns employed, nor indeed can it be said that any exact number was employed, as the conditions of the battle changed at every moment. Not less than one-fourth must be thrown out of consideration, as mounted too badly for efficient or even safe use.

The mortars played, as has been stated, a very insignificant part in the engagement.

Including one of the Inflexible's turrets, the working broadside of the offshore squadron opposed to these batteries consisted originally of the following heavy guns:

16-inch M. L. R. of 81 tons	2
12-inch M. L. R. of 25 tons	1
10-inch M. L. R. of 18 tons	15
9-inch M. L. R. of 12 tons	2
8-inch M. L. R. of 9 tons	6
In all	26

These were supplemented later by three more of 25 tons and two of 18 tons (the Temeraire's effective battery), and by the two 81-ton guns in the Inflexible's forward turret. These thirty-three guns were all used against Ada and Pharos.

The inner line proper (not taking Marabout into consideration) could bring to bear the following pieces, viz:

10-inch Armstrong, M. L. R	1
9-inch Armstrong, M. L. R	1
8-inch Armstrong, M. L. R	5
40-pdr. Armstrong, B. L. R	1
XV-inch S. B.	4
X-inch S. B.	33
6½-inch S. B.	39
XIII-inch mortars	9
XI-inch mortars	5
X-inch mortars	4
In all	102

The eleven heavy modern guns were all manned and fired, but hardly more than one-half of the smooth-bores were fit for use, while men were lacking to properly work even this small proportion of serviceable guns. Twenty-five may be regarded as a fair approximation to the number of the smooth bores served steadily at the outset.

The inshore squadron could employ the following heavy guns (considering only the broadside engaged), viz:

12-inch M. L. R. of 25 tons	*4
9-inch M. L. R. of 12 tons	5
8-inch M. L. R. of 9 tons	4
In all	13

* In the beginning of the action the Temeraire assisted with her two barbette 25-ton guns of 12-inch caliber.

The bow and stern guns of the Monarch were of great value, and may certainly be counted as worth one more 9-inch gun.

The fact that the attacking force could concentrate its whole fire against any single work on shore must not be lost sight of. It is thus possible to express the phases which the engagement either assumed, or might have been made to assume, in the form of numerical ratios.

Fort Pharos.. 4 to 33 (actual).
Fort Ada.. 5 to 28 or 33 (actual).
Ras-el-Tin Lines... 7 to 26.
Light-House Fort.. 4 to 26.
Fort Mex... 5 to 14 or 16 (actual).

These ratios for the northern front might be almost indefinitely increased if allowance were made for the enormously superior weight of some of the British guns. They will, however, have sufficiently served their purpose if they convey a general, and not altogether inaccurate, notion of the relative strength of the opposite sides in the action of July 11.

III.

THE ATTACKING FLEET.

Admiral Seymour had at his disposal eight iron-clads and five wooden gun-boats. Of the former, five attacked the outer line of defenses, while the remaining three operated inside of the reef stretching from the breakwater to Fort Marabout. The gun-boats were variously employed, their most serious effort being directed against Fort Marabout.

It is thought that a brief description of each vessel will result in a clearer conception of its powers of offense and defense.

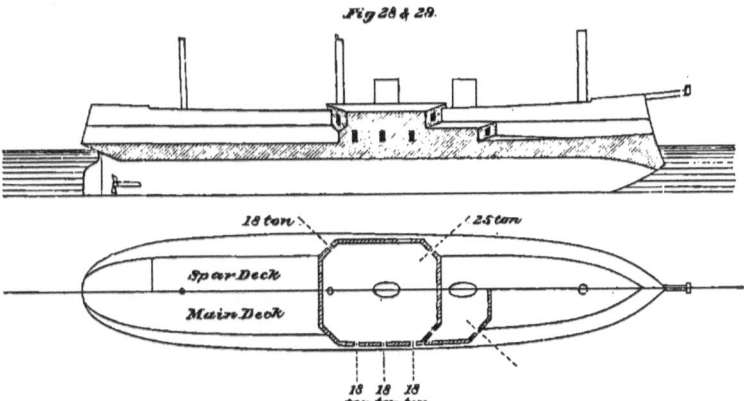

The outside squadron was composed of the Alexandra, Inflexible, Sultan, Superb, and Temeraire, and was under the command of Captain Walter J. Hunt-Grubbe, C. B., A. D. C., as senior officer.

The Alexandra, completed in 1877, is of 9,490 tons displacement, and 8,610 horse-power (indicated). A conventional view of her is given in Fig. 28. The armored parts are shaded. In Fig. 29 are half plans of her spar and main decks. She is a belted casemate ship, but possesses ample bow and stern fire. Her armor is 13¼* inches thick at the water-line amidships, and tapers fore and aft to 10 inches. The lower casemate has 9½ inches of armor, and the upper, 6 inches. The main-deck battery consists of eight 10-inch M. L. R. of 18 tons, the two forward ones being in corner ports and therefore capable of delivering their fire either ahead or abeam. The spar-deck battery comprises two 12-inch M. L. R. of 25 tons, and two 10-inch M. L. R. of 18 tons, all mounted in corner ports. The larger guns can fire from ahead to a little abaft the beam, and the smaller from a little forward of the beam to directly astern. Forward of the casemate, the ship's side tumbles home to allow bow fire from both main and spar deck batteries; abaft the casemate, the same construction is adopted at the height of the spar deck.

The Alexandra is well sparred, and is rigged as a bark. She carried a crew of 670 men. She was Admiral Seymour's regular flagship, from which he had temporarily shifted his flag to a lighter vessel, capable of readily entering the harbor of Alexandria.

The Inflexible is a double-turreted sea-going ship of 11,880 tons displacement, and 8,010 indicated horse-power. Figs. 30 and 31. She

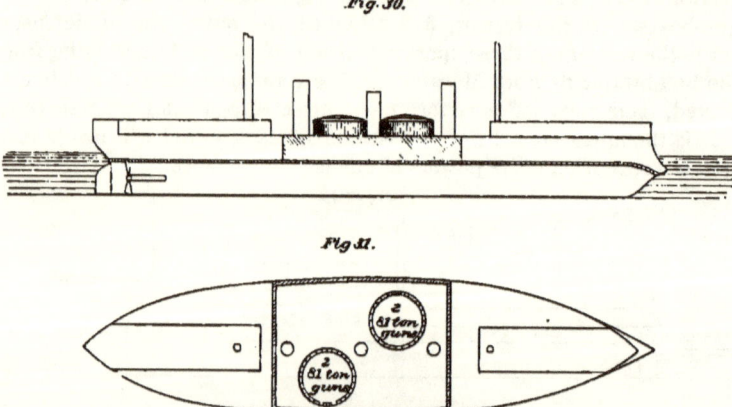

Fig. 30.

Fig. 31.

has a central casemate, reaching to the spar deck and protecting the vital parts of the vessel. The armor of this casemate is on the sandwich principle. At water line 12 inches of iron, 11 inches of wood, 12 inches of iron, 6 inches of wood, inner skin of 2 inches of iron. Above water line 12 inches of iron, 11 inches of wood, 8 inches of iron, 10 inches of wood, and an inner skin of 2 inches of iron. Below water 12 inches of iron, 11 inches of wood, 4 inches of iron, 14 inches of wood, and an

---

*The inner skin is included in the thickness of the armor.

inner skin of 2 inches of iron. An underwater armored deck, 3 inches thick, extends from this casemate to the bow and stern. The turrets are set at diagonally opposite corners of the citadel, so as to give complete fore-and-aft fire to all the guns. The turret armor is also on the sandwich principle, consisting of an outer compound plate of 4 inches of steel on 5 inches of iron, 8 inches of wood, 7 inches of iron, in all 16 inches of metal. In each turret are two 16-inch M. L. R. of 81 tons weight.

Forward of and abaft the turrets are comparatively narrow superstructures (21 and 30 feet wide), each about 100 feet in length, and built, for the accommodation of the crew and officers, inside the lines of fire. On top of the superstructures are a few small pieces, B. L. R. 20-pdrs., Nordenfeldts, &c.

The elevating and depressing of the 81-ton guns is performed automatically. These guns have no top carriage, properly speaking. The trunnions rest on blocks traveling on fixed slides, the recoil being taken up in hydraulic cylinders. The breech rests on a third block, sliding on a beam, which is capable of being turned about one end by a third piston. The gun is worked entirely by hydraulic power.

The Inflexible is brig-rigged, and, though the largest man-of-war afloat to-day, carries only 484 men.

The Sultan, launched in 1870, is represented in Figs. 32 and 33. She

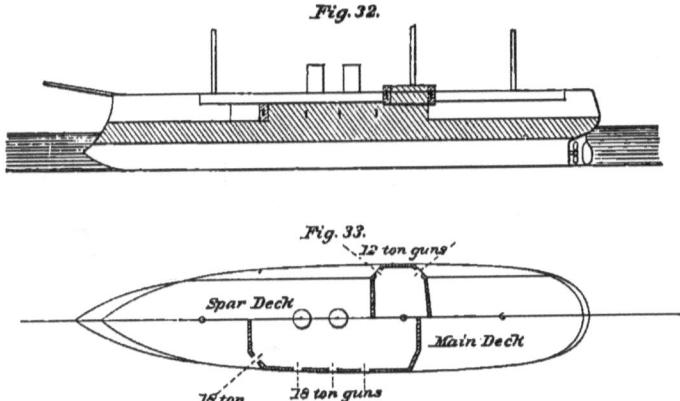

is of 9,290 tons displacement, and has engines capable of developing 7,736 horse-power. She is bark-rigged. She has an armored belt around the water-line and an armored citadel on the main deck, at the forward end of which is a recessed port for obtaining bow fire. In this casemate are eight 10-inch M. L. R. of 18 tons weight. On the upper deck is a smaller casemate containing four 9-inch M. L. R. of 12 tons weight, for which fore-and-aft fire is obtained by carrying the spar-deck rail inboard out of the line of fire. The armor varies in thickness from 11 to 7 inches.

The Sultan had but recently gone into commission, with a crew of 400 men.

The Superb, of 9,170 tons displacement and 7,430 indicated horsepower, was originally designed for the Turkish Government. She was completed in 1878, and sold by the builders to the English Government and equipped for sea-service in 1880. She is represented in Figs. 34

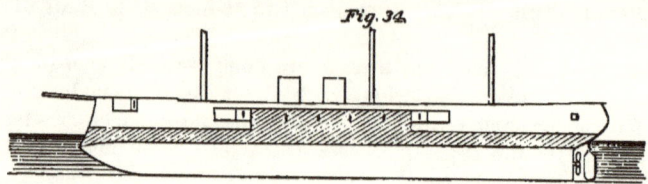

Fig. 34.

and 35. She has an armored belt at the water-line and a casemate amidships, on the main deck, in which are mounted twelve 10-inch M. L. R. of 18 tons weight. The corner guns are in recessed ports, giving

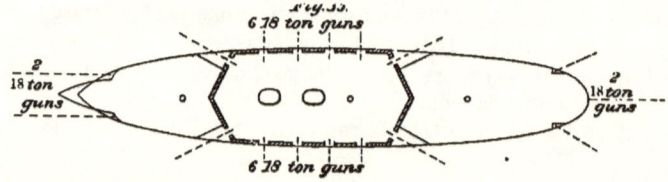

fire nearly ahead and astern. Four 10-inch M. L. R. of 18 tons weight complete her battery, two being carried in the bow and two in the

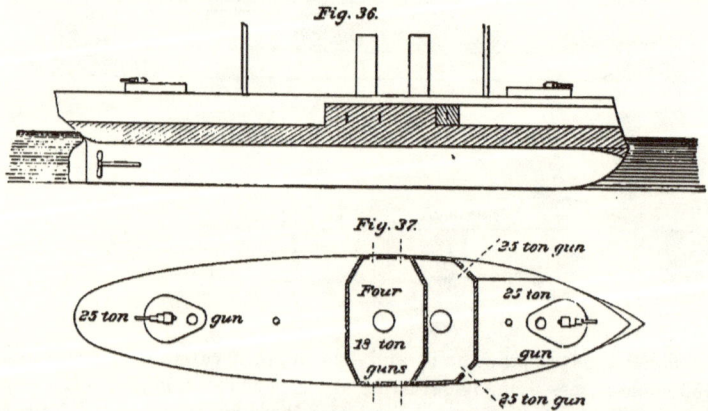

stern. The armor is 13½ inches thick; that on the belt tapering to 7¼ inches forward and 5½ inches aft. The Superb is bark-rigged, and she has a crew of 620 men.

The Temeraire, shown in Figs. 36 and 37, is a belted casemate vessel, carrying on the upper deck two fixed pear-shaped open turrets. In the casemate are four 10-inch M. L. R. of 18 tons, and two 11-inch M. L. R. of 25 tons, the latter firing from corner ports, either ahead or abeam. The turrets have each a 25-ton gun mounted on the Rendel system. The guns are fired *en barbette*, then disappear by their own recoil; are loaded under cover and raised again to the firing position. The forward turret is protected by 11½ inches of armor, the after one by 9½ inches. The armored belt is 12½ inches thick amidships and tapers towards the bow and stern. The casemate armor varies from 10 to 8 inches in thickness. This very efficient vessel displaces 8,547 tons, and has engines capable of developing 7,520 horse-power. She is officially stated to have cost less than $2,000,000. Like the Inflexible she is brig-rigged. Her crew numbered 534 men.

The inshore squadron of armored ships under the more immediate command of the Admiral consisted of the Invincible (flagship), the Monarch, and the Penelope.

The Invincible, of 6,000 tons displacement, and engined up to 4,800 horse-power, was designed in 1867. She is represented in Figs. 38 and 39.

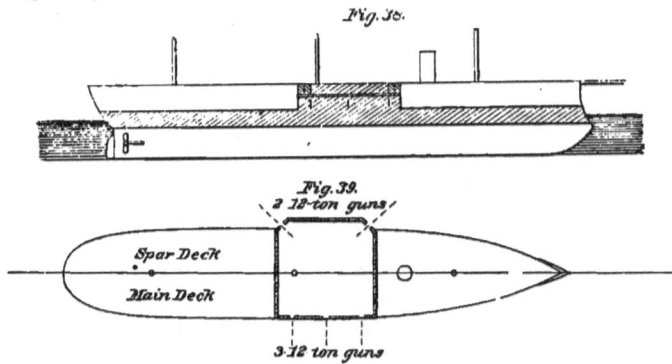

She has an armored belt and a short casemate. The main-deck casemate mounts six 9-inch M. L. R. of 12 tons weight. The spar-deck battery is composed of four similar guns, carried in a redoubt which projects sufficiently clear of the ship's side to give the desired fore and-aft fire from corner ports. In addition are four unprotected M. L. R. 64-pdrs. Her armor ranges from 9¼ to 5¼ inches in thickness. Her crew was 450 strong.

The Monarch, Figs. 40 and 41, is a masted sea-going, double-turreted monitor with high free-board, of 8,320 tons displacement and 7,840 indicated horse-power. She has an armored belt, an armored citadel, and armored ends. In the turrets are four 12-inch M. L. R. of 25 tons weight, protected by 11½ inches of iron. In the bow are two 9-inch M. L. R. of 12 tons weight, and in the stern one 7-inch M. L. R. of 6½ tons weight. On her hurricane deck, which extends fore and aft above the turrets, are eight Nordenfeldt guns. Her crew is composed of 515 men. Her belt armor varies in thickness from 8½ to 5 inches.

The Penelope, the smallest of the iron-clads which took part in the engagement, is of the same general type as the Superb, but smaller (see Figs. 34, 35). The Penelope is classed as a corvette. She displaces 4,470 tons, and is engined up to 4,700 indicated horse-power. She is a belted casemate cruiser, mounting eight 8-inch M. L. R. of 9 tons. She also carries three B. L. R. 40-pdrs. The maximum thickness of her armor is 6 inches, and her draught only 17 feet 6 inches. Her crew is 223 men.

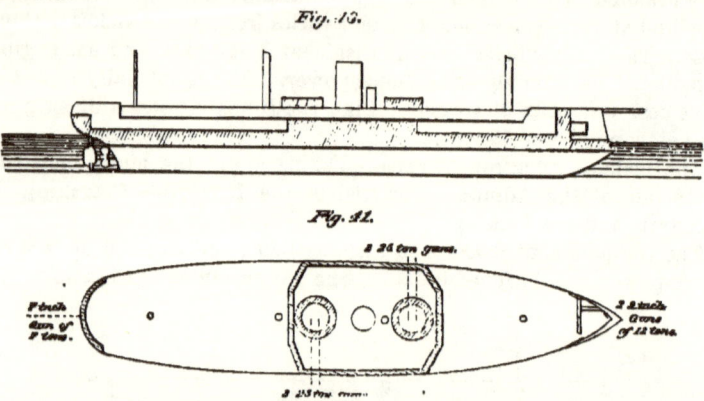

In addition the ships carried some B. L. R. 20-pdrs., and were well supplied with Nordenfeldts and Gatlings. The ships themselves, although spoken of by the popular name of iron-clad, are all iron-armored vessels.

The gun-boats present at Alexandria during the bombardment are all of composite construction. The larger ones are bark-rigged.

The Bittern displaces 805 tons, can develop 850 horse-power, and carries one 7-inch M. L. R. pivot, and two B. L. R. 40-pdrs. Her crew is composed of 90 men.

The Condor is of about the same size. She carries one 7-inch M. L. R. pivot, and two M. L. R. 64-pdrs. Her crew is 100 strong.

The Beacon displaces 603 tons, develops 510 horse-power, while the Cygnet and Decoy are of but 440 tons displacement. Their crews were 75, 60, and 50 men, respectively. They were armed with two 64-pdr. M. L. R. and two B. L. R. 20-pdrs. The Cygnet and Decoy are barkentine-rigged.

July 10 was spent in clearing the ships for action. The lower rigging was "come up" in the line of fire and was carried inboard. The topgallant masts were struck, bowsprits rigged in (on board the armored ships) until the cap touched the stem, leaving the whiskers and head rigging outboard. The lower and topsail yards were kept aloft.

On board the gun-boats all the yards were sent down, and the topmasts housed, in addition to the other preparations usual on such occasions.

IV.

THE BOMBARDMENT.

During the night of July 10 and 11 the vessels of the British fleet took up the positions to which they had been severally assigned. At daybreak of the 11th the nature of the attack became evident. The heavier ships were placed to engage the northern line and the lighter ships the inner line. By referring to Plate 1, these original positions may be seen plotted at E, F, G, H. The Alexandra, Sultan, and Superb maneuvered under way at the outset, firing at the Light-House Fort and Ras-el-Tin Lines. The Inflexible was at anchor, directing the fire of one turret against the Light-House Fort, that of the other against Oom-el-Kabebe. The Temeraire was aground during the early part of the day firing at Mex. The Invincible, Monarch, and Penelope were under way out of the line of the Temeraire's fire, engaging Mex and Marsa-el-Khanat.

The day was perfectly clear and the sea smooth. The wind was light from the northward and westward, blowing the smoke from the ships towards the shore and thus *obscuring the target for a long time after each fire and making it difficult to watch and profit by the fall of the shot.* A gun captain can correct his aim much better when he sees himself where the shot strikes than when it is reported from aloft by an observer. This circumstance and the fact that *the sun at the beginning of the action was in the eyes* of the British gunners were the only disadvantages under which the attack labored. Otherwise it would have been impossible to select more propitious conditions.

Admiral Seymour's order of battle is here quoted at length:

INVINCIBLE, *at Alexandria, July* 10, 1882.

MEMORANDUM.

In the event of my not receiving a satisfactory answer to a summons which I shall send to the Military Governor of Alexandria, calling on him to deliver up to me, temporarily, the works on the southern shore of the harbor, and those on the Ras-el-Tin Peninsula, the squadron under my command will attack the forts as soon as the twenty-four hours given to neutrals to leave the place have expired, which will be at 5 a. m. of the 11th. There will be two attacks:

1. From the inside of the harbor, in which the Invincible, Monarch, and Penelope will take part.
2. By the Sultan, Superb, Temeraire, Alexandra, and Inflexible, from outside the breakwater.

Action will commence by signal from me, when the ship nearest the newly-erected earthwork near Fort Ada* will fire a shell into the earthwork.

On the batteries opening on the offshore squadron in reply, every effort will be made by the ships to destroy the batteries on the Ras-el-Tin Peninsula, especially the Light-House Battery bearing on the harbor. When this is accomplished, the Sultan,

---

* The Hospital Battery, Plates 21 and 22.

Superb, and Alexandra will move to the eastward and attack Fort Pharos, and, if possible, the Silsileh Battery.

The Inflexible will move down this afternoon to the position off the Corvette Pass assigned to her yesterday, and be prepared to open fire on the guns in the Mex Lines, in support of the inshore squadron, when signal is made.

The Temeraire, Sultan, and Alexandra will flank the works on Ras-el-Tin.

The gun-vessels and gun-boats will remain outside and keep out of fire until a favorable opportunity offers itself of moving into the attack of Mex.

Ships must be guided in a great measure by the state of the weather, whether they anchor or remain under way. If they anchor, a wire hawser should be used as a spring.

The men are to have breakfast at 4 30 a. m. and are to wear blue working rig.

The inshore squadron will be under my personal command; the offshore ships under that of Captain Hunt-Grubbe, C. B., of the Sultan.

The Helicon and Condor will act as repeating ships.

Finally, the object of this attack is the destruction of the earthworks and dismantling of the batteries on the sea fronts of Alexandria. It is possible that the work may not be accomplished under two or three days.

Shell is to be expended with caution, notwithstanding that the Humber, with a fair proportion of reserve ammunition, may be expected here on the 12th.

Should the Achilles arrive in time, she is to attack Fort Pharos, or place herself where the senior officer of the offshore squadron may direct.

BEARINGS.

Line of ships NE. by E., 2¼ cables apart.

Alexandra.

Eunostos* light-house SE. by E. ¼ E.
Breakwater light-house S. ¾ W.
Black Rock† Battery, distance, 1,500 yards.

Sultan.

Eunostos light-house E. by S. ¼ S.
Breakwater light-house S. ¼ W.
Barrack Point,‡ 1,750 yards.

Superb.

Eunostos light house E. ⅜ S.
Breakwater light-house S. ¼ E.
Light-house, 1,950 yards.

ADDITIONAL BEARINGS.

Inflexible, 3,700 yards N. by W. of Mex.
Temeraire, 3,500 yards NNW. of Mex.
Penelope, }
Invincible, } 1,000 to 1,300 yards W. by N. of Mex.
Monarch, }

I have, &c.,

F. BEAUCHAMP SEYMOUR,
Admiral and Commander-in-Chief.

To the CAPTAINS and OFFICERS
Commanding H. M. Ships at and off Alexandria.

---

* The principal light-house of Alexandria.

† Afterwards known as Central Battery, Ras-el-Tin Lines.

‡ Half way between the Tower Battery, Ras-el-Tin Lines, and the Light-House Fort.

PLATE 1.

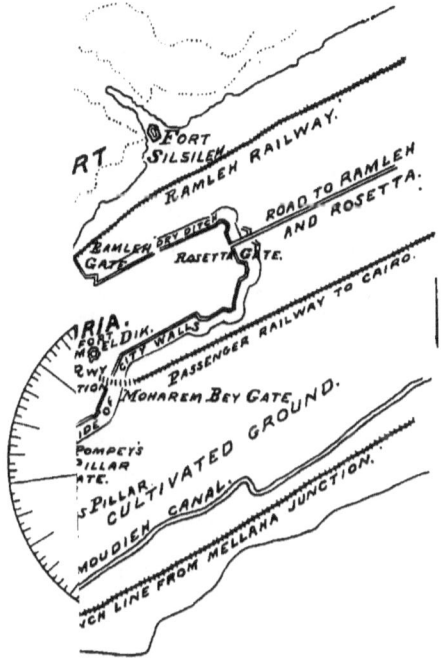

'PTIEH (POLICE STATION.)
GTHE RUE FRANQUE.
CARACOLS (STATION HOUSES)
MERICAN CONSULATE.
Fort BY THE OUTSIDE SQUADRON.
N BY THE INFLEXIBLE.
" " TEMERAIRE.
D BY THE INSHORE SQUADRON.

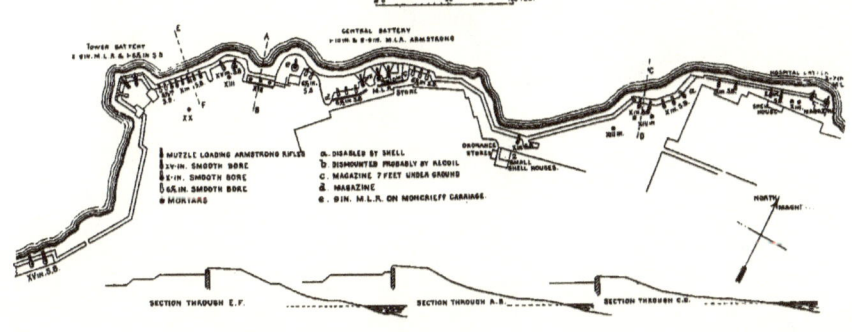

To the foregoing may be added the general instructions to commanding officers to fire back at any fort that might open on them.

The following is the official report of the action as given by Admiral Seymour. The paragraphs relating to individuals only are omitted:

INVINCIBLE, at *Alexandria*, *July* 20, 1882.

SIR:

1. In continuation of my official report of proceedings, dated the 19th instant, I have the honor to submit, for their lordships' information, a more detailed account of the action which took place on the 11th, between the squadron under my command and the forts which defend Alexandria, than I was enabled to forward at that time.

2. As will be seen by the inclosed order of battle, a copy of which was supplied to each captain, I had decided to make two attacks, one by the Sultan, Superb, and Alexandra on the north face of Ras-el-Tin, supported by the fire from the after-turret of the Inflexible, anchored off the entrance to the Corvette Pass, thus enfilading the Light-House batteries; the other, by the Invincible, Monarch, and Penelope from inside the reefs, aided by the fire of the Inflexible's forward turret and the Temeraire, which took up a position close to the fairway buoy of the Boghaz or principal pass leading into Alexandria Harbor. The Helicon and Condor were detailed for duty as repeating ships, and the Beacon, Bittern, Cygnet, and Decoy were employed as directed by signal during the day.

3. At 7 a. m. on the 11th I signaled from the Invincible to the Alexandra to fire a shell into the recently-armed earthworks termed the Hospital Battery, and followed this by a general signal to the fleet, "Attack the enemy's batteries," when immediate action ensued between all the ships, in the positions assigned to them, and the whole of the forts commanding the entrance to the harbor of Alexandria. A steady fire was maintained on all sides until 10.30 a. m., when the Sultan, Superb, and Alexandra, which had been hitherto under way, anchored off the Light-House Fort, and by their well-directed fire, assisted by that of the Inflexible, which weighed and joined them at 12.30 p. m., succeeded in silencing most of the guns in the forts on Ras-el-Tin; still some heavy guns in Fort Ada kept up a desultory fire. About 1.30 p. m. a shell from the Superb, whose practice in the afternoon was very good, blew up the magazine and caused the retreat of the remaining garrison. These ships then directed their attention to Fort Pharos, which was silenced with the assistance of the Temeraire, which joined them at 2.30 p. m., when a shot from the Inflexible dismounted one of the heavy guns.* The Hospital Battery was well fought throughout, and, although silenced for a time by a shell from the Inflexible, it was not until 5 p. m. that the artillerymen were compelled to retire from their guns by the fire of the offshore squadron and the Inflexible. The Invincible, with my flag, supported by the Penelope, both ships being at anchor, the latter on one occasion shifting berth, and assisted by the Monarch, under way inside the reefs, as well as by the Inflexible and Temeraire in the Boghaz and Corvette Channels, succeeded, after an engagement of some hours, in silencing and partially destroying the batteries and lines of Mex. Fort Marsa-el-Khanat was destroyed by the explosion of the magazine after half an hour's action with the Monarch.†

About 2 p. m., seeing that the gunners of the western lower battery of Mex had abandoned their guns, and that the supports had probably retired to the citadel, I called in the gun-vessels and gun-boats, and under cover of their fire landed a party of twelve volunteers, under the command of Lieutenant B. R. Bradford of the Invincible, accompa-

---

*This remark is an error. No "heavy gun," if by that is meant a rifled gun, was dismounted in Fort Pharos.

†It was subsequently discovered that the explosion caused by the Monarch's fire was of a store of gun-cotton some distance in rear of the fort. The latter was unharmed.

nied by Lieutenant Richard Poore of that ship, Lieutenant the Honorable Hedworth Lambton (my flag lieutenant), Major Tulloch, Welsh Regiment, attached to my staff, and Mr. Hardy, midshipman in charge of the boat, who got on shore through the surf and destroyed, with charges of gun-cotton, two 10-inch M. L. R. guns, and spiked six smooth-bore guns in the right-hand water battery at Mex, and returned without a casualty beyond the loss of one of their boats (Bittern's dinghy) on the rocks. This was a hazardous operation very well carried out.* Previous to this, after the action had become general, Commander Lord Charles Beresford, of the Condor, stationed as repeating ship, seeing the accuracy with which two 10-inch rifled guns in Fort Marabout were playing upon the ships engaged off Fort Mex, steamed up to within range of his 7-inch 90 cwt. gun, and by his excellent practice soon drew off the fire.† I then ordered him to be supported by the Beacon, Bittern, Cygnet, and Decoy, the Cygnet having been engaged with the Ras-el-Tin forts during the early part of the day. I am happy to say, during the action, no casualties happened to those vessels, owing, in a great measure, to the able manner in which they were maneuvered, and their light draught enabling them to take up their position on the weakest point of the batteries. The action generally terminated successfully at 5.30 p. m., when the ships anchored for the night.

4. The force opposed to us would have been more formidable had every gun mounted on the line of works been brought into action, but in the Ras-el-Tin batteries few of the large smooth-bores and fewer of the French 36-pounders, bought in the time of Mehemet Ali, were manned, the Egyptians preferring to use the English 10-inch, 9-inch, 8-inch, and smaller muzzle-loading rifled guns. These guns are precisely the same as those which Her Majesty's ships carry, and no better muzzle-loading guns can be found. They were abundantly, even lavishly, supplied with projectiles of the latest description, chilled shot, and the sighting of the guns was excellent. The same may be said of the guns in the Mex Lines, excepting that in them the 36-pounders were more used, and that one, if not two, 15-inch smooth-bores ‡ were brought into action in addition to the 10-inch, 9-inch, and smaller M. L. R. guns fired. Fort Marabout brought two 10-inch M. L. R. guns† into action at long range, shell after shell of which came up towards the inshore squadron in an excellent line, falling from ten to thirty yards short. Not one shell from the guns in the southern batteries burst on board Her Majesty's ships during the day.

5. I forward for their lordships' perusal the official report of Captain Walter J. Hunt-Grubbe, C. B., A. D. C., of Her Majesty's ship Sultan, who most ably commanded the outside squadron, which bore the brunt of the action, as the accompanying statements of the damages sustained by the Sultan, Superb, and Alexandra fully testify. I have no account of the damage sustained by the Penelope, as that vessel was shortly

---

* In Fort Mex was but one 10-inch M. L. R. This and its neighbor, a 9-inch gun, were disabled by the landing party (see Plate 37). The wind had freshened slightly, making quite a surf at the spot where the party landed—marked *a* on Plate 37—and adding a sensible risk to the peril of the undertaking.

† These "10-inch rifled guns" are, in reality, 9-inch guns, on the east face of Fort Marabout, and are shown on Plate 32. The handling of the Condor was most seaman-like. Commander Lord Charles Beresford selected a position on the prolongation of the capital of the northeast bastion, where the guns of the fort could only be brought to bear upon him with great difficulty. Here, at 1,200 yards from the fort, he dropped a kedge and, keeping his ship constantly in motion either by paying out or hauling in his warp, he succeeded in evading the enemy's heavy shot, any one of which might have inflicted serious if not fatal damage. In addition, he made sharp use of his machine guns. When the risk this ship incurred is considered, it is impossible not to couple her share in the action with the operations of the landing party from the Invincible as the two brilliant episodes of the day.

‡ See page 17.

afterwards detached from my flag. The upper works of the Invincible and Inflexible were a good deal knocked about, but no serious injury was inflicted. No damage was done to the Temeraire or Monarch.

* * * * * *

It is quite impossible for me to account for the very small loss sustained by Her Majesty's ships on this occasion, considering the amount of shell and shot which struck them, and the injuries inflicted on the hulls of the Sultan, Superb, and Alexandra, and in a lesser degree on those of the Invincible, Penelope, and Inflexible, but I may here express my deep regret that Lieutenant Francis Jackson and Mr. William Shannon, carpenter of the Inflexible, should have fallen. The wounded, who when last heard from were doing well, were sent to Malta in the Humber.

* * * * * *

I have, &c.,
F. BEAUCHAMP SEYMOUR,
Admiral and Commander-in-Chief.

To the SECRETARY OF THE ADMIRALTY.

The special work done by the offshore squadron is thus described in the official report of its senior officer:

JULY 14, 1882.

SIR:

1. In compliance with your memorandum of the 10th instant, I have great pleasure in reporting the successful manner in which the offshore squadron, under my personal command, consisting of, at first, the Sultan, Superb, and Alexandra, and afterwards the Temeraire and Inflexible, attacked and silenced the earthworks and batteries on the 11th instant, comprising Forts Pharos and Ada, the batteries at Hospital Point, the new earthwork, which was of formidable nature, and the Light-House batteries bearing on the harbor.

2. The action was commenced at 6.59 a. m., by the Alexandra firing a shell at the earthwork near Fort Ada, and a few minutes after all the forts replied and the action became general.

3. At this time I was steaming in close order, at about 1,500 yards, past the batteries, and was turning in succession with a view to anchor in the order prescribed by you, but before doing so I again repassed. Finding, however, that the batteries were stronger than was anticipated, and that the Egyptian gunners were far from despicable, making, indeed, very good practice, I deemed it advisable to anchor and obtain the exact range. This was executed with great precision by the squadron, and we soon appeared to be dismounting their guns.*

4. At 10.30 a. m. the Light-House Battery, which had been, earlier in the day, severely handled by the Inflexible, ceased to return our fire, their last rifled gun being disabled, though not before it had given us much trouble.

5. At 12.45 p. m. the Temeraire and Inflexible (you no longer requiring their services) began to assist in our attack, shelling Forts Pharos and Ada with great effect.

6. By this time the fire was considerably less, but one rifled gun† on the Hospital earthwork, which it was impossible to dismount, being invisible from the ship, did us great damage.

7. At 1.32 p. m. a shell from the Superb blew up the magazine by Fort Ada,‡ and that fort and Pharos were hurriedly evacuated.

8. After this the enemy's firing ceased, and, on our side, it was confined to dislodging parties of men, reported from time to time from the tops as reassembling in rear of the earthworks.

---

* More appearance than reality, as will be afterwards shown.
† A 7-inch Armstrong M. L. R.
‡ This magazine was inside the fort.

9. The ships were handled and fought in a manner reflecting great credit on their officers and ships' companies.

* * * * * * *

I have, &c.,

W. HUNT-GRUBBE,
Captain.

To Admiral Sir F. BEAUCHAMP SEYMOUR, G. C. B.,
Commander-in-Chief.

The parts omitted above are personal mentions and recommendations. In a dispatch of July 14, Admiral Sir Beauchamp Seymour further says:

On the morning of the 12th I ordered the Temeraire and Inflexible to engage Fort Pharos, and after two or three shots had been fired, a flag of truce was hoisted on Fort Ras-el-Tin,* and I then sent my flag lieutenant, the Honorable Hedworth Lambton, in to discover the reason, and, from his report, there is no doubt it was simply a ruse to gain time; and as negotiations failed, my demand being to surrender the batteries commanding the Boghaz Channel, one shot was fired into the Mex Barracks† Battery earthwork, when a flag of truce was again hoisted. I then sent Lieutenant and Commander Morrison into the harbor in the Helicon, and on his going on board the Khedive's yacht, the Mahroussa, he found she had been deserted, and he reported on his return after dark his belief that the town had been evacuated.

To these official reports little need be added. The practice was, in the main, excellent. The fire of the Inflexible and Temeraire appeared to the writer, who was not far from either at the beginning of the action and during the forenoon, to be particularly good. The Inflexible seemed to use her small 20-pdrs. as range-finders, so as not to waste her valuable shot. A shrapnel burst prematurely inside of one of her 81-ton guns, inflicting no damage, its scattering pieces being plainly visible on the water.

On board of the Superb the fire from her small guns was stopped on account of the smoke they occasioned.

The projectiles from the offshore squadron were heard to "wobble" greatly—noticeably in the cases of the broadside vessels—as indicated by a prolonged and heavy rumbling sound, like that of a distant railway train.

The Egyptians were overmatched in guns both as to size and number, but the way that they responded to the heavy fire from the English fleet was marvelous, standing to their batteries with unexpected and admirable courage. When the Inflexible's 1,700-pound projectiles struck the scarp of the Light-House Fort, immediately underneath an embrasure, they would throw up a cloud of dust and fragments of stone as high as the light-house itself. To the looker-on it seemed impossible to live under such a fire, yet after a few minutes the dust would clear away and the gun's crew would pluckily toss another shell back at their huge opponent. The Egyptian practice was naturally subjected to keener criticism than the British, as the fall of each shot that failed of its tar-

---

* The Light-House Fort.
† Mex Citadel.

get could be distinctly seen. The error was, generally speaking, caused by too much elevation. Certain of the guns were pointed with "consummate skill," notably one 36-pdr. (6½-inch S. B.) in the citadel of Mex, which hulled the Invincible with persistent accuracy.

Of the fuzes used by the British, the greater part were the "general-service percussion." *It is impossible to exaggerate the misbehavior of this fuze on the occasion of the bombardment.* The most careless witness of the action could not help noticing the frequency of premature explosions, and of failures to explode at all. It is not beyond the limits of fair estimation to set down the number of the latter as reaching several hundred, while some British officers think the proportion no less than four-fifths of all fired. In several instances fuzes were driven bodily into the bursting charge without exploding the shell. The stoutest apologist for this fuze, urging that it was designed for use against armored ships, and therefore given a retarded action, could neither expect nor desire a more violent impact than is shown by this fact to have taken place. As a result of the unreliable nature of these fuzes, it may be mentioned that one of the Penelope's 8-inch shell was afterwards found lying harmless in a magazine containing over four hundred tons of powder.

One or two of the British shell were split longitudinally into two parts, doubtless by the force of the blow they delivered, which was, however, not sufficient to ignite the fuze.

It is proper to remark that the entire subject of fuzes is now being overhauled in England, in response to the universal and loudly-expressed dissatisfaction at their performance during the bombardment.

It has been already stated that the fire was ordered to be slow and deliberate, with the object of husbanding the supply of ammunition. Difficulty was experienced in obtaining the exact number of charges expended, or indeed accurate particulars of many interesting professional matters connected with the bombardment, a spirit of mystery appearing to have prevailed. The following figures may be relied upon as approximately correct.

The Monarch fired as follows: 117 12-inch shell from her turret guns; 103 9 and 7 inch shell from her bow and stern guns.

The Penelope fired 157 common shell, 38 shrapnel, 36 Palliser shell. She used 1 20″ time fuze, 114 10″ time fuzes, and the remainder, general-service percussion fuzes.

The Superb fired 200 10-inch shell, mostly common, 10 10-inch shrapnel, and a few 20-pounder shell.

The Invincible fired about 220 shell of various kinds, mostly common (as distinguished from shrapnel). A few only were shrapnel and Palliser shell. The fuzes were chiefly percussion. She expended between two and three thousand rounds of Nordenfeldt ammunition.

The Inflexible's stock of ammunition was currently reported to have been reduced to 40 *battering shell at the end of the day.*

As regards the Sultan, the statement was made, and credibly too, that *"she could not have continued the action for more than an hour longer, as the ammunition was nearly exhausted."* What is true of the Sultan is also doubtless true more or less of the other vessels—an important point, that should be kept in mind.

The outside squadron, as will be observed, began the action under way, at the minimum distance of about 1,500 yards, and anchored after passing the batteries a second time, *the advantage of knowing the range exactly prevailing over the increased risk of being hit.* It then moved, from time to time, concentrating its fire on each work in succession until the close of the day.

In the inshore squadron the flagship was anchored for the most part at 1,300 yards from Mex, a position from which a clear view could be had, and was kept broadside to the wind on one side, and the batteries on the other, by a kedge carried out to windward. The Monarch and Penelope remained under way, passing and repassing the forts. The Penelope adopted the plan of steaming out three-quarters of a mile towards the reef and then drifting in, broadside on, until within about 700 yards, while the Monarch appeared to keep more way on, moving in a line parallel with the shore. These ships exchanged a few shots with Fort Marabout, but at so great a range that they could neither inflict nor receive much damage. Later in the day, when the offshore squadron moved to the eastward to attack Fort Pharos, these two ships passed inside the breakwater and shelled Saleh Aga and the battery between Saleh Aga and Oom-el-Kabebe. They would have gone up to the city had they not been recalled by signal.

Machine guns were largely employed by the fleet. It is quite impossible to determine their exact value at Alexandria, for no record was kept by the Egyptians of their losses. The appearance of the buildings immediately in rear of the batteries, scarred and pitted by Nordenfeldt and Gatling bullets, proves that these weapons must have had some effect. This appearance is more marked at Mex than in the Ras-el-Tin Lines, a fact which might have been presupposed, the average range being in the former case about one-half that in the latter, and the number of machine guns brought to bear being greater through the reinforcement of the inshore squadron by the gun-boats after noon. Had machine guns contributed in any great measure to the result of the fight, they would have left more traces on the guns. Their value against properly-constructed forts can hardly be problematical. *If mounted in the tops, and used at short range, against low parapets,* as at Mex, *they may be very useful, but in a general engagement at long range,* as in the case of the outside fleet, where the fall of the bullets could not be observed and the aim corrected, owing to the distance of the object aimed at and the thickness of the smoke, *they cannot be considered as really formidable.*

The English loss on July 11 is given in the following summary:

Ships.	Killed.	Wounded.
Alexandra	1	3
Inflexible	2	1
Invincible		6
Penelope		8
Sultan	2	8
Superb	1	1
Total	6	27

The Egyptian forces at Alexandria were under the immediate command of Toulba Pasha. From the best sources of information accessible it is gathered that the defenses contained less than 2,000 artillerists. Of infantry and of civilian volunteers there was no lack. The disposition of these troops has not been positively ascertained. It is known that the important post of Mex was commanded by an adjutant-major, who had with him one captain, three lieutenants, and 150 men. Of this small force one lieutenant was mortally wounded, 50 men killed, and 48 wounded. Another account gives the loss as very much less. In this land it is hard to obtain the truth.

Oom-el-Kabebe, as already mentioned, was subjected to the Inflexible's fire during the forenoon. Its garrison consisted of 75 men, aided by a considerable number of Arab volunteers. Eighteen of these were wounded by splinters of masonry. In all, along the southern or inside line, from Saleh Aga to Marabout, 65 men were killed and from 150 to 200 wounded. Among the latter were several officers.

In the northern line of defenses, one officer was killed in the Light-House Fort and one in the Ras-el-Tin Lines. In each of the foregoing, and in Fort Ada, one was wounded. At least 50 men were killed and 150 wounded in these lines, but the record is very vague. Stray pieces of shell are reported by the chief of police to have killed and wounded between 150 and 200 citizens, but this statement must be accepted only for what it is worth.

It is thought that in the interest of impartiality the native Egyptian semi-official report of this engagement should be given. The following, taken from the London Times, is a translation of the account of the bombardment published in El Taïf, an Arabic newspaper, the organ of Arabi Pasha:

WAR NEWS.—On Tuesday, 25 Shaban, 1299, at 12 o'clock in the morning (July 11, 7 a. m.), the English opened fire on the forts of Alexandria and we returned the fire.
At 10 a. m. an iron-clad foundered off Fort Ada.
At noon two vessels were sunk between Fort Pharos and Fort Adjemi.
At 1.30 p. m. a wooden man-of-war of eight guns was sunk.
At 5 p. m. the large iron-clad was struck by a shell from Fort Pharos, the battery

was injured, and a white flag was immediately hoisted by her as a signal to cease firing at her, whereupon the firing ceased on both sides, having lasted for ten hours without cessation. Some of the walls of the forts were destroyed, but they were repaired during the night. The shots and shells discharged from the two sides amounted to about 6,000, and this is the first time that so large a number of missiles have been discharged in so short a time.

At 11 a. m., on Wednesday, the English ships again opened fire and were replied to by the forts, but after a short time the firing ceased on both sides, and a deputation came from Admiral Seymour and made propositions to Toulba Pasha, which he could not accept.

* * * * * * *

No soldiers ever stood so firmly to their posts under a heavy fire as did the Egyptians under the fire of twenty-eight ships during ten hours.

* * * * * *

At 9 a. m., on Thursday, an English man-of-war was seen to put a small screw in place of the larger one which she had been using, and it was then known that her screw had been carried away by a shot from the forts.

On examining other ships it was observed that eight had been severely battered on their sides and that one had lost her funnel.

V.

THE EFFECT UPON THE SHIPS.

Two of the armored ships, the Monarch and the Temeraire, were not injured at all. This immunity was due in the case of the former to her being kept continually in motion; in the latter, to the fact that she was very distant from the enemy's batteries all the forenoon, being brought within short range later in the day, after the Egyptian gunners had become demoralized under the severe fire of the five preceding hours.

The Condor was struck once, receiving a slight wound in the bow. Otherwise, the unarmored vessels were not touched, although the Cygnet took a noticeable part in the morning's attack on the Light-House Fort, engaging from a point well outside of the line, followed by the offshore squadron, and all were exposed at Marabout and afterwards at Mex.

The official report of the damage sustained by the Alexandra is given below. This vessel was struck sixty-odd times. It is proper to recall the fact that she is the regular flagship of the British Mediterranean fleet.

H. M. S. ALEXANDRA,
Alexandria, July 21, 1882.

LIST OF DAMAGE TO HULL AND RIGGING SUSTAINED ON THE 11TH INSTANT.

1. Three shot-holes in recesses on mess deck, two on port side, one on starboard, the shot or shell carrying away several frames, disabling pump-gear, supporting-stanchion of deck, shield by fire-hearth, ladders, two mess-tables and their stools and fittings, knocking away soil-pipe of water-closets, besides several small defects caused by shell bursting.

2. Shot-hole in torpedo-lieutenant's cabin, damaging frames, edge-straps, bulkhead of cabin, furniture, and engine-room coamings.

3. Shot-hole through netting, after part of quarter-deck, port side, carrying away part of wardroom skylight, sashes, rails and stanchions of after-ladder, and stanchions of standard compass started.

4. Shot-hole through cabin of staff-commander, completely destroying some furniture and damaging more.

5. One shot-hole in captain's cabin on port and one on starboard side, completely destroying furniture in bed-cabin, and partially destroying furniture in sitting-cabin.

6. Trunk of admiral's skylight completely destroyed. The shell, in falling, damaged captain's table in admiral's fore-cabin.

7. Two shot-holes in commander's cabin, completely destroying cabin and all furniture, shell bursting in cabin.

8. Steam-pinnace, port quarter, utterly destroyed; stern broken and bows shattered.

9. Several loading-scuttles in upper and main batteries blown away and glasses broken, damaging chains, levers, &c.

10. Sailing-pinnace: shell carried away starboard quarter and port gunwale.

11. Lower part of ventilator to stoke-hole blown away.

12. Fore and aft bridges blown away, and several ridge-stanchions damaged and blown away.

13. Several awning-stanchions broken and blown away, and stanchions in forecastle damaged, &c.

14. Two shot-holes in fore part of upper deck forward.

15. Sashes of chart-house broken and furniture damaged.

16. Seven streaks of upper deck forward much shattered.

17. Several water-closets slightly damaged.

18. Chock of naval-pipe forward slightly damaged.

19. Main royal yard and fore top-gallant yard badly bruised.

20. Shot-hole through starboard side of quarter-deck.

21. Three streaks of deck in staff-commander's cabin badly shattered.

22. Post-office and fittings damaged.

23. Casing of soil-pipes, wardroom closets, blown away.

24. Several side-steps, port side, blown away.

25. Several plates of crown of lower glacis rivet-heads blown off and plates started.

26. Outside plating in wake of mess-shelves on mess deck, port side, broken.

27. Heel of fore-bitts damaged and iron safes in galley broken.

28. Several streaks of deck on mess deck shattered.

29. Plate under upper deck in torpedo-flat cracked.

30. Several tubes through wings leaky.

Twenty-four shot and shell penetrated the ship above the armor-plating, causing a considerable amount of damage to lower deck, galley, cabins, &c. Several shot and shell struck the armor-plating without doing any appreciable damage, but one which impinged on the upper edge of armor-plating just abaft mainmast, port side, indented the plate and made some jagged marks and holes to the depth of from one-half to one inch. The foremost funnel was struck in three places, the standing rigging in eight, and running rigging in twenty-one places.

RICH'D T. GRIGG,
Carpenter, H. M. S. Alexandra.

ALEXANDRIA, *July* 21, 1882.

LIST OF RIGGING SHOT AWAY.

Fore rigging.—Fourth, fifth, and sixth shrouds shot away on port side just above deadeye.
Main rigging.—Second shroud, port side, six ratlines up from sheer-pole; eighth shroud, port side, twenty-three ratlines up from sheer-pole; third shroud, starboard side, nine ratlines up from sheer-pole.
Mizzen rigging.—Fourth shroud, starboard side, nine ratlines up from sheer-pole; main top-gallant stay; main royal stay.
Running-rigging.—Port fore tack, topmast staysail halliards, fore-truss falls, fore truss tricing lines, foresail tackle, mainsail tackle, main-truss falls, main-truss tricing lines, whips for main buntlines, main vangs, fore vangs, mizzen vangs, main leechlines, cross-jack lift, starboard main topsail clewlines, port boat's purchase falls, fore and aft, wire, pendant, for placing boats.

H. T. BURNETT,
Boatswain.

No mention, of course, is made of the fact that three of the guns were badly scored by shells bursting within them, and that in two guns the A-tube was split. These guns were carefully inspected after each round, and were used until the end of the action. The loss of time through this enforced precaution might have proved extremely awkward under other circumstances and in a more evenly-contested engagement.

All the recorded damage is such as might naturally be expected in action except, possibly, No. 9 of the carpenter's report. Assuming that this was due to concussion and not to the entrance of a hostile shot into the Alexandra's casemate, an assumption warranted by the wording of the report, it falls at once into the same category as the others.

In no respect were the Alexandra's powers as a fighting machine impaired by the injuries she received.

The official report of the damage sustained by the Inflexible is a "confidential" document. It is known, however, that she suffered a good deal aloft, and that she was pierced under water, presumably, of course, outside of her casemate. The latter wound is said not to have been of a serious nature, but as it involved docking the ship when she arrived at Malta, it must have been too serious to have been repaired by the mechanics on board. Its size and location were kept a secret. The after superstructure was perforated by a 10-inch Palliser shell just above the spar deck, on the starboard side. This shell first killed the carpenter, who was at work on a bulkhead in the officers' quarters, then struck a bitt inside, glanced up and a mortally wounded Lieutenant Jackson, who was directing the fire of a B. L. R. 20-pdr. mounted on the hurricane deck.

The Inflexible's boat-davits are rigged to bring the boats during action above the superstructure and clear of the line of fire. The concussion of the discharge of her turret guns, burning 370 pounds of powder, was so great, when the guns were fired fore and aft, or nearly so, that several of her boats were badly hurt, the planking being torn bodily from the frames.

The following is the official report of the injury sustained by the Invincible. Being in a fixed position all day, her range was soon gotten by the Egyptians, who hulled her repeatedly. Reference has been made to a certain 6½-inch S. B. in Mex Citadel as particularly well served. On account of its masked situation great difficulty was experienced on board the Invincible in obtaining the range in return. A large number of the hits recorded are due to this one gun.

H. M. S. INVINCIBLE,
At Alexandria, July 21, 1882.

LIST OF DAMAGES RECEIVED IN ACTION JULY 11.

(Commencing forward and working aft.)

1. A dent in the doubling-plate, under hawse-pipe, 2 inches in depth and 9 inches in circumference; the doubling-plate is ¾ inch thick on side, plating ⅝ inch.
2. A puncture made by a shot striking the head chute and bringing up against the water-way of the mess deck, about 3 feet 6 inches above water.
3. A hole made by a shot passing through the ship's side, gouging the deck, carrying away the lockers and bulkhead of the chief petty officers' mess, finally lodging in the fire-hearth.
4. A very large dent, about 3 feet farther aft and 3 feet above, starting the plate badly above, 5 feet 6 inches deep between the frames, showing quite an angle where the frames are situated from the outside.
5. A hole on the upper deck, passing through the side, tearing away the wooden water-way and angle-iron of the gutter-way, stopping on the opposite side, slightly damaging the shot-racks and spirketing.
6. A hole about 1 foot abaft, on a level with the mess-deck ports, passing through the side, carrying away a mess-shelf, a table leg (or crow's foot), iron stanchions, and torpedo air-pipes, passing on, striking a mess-stool and lockers, finally stopped by striking the iron plating, which is bulged out on the other side.
7. A shot passing through lower half-port, striking and gouging a piece out of the iron ballards.
8. A hole on the lower deck just before the funnel casing, caused by a shot which passed through the side, carrying away a mess-shelf, hammock bars, two pump stanchions, and the rack in which they were stowed, passing through string of iron ladder, and severely damaging an iron ventilator.
9. A hole just before the upper battery, caused by a shot passing through side, carrying away cistern-pipe of gun-room officers' water-closet, buckling up the iron bulkhead $\frac{3}{16}$ inch thick, smashing the jamb of the doorway and the cat-block, and striking the port foremost battery door (armor plated), which was open.
10. A hole just before the bridge, caused by a shot passing through the glacis-plate and the ship's side, and gouging the teak, ½ inch thick, and wood water-way.
11. A hole in the captain's galley, apparently caused by a rocket or splinter, just abaft the fore deadwood.
12. A shot struck the fish davit, carrying away an iron stanchion and part of the fore and aft bridge, then struck the fore bitt-head, which it splintered.
13. Molding on starboard quarter injured by shot or piece of shell.
14. Several ropes aloft were cut away by shot.

ROB. H. M. MOLYNEUX,
Captain.

The Penelope was hulled eight times during the action, but no serious damage was done. Her commanding officer thought she was not struck by the rifled shell. One 36-pound shot entered the cabin and made an extraordinary corkscrew journey through store-rooms and state-rooms until it finally came to res The muzzle of No. 2 gun on the port side was hit by a large round shot which took off a tapered flake about six inches long and six inches wide outer end, without disabl or indeed really damaging the gun. Figs. 42 and 43. On board of the Penelope this bruise was supposed to have been the work of a XV-inch shell.

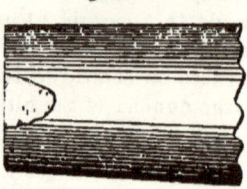

Fig. 42.   Fig. 43.

Many ropes were cut aloft, and the main yard was so injured that it had to be replaced.

The following is the official report of damages sustained by the Sultan:

H. M. SULTAN,
Off Alexandria, July 14, 1882.

1. Four plates on starboard side in wake of sheet-anchor partly shot away; one frame broken, one frame bent in, and inside lining smashed in; tumbler of sheet-anchor broken and part shot away; side scuttle broken; bulkhead of gun-room closet shot away; the fore end of hammock berthing shaken and splintered by shell; voice-pipe from upper battery deck shot away; gun-room water-closet and connections broken and part shot away; fore part of fore channel, starboard side, gone; shutters to billboard broken.

2. Upper part of coamings to fore ladder-way shot away.

3. Transporting chock at knighthead, port side, splintered and part gone; bow port gone; upper part of bow port, starboard side, gone.

4. Bulkheads of seamen's head and officers' water-closets, port side, much damaged and part blown away; hole in lower edge of plate 16 inches by 12 inches; upper edge of plate beneath torn down and edge strip broken.

5. Three steps of the side of the port fore gangway shot away.

6. Hole in side plating of sick-bay, port side, about 8 feet above water-lines, 15 inches in diameter; one frame broken and bent in; water-way gone; gutter angle-iron bent in, and ten streaks of inside lining broken; framing of water-closet in sick-bay, port side, blown away and closet damaged; bulkhead of sick-bay much damaged by shell; two rifle-racks on aft deck broken.

7. Two ward closets much damaged; hole in side of plating 12 feet above the water-line, 14 inches in diameter; frame broken, lining smashed in, and two side scuttles broken.

8. Armor plate about 22 feet abaft after gangway and 1 foot above the water-line dented by shot, and plate started.

9. Armor plate under main-deck battery, 1 foot 6 inches, dented by shot.

10. Berthing starboard side quarter-deck, cowl-head to ventilator to shaft-alley, starboard side quarter-deck damaged by shell.

11. Hole 16 inches by 10 inches through mainmast, 17 feet from upper battery deck; voice-pipe from upper battery deck to main top shot away.

12. Main topmast grazed by shot and lightning-conductor partly gone.

13. Mizzen topmast head and royal truck shot away.
14. Four boats damaged by shell.
Running rigging cut through by shot and shell.
                          Approved.
                                        W. HUNT-GRUBBE,
                                                    Captain.

The report of the Superb's wounds is quoted below.

DAMAGE TO HULL AND RIGGING OF SUPERB DURING ACTION WITH THE BATTERIES AT ALEXANDRIA.

1. The ½-inch plating close before the battery on the port side shot through, the projectile (a 10-inch shell) passing through all the frames (ten in number) forming the lower part of the embrasure for the battery port, starting the upper plating about 2 feet in an upward direction, and starting the outside plating, making a hole in the side 10 feet long by 4 feet deep down to within 3 feet of the water-line, striking the armor plate and bursting.

2. The ½-inch plating a few feet before the fore torpedo-port, port side of mess deck, shot through about 4 feet above the water-line, making a hole 10 inches in diameter.

3. The ½-inch plating close abaft the battery on port side shot through, carrying away the frame angle-iron, and making a hole in the side 12 inches in diameter 5 feet above the water-line. This was a 10-inch solid shot, now on board.

4. The armor plates were struck in two places on the port side about 4 feet above the water-line, the one indenting the armor 3 inches; in the other the mark of the explosion of the shell is visible, and the plate is slightly started, breaking 14 rivet-heads of the plating forming the port sill.

5. The foremast was shot through, making a hole about 12 inches in diameter close to the awning hoop.

6. Stanchion for after bridge shot away.

7. Hammock berthing shot through in two places, carrying away three voice-tubes.

8. Iron plating at lower part of embrasure port on port side under the poop, shot through close to the drop-bolt, breaking the port sill and starting the inside plating, and destroying the buckler port.

9. Both platforms for accommodation-ladders shot away.

10. Leadsman's stools shot away.

Standing and running rigging.

11. One 6-inch-wire shroud with iron ratlines shot away; one top-gallant and one topmast backstay shot away; one fore brace, fore top-sail halliards, runner of jib-stay and fore guy, fore top-gallant sheet, fore topsail buntlines, and fore top-gallant lift shot away; main sheet, after-boom topping-lift, and mizzen top-mast rope and cross-jack truss shot away.

                                        THOMAS LE H. WARD,
                                                    Captain.

The Superb's wound, numbered 1 in the foregoing report, was to the observer the most striking of all in the fleet. In even a moderate sea the hole described would have been most annoying, resisting temporary plugging, and admitting water into an important compartment.

The result of the damages just detailed was very slight. Viewed in relation to the circumstances in which the fleet was placed they were practically nothing. Not a gun was really disabled, nor the fighting qualities of a single ship affected. The following day all were ready and the crews eager to resume the engagement, which could have been continued just so long as the powder and shell held out.

VI.

THE FORTIFICATIONS AND THE DAMAGE SUSTAINED BY THEM.

In this section the fortifications are described in detail and an account given of the part each took in the action, together with the effects upon it of the fire from the British fleet.

Reverting to Plate 1, it will be seen that Fort Silsileh is the most eastern of the immediate sea defenses of Alexandria. It stands at the base of a long rocky spit which shuts in the eastern harbor, called generally the New Port. The fort is a small work built around an old martello tower. Plate 2. It comprises two concentric batteries on the north face. The terreplein of the upper battery, it will be observed, has been widened and the parapet thickened from 15 feet to 36 feet. The proper embrasures have been cut, and two M. L. R. guns, one 8-inch and one 9-inch, have been mounted. These guns point towards the mouth of the harbor, at which place their fire crosses with that from the eastern face of Fort Pharos. Two X-inch shell guns are mounted *en barbette* on the east face of Silsileh, and more would have been put into position had time allowed. A XIII-inch mortar completes the armament of this fort, which is said to have fired " a few well-directed rounds" at the Temeraire when she came around to shell Fort Pharos. The Temeraire made no reply, however, and the fort is unscratched.

The first fort in the northern line of defense is Pharos, admirably placed to command the eastern harbor and the approaches from the east and north, while the guns on its southern face may be trained directly upon the city itself. It stands upon the site of the famous light-house of Ptolemy Philadelphus, one of the seven wonders of the ancient world. The old castle or keep is a fine specimen of mediaeval Arab architecture, erected at the close of the fifteenth century. The modern fort, built around it, was considerably strengthened in 1852. Its general appearance at the present moment, as seen from the shore to the southward and westward, is given on Plate 3. It is connected with the city by a long causeway, shown in Plate 12. Plate 4 is a view of the northwest sea-face. From this it will be seen that there were two tiers of guns on this side, the lower in a casemate *à fleur d'eau*, the upper uncovered. Plate 5 gives the plan of the fort as a whole, a horizontal section through the casemate, and horizontal and vertical sections of the magazine. Fig. 48 is a principal section along the line A B, and Fig. 47 an enlarged section of the casemate. These last figures are on Plate 6, which also contains sections through the east and west faces, and an index sketch to the principal hits on the northwest scarp.

The casemate was chiefly armed with $6\frac{1}{2}$-inch S. B. guns on garrison carriages. Two embrasures in the west tower and that marked 17 on the plan, Plate 5, were unoccupied. In embrasures Nos. 3 and

8 were the 40-pounder B. L. R. Armstrong guns already mentioned. Of this casemate it may be said that its walls, only 10 feet in thickness, could offer no adequate resistance to the heavy projectiles thrown at them, and that to work its guns under the fire of the British fleet required great pluck and no prudence.

The main strength of Fort Pharos lay in its upper battery. Here the thin walls of the old fortress have been thickened from 7 to 28 feet (measured through the base of the superior slope), and M. L R. guns mounted—two 8-inch and one 10-inch on the northwest face, one 9-inch on the north face, and two 9-inch on the northeast face. The last two were not used during the bombardment. Plate 7 gives a large-scale plan of this upper battery of rifled guns. Plate 8 shows the additional protection provided for them. The method, so clearly shown here, was adopted in the case of the other and heavier guns not included in the pictures.

The west face was armed with four X-inch S. B. guns, of little or no value, even if they could have been brought to bear.

The south face mounted a formidable-looking battery of fourteen 6½-inch S. B., bearing on the town.

Four XIII-inch mortars completed the armament.

The series of plates numbered 3, 4, 8, 9, 10, and 11 exhibit the general condition of the masonry of Fort Pharos after it had been subjected to the pounding of the British fleet. Particular attention is called to the ample breaches made in the west face, as seen in Plate 3. The one to the extreme left is doubtless due to several well-directed and concurrent shells, exploding with unwonted accuracy after being fairly buried. Just to the left of the old castle or keep is another breach through which the Armstrong guns on the northwest face may be seen. Different views of these breaches are exhibited in Plates 8, 11, and 12. (Plate 11 is a view of the ditch between the fort proper and the outer gallery.) As a result of the large breach shown more clearly in Plate 12, the platform under a X-inch S. B. gun is totally ruined, although the gun itself is unharmed. Recurring to Plate 3, a still wider breach is seen in the parapet of the west face, exposing a second X-inch S. B. gun, likewise put *hors de combat*. The shot-hole, just above the water, is 15 feet wide and 11 feet high.

The scars on the northwest face, the principal one engaged, are given in Plate 4. For the sake of clearness, the sketch, Fig. 44, Plate 6, is added as a key.

Hit No. 1 is due to two shots, one above and to the right of the embrasure (No. 11 on plan of casemate, Plate 5), the other at the left lower corner. Their effect has been to peel off the outer courses of masonry to the depth of 2 feet or so quite uniformly, and to block the gun inside the casemate by a large mass of splinters.

Hit No. 2 has knocked away 7 feet of the cordon, but has had no serious effect.

No. 3 appears to have been done by several hits in the same neighborhood. Of these, one is worthy of special notice. The shell entered the masonry to the depth of about 3 feet and then burst, blowing out a fine crater and making a huge pile of *débris* at the foot of the scarp.

No. 4 is the result of two 10-inch Palliser shell, one striking the cheek of the embrasure, the other immediately beneath the sole. Both projectiles entered the casemate and wrecked the gun and carriage beyond imagination.

No. 5, a shell cut out a portion of the cheek of the embrasure and burst inside the casemate, disabling the gun by masonry splinters.

No. 6 is a deep hole. The projectile is doubtless lodged inside unburst. The splinters of masonry falling behind it have so plugged the hole as to prevent probing.

No. 7, a slice is cut out of the cheek of the embrasure. The gun was probably not seriously affected by this shot, but it was totally wrecked by the bursting of a shell underneath the carriage.

Nos. 8 and 9, a series of surface wounds, due to several shell.

No. 10 shows what is left of an embrasure. The gun and carriage inside are hopelessly and shockingly wrecked.

The remaining embrasure on the right exhibits no scar, but enough masonry has been knocked off the inner edges to block the gun.

The other casemate, Plate 5, in the northeast face, was less injured, not being subjected to so severe or so direct a hammering. Only that embrasure, No. 17, in which no gun was mounted, was struck.

These galleries were simply slaughter-houses, a large number of men being killed and wounded, mostly by splinters of stone. The thinness of its walls and the lightness of its ordnance have been already remarked upon. Nearly all of these guns were used.

The condition of the casemate battery is given in the following schedule, the numbers being as on Plate 5:

1. The gun is not hurt, but is unserviceable, being blocked by pieces of stone from the embrasure. •
2. The gun and carriage are wrecked.
3. 40-pdr. Armstrong B. L. R. is still serviceable. The left rear pier of the casemate is knocked away.
4. Gun wrecked by a shell which burst under the platform.
5. No damage.
6. Embrasure is broken and beaten in on the gun.
7. See No. 4, page above.
8, 9, and 10. In good condition.
11. Total destruction of gun-carriage.
12. Carriage blocked by *débris* of the masonry.

Passing to the upper or uncovered battery Plate 5, it is found that the rifled guns were not directly harmed by the British fire. The heaviest, a 10-inch gun, was blocked by the fall of pieces of masonry from the corner tower of the keep, under which it had been very indiscreetly mounted. In addition, the sill of the embrasure was dislodged by a well-burst shell. The pivot is unshipped, but this could have been quickly remedied. (Plate 13.)

The perfect condition of the 8-inch guns to the westward is shown in Plates 8, 9, and 12.

The 9-inch guns to the eastward, not being engaged, were unharmed.

In the northwest angle of the fort were two X-inch S. B. *en barbette*, which were worked during the bombardment. A well-placed shot has overturned one of the two. (Plate 8.) This is probably the gun referred to in the Admiral's report as having been dismounted by a shell from the Inflexible. Its neighbor, still standing, is said to have been the last gun fired by the Egyptians as the Inflexible steamed away at the close of the day.

Of the four guns originally mounted on the west face, two are still serviceable.

The smooth-bores on the south front, which overlooks the eastern harbor, were destitute of cover against a rear or enfilading fire. Two of them, in consequence, were disabled. Gun No. 8 of this battery, counting from the eastward, was put *hors de combat* by the destruction of its platform. (Plate 13.) The place of the gun adjoining is marked on the same plate by the ends of the brackets of the carriage standing on end. The gun itself received a blow square in the breech, which knocked it out of its carriage and over the parapet. It passed through the roof of the kitchen beneath (Plate 5) and planted itself vertically, with the muzzle down. (Plate 14.) The directness of the blow is indicated by the straightness of the path described by the gun in its flight and the absence of the cascabel.

The rear face and keep show unmistakable traces of at least twelve good hits each, the rifle-gun battery eight, the left or west face eleven, the casemate, as judged from the inside, eleven, from the outside, eighteen. Many of these marks may have been duplicated, the destruction of the masonry rendering an accurate identification quite impossible. No traces of Gatling or Nordenfeldt bullets or of shrapnel could be discovered.

The practice on Fort Pharos, it will be remembered, was due to the combined efforts of the five heaviest ships in the fleet.

Thirteen blind shell were found in Pharos and two *broken* 11-inch common shell. The serge bags containing the bursting charge were white and clean. The powder itself was hard and caked.

Summing up the damage done to this fort, it is seen—

1st. That one rifled gun, the heaviest of all, was put *hors de combat*. On account of the proximity of the keep, it could not have been permanently served at any time.

2d. That one X-inch S. B. gun* in the upper battery was dismounted.

---

*Those on the west face are not considered.

3d. That, in the northwest casemate, seven out of twelve guns were more or less disabled.

4th. That the old-fashioned batteries, whether barbette or casemate, afforded very inadequate protection.

On the other hand it is also shown—

1st. That five out of six, or, more justly, three out of four, rifled guns were unharmed.

2d. That one X-inch S. B. in the upper battery was still serviceable.

3d. That the four $6\frac{1}{2}$-inch guns in the north casemate were uninjured.

4th. That two B. L. R. 40-pdrs. and three $6\frac{1}{2}$-inch S. B. in the northwest casemate, five guns out of twelve, were not hurt.

5th. That the modern batteries with thickened parapets gave ample protection against almost the heaviest guns now afloat.

In Plate 8 a distant view may be had of Ada, the next fort to Pharos in the northern line of defense.

Like Fort Pharos, Ada is built upon an outlying ledge of rocks and is connected with the mainland by a stone causeway. It is an irregular four-sided work so placed that its principal faces point northeast and northwest, delivering cross-fires in front of Pharos on one hand and of the Ras-el-Tin Lines on the other. The former face is lightly armed with seven X-inch S. B. guns. Back of the north angle of the fort is a cavalier, B, with a solid masonry scarp, mounting one 8-inch M. L. R., capable of a certain amount of train on either front, with a X-inch S. B. mounted on each side. In the northwest face lies the strength of the fort, a modern cavalier with thickened walls (28 feet) carrying one 10-inch and three 9-inch Armstrong M. L. R. Between this and the bastioned north angle is a low battery of X-inch S. B. guns. In addition to the guns enumerated, there are as usual some mortars (five XIII inch). Plate 15 gives a general plan of the fort, and Plate 16 the details of the larger rifled-gun battery, Cavalier A.

The northeastern face points towards Fort Pharos, and therefore was not exposed to the attack, which was directed mainly against the western battery where the heavy modern guns were mounted.

On Plate 17 is a sketch, Fig. 49, of the principal scars on Cavalier A.

No. 1 is a hole made, probably, by a Palliser shell, which penetrated too deep for probing and now lies at the bottom unexploded.

No. 2 is similar to the foregoing. The wall is shattered for over 3 feet across, and the crater is 4 feet deep.

Nos. 3, 4, 5, and 6 are similar to No. 1, scaling off the outside stone work to the depth of about a foot and making a broad scar 9 feet in width extending from the cordon down.

Nos. 7 and 8 are like No. 1.

No. 9 is particularly noteworthy. One of the Inflexible's shells has entered to the depth of over 8 feet, bursting inside and blowing out the mass of *débris* 12 feet across, seen lying beneath.

Nos. 10, 11, 12, and 13 resemble No. 1.

No. 14 has burst on the cordon and cut down the scarp about 2 feet. This scarp was pitted all over by shrapnel balls. No machine-gun bullet-marks were detected.

The hits on the superior and exterior slopes are sketched on Plate 16.

No. 1 is the No. 14 just described. It made a good crater, blowing out behind it the material it dislodged on entering.

No. 2. The shell struck the exterior slope and burst well, making a large crater, which laps over upon the superior slope, and blowing down a part of the cheek of the embrasure. The damage is more apparent than real.

Nos. 3, 4, and 5 are fine craters of various sizes. None, however, are of a serious nature.

No. 6 is the best of this series of hits, having been made by a plunging shot, which, if it had fallen a few feet either way, would have ruined a 9-inch M. L. R. This crater is 7 feet wide and 9 feet long.

No. 7 resembles No. 3.

On the superior slope, near hit No. 5, was one of the Inflexible's 16-inch Palliser shell pointing straight out to seaward. Such a position would seem to indicate that the shot had been fired at long range, had become unsteady in its flight, had capsized as it struck, and that enough velocity of rotation was left to roll it out of its bed up to the crest of the parapet. The general good behavior of these shell renders this case interesting because exceptional.

The injuries received by the southeastern or shore side of this fort from plunging shot that had passed over the batteries are shown on Palte 18.

There are two good hits on the parapet of Cavalier B and ten on its northwest scarp back of the water battery. The latter shows two hits on the parapet.

Plate 19 is a view of what was left of the magazine after its explosion at 1.32 p. m. This catastrophe, rendered possible by the absurdly insecure position of the magazine, silenced the fort. The number of killed and wounded by this accident could not be ascertained, but it must have been a fair proportion of the garrison. The occurrence itself was a magnificent specimen of pyrotechnics, resembling the eruption of a volcano. It is hardly to be wondered at that the fort was "hurriedly evacuated" by the survivors. The high battery seen on the right in this plate is Cavalier B.

Passing to the guns, it is found that the largest, a 10-inch Armstrong, was disabled. A shot had struck it on the muzzle, carried away the holdfasts, and knocked the slide trucks off the tracks. The crew were evidently making an attempt to get the gun into position again at the time of the explosion, for the jacks were found under the slide after the action. The adjoining 9-inch guns were unharmed.

In Cavalier B, one X-inch S. B. was dismounted by a shell from the fleet. (Plate 20.)

In the lower sea battery, one X-inch S. B. was dismounted by a shell, and a second was wrecked through the smashing of the slide by a plunging shot.

Besides the shell from the 81-ton gun, already mentioned, three others were found unburst, one 9-inch Palliser, one 10-inch Palliser, and one 10-inch common shell.

Summing up the damage done, we find—

1st. That one 10-inch M. L. R. was put *hors de combat* by the British fire.

2d. That of the smooth-bores which could be brought to bear, three out of seven were disabled if not dismounted.

3d. That the magazine was exploded, and the fort, in consequence, abandoned.

On the other hand—

1st. Four out of the five rifled guns were still serviceable.

2d. The disabled rifled guns could have been restored to efficient working order in a very short time.

3d. The damage done to the walls and parapet was practically insignificant and could have been repaired, where necessary, in a few hours.

Immediately southeast of Fort Ada, lying between it and Fort Pharos, and placed, so to speak, at the apex of the re-entering angle formed by the coast as it runs from one to the other, is a new work known as Fort Ada Lunette. (Plate 12.) It took no part in the bombardment.

Passing to the westward the coast recedes and assumes the shape of a narrow bight, about one thousand yards in length, being, for the most part a shelving, sandy beach, unprovided with defenses. At the western end of this bight begin the Ras-el-Tin Lines, in a new unfinished fortification, called, in Admiral Seymour's report, the Hospital Battery. By glancing at Plates 1 and 21 it is seen that these lines are a succession of open works, on the northwest side of the city, connected by a low parapet of varying form. The position is a strong one by nature, there being sufficient salients to permit, if properly utilized, concentration of fire at any desired point within range. A direct landing is out of the question in view of an outlying reef and of the height and steepness of the bank. An attendant drawback arises from the proximity of the city, into which any hostile shell, ricocheting upwards from the parapet, or fired with too great an elevation, must inevitably fall. This disadvantage is, however, common to all the sea defenses of the northern line.

The Ras-el-Tin Lines comprised three rifled-gun batteries, known as the Hospital, Central, and Tower Batteries, the curtains between being provided with smooth-bore guns and mortars. The total armament consisted of one 10-inch, two 8-inch, and two 7-inch Armstrong M. L. R.,

four XV-inch S. B., sixteen X-inch S. B., of various types, eleven 6½-inch S. B. (or 36-pdrs.), and one XX-inch, seven XIII-inch, and one X-inch mortars. All of these rifled guns and most of the smooth-bores were worked. In addition were the 9-inch M. L. R. on a Moncrieff carriage, and the B. L. R. 40-pdr. Armstrong, on Kennon's lift-carriage already mentioned. This last gun is not shown on either plan. It stands about one hundred yards to the eastward of the Light-House Fort. The mounting of this piece is on a simple and ingenious plan, which may be described in a few words. The gun on an ordinary carriage is borne on a counterpoised platform capable of being raised and lowered in a deep pit. (A gasometer will give a rough idea of the system of counterpoises.) At the bottom of the pit are the magazine and shell-room and the loading chamber. After firing, the gun is lowered for loading, then raised and fired over the bank. The cost of this system must be very great, and might find its justification in the case of a muzzle-loading gun in an exceptionally exposed position.

The Ras-el-Tin Lines were deficient in traverses, while the magazines were subject to the disadvantage of inadequate protection. In rear, at various points, were ample barracks, shell-houses, &c. Incidentally, these served the purpose of defining, with extreme clearness, the target aimed at by the British gunners, to the detriment of the garrison.

The details of the Hospital Battery are given in Plate 22. It was unfinished at the time of the bombardment, so that its guns did not enjoy the full measure of protection which it was designed to give them. This battery was very severely handled, the masonry battered in, and the guns blocked. It is simply impossible to note or even fairly estimate the number of hits. The left flank is completely breached and the top of the new expense magazine deeply scored by shells. The wreckage of the right embrasure was caused by a 16-inch Palliser shell. The battery mounted two 7-inch M. L. R. The guns themselves were uninjured. Subsequently they were transported to Ramleh and mounted there in the British lines of defense. Upon one of them no less than 49 shrapnel marks were counted, some as deep as half an inch. This, a 10-inch shrapnel, must have burst directly in front of the muzzle of the gun and have inflicted terrible damage upon the gun's crew. A shell burst under the front track of this gun, tore it up, and twisted the left front truck in its socket. In spite of all these disasters, and of the heavy machine-gun fire to which it was subjected, the Hospital Battery was fought until 3 p. m., or for eight hours. This circumstance alone would prove the stubbornness of the defense. It is proper to recall the words of Captain Hunt-Grubbe's official report: "One rifled gun in the Hospital earthworks, which it was impossible to dismount, being invisible from the ship, did us great damage."

The smooth-bores to the westward of the Hospital Battery were nearly all worked more or less. One X-inch gun, marked a on Plate 21, was dismounted by a shell, and another, b, by its own recoil, having probably been overcharged.

The buildings and walls in rear bear evidence of the use of Nordenfeldt and Gatling guns by the fleet.

The large modern work, called for the sake of clearness the Central Battery, is drawn on Plate 23, where the principal scars on the parapet are marked. Its relation to its neighbors appears on Plate 21. It suffered very severely, receiving the full attention of the broadside vessels in the offshore squadron.

No. 1 is a deep cut on the right cheek of the embrasure, but of no practical damage.

No. 2 is a similar wound on the other cheek.

No. 3 is a good hit under the muzzle of the gun, wrecking the holdfast.

Nos. 4 and 5 are mere scores on the cheek, and may even be due to shrapnel.

No. 6 is a fine crater, 11 feet in diameter, made by a well-burst shell. It cannot, however, be considered as a serious wound.

No. 7 is a trench 6 feet long, 4 feet wide, and 1 foot deep, scooped out by a glancing shell.

No. 8 is a severe wound in the sill of the embrasure, which was totally wrecked. The revetment of the interior slope is gone between the points marked d and e.

No. 9 is a scooped trench like No. 7.

The 10-inch rifled gun was put completely *hors de combat*. The right front truck is gone. The compressors appear to have failed, for the gun has recoiled violently and damaged the buffers. The masonry at the pivot has been battered in and the slide trucks are nearly off their tracks. The gun itself was struck on the chase, and the outer tube split 2 feet from the muzzle.

Its immediate neighbor, a 9-inch M. L. R., is uninjured. The holdfast shows a tendency to rise off the pivot.

The remaining gun in this battery experienced a complication of troubles. It was rendered useless through the jamming of a shell in the bore. It was badly hit on the trunnion and on the right carriage-bracket 6 inches in rear of the trunnion. The holdfasts had begun to give way, and the pivot was bent, while the trucks were blocked by the fragments of the ruined embrasure.

The third modern battery in the Ras-el-Tin Lines is distinguished by a martello tower around which it is built, and through which it is known as the Tower Battery. It is shown in detail on Plate 24, where the principal hits on the parapet are sketched in.

No. 1 was probably made by a glancing shell which cut 2 feet out of the right cheek of the embrasure of the easternmost 8-inch M. L. R.

No. 2 appears to be due to two well-burst shell. The right cheek is knocked away.

No. 3 is a very good hit. The masonry at the angle is torn out and thrown down on the tracks, thus blocking the carriage.

No. 4. Several light hits on the superior slope.

No. 5 is a crater about 9 feet across and 3 feet deep, made by a shell which burst after getting fairly buried. The end of the cheek of the embrasure is destroyed, but the gun was not damaged and the resisting power of the battery was unaffected.

No. 6 is a breach 10 feet wide in the parapet, and is shown in section on Plate 24. It did no harm to the guns.

No. 7 is a large crater, 10 feet in width by 6 feet in length and 3 feet in depth, caused by a well-burst shell.

No. 8. The right cheek of the embrasure is cut away.

The 8-inch Armstrong M. L. R. on the right of the battery was struck under the chase, but was not injured. The right front truck of the top carriage was smashed, and the left bracket was cut through by a splinter of masonry. The gun could have been used again.

The other rifled gun was hopelessly wrecked. A shell had apparently fairly entered the embrasure, striking the chase and third coil, and, passing underneath the gun, had exploded inside the carriage. The brackets were blown clean out and the gun permanently disabled.

A portion of the Ras-el-Tin palace buildings, erroneously termed the harem, was set on fire by shells which were directed against the Tower and Central Batteries, but which overshot the mark and exploded inside this house. It is believed that this is the only building in Alexandria thus fired by British shells.

In the Ras-el-Tin Lines the practice of the British fleet is seen to have been vastly more disastrous to the rifled guns than in either Pharos or Ada. Of the seven in all, mounted, the 10-inch, one each of the 9 and 8 inch and both 7-inch guns were disabled, the latter being blocked by masonry splinters. There were thus left but one 9-inch and one 8-inch gun still serviceable.

The parapets could all have been restored, temporarily at least, in a single night, and the 10-inch, possibly the 9-inch, and both 7-inch guns made capable of use in a very short time.

The smooth-bores suffered but two wrecks, both near the Hospital Battery. The parapet here is so low that the crews could be readily driven from the guns by smaller pieces of ordnance, leaving the heavy guns of the fleet comparatively free to devote their entire attention to the rifled guns. The smooth-bore, bowled off its carriage, was, however, struck by a heavy shell. In spite of 20-pdrs., Nordenfeldts and Gatlings, these old-fashioned guns were vigorously served, doing much damage to the ships.

The Ras-el-Tin Lines terminate to the westward in a well-designed bastioned fort, surrounding the modern light-house of Alexandria. The point on which the fort is situated is called Eunostos Point, and the fort itself has been termed variously as Eunostos, Ras-el-Tin, and the Light-House Fort. Plate 1, exhibits the general command of this work: northwest to seaward, west to seaward, in the direction of the channels, across the bar, south and southeast over the harbor. It is built on solid rock, the scarp rising abruptly from the level of the sea, above which, at the height of 28 feet, is the terreplein. The plans and sections of the fort are given on Plate 25, which also shows an enlarged plan of the west or main sea face. The parapet of the original fort had been greatly thickened prior to the mounting of the modern guns, and at the time of the bombardment the process of further increasing its defensive qualities was still going on.

A landing pier and sally-port are on the south side. The main magazine is at *b* on the plan, smaller expense magazines being indicated by dotted lines in most of the traverses.

The eastern part of the walled inclosure is a fortified barracks, affording ample accommodation for a thousand men. The land approaches to the fort are commanded by loop-holed chambers, thrown forward Portions of the northern and southern walls are similarly pierced for musketry.

The Light-House Fort mounted one 10-inch, four 9-inch, and one 8-inch Armstrong M. L. R. Of these the latter and one of the 9-inch guns could not be brought to bear on the British fleet. The west curtain carried two XV-inch and two X-inch cast-iron S. B. guns, which, however, were not manned or fired on July 11. On the north front are three more X-inch S. B. guns, and on the south front a large battery of twenty-one $6\frac{1}{2}$-inch S. B.

The four rifled guns on the west face were alone employed on the day of the bombardment. They were subjected to an extremely heavy fire (practically from all five ships of the offshore squadron), which has left well-marked traces. They were all, especially those in the south bastion, most indifferently protected, the parapet being dangerously low.

On Plate 17, Fig. 51, is a sketch of the west face of the right or northern bastion, showing the principal scars.

No. 1 is a large pile of *débris* knocked down by several shells. It is impossible to ascertain the exact number of hits that combined to produce this effect.

No. 2 is a hole 15 feet wide, the work of not less than two well-burst shell. The crater is 5 feet deep.

No. 3. A shell burst well in the exterior slope, making a gap 9 feet 7 inches wide.

No. 4 is a clearly defined crater, 4 feet 6 inches wide, 4 feet high, and 3 feet 6 inches deep.

On the scarp of the curtain are eleven hits. The largest, made by a shell from the Inflexible, is shown in Fig. 52, Plate 17. The average depth over the surface is 4 feet and at the hit 8 feet. The effect of the explosion is certainly extensive, but very little of the exterior slope is brought down, and the parapet is in no way weakened. The other hits on the scarp are of very slight importance; the projectiles have entered to the depth of about 3 or 4 feet each. All these wounds were occasioned by stray shell aimed at the guns in the bastions.

Passing to the curtain parapet, we find (see Plate 25) a number of good hits.

No. 5 is a large, well-formed crater, about 9 feet in diameter, extending half way across the parapet.

No. 6 is a cut clear down to the cordon from 4 feet above the exterior crest.

No. 7 is a trench scooped out of the top of a traverse containing an expense magazine. The trench is $8\frac{1}{2}$ feet long and 6 feet 9 inches wide.

No. 8 is a beautiful breach, made by a plunging shot, cutting down the crest of the parapet along a distance of 12 feet. Fig. 53, Plate 17, is a section through the middle of the gap. The shell must have exploded as soon as fairly buried. The mean thickness of the parapet is 18 feet. The path of the shot through it is 12 feet.

No. 9 is a practicable breach at the angle between the curtain and the southern bastion.

No. 10 is a good crater in the exterior slope, overlapping the superior slope.

Nos. 11, 12, and 13. The corner is knocked down, but little real damage done.

No. 14 is a scar on the right cheek of the bastion.

No. 15. The shell burst well, blowing away the outer corner of the left cheek.

No. 16 is a large, but not serious, crater in the traverse.

Nos. 17 and 18 are good craters in the slopes running down over the cordon into the scarp.

No. 19. Wrecked the embrasure.

The right face of the south bastion is shown in Fig. 50, Plate 17.

Hit No. 1 is the same as No. 18 just described.

No. 2 is a hole 3 feet deep, 3 feet 6 inches high, and 2 feet 6 inches wide.

No. 3 is similar to No. 2. On the ground, 6 feet distant, lies a 10-inch common shell pointing towards the hole.

No. 4 is a hole into which a projectile has penetrated to the depth of at least 8 feet.

No. 5 burst on the cordon, making a good crater 7 feet 6 inches long and 4 feet wide.

No. 6 is similar to No. 2.

No. 7 is a scar made by a 10-inch common shell which burst on impact, scaling off the wall over an area $7\frac{1}{2}$ feet long and 4 feet wide to the depth of a foot.

Nos. 8 and 9 are two connecting craters made by blind shell.

Passing to the inside of the northern bastion, and referring to Plate 26, the damage sustained becomes evident at once.

The 9-inch gun, mounted in the capital of the bastion, has been rendered useless by excessive and improperly controlled recoil. A stouter forelock through the pivot would have resisted the shearing action of the sudden bump with which the gun came in, would have retained the holdfasts in place and the gun in serviceable condition. The state of its neighbor is the work of, perhaps, the best shot of the day. The gun itself is deeply scored under the chase. After inflicting this wound the shell probably passed inside the carriage and burst, throwing the gun over backwards on top of several of the crew, who were found in that position on the following day. It is possible that the smashing of the trunnion band may have been due to another and previous shell.

In the left, or southern bastion, the 10-inch M. L. R. gun was the last to be silenced. It was this gun that killed Lieutenant Jackson on board the Inflexible. The gun was hit on the A-tube but not damaged, being eventually placed *hors de combat* by the wrecking of the embrasure.

Its neighbor, a 9-inch M. L. R., is said to have been the first gun disabled. It is shown in Plate 27. The embrasure is ruined, the pivot gone, and the gun is on end. It is not impossible that this result may have followed upon the knocking in of the sill of the embrasure, but it is more likely to have been due to a weak pivot and thus to be a mere duplication of the experience in the northern bastion.

The third gun in this bastion, a 9-inch M. L. R., was not worked during the engagement. It bore upon the harbor. Being well masked, it escaped injury.

The remaining rifled gun in the fort, an 8-inch Armstrong, mounted on the southern or inner face, was not worked. It is seen in Plate 28. It suffered badly from reverse fire. The left training truck is gone and the embrasure wrecked.

The masonry in the neighborhood and the walls of the buildings bear the impression of many Nordenfeldt bullets, shrapnel balls, &c. The buildings within the fort are terribly breached and damaged. The light-house itself did not escape; several holes of various sizes having been made in it by stray shell and shell fragments. The general state of affairs shown in Plate 29 is insignificant in comparison with that of the large shell-houses marked *d* and *e* on Plate 25.

This fort ceased fire at 10.30 a. m.

Extensive as are the damages noted as sustained by the masonry in the Light-House Fort, due to the combined efforts of the offshore squadron aided by the Temeraire and the after or starboard turret of the Inflexible, it is impossible to avoid the conclusion that in the main the thickened parapets resisted the impact extremely well, the sole practicable breach being made in the thin 15-foot wall of the curtain, where, also, was cut the noteworthy gap already sketched and described. They failed to yield sufficient protection to the garrison, and they suffered greatly about the crests and about the cheeks of the embrasures, but through being too *low*, not too thin.

If it is borne in mind that here were four guns whose positions could be unmistakably marked by ranges on high and conspicuous objects in rear, engaged with no less than twenty-six* guns, of which fifteen were as large as the largest gun in the fort and three were larger, the result of the work done can be readily understood.

But two guns, one 10-inch and one 9-inch M. L. R., can be considered as promising an immediate period of renewed usefulness. One 9-inch gun is ruined beyond redemption and the other can only be restored to working condition at the expense of much time and labor. Through the fire of the fleet, three out of four are rendered unfit for employment. But, however, two of the four guns could have been gotten ready for fighting the next day.

The lines on the southern shore of the bay begin close to the town at Fort Saleh Aga. Plates 1 and 30.

This is an old work near the shore, consisting of a water battery and a square redoubt, the latter surrounded by a dry ditch. One face of the redoubt, mounting four 6½-inch S. B., is designed to command the shore approaches from the westward. The other faces bear upon the harbor, and mount, in all, five X-inch and twelve 6½-inch S. B., with one XI-inch mortar. Being an inner defense, Saleh Aga was not attacked until late in the afternoon of the day of the bombardment, being under the fire of the Monarch and Penelope for a very short time. The parapets are practically untouched. A 6½-inch S. B. gun was dismounted by the ships.

Southwest of Saleh Aga, and distant from it about 800 yards, is an old-fashioned open battery, adjoining a martello tower, and mounting two X-inch S. B. and two 6½-inch S. B. guns. The parapet shows five or six good hits, and the scarp one more. None of them are at all serious. The extreme western gun of the four, one of the smaller type, has, unquestionably, been struck by a shell. The gun is cut in two, and the muzzle portion thrown many yards to the front. It is difficult to reconcile the situation of this fragment with the evidence of the blow.

At a second interval of about 800 yards is a closed work, known as Fort Oom-el-Kabebe, in many respects one of the most interesting of the forts about Alexandria. It stands back from the water on the comparatively high ground, about 80 feet in elevation, that lies between the harbor and Lake Mariout (ancient Marœotis). The fort commands the inner harbor (see Plate 1), the Corvette and Boghaz Passes. After crossing the bar any vessel would still be continually under its fire until it actually reached the city. Plate 31 is an interior view of this fort, looking east, with the inner harbor as a background. On Plate 32 is a general plan of the fort, a large irregular work, whose principal front is turned towards the northwest. The southern face is thrown back to command the land approaches from Mex. The eastern side recedes towards the center, narrowing the work at this point.

---

*The Temeraire's share in the operations against the Light-House Fort was inconsiderable.

Practically it consists of two connecting courts, with barracks and other buildings in each, two sides of which mount guns, the whole surrounded by a dry ditch 30 feet in width and of varying depth. A miter-shaped detached work at the eastern extremity contains a large defensible barracks. At one point of the principal face the old parapet has been thickened to about 27 feet, the terreplein widened, and two 8-inch Armstrong M. L. R. mounted in embrasures. In addition to these are six X-inch S. B. and ten 6½-inch S. B., one XIII-inch and two XI-inch mortars. Plate 33 is an interior view at the western end, which includes, incidentally, the land between Oom-el-Kabebe and Mex.

The professional interest which this fort offers is derived from the fact that, being engaged by the Inflexible at the long range of 3,800 yards, the shot struck the work at a considerable angle of fall. The most noticeable of the wounds inflicted by this vessel are marked on Plate 32.

No. 1 is a fine breach in the counterscarp, 10 feet wide and 6 feet deep. The descent into the ditch, through this gap and over the *débris* at the bottom, would be very feasible.

No. 2 is a small scar on the cordon. Near it are three small hits on the gorge of the work.

No. 3 is a fine hole in the retaining wall of the scarp. The angle is cut away for 10 feet along each face, making an almost practicable breach. The shell has burst at exactly the right depth.

No. 4, a small gouge out of the counterscarp, appears to have been done by the same shell which inflicted wound No. 3, in its flight.

No. 5 is a splendid crater. The shell has fallen at an advantageous angle, and burst when well buried, blowing out the earth of the superior slope from a hole 17 feet long, 14 feet wide, and 5 feet deep.

No. 6 is similar to the above, but a trifle smaller superficially and 6 inches shallower.

No. 7 is best seen in Plate 31, immediately beyond and under the muzzle of the nearest gun. This was a dangerously effective shot, and must have inflicted great injury upon the garrison, through the splinters of the masonry it dislodged. It lacked but a few feet of lateral deviation to be by far the best shot of the day.

No. 8 is a large breach in the counterscarp, measuring 12 feet across and reaching 3 feet down. As in the case of No. 1, the pile of *débris* beneath, together with the gap itself, forms an easy descent into the ditch.

No 9 is an almost practicable breach in the scarp. It measures 10 feet along the cordon.

No. 10 is a shallow irregular crater in the superior slope, 2½ feet across and 9 inches deep.

No. 11 is a good crater, 7½ feet in diameter and nearly 5 feet deep.

No. 12 is another serious hit, cutting down the parapet at the embrasure nearly to the terreplein. The gun in the embrasure is broken up. These two results may be due to different shell.

No. 13 is a deep trough plowed in the superior slope, 7 feet wide at its greatest breadth and 12 feet long. It reaches to the crest of the parapet, along which it measures 3 feet.

Reference will be made later to these craters, whose extensive and dangerous character should be remembered.

To the guns in Oom-el-Kabebe very little damage was done. The 8-inch rifles were untouched, although literally covered with dust and gravel, tossed about by the shell as they landed. (The injury to the muzzle of the gun seen in Plate 35 was done by gun-cotton after the occupation of the place by the British.) The X-inch S. B. on their right, is dismounted and thrown in rear of the terreplein (Plate 31), probably by its own recoil. The first $6\frac{1}{2}$-inch S. B. on their left, beyond the traverse shown in the plan, Plate 32, has come to an extraordinary end. The breech of the gun is seen in Plate 34 lying in the middle of the western court. It was, doubtless, knocked off its carriage and smashed by a Palliser shell. The fracture, as inspected on the spot, is not that of a burst. A portion of the muzzle went through the air over the roofs of the intervening buildings and lodged in a wall at a, at the western end of the fort (see plan). The guns seen in the various plates to be lying alongside of their slides were capsized by blue-jackets from the fleet after the bombardment.

Oom-el-Kabebe is stated to have been "most troublesome." Its practice was certainly good.

A large number of blind shell were found here.

The firing of the Inflexible against this work, both as witnessed from the outer anchorage during the day and as seen in the results enumerated, was admirable.

After all, but one gun was disabled by the fleet, and the damage to the parapet could have been repaired in a very short time. The parapet itself was too low to give proper shelter against modern projectiles.

Reverting to Plate 33, the cage beacon in the half distance is one of the leading-marks for entering the Boghaz Pass. Immediately in front of it is a small detached work, known as Fort Kumaria, which took no part in the engagement. To the right is the outer harbor, bounded beyond by the shoulder of land which terminates at Fort Adjemi. Just over the right of Kumaria is the martello tower in the battery which begins the Mex Lines. The lateen yards belong to native craft at Mex, the buildings of which place appear close to the beacon. The minarets are on an unfinished and long-deserted summer palace of the Khedive, to the left of which is seen the citadel of Mex.

Plate 1 shows that the Mex Lines extend along the shore for a distance of 2,000 yards, beginning with the Martello Tower Battery, just pointed out, and ending in Mex Fort and the land lines which stretch across the isthmus from shore to shore.

As every vessel entering the harbor must approach Mex, pass close to it, and remain for a long time within easy range of this series of fortifications, it naturally received great attention in the original design. The construction, having been effected in the early part of the century, falls far below the requirements of to-day. The guns are all mounted *en barbette* behind thin, old-fashioned walls in wretched condition.

The trace of these lines is given on the conventional plan, Plate XL.

In the lines proper, not including the fort of Mex, were mounted four XV-inch S. B., eleven X-inch S. B., and eight $6\frac{1}{2}$-inch S. B.

In the Martello Tower Battery, B C, one X-inch gun was knocked over backwards by a shell, and one was dismounted by its own recoil.

Near this, at G H, is a pair of XV-inch S. B., intact, on very rotten carriages. They were not served on July 11.

The whole length of these lines was subjected to a very searching fire of machine guns throughout the day, particularly after the gun-boats came inside. The walls bear testimony to the sharpness of the fire.

Back of the Mex Lines are two or three old forts, designed to guard the land approaches. One of them had been turned into a magazine, where no less than 7,000 barrels of powder were stowed. Among them lay the Penelope's unexploded shell.

To the eastward of the village of Mex the land projects slightly into the sea, affording a site for a fort, whose only disadvantage is lack of elevation. On Plate 37 is a general plan of the fortification.

The front is twice broken at a wide angle. The parapet of the western portion has been greatly thickened and heightened, embrasures cut, and substantial emplacements prepared for two rifled guns. In Plate 38 the line of separation between the new and the old work on the retaining wall is clearly shown.

To the left and rear of the new rifled-gun battery is a smooth-bore battery, facing in the same general direction. It can be seen in Plate 39. The third battery of Fort Mex lies to the eastward of the heavy rifled-gun battery, and contains a number of guns of various calibers and types. Plate 40 is of special value in several respects. It shows the relation between this and the other lower battery, the low nature of the land, and the appearance of the harbor between Mex and Alexandria. Its chief merit, however, is in making clearer than is possible by any verbal description the inadequate protection enjoyed by the Egyptian guns and gunners during the bombardment, the total lack of overhead protection, the lack of traverses, the soft, friable character of the material used in the construction of the forts, and the brittleness of the mortar revetting employed on the slopes. It will be observed that nearly all of this revetment, which the picture shows to have been knocked off near the muzzles of the guns, is simply blown away by the concussion of the Egyptian firing, but little being destroyed by impact of the British shell. The integrity of this thin coating of plaster on the crest of the parapet in any of the fortifications at Alexandria is unfailing evidence that the gun immediately above it was not fired during the action.

At Mex preparations were making just before July 11 for the mounting of two more 10-inch and two more 9-inch Armstrong M. L. R., the guns, carriages, and slides being in readiness on the spot. (Plates 40 and 41.) The guns actually in place comprised one 10-inch, one 9-inch, and three 8-inch M. L. R. guns, four X-inch and five $6\frac{1}{2}$-inch S. B. guns, six XIII-inch, two XI-inch, and two X-inch mortars.

The chief scars on the rifled-gun battery are sketched in on the plan of the fort, Plate 37.

No. 1 is a small trench in the superior slope.

No. 2 is a large but unimportant wound on the angle.

No. 3 is a deep score in the exterior slope, due probably to shrapnel.

No. 4 is a crater about 6 feet in diameter and 16 inches deep.

No. 5 is a series of small hits, knocking off the crest of the parapet and cutting away pieces of the interior slope. (Plate 39.)

No. 6 is a small trench like No. 1.

No. 7 is a cut down the exterior slope to the cordon, and is a good crater made by a well-burst shell.

No. 8 is an excellent gap. (Plate 38.) The interior slope is knocked away for a distance of 12 feet measured along the crest.

Nos. 9 and 10 are craters made by good bursts. The former is 12 feet long by $8\frac{1}{2}$ feet wide, and is 2 feet 6 inches deep.

No. 11 is a long, deep breach in the jetty-like wall, the prolongation of the scarp (but unbacked by earth filling). The splinters from this wall must have proved very harassing to the people in the fort. The gap itself extends into the scarp of the fortification, which is cut away to 5 feet below the cordon.

The serious character of the pieces of stone hurled about by the impact of the ships' shells can be best appreciated from an inspection of Plates 39 and 42. The former shows how complete was the wreck of the 10-inch-gun embrasure.

In Plate 40 is seen the damage sustained by the eastern battery, and in Plates 39, 40, and 41 the nature of the injuries received by the buildings within the enceinte. These were frightfully battered to pieces by shell that glanced up from the parapet or over shot their mark.

In view of the tremendous fire to which Fort Mex was subjected and the comparatively short range at which all the ships, except the Temeraire, engaged it, it is almost impossible to believe the fact that not a single gun here was dismounted or disabled during the action proper. The 10-inch and the 9-inch rifles (Plates 38 and 43) were wrecked with gun-cotton. The 8-inch gun, seen on the ground in Plate 41, was bowled over by the Penelope, long after the fort had ceased firing, and from a distance stated to be about 300 yards. The successful shot was the thirtieth of this series, and was aimed by the gunnery-lieutenant. The gun in going over has taken the top carriage with it and overturned the slide. The blow was received under the left side of the first coil, tearing out a strip 2 feet long by nearly 5 inches wide, and starting the whole coil from the chase on the other side. The B-tube has a well-marked transverse split about 33 inches from the muzzle.

The 10-inch rifle bears two scars from shells on the coils on the left side and several marks of Nordenfeldt bullets. One of the latter has scooped out a fine track 4½ inches long on the breech, and another has entered the breech-coil to the depth of half an inch.

The 9-inch rifle was struck on the right side just in front of the trunnions by a fragment of shell, and on the breech-coil by a shell, which made a furrow a foot long, 7 inches wide, and an inch and a quarter deep, and then glanced off. (See Plate 42.)

The carriage of the left X-inch S. B. in the lower battery was hit by a piece of shell, and the gun itself by many shrapnel balls, but neither was injured.

The adjoining 8-inch rifled guns were struck by shrapnel balls, one showing twelve hits, the other nine.

Mex was the only fort at Alexandria which could not have resumed the action on the following day, for the party which landed from the Invincible, at the spot marked *a* on Plate 37, completed the work of destruction but just began by the fleet, ruining the carriages of the two heavy guns by exploding gun-cotton inside the brackets, and spiking the remaining guns in the lower batteries. Except for this gallant and eminently successful exploit, the parapets might have been sufficiently repaired during the night by heavy gangs of natives to enable the garrison to reopen fire. The Egyptians here had lost so severely that only men of a high order of bravery could have been induced to expose themselves to a repetition of the hammering they had endured on July 11. The actual garrison was whipped, and thoroughly whipped, after a most creditable and determined resistance, but it is hardly to be doubted that if it had been of a *personnel* similar to that on board the attacking fleet the spiking party would have had difficulty in executing their task, and on July 12 the challenge from the ships would have been promptly accepted.

Mex Citadel, so called, is a large square fortified barracks, with a deep, wide ditch around it, situated on the top of the ridge back of Mex Fort. Adjoining the citadel on the northwest face is a small open battery mounting four 6½-inch guns. An embrasure was improvised in the western angle for a 40-pdr. Armstrong B. L. R. These guns were well served. The practice of one of the smooth-bores against the Invincible received especial praise from Admiral Seymour. The walls show the traces of heavy return fire. The crew of the Armstrong gun suffered severely from a well-directed and well-burst shell. No real damage, however, was done to the guns or the fortification.

Three thousand yards to the westward of Mex is a small old-fashioned fort, close to the sea, called, by Admiral Seymour, Marsa-el-Khanat. It mounted three X-inch S. B. and one 6½-inch S. B. In a yard near by were found three 9-inch Armstrong M. L. R., ready for mounting. The fort thus strengthened would have been a formidable addition to the defenses of the Marabout Passage. The fort did not bear a scratch. Two of the X-inch guns had been, by this recoil, capsized. They were of the lightest pattern, and could not stand the heavy charges and solid shot with which they had evidently been fired.

Fort Marabout, the westernmost of the forts bearing on the bay, is on the rocky island of the same name. It is an old-fashioned work with a steep scarp. The trace is long and narrow. (Plate 32.) Its northeastern corner was prepared, in the same manner as elsewhere, for the reception of modern guns. It is well supplied with barracks, shell-stores, &c.

In a were found large quantities of filled cartridges. As the building projected well above the crest of the parapet, the wonder is but natural that these cartridges should have escaped explosion. The room served as an expense magazine.

b is a kitchen; c a store-house full of oil, in jars; d is the principal magazine also well supplied with made cartridges; e is a filling room for smooth-bore shells; f is a fuze store-house; in g were stores of timber; h is a filling room for shells; i is a store-room containing mortar implements and stores; l and m are large and well-furnished stores of empty shells, both rifled and smooth-bore, together with ordnance stores of every description.

The liberal scale of equipment observed in this fort is due to its remoteness from the base at Alexandria and its insular position.

Close to the entrance of the fort is a small landing pier. The armament consisted of three 9-inch M. L. R., and of nine X-inch S. B. and sixteen $6\frac{1}{2}$-inch S. B. guns.

Five additional Armstrong M. L. R. were found in the fort awaiting the preparation of gun emplacements. These were one 10-inch, two 8-inch, and two 7-inch guns. At least two would have been plac d on the east front to command the Marabout Channel.

The northeastern corner received the fire of the Condor and other gun-boats, and the southeastern a few shots from the inside fleet, notably the Monarch. The scarp of the former is well pitted. It shows about twenty hits in all. The damage is, however, all apparent, none real.

The rock on which the fort is built is plastered up to a smooth surface. This coating of plaster, which is about a foot thick, has peeled off freely where the shot have struck. A 64-pdr. shell, for instance, has made a hole 10 feet in diameter in this sham scarp. One small building was set on fire, a notable result in view of the large number of blind shell found in the fort.

The irregular scarp at the southeast corner is natural. It has received several hits, thought to be due to the Monarch.

The guns in this fort were uninjured.

Of the neighboring fort, Adjemi, it is merely necessary to state that it is commenced on a large scale. Unfinished as it is, Adjemi mounts three 10-inch, five 9-inch, and one 7-inch Armstrong M. L. R. behind a 50-foot parapet, while the magazines, barracks, &c., are excellent in design. Being quite useless from its position, Adjemi was not engaged on July 11. A similar work near the city would have proved a serious antagonist to the British fleet.

In considering the state of the southern line of defenses of Alexandria after the bombardment, it is more than ever necessary to distinguish between the real and the apparent damage done to them; the former being those wounds which immediately affected their fighting qualities, in the disabling of the guns, the fatal breaching of the parapets, the wrecking of the gun-pivots, or the destruction of vitally important stores of ammunition; the latter being shell marks on the parapets, not necessarily fatal, however large, and especially shot wounds and holes in the buildings within the enceinte. Self-inflicted harm on each side is, of course, excluded.

Applying this test and summing up the injuries received by the fortifications of this line, one is amazed to find how slight they were in reality.

Including even the rifled gun in Mex, which was dismounted by the Penelope at leisure after the fort had ceased firing, the following is the loss of offensive power occasioned directly by the fleet:

In Saleh-Aga, one 6½-inch S. B. dismounted.
In the next battery, one X-inch S. B. dismounted.
In Oom-el-Kabebe, one 6½-inch S. B. dismounted.
In Martello Tower Battery, one X-inch S. B. dismounted.
In Mex Fort, one 8-inch M. L. R. dismounted.

These make a total of but five guns in the sea batteries extending from Saleh Aga to Marsa-el-Khanat, and including both works.

In the foregoing description of the effects on the fortifications at Alexandria of the bombardment by the vessels under Admiral Sir Beauchamp Seymour, great prominence is given to the Inflexible's practice. This is due partly to the magnitude of the wounds she inflicted, but partly also to the fact that the guns she carried were the only ones of their type in the fleet, and that her projectiles were in consequence readily recognized even when in small fragments. The same facility of identification was impossible in the cases of the other ships. An 11-inch shell, for example, if found in the northern line, might have come from either the Temeraire or the Alexandra. The confusion is still greater when the smaller shell are considered, for 10-inch guns were mounted by all the members of the offshore squadron, and 9-inch guns were carried by several in both squadrons.

It is worthy of mention that the credit for best shooting seemed to be divided between the Temeraire and Inflexible, the only ships in which the guns were worked by hydraulic power.

POSTSCRIPT.—Since the foregoing was written a very interesting article has been read before the United Service Institution by Captain

Walford, R. A., in which the expenditure of ammunition by the British fleet is given in detail. From Captain Walford's article the following tables are extracted:

Ship.	Filled shell.				Empty shell.	Shot.	Case.	Total.
	Common.	Palliser.	Shrapnel.	Segment.				
Alexandra	379	23	1			4		407
Sultan	247	24	3	44	10	10		338
Superb	257	83	25	34		12		411
Penelope	241		45	32		62		380
Monarch	227	5	129			6		367
Temeraire	139	70	13	6				228
Invincible	221		25		2	2		250
Inflexible	139	21	11	37				208
Beacon	21			1	61	18		101
Condor	162		8		31			201
Bittern	66	7	1			12	3	89
Cygnet	72				71			143
Decoy	69							69
Helicon	6							6
Total	2,246	233	261	154	175	126	3	3,198
Percentage	70	7	8	5	5.5	4.5		

Average number of rounds per heavy gun.

Ship.	Gun.							General average.
	16-inch.	12-inch.	11-inch.	10-inch.	9-inch.	8-inch.	7-inch.	
Alexandra			24.00	22.1				22.4
Sultan				17.12	12.5			15.5
Superb				19.37				19.3
Penelope						28.8		28.8
Monarch		29.25			24.00		21	26.57
Temeraire			34.00	21.00				27.5
Invincible					12.6			12.6
Inflexible	22							22.0
General average	22	29.25	30.00	19.79	14.00	28.8	21	20.6

Expenditure of ammunition—shot and shell.

Ship.	Gun.							Total heavy guns.
	16-inch.	12-inch.	11-inch.	10-inch.	9-inch.	8-inch.	7-inch.	
Alexandra			48	221				269
Sultan				137	50			187
Superb				310				310
Penelope						231		231
Monarch		117			48		21	186
Temeraire			136	84				220
Invincible					126			126
Inflexible		88						88
Beacon						16		16
Condor						65		65
Bittern						33		33
Cygnet								
Decoy								
Helicon								
Total		88	117	184	752	224	231	135	1,731

Ship.	Gun.					Grand total.	Martini-Henry.	Nordenfeldt.	Gatling.	Rockets.
	64-pounder.	40-pounder.	20-pounder.	9-pounder.	7-pounder.					
Alexandra			138			407		4,000	340	
Sultan			139		12	338		1,800	2,000	
Superb			60	41		411		1,161	880	
Penelope		96	23	30		380	5,000	1,672		
Monarch				153	28	367	1,800	3,440	2,680	21
Temeraire			8			228		160		
Invincible	106		18			250	2,000	2,000	1,000	
Inflexible			120			208		2,000		
Beacon	22		53		10	101	320			3
Condor	128				8	201	1,000		200	13
Bittern		56				89				
Cygnet	101		42			143				
Decoy	49		20			69	40			
Helicon	6					6				
Total	412	152	621	224	58	3,198	10,160	16,233	7,100	37

The amount of powder fired away was 131,856.5 pounds, of which amount the Inflexible used 39,000 and the Superb 22,897.75 pounds.

VII.

GENERAL CONCLUSIONS.

Such an occurrence as the bombardment of the fortifications at Alexandria is so rare in recent naval annals that a proper consideration of its results must yield valuable lessons for the guidance of all interested in either offensive or defensive methods of warfare. Certain points suggest themselves naturally and almost inevitably. In other cases the inference drawn may be erroneous, but the arguments advanced are believed to warrant the deductions. The term "fort" is limited to the defensive works designed to protect a harbor from the entrance of an inimical fleet.

1. The command of a fort, or its height above the level of the sea, is of enormous importance.

A difference of a few feet in this respect may so change the angle of fall of a well-directed shot as to cause it to be received along the line of greatest instead of along the line of least resistance of the parapet, while, on the other hand, it gives the defense an increased chance of returning plunging shot that may strike a ship's deck, the part where she enjoys a minimum of protection.

A comparison of the damage done on the masonry of the upper and lower batteries of Fort Pharos is instructive in this connection. In Fort Ada, again, the dismounted guns were all in the two lower batteries; and at Fort Oom-el-Kabebe, to contend against the unusually good command on the part of the fort and to secure a proper direction of descent for the projectile, the fleet was obliged to engage it by powerful guns at great range. Now, great range is another expression for lessened probability of successful practice. Lastly, can any reasonable doubt be entertained that the Light-House Fort suffered more severely than Fort Pharos partly and largely, but not exclusively, because it was fourteen feet lower?

2. As to the requisite thickness of the parapet.

The British have no gun afloat which can send a projectile through, or seriously damage, a good earthen parapet 30 feet in thickness at ordinarily practicable ranges. This statement may, it is thought, be extended to embrace, as well, the 71-ton Krupp steel B. L. R., with its 34,000 foot-tons of total energy, and even the 100-ton Armstrong M. L. R., which throws a shell having 41,000 foot-tons of stored-up energy, the additional 7,000 foot tons of energy not appearing to be sufficient to take its shot clean through where the first failed so completely.

For the present, at least, 30 feet of well-packed loam may be accepted as yielding adequate protection. At the embrasure proper a small amount of heavy armor might be advantageously applied, in ways that would naturally suggest themselves to the military engineer, who could thus secure cheap and efficient protection.

3. The parapet must be high above the sill of the embrasure. If low, it may be gradually cut down to a dangerous extent, as at Mex (Plate 38). At Oom-el-Kabebe, where the crest was of the same height (6 feet above the terreplein), a comparatively large percentage of the garrison were wounded by masonry splinters alone, and the guns covered with *débris*. The Light-House Fort suffered badly through the same defect in design. The condition of the 8-inch guns in Fort Pharos, mounted behind parapets 2 feet higher, may be instructively studied in Plates 8 and 9. With flat trajectories more damage must be expected from flying pieces of masonry than from the enemy's shell. By means of the former the horizontal motion of the shot is changed into vertical motion, which is vastly more dangerous to the people inside the fort.

4. In constructing a fortification nothing should be allowed to appear above the crest of the parapet, and the latter should be an unbroken line.

If this rule is not followed, the attack is furnished with an excellent target, or with means of readily identifying the position of the guns in the battery, and of concentrating its fire with ease upon any desired point.

5. For this reason, among others, the system of mounting guns *en barbette* should not be followed. In fact, the barbette guns suffered most at Alexandria, being much more roughly treated than those in embrasures, thus proving practically their theoretical deficiencies. Merlons, therefore, would appear to be indispensable in the uncovered batteries of any well designed fortified work.

6. The British gunners were greatly aided in the task of pointing by having the black muzzles of the Egyptian guns clearly defined against the light-colored masonry of the parapet. *Would it not be well to paint the guns of a color indistinguishable from that of their surroundings?*

7. The average value of armor has been greatly underrated.

The resisting power of armor plates is determined under conditions which are in the highest degree favorable to the gun and unfavorable to the armor, the latter being placed so that the impact shall be normal, and at a distance permitting the exhibition of the full effect of the energy stored up in the projectile. Moreover, the plate is ordinarily braced rigidly against the blow. That the first two conditions are just no one can deny. The last, however, does not hold in practice, a certain amount of elasticity, correctly, if vulgarly, known as "give," always existing. This "give" is certain to transmit the shock over a more or less extended surface, and thus to aid in keeping out the shot. Practically, the question assumes this form: "Is it not both right and expedient for the naval architect to give a numerical expression to the risk which experience has demonstrated may be incurred with impunity, and claim, for instance, that a 10-inch plate will resist a 10-inch shot fired under all the likely or even remotely probable conditions of battle?" For we see that battering shell of this caliber were freely used by the Egyptians, one actually stopping on board of the Inflexible; we know that all the ships of the fleet were exposed to their fire; that in the Invincible and others they had even a stationary target; that in no case was the armor of any of the ships pierced, although the range was not excessive, and the armor plates, in most instances, of about 6 inches in thickness. It cannot, of course, be affirmed that a 10-inch Palliser shell struck and failed to penetrate a 6-inch plate. Among the multititude of these projectiles fired it is fair to assume that some of them did strike harmlessly upon the thinner plates carried by the older vessels of the fleet, in spite of the fact that their penetration at 1,500 yards may be justly set at 11 inches of iron, starting with a muzzle velocity of 1,360 feet per second and a penetration of $13\frac{1}{2}$ inches of iron. It is certain that the 6 and 8 inch armor of the Alexandra, and the 6-inch armor of the Sultan, were only dented to a slight extent by the heaviest blows they received.

8. *Recent high-powered guns are not adapted to bombarding earthworks.*

These guns possess a flat trajectory and send their projectiles along the line of greatest resistance of the fortification. The best work done at Alexandria was on the parapet of Fort Oom-el-Kabebe, which was shelled by the Inflexible at nearly 4,000 yards. In this case, the shell having a considerable angle of descent, buried themselves well, and, in exploding, blew out large craters, one of which was 17 feet long by over 5 feet deep. The great distance would forbid the placing of a sufficient number of these hits so close together as to breach the parapet, and the fire of the ships was too slow to keep the crews entirely away from the guns.

If, however, in this sense, the best results from these modern weapons are only to be obtained by indefinitely increasing the fighting distance, the value of the high power and flat trajectory is unquestionably negative.

To the unprejudiced observer, the most striking characteristics of the bombardment are, without doubt, the excessive apparent and the slight real damage done to the fortifications.

9. As a corollary to the above, the batteries of ships must be composite. Unless the ships themselves are to be armed for the purpose of either engaging other ships or batteries exclusively, they should be prepared for both classes of work.

If Admiral Seymour had possessed a vessel carrying both heavy modern high-powered guns and large howitzers or other shell-guns capable of great elevation, and thus somewhat similar to the mortar in application, she would have been of immense value, for she could have run close into the forts. With her shell and machine guns she could have driven the Egyptians away from their batteries, dismounting the latter with comparative ease at short range with her powerful ordnance. Valuable as Gatlings and Nordenfeldts may be, under certain circumstances, it cannot be denied that they lack the moral effect of well-burst shell. Something approaching vertical fire must be secured for operations of this nature.

A British naval officer of standing, present at the engagement, stated that, in his opinion, an old line-of-battle ship, with her numerous, if smaller, guns, would have been more effective than the modern ships which took part in the bombardment.

It may be urged, in reply, that these recent guns possess the ability to use shrapnel and canister. But any one familiar with these projectiles must know that the former is useful only when the range is accurately known and the fuze is capable of adjustment within very narrow limits; that the latter can only be employed at extremely close quarters; and that, unless fired at high elevations and with reduced charges, involving different range tables and vast inconvenience, the objection of too great flatness of trajectory will still hold; *nor do the gun-carriages and ports of to-day admit of an elevation sufficient to secure the desired advantage.*

10. The necessity of a thorough determination of the possibilities of vertical fire must be patent to the most careless reader of this report. It is hardly an exaggeration to suggest that of all the directions open to the development of ordnance, at the present time, this is by far the most promising and important.

The writer feels strongly the desirability, not to say imperative obligation, of working out this old problem under the new conditions of the moment, and unhesitatingly recommends it as worthy of serious consideration and practical investigation.

11. The system of imparting rotation to a shot by means of an expanding base ring *was established as thoroughly trustworthy* even when applied to so large a projectile as the Inflexible's 16-inch, 1,700-pound shell.

All that were found by the writer had lost the copper gas check, but the latter *was generally not far distant from the spot where the shell landed.* The track of the projectile over the water was not observed to have been marked by scattering pieces of the expansion ring that had stripped off. Official statements on this point, by those in a position to notice, are wanting.

12. The question is not unlikely to arise in the mind of the naval officer, whether the good shooting of the Temeraire may not have been in a measure due to the unobstructed view had by the captains of her barbette guns. On this point no possible doubt can be entertained.

To obtain really good aim without inconvenient straining, the eye must embrace, at will, the surroundings of the individual point selected as a target. This condition is admirably secured in open-top turrets, and may be legitimately urged among the advantages they offer.

13. The range at which the fleet engaged seems to have been needlessly great. The outside vessels could have gone to within 1,000 yards on the northwest side of the Light-House Fort, and 800 yards abreast the Ras-el-Tin Lines; to within 500 yards of Fort Ada and 200 yards of Fort Pharos. Along the southern line the ships could easily have gotten within 400 yards of all the batteries. This would have prevented the Temeraire from shelling Mex, but it is believed that the gain would have outbalanced the loss. It can hardly be doubted that the boldness of this move would have been rewarded by the speedier and more extensive dismounting of the guns, which was confessedly the chief object of the attack. Shrapnel and canister from a portion of the ships' batteries, supplemented by the machine guns at a more appropriate range than that originally adopted, would have prevented return fire from the shore, and the remainder could have been concentrated on each gun in the forts in succession until bowled over. Close range and a stable platform, however, are necessary for such refinement of practice.

It must be remembered that the target in each case at Alexandria was the muzzle of a gun—a mere pin's head at the distance at which the ships engaged—and that a successful hit meant either good luck or phenomenally good shooting.

Hammering away "at long taw" was very skillful, and, in the end, was tolerably fortunate, but it is certain that the length of the action, while abundantly foreshadowed in Admiral Seymour's order of battle, was a disappointment to those who expected short work to be made of the Egyptians, while it *drained the stock of ammunition to a dangerously low ebb.*

14. The outside squadron having tried both modes of attack, under way and at anchor, definitely solved one important problem. *There remains no possible doubt that ships engaging forts not superior to them in force gain more in accuracy of fire by anchoring than in safety by keeping under way.*

A private account of the bombardment, written on board of the Invincible and published in the London Standard newspaper, refers to the Monarch as delivering a less effective fire, in consequence of keeping under way, than her neighbors. Her best work was at Marsa-el-Khanat, but the gun-cotton she blew up there was hundreds of yards in rear of the fort she aimed at.

It is proper, at this place, to suggest that the slight damage done to the guns in the fort at Mex can probably be accounted for by the fact that the Invincible, although at anchor, was too distant, and the other ships were under way.

15. One fact which struck the observer in passing through the forts at

Alexandria, in the northern line, is the lessened injury inflicted by the ships as they moved to the eastward.

The Light-House Fort was entirely disabled; the batteries in the Ras-el-Tin Lines were silenced, but not entirely put *hors de combat*. Only one rifled gun was disabled in Fort Ada and one in Pharos. As the attacking squadron grew in strength, as it advanced against these works in the order named, *and as the sun had moved out of the gunners' eyes to shine more fully on the target*, an explanation (not the only one, however) is found in the fact that the steady northwest breeze of that day had gradually raised *a slight swell, making* the afternoon practice less effective than that of the morning. This sea can be best described as slight and short, but its influence upon the bombardment is unmistakable.

16. It follows, as an inference from what has just been stated, that an additional advantage, not generally claimed for vessels with complete *fore and aft fire*, lies in their ability to ride at anchor, *head to sea*, and engage a fort, either ahead or astern, from a platform which is as steady as the circumstances can possibly permit.

17. Besides the hints which may be incidentally derived from the foregoing notes it is well to add, for the guidance of officers commanding vessels assigned to the task of demolishing fortifications, that there can be but two targets at which it is worth while to direct their fire. *Te first is the muzzle of any gun actually served;* the second is *any building known or believed to be a magazine or shell-house*, which is visible above the parapet.

All shot not placed in accordance with these rules are shot thrown away. They may make deep holes in the parapet and wound members of the garrison by splinters, but they are without real effect on the powers of the work either for offense or defense. It is advisable not to waste time and effort on a gun which may prove to be a quaker or unserviceable, but to confine the attack to the enemy's weapons in use. On the other hand, if an enemy allows an undue accumulation of inflammable or explosive material in an exposed situation, it will probably be under a roof of some kind. Here lies the chance of igniting it by a well-burst shell. *Lightning-conductors, as marking the site of the magazine*, should be specially sought for, and, if found, fired at. Generally speaking, however, the most vulnerable parts of a fortification are the guns mounted in it, and to them most attention should be devoted.

18. Having the essential facts of the last engagement between ships and earthworks at hand, it is impossible not to draw one broad inference—*that vessels are not yet and never will be able to fight on even terms with forts.*

The responsibility of the attack belongs to the former, while the latter gain the credit of a drawn battle. The former cannot continue the action beyond a certain time, *limited by the capacity of shell-rooms and magazines*. The garrisons of the latter may wait quietly under cover until the fire slackens, can then return it with interest, and continue it indefinitely, and absolutely at their own leisure.

This disadvantage, and the obligation of assuming the initiative, should be recognized and well weighed before commencing operations.

19. These deductions in no way touch the question of *the ability of forts to stop the progress of modern ships.* In this respect, and unaided by other modes of defense, by obstructions, &c., *the works at Alexandria would have been utterly powerless against the British fleet,* which need hardly have paid them the compliment of a passing shot.

20. The success which attended the efforts of the spiking party at Mex inspires the regret that similar work was not generally attempted by the fleet.

It is easy to be wise after the event, and therefore it cannot now be doubted that, in this way, the true state of the *morale* of the garrison would have been revealed, and possibly such measures taken as might have prevented the burning of the city. A few hundred men could have seized and held the place on July 12, so great was the fear on the part of the Egyptians, both soldiers and citizens, caused by the bombardment—a fear not known, at the time, to the British commander-in-chief. In consequence of the lack of information, this memorable battle was followed by one of the most shocking, wanton, and deplorable catastrophes of the century.

21. The forts at Alexandria were badly bruised, but the more modern parapets were not seriously harmed. In the generality of cases the real damage they sustained could have been easily repaired in a single night. If the bombardment was directed against the forts in this, their defensive capacity, it must be pronounced a failure. If its object was the dismounting of the new rifled guns, it must be conceded that such results as attended the work of the inshore squadron (only one gun of this type being seriously affected), or even such as were achieved by the offshore squadron (less than one-half being permanently disabled), do not justify the verdict of success.

In the wider sense of having driven the garrison from their batteries, and having silenced the forts, the fleet was unquestionably victorious.

Into this product, however, enters the important element of *morale.* *The British, while surprised by the tenacity of their opponents, were the first to confess that men of a stamp at all similar to their own would have accepted the gage thrown down the next day, and have renewed the fight.*

With a heavier sea running to render the fire of the fleet less accurate, and to embarrass the operation of replenishing its almost empty magazines and shell-rooms from the ammunition vessels in the outer roadstead, can any doubt be reasonably entertained that the struggle would have been vastly prolonged even if the final result had been unaltered?

PART II.

THE WAR IN EGYPT.

VIII.

OPERATIONS BY THE BRITISH NAVY AT ALEXANDRIA SUBSEQUENT TO THE BOMBARDMENT.

The events of the day immediately following the bombardment have been already briefly referred to (p. 36). To give a clear idea of the demands of Admiral Seymour, and of the policy adopted by the Egyptians, the following letter is quoted at length. It is the report, to the admiral, of the officer sent to communicate with the military authorities ashore in response to their hoisting a flag of truce on the Light-House Fort.

H. M. S. INVINCIBLE,
Off Alexandria, July 12, 1882.

SIR: I have the honor to inform you that on arriving on board the Egyptian yacht Mahroussa I informed the captain that I had your orders to communicate with the military governor of Alexandria.

His excellency Toulba Pasha, military governor, just then came alongside in a steam launch. He told me he was on the point of going out to the British admiral.

I told him you could not hold any communication with him until, as a preliminary, Mex Batteries and Adjemi were surrendered, the former to be temporarily occupied by your forces, the offensive defenses of the latter to be destroyed.

I carefully pointed out to the Pasha that these positions were practically in your power, that you did not intend to hoist the British flag or do anything to hurt the susceptibilities of the Egyptian nation, but you required the peaceful surrender as a guarantee of good faith.

The Pasha, after a deal of temporizing and begging the question, said he had not the authority to comply with your demands, but must communicate with the Khedive, at Ramleh palace, four or five miles distant. I asked him to do so by telegram. He replied, "There is no telegraph wire"—a mistake on his part. I then (at twenty minutes past 12) informed the Pasha he must give written surrender by 2 p. m. He begged for 3 p. m., pointing out the physical impossibility of communicating with Ramleh under that time. I informed him that I could not alter the time, and replied I was convinced that he, the gallant defender of Alexandria, had the power to surrender what was required, pointing out to him that the forts in question had been silenced by our ships, and were no longer in a position to offer any resistance. He then asked, "What will the English admiral do if we cannot accept his terms?" I replied, "Destroy the whole of the fortifications."

He then said, "There will be no men in them," to which I replied, "You would be delighted to hear that, as your object was the demolition of the forts, not the destruction of men."

The interview then ended, the Pasha ostensibly hurrying to Ramleh to consult the Khedive. The Bittern weighed at 2 p. m. I returned to the Mahroussa, compared watches with the captain (2.15 p. m.), and informed him, as time was up and no answer to your demand had arrived, you would recommence fire at 3.30 p. m.

He asked me to wait a little longer, as the answer would come directly. I told him I would wait on board the Mahroussa till 2.30 p. m., but had not the authority to change the time for recommencing the fire on the forts, viz, 3.30 p. m.

He hurried ashore to inform Admiral Kamil Pasha (sub-minister of marine).

At 2.30 p. m., seeing my boat alongside, he returned and wished for further delay, which I declined and returned to the Bittern.

In my opinion the sole object was to gain time to enable the soldiery and rabble to pillage and burn the town without the danger of a stray shell disturbing their operations.

Commander Brand of the Bittern informed me at least 500 troops in heavy marching order had evacuated Ras-el-Tin while I was on board the Mahroussa.

I have, &c.,

HEDWORTH LAMBTON,
To *Lieutenant.*
Admiral Sir F. BEAUCHAMP SEYMOUR,
Commander-in-Chief.

The following extracts are from Admiral Seymour's official dispatches of the dates mentioned:

[Of July 14.]

As negotiations failed * * * one shot was fired into the Mex Barracks Battery earthwork,* when a flag of truce was again hoisted. I then sent Lieutenant and Commander Morrison into the harbor in the Helicon, and on his going on board the Khedive's yacht, the Mahroussa, he found she had been deserted, and he reported to me on his return after dark his belief that the town had been evacuated.

This belief was quite correct. Under cover of the white flag, Arabi succeeded in getting his troops safely out of the city, which was given over to the mob for pillage and burning. Some smoke had been observed rising from the place before sunset, but after dark the flames were but too apparent. Alexandria had been fired in at least two quarters.

[Of July 19.]

At daylight [of the 13th] the [inshore] squadron was under way, and I proceeded up the harbor and found that the town was on fire in several places; that the harem of the Ras-el-Tin palace was burning, and that the forts were evacuated.

As by the most reliable authority I learned that the force of Arabi Pasha had only moved out as far as Pompey's Pillar, where they were said to be awaiting us, I had to be cautious in our proceedings, and, as a first measure, I landed a party from the Invincible and another from the Monarch, under Captain Fairfax, C. B., A. D. C., to spike or burst the guns between Gabarri and Tsali which bore upon the harbor.

While this was being accomplished the gun-boats were sent to the ships outside to bring in the marines. Ras-el-Tin itself was occupied and many of the guns bearing on our ships spiked. About the same time I received a visit from Ahmet Tewfik Effendi, A. D. C. to his excellency Dervish Pasha, who, accompanied by Colonel Zohrab Bey, A. D. C. to H. H. the Khedive, had come in from Ramleh palace, about 4 miles from Alexandria, asking me if I would undertake to receive the Khedive, whose safety from the mutinous regiments surrounding him gave rise to much apprehension. I at once expressed my readiness and anxiety to be of service to His Highness, and at about 4 p. m. I had the honor to receive him at the gate of the palace, which fortunately had suffered only to a very slight extent from the fire of the ships on the 11th instant.

[Of July 14.]

I regret to say that the city of Alexandria has suffered greatly from fire and pillage. At the same time the guns on the southern shore were being spiked. We occupied the Ras-el-Tin Lines with such men as we could spare.

* This, the last shot of the engagement, struck the northeast angle of Mex Citadel.

[Of July 14.]

In the evening [of the 13th] a party of blue-jackets landed with a Gatling gun and cleared the streets of the Arabs, who were setting fire to and pillaging the town.

[Of July 20.]

In the evening [of the 13th] we landed all the marines from the offshore squadron and got a small patrol into the streets, but they were of little service.

As explanatory of these brief notices, it is proper to state that the first party which landed from the ships was composed of 160 marines and 250 blue-jackets from the Monarch, Invincible, and Penelope, under the command of Commander Hammill, of the Monarch. They reached the Ras-el-Tin palace at 10.30 a. m., seized the western end of the peninsula, and threw out a line of sentries north and south extending from shore to shore. At half-past twelve a small party of marines and a Gatling gun's crew from the Monarch pushed on towards the town, occupied the arsenal, and guarded the streets in the immediate neighborhood, making prisoners of the natives who were seen looting just outside of the gates, and firing upon those more remote. The arsenal then became a point of refuge for the Europeans still left alive in the city, who came down some seventy in number to seek protection. The Gatling gun was planted to command the principal street leading to the water-front through this part of the place, where there were many buildings burning and in ruins.

During the afternoon the blue-jackets were re-embarked, and the marines of the Superb, Inflexible, and Temeraire landed in their stead.

The patrolling of the city was begun, a company of Royal Marine Artillerymen, armed as infantry, marching through the Arab and European quarters of Alexandria. They shot one or two natives caught in the act of setting fire to houses, and they shot three of the native police who were pillaging a house after having cruelly maltreated the doorkeeper, an Arab faithful among the faithless.

In the evening the marines were also landed from the Achilles and Sultan.

The Inflexible, Temeraire, and the Achilles, an armored ship which arrived on the 12th, were stationed off Ramleh to command the land approaches to Alexandria from the southward and eastward.

Of the events of July 14, Admiral Seymour says:

Employed during the whole of the day landing as many men as we could spare from the squadron, and by evening we had occupied the most important positions.

Appointed Captain John A. Fisher to take charge of the naval brigade.

The fires had occasioned enormous damage in the European quarter, where had formerly stood many fine buildings, for the most part of French and Italian styles of architecture. The incendiarism was still going on. Not a street here was passable for any distance, all being more or less blocked by the smoking ruins of the fallen houses; walls were still tumbling down, and the hot air was opaque with lime, dust, and smoke.

Several ships of the Channel squadron having arrived, their marines were at once landed. The entire city was now occupied.

Alexandria being a walled town, the distribution of the force at Captain Fisher's disposal was naturally governed by this fact, and was practically as follows:

At the Ramleh gate were marines from the Monarch.

At the Rosetta gate were marines from the Temeraire.

At the Moharem Bey gate were marines from the Alexandra and Inflexible.

At the Fort Kum-el-Dik gate were marines from the Sultan.

At the Pompey's Pillar gate and Dead gate were marines from the Superb.

At the Caracol (B. on map) gate were marines from the Achilles.

At the Gabarri railway station were marines and blue-jackets with Gatlings from the Alexandra.

At the Zaptieh (A. on map) and the arsenal were marines from the Invincible.

It was on this day that an armed force from the United States ships Lancaster, Nipsic, and Quinnebaug, composed of a Gatling gun and crew, a 3-inch B. L. R. and crew, and a company of marines, the whole under the command of Lieutenant-Commander Goodrich, landed, occupied the United States consulate, and patrolled a large section of the European quarter of the town, extending to the Ramleh gate. The details of this service and of the later service performed by Lieutenant Hutchins, are the subject of other official reports.

On July 15, in view of a rumor that Arabi meant to attack the city, a large number of blue-jackets and marines with Gatlings were landed from the British ships, each, as a rule, reinforcing its own detachment ashore. The Minotaur's marines strengthened the post at the Ramleh gate, and her blue-jackets the weak part of the defense between Pompey's Pillar gate and Miniet-el-Bassal, the Alexandra's blue-jackets being stationed in the latter quarter to guard the bridge over the Mahmoudieh Canal. It is now, however, believed that at about this time Arabi withdrew from the immediate neighborhood of Alexandria and encamped towards King Osman and Kafr Dowar, across the isthmus which connects the Alexandrian peninsula with the mainland.

The police of the town was placed under the charge of Commander Lord Charles Beresford, of the Condor, with headquarters at the Zaptieh. To him all offenders were sent for investigation of charges and for punishment. This as well as all subsequent action on the part of the British, whether by the army or the navy, was in the name and by the authority of the Khedive, and had for its aim the re-establishment of the latter's shattered power.

On July 17 the 17th company of the Royal Engineers, 90 men, under Captain E. Wood, and the 1st battalion of the South Staffordshire Regiment (late 38th foot), 860 strong, under Lieutenant-Colonel Thackwell, which had come from Malta, arrived in H. M. S. Northumberland and were landed. The former went to Miniet-el-Bassal and began at once the work of improving and repairing the existing defenses. The technical details will be found in the section treating of the work done by the Royal Engineers.

The 38th marched to the Moharem Bey gate and relieved the marine sentries between Pompey's Pillar gate and the Ramleh gate. This relief was sadly needed, for the men were nearly tired out. No small part of their physical exhaustion was due to the attacks of insects, fleas and mosquitoes, which deprived them of proper sleep. Up to this time a few hundred men had held the city against a force estimated to be ten times as strong, and in the presence of an inimical and violent population.

The troop-ship Tamar arrived at 2 a. m. of this day, having on board the marine battalions, 600 Royal Marine Light Infantry under Lieutenant-Colonel Ley, and 300 Royal Marine Artillery under Lieutenant-Colonel Tuson. In the afternoon these troops were landed at Miniet-el-Bassal and took immediate charge of the western lines; that is, from Pompey's Pillar gate to the Mahmoudieh Canal.

These battalions formed the advance of the British expeditionary force, and Major-General Sir Archibald Alison, K. C. B., had arrived to conduct their operations.

On July 18 the 3d battalion of the King's Royal Rifle Corps (late 60th foot), 960-odd men, which had reached the outer roads the day before, in the Agincourt, were landed from that ship in a smaller transport, the Nerissa, by the same method as was employed in the disembarkation of the 38th. The 60th went to Moharem Bey gate, relieving the posts of the 38th, which concentrated at the Rosetta gate.

The land defense of the city was now definitely assumed by the army, assisted at the Ramleh gate by the marines from the Alexandra, Superb, and Temeraire, and elsewhere by the blue-jackets and their Gatling guns. The other bodies of marines landed from the ships were employed in patrolling and policing the town, being stationed as follows:

Ras-el-Tin palace, half of Agincourt's party.
Coast-guard station,* Sultan's party.
Zaptieh, Monarch's party.
Tribunal,† Minotaur's party.
Caracol (C. on map), half of Agincourt's party.
Caracol (B. on map), Achilles' party.
Gabarri station, Inflexible's party.

The whole of the marines now ashore were under the command of Lieutenant-Colonel F. G. Legrand, R. M. L. I., who had come out from

---
* Near the arsenal.
† Diagonally across the street from the American consulate.

England for this purpose. These carried on the duty of constables, cases being tried at the Tribunal and Zaptieh, in the Rue Franque, and then sent to the arsenal for punishment. Strong measures had to be resorted to to keep the large population in order, especially in view of the great temptations and opportunity for looting.

Efforts were, however, made to secure a native police force as a substitute, but the unsettled condition of things and the difficulty of getting trustworthy Egyptians rendered this a long and tedious process.

It is impossible to give more than a general account of the work of the navy done ashore in and about Alexandria, for the number of men landed varied from day to day with the actual necessity or in accordance with the anticipation of offensive operations by the Egyptians. The term "naval brigade," as meaning a fixed organization, is, therefore, incorrect in this instance.

The matter of rationing these bodies of seamen and marines serving on shore was only difficult in the early days of the occupation, when wheeled and other transport was not easy to obtain and when the streets were blocked by *débris*. Each ship, therefore, at the outset kept its own landing party supplied with food, the task being performed by those still on board.

When the necessity of a more permanent and methodical arrangement became evident, a depot of supplies was established on shore, to which each ship contributed its quota. At this store, rations, as needed, were drawn by the several parties. The grog ration was maintained, and on occasion, after hard work, an extra "tot" was served out. It seemed, however, to be the experience of those officers best placed to judge, that an extra ration of cocoa was of more practical benefit than an extra ration of rum.

The original landing parties carried two days' supplies in their haversacks.

All hands were dressed in blue, and wore the blue cap, in its white cover, to which was attached a cape or havelock.

The riflemen were equipped in heavy marching order, carrying their Martini-Henry rifles, sword-bayonets, and from 100 to 120 rounds of ammunition per man.

The equipment of the British sailor landed for operations on shore is detailed in the section entitled "The Naval Brigade."

To each gun's crew, 9-pdr. or Gatling, and to each infantry company landed at Alexandria was attached a mess-cook, and each detachment had two pioneers, carrying shovel, pick-ax, &c., four stretchermen, and a hospital steward. The subdivisions or pieces were commanded by sub-lieutenants or midshipmen, and the companies by lieutenants.

Three 9-pdrs. were mounted in Fort Kum-el-Dik, as part of the permanent defenses of the city, and were manned by blue-jackets from the fleet.

After the advance of the army to Ramleh, the marine artillerymen of the Inflexible were sent out to assist in mounting and working the guns there.

Between July 18 and 26 the blue-jackets ashore were stationed at the Pompey's Pillar, Moharem Bey, and Rosetta gates, the Alexandra's detachment occupying the Ras-el-Tin peninsula.

On July 26 the seamen from the Alexandra, Monarch, Sultan, and Superb went out to Ramleh, planting and manning six 9-pdrs., two 7-pdrs. and four Gatlings. This large detachment was under Commander Thomas, of the Alexandra, who was relieved a few days later by Commander Hammill, of the Monarch.

On July 30 all the marines were withdrawn to their ships, but three days afterwards about 200 were again landed from the Alexandra and Superb. They were placed at Mex, under Lieutenant-Colonel Legrand, to guard that important outpost. On August 12 they were relieved by a company of the Royal Marine Artillery battalion.

Immediately after the bombardment, the work of destroying the offensive capacity of the fortifications bearing on the sea was begun. Parties of men, mainly from the Hecla (torpedo-supply ship) and the Condor, destroyed the ammunition in the forts, throwing the powder and shell into the sea. Torpedo detachments from various ships wrecked the guns, all of which were thoroughly spiked. The light guns ($6\frac{1}{2}$-inch S. B.) were hove off their carriages and the rifled guns treated with gun-cotton. If the various plates giving views of these guns are studied, it will be seen that every one of the latter exhibits a slight bulge near the muzzle. The official report on this subject is, unfortunately, a confidential document, but it is believed that no gun resisted the detonation of a pound of gun-cotton placed about 18 inches inside of the bore. The result is a distortion sufficient to prevent the introduction of the shell, while the external appearance is only altered to the eye of the close professional observer. A much larger charge than usual must have been employed in the 8-inch gun at Oom el-Kabebe, whose muzzle is absolutely blown off.

Hundreds of tons of gunpowder were ruined, and scores of valuable guns rendered useless. The object or necessity of this destruction is hardly evident.

The torpedo stores at Mex received a similar treatment. The cases were punctured freely with pick-axes.

On about August 20 the defenses of Ramleh were strengthened by the mounting of three 7-inch Armstrong M. L. R. Two were taken from the Hospital Battery, and the third was found unmounted near Mex. Their position is given on Plate 45, at *p*. They were conveyed to their site by rail from the railway station at Moharem Bey, and skidded into place, the parbuckles being hauled on by a locomotive. The gun-platforms were constructed of heavy balks of timber, sided 8 inches by 10 inches, laid longitudinally and transversely. An anchor for the pivot-bolt was improvised by sinking a smooth-bore gun, muzzle up, in the sand. The railway embankment was used as a parapet, the guns being mounted *en barbette*. The easternmost of the three guns was placed so as to command a long stretch of road, and therefore needed no lateral train. It was probably the one whose carriage-truck had been injured on July 11. Its slide was lashed in place and backed by heavy timbers against the recoil. A pit was dug in the embankment and a rude magazine built in it, upright and cross timbers forming the sides and top. Sand-bags and earth were piled about it and above, as a protection.

This battery was brought up in answer to a 15^{cm} Krupp gun mounted at King Osman, Plate 44, but it was very little used, since it had the effect of drawing the Egyptian fire in the direction of the water tower and reservoir immediately in rear, serious damage to which would have been a real calamity.

On a slight elevation back of the water tower were the other pieces in the naval battery, two 9-pdrs. on field carriages, firing through a low parapet of sand and sand-bags. This battery was manned by about eighty men, from the Inconstant, under Commander Parr. They lived in tents and had a regularly organized camp near their guns.

The armed train is described elsewhere.

On the water the navy was constantly engaged in landing troops and stores and in patrolling the approaches to the westward of Mex and the eastward of Ramleh. In the latter quarter, at certain points, the land is so low as to permit a ship anchored off the coast to throw her shell well up in the direction of Kafr Dowar. Never less than one iron-clad was kept here to prevent an advance from Aboukir or King Osman. The electric light was useful in the former connection.

The navy, it will be seen, took a notable part in the passive defense of Alexandria, as well as in the various skirmishes and reconnaissances between Ramleh and Kafr Dowar. Its part in the reconnaissance in force of August 5, is contained in the account of that action given later.

A fitting conclusion to this section is the testimony as to the efficiency of the aid rendered by the navy to the army, which is contained in the following letter:

RAMLEH, *September* 20.

To the Chief of Staff:

SIR: I have the honor to request that you will be good enough to bring to the notice of the Commander-in-Chief in Egypt the excellent work performed on shore by the officers and men of the Royal Navy and Royal Marines during the period I have been in command at Alexandria. All requests from me for their employment on shore have been met with the utmost alacrity and good feeling by Admiral Dowell, C. B. The work performed by the several parties has been of an arduous and varied nature, but I particularize the following: Commander Hammett, R. N., with a party of bluejackets from the Minotaur, landed on the nights of the 31st August and the 1st September, and demolished by gun-cotton a house near our advanced posts on the canal, which afforded cover to the enemy. Commander Morrison, R. N., was relieved shortly after my assuming command by Commander Parr, R. N., whose men, under the direction of Lieutenant Scott, R. N., worked in a most praiseworthy and successful manner in mounting three 7-inch M. L. R. guns on the water-tower position. The sand being very heavy rendered the work most difficult. These guns were effectively used against the enemy's earthworks under the direction of Commander Parr and Lieutenant Wrey, R. N. It is right that I should add that Major-General Alison had, previous to his departure, spoken to me of Lieutenant Scott's work in the highest terms of praise. We derived great assistance from a party of blue-jackets under Commander Henderson, who, with the twenty-first company Royal Engineers, all being under the command of Captain Puzey, R. E., repaired the rail between Kafr-el-Dowar and Alexandria. The destruction of a heavy piece of masonry thrown up across the line demanded great exertion. The cutting of the Mex dam was an arduous piece of work performed by Lieutenant Scott, R. N., and a party of blue-jackets. They also built a retaining wall measuring 170 yards long, 12 feet broad at the top, and 15 feet broad at the bottom. Good service was done by the Royal Marines while in garrison at Alexandria, under the command of Major French, R. M. A.

I have, &c.,

EVELYN WOOD,
Major-General, Commanding at Alexandria.

IX.

OTHER OPERATIONS PRECEDING THE CHANGE OF BASE..

In anticipation of the necessity of landing an armed force on Egyptian soil, the British Government had previously embarked the infantry and marine battalions, whose arrival at Alexandria has been already noted, and had sent the vessels conveying them to Cyprus, where they were to be held as a reserve in case of emergency. These troops had been summoned by Admiral Seymour to Alexandria shortly after the bombardment of the fortifications and the occupation of the town by the seamen and marines of the fleet. That they were not on hand to take possession of the place on the morning of July 12 is to be regretted. *Had they, or indeed almost any number of men, greater than a mere handful, been landed at that time, the burning of the city, one of the greatest disasters of the age, would have been averted.* It is so easy, however, to judge after the fact, that to many persons it is hard to understand that such an occurrence could have scarcely been foreseen, as a necessary consequence of the successful engagement of the forts and therefore as necessitating preparation on his part for the immediate disembarkation of armed men. Nor, in fact, does the discussion of the question properly belong to a report of this nature. Nevertheless, viewed in the light of subsequent events, it conveys the lesson that, under similar circumstances, in the future, *such prevision and preparation will be obligatory on the side of the attack* to properly defend the interests of neutrals against the ravages of a semi-civilized enemy smarting under the sense of defeat.

The rôle played by the British army at Alexandria was of a negative character, in the main consisting in an efficient if passive defense of the city against the Egyptians encamped and intrenched at Kinq Osman and Kafr Dowar.

Possessing an ample port and exceptional dock facilities, Alexandria would have well served the purpose of a base in an advance into the interior, but certain strategic considerations relegated it to a position of minor importance. What those considerations were will transpire later. For the present, it is only necessary to study the needs of the defense and the measures taken to supply them.

Referring to Plate 44, it will be seen that the city occupied a very exposed situation with an enormously long line to defend. At the eastern extremity of the Alexandrian peninsula were Aboukir and its nest of powerful forts, still in the hands of an Egyptian garrison of about 5,000 men. This garrison was in constant and direct communication with the main body at Kafr Dowar. To command the approach from both of these quarters, possession of Ramleh was indispensable. The map, while indicating the location and general character of Lake Mariout (ancient Mareotis), fails to show that it is a variable quantity, depending for its maximum depth upon the high water in the Nile, during the month of October, while in the summer its bed is a succession of shallow pools, quagmires, and dry places, and is readily passable in all directions by those familiar with it, so that the Egyptian army at Kafr Dowar was able at any time to march across it upon Alexandria. The approach would not have been attended by any special difficulty, for competent guides could have been secured by the hundred.

The city walls on the southern side were in bad repair and were surrounded by villas, gardens, and villages which would have completely masked a night attack until too late to reinforce the point struck, while, at the southwestern part of the city, they had been removed to make way for the new suburb of Miniet-el-Bassal, where were the steamer docks and the Gabarri freight station.

Even at this place the trouble did not cease. It was necessary to hold, as far as Mex, the strip of land which divides the harbor from Lake Mariout, if vessels were to enter and leave the port unmolested. The entire length of this line is between ten and eleven miles. At both ends of it the ships lent efficient aid, by their presence, but over the greater part nothing but troops could suffice.

On July 24, Ramleh was seized and occupied. The following is the official dispatch on the subject sent by Sir Archibald Alison to the Secretary of State for War:

JULY 24—11 p. m.

Malabar, with one half battalion, arrived last night. At 3 o'clock this morning mounted infantry marched for the position in front of Ramleh barracks [see Plate XLIX], which I intended to occupy at 6 o'clock. I followed by train, with Rifles [60th], two 7-pdr. naval guns, and some sappers. On arriving at Ramleh, I found the ridge occupied by the mounted infantry. This ridge lies half-way between the Khedive's palace on the sea and the Mahmoudieh Canal. It commands the bridge by which the Cairo Railway crosses that canal, and the point at which the canal, running from Alexandria parallel to the sea, turns off at right angles inland towards Arabi's position. The key of this ridge is the tower of the Ramleh water-works, a strong, defensible building. I occupied this position at once with the Rifles, under Ashburnham, and guns, and established outposts at the railway bridge and in front of the canal bend. Shortly after we were in position, a small force of Arabi's cavalry, followed by infantry, advanced towards the railway bridge, within four hundred yards of the Rifles. After exchanging shots for some time, the cavalry retired rapidly on the Mahmoudieh Canal. The enemy's advance was more decided; considerable force of cavalry, with two horse-artillery guns, pushed on rapidly, the guns coming into action briskly; infantry followed, and the movements of a considerable body of troops were observed upon the high ground behind. Arabi's attack was not pushed home, and the fire of his guns, brisk for some time, gradually died away. Firing ceased. There were no casualties on our side.

This bloodless operation was the first encounter between the land forces on the two sides.

The work of fortifying Ramleh was begun at once and prosecuted with vigor, for the force opposed to the British far outnumbered the latter at all times, and the need of the moment was to hold on until the army corps under General Wolseley, definitely ordered to Egypt on July 21, could be collected and transported to Alexandria.

The measures taken to strengthen the position already seized at Ramleh can be readily comprehended by the aid of Plate 45. It may be well to mention that Ramleh is not a village or town, but a species of summer resort for the European residents of Alexandria, who have built houses and villas upon the sandy neck of lowland lying between Lakes Mariout and Aboukir on the one hand and the Mediterranean on the other. These houses are distributed over a length of several miles, and are mostly surrounded by high-walled inclosures, where with much effort in the direction of irrigation a few shrubs are made to grow. Between these scattered country places the sand lies everywhere ankle deep. There is an occasional pretense of a road, like that, for instance, leading to Rosetta, but, generally speaking, communication between any two points is in the straightest possible line and through the sand.

To supply the needed transit to and from the city, a private company has built the Ramleh Railway. This has no connection, material or otherwise, with the Egyptian Government lines. An incidental advantage due to the occupation of Ramleh was the protection enjoyed by the Ramleh Railway and by the other owners of property in this quarter.

The water-works contain the pumping engines which deliver the fresh water for distribution from the Mahmoudieh Canal to the tower and reservoir just back of them on higher ground. These two points, the water-works and the water-tower, were the center of the defense. A strong detachment was always maintained at the former, while the headquarters were established at the latter. An elevation immediately in rear of the tower was strengthened, a trench dug, and a number of guns mounted, viz, five B. L. R. 40-pdrs. and two 12-pdrs. The magazine was sunk at n (Plate 45). At first, working parties ran a shelter trench along the crest of the rising ground, and this was gradually converted into a musketry parapet 4½ feet high. Emplacements for the 40-pdr. and other guns were made, the platforms being of railway sleepers, and the parapets strongly revetted with sand-bags or timber. Small musketry redoubts were thrown up on the flanks of the position.

To the east and west, at *s* and *t*, were intrenched infantry camps. The naval detachment was encamped at *u*. Their two 9-pdrs were mounted in the adjoining earthwork, while their 7-inch Armstrong M. L. R. were at *p*, near the water-tower.

The extreme eastern picket was in a fortified house a mile and a half distant. Its object was to act as a feeler in the direction of Aboukir. It is not shown on Plate 45. Other pickets were established as indicated on the plan, where *l l* are shelter trenches; *j* a small redoubt for musketry, and *k* the chief battery, mounting the guns already enumerated.

The Egyptians could advance from King Osman either by the road on the canal bank or that on the railway embankment. The outpost on the former line was called, and is marked on the plate, Dead Horse Picket; on the latter, no regular picket was maintained beyond the iron railway bridge over the Mahmoudieh Canal, although vedettes were constantly thrown out in the direction of Mellaha Junction.

As a barrier against a movement along the southern branch of the railway, that coming from the Gabarri station, a strong force was established at the Villa Antoniades on the canal, with strict orders to hold on, in the event of attack, whether reinforced or not.

On Plate 45 is an enlarged view of this outpost, giving the details of the means employed to strengthen it. As a good piece of extemporized defense these means merit special mention.

The men's tents were pitched on the roadway along the Mahmoudieh Canal, outside of the garden, the horses and mules being picketed at *k*, a stable yard; *a* is a tower utilized for signals and lookouts. From this point signals could be exchanged with headquarters at the Ramleh water-tower, while the view it commanded extended across the bed of Lake Mariout to King Osman, and swept on to the left to Ramleh. At *b* in the plan, inside of the entrance to the garden, was a semicircular breastwork facing the villa and reaching across the gateway. The front fence is of iron on a stone foundation. Upon the coping of the latter were piled stones, breast-high (see section), to make a shelter for riflemen. At *c* was a stockade across the road, with an earthen parapet at the end adjoining the canal, where two B. L. R. 40-pdrs. were permanently mounted on field carriages. These commanded the approach along the railway embankment. At *d d* are other stockades built across the road to protect the rear. At *e e* were temporary bridges across the canal. At *l* was a substantial palisade, a sort of *tête-du-pont*; *f* was a deserted Arab village, the houses of which were loopholed and otherwise defended. A dry ditch was dug at *m*. On the roofs of the houses were piled sand-bags for a breastwork, with a higher tier in rear to protect the men against accidental reverse fire from the sharpshooters on top of the house n in the corner of the garden. g was an outlying house thoroughly loopholed and strengthened; h h are shelter trenches, and i a redoubt where two 12-pdrs. were mounted during the day-time. These guns were withdrawn to the other side of the canal at nightfall and put at c, beside the 40-pdrs.

The garrison at this point were composed of five companies of the Royal Sussex Regiment, 1st battalion (late 35th foot), under Lieutenant-Colonel Hackett, and about 75 artillerymen. They managed their own transport, having a lot of Cyprus mules under their control, had good drinking-water from a well near by, and were able to supplement the army ration with milk, fruit, and vegetables brought in daily by natives. Under the shade of the trees on the bank of the canal, which furnished them with fresh water for washing and cooking, they were as comfortable as the flies and mosquitoes would permit, except for an occasional shell sent from King Osman by the largest Krupp gun at a range of 8,000 yards.

The general defense profited by the presence of the Mahmoudieh Canal, with its high banks, and by the railway embankment, which stretched from the Antoniades garden towards Ramleh.

For night work an electric light was placed on the roof of a house at Fleming station, so as to illuminate the approaches from Aboukir and Kafr Dowar.

The following notes are by Captain E. Wood, commanding the 17th company Royal Engineers:

The advanced posts were put in a state of defense. In some cases well-situated houses were selected; in others breastworks were constructed. Fascines of long reeds, picketed down with ribs of palm leaves, were used for revetting the interior slopes.

Norton tube wells were driven, and wherever good water was found, wells from 4 to 5 inches in diameter were sunk to depths varying from 8 to 20 feet. Light octagonal wooden curbs were used, behind which sheeting was driven.

An infantry bridge 120 feet long was thrown over the Fresh-Water Canal one day. The water was only 3 feet deep, but the mud was so soft that a rod was easily pushed 6 feet into it. Some old boarded roofing was cut into squares of 6 feet. On these stout trestles were fixed, the wide bases preventing the piers sinking into the mud when the load came on. The shore piers were formed of tables found in neighboring cottages; palm-tree logs were laid on the mud, the legs of the tables put astride of them and driven well home.

Light pontons of canvas over framing of inch stuff were made, and a special superstructure with projecting ends, strongly braced, for rafting, was provided to suit the shallow muddy sides of the canal. The intention was to "track" the raft up the center of the canal by ropes on each bank, so as to use it as a floating bridge, or to complete the bridge from bank to bank by means of light composite beams (made by the sappers) thrown from shore piers; the materials for these piers would be carried on each bank by cart or otherwise.

The company was moved before this scheme could be tried, but the want of it had been strongly felt when a reconnaissance against the enemy had been pushed on both banks of the canal.

Passing to the inner line of defense, the gates of the town were guarded by strong parties, and the 6½-inch S. B., mounted on the walls here and there, were manned, as well as the Gatlings. At the various gates draw-bridges over the dry ditch were fitted and the approaches mined. The mines of gunpowder were made of suitable metal cases, and were provided with electric fuzes from which the wires, concealed, passed inside the walls to a battery and firing key.

Inside the town are two small old forts, Kum-el-Dik and Napoleon (Plate 1). These were garrisoned. The former commands the eastern approaches to the city, and mounts twelve 6½-inch S. B. (36-pdrs). In addition, were the three naval M. L. R. 9-pdrs. already mentioned.

Fort Napoleon is placed to overlook the directions southward and westward from the city as well as the harbor. It mounted six 6½-inch guns *en barbette*. It was of most value as a signal station, its position and elevation rendering it useful for speedy communication between the fleet and the troops on shore.

These interior works supplemented the defense of the *enceinte*, of which the walls are high and bold. Outside of them runs a ditch from 20 to 40 feet wide and half as deep. At the different gates the walls are thickened and guns mounted to sweep the road, while outside are advanced works on a large scale.

Within the town, at the principal street corners, were plainly-marked sign-boards indicating, in English, the name of the street and the place or quarter to which it led; and towards the southwestern part of the city, where walls are lacking, the streets were strongly barricaded. The barricades in the principal thoroughfares were so arranged that passage through them was possible at will. The bridge crossing the Mahmoudieh Canal at Miniet-el-Bassal was particularly defended, the barrier here being of iron plates with stone backing. A cob-work of stone surmounted the whole.

The presence, within the walls, of a numerous and inimical population necessitated strong police measures to maintain a proper state of subjection, for the garrison was rarely more than from three to five thousand men, and much dependence had to be placed on a healthy *morale* on the part of the natives.

Another serious menace lay in the shortness of the supply of water, for which Alexandria is almost exclusively dependent on the Mahmoudieh Canal. The latter had been dammed by Arabi, soon after his evacuation of the city, at a point near King Osman. The water left in the canal below the dam, together with what might seep through it, and what was contained in the few wells and cisterns in and about Alexandria, was all that the inhabitants could rely upon. This stock was increased by large distillers ashore and afloat, but, even at best, the scarcity of this vital element was always felt as a present hardship and contingent calamity. The distribution of water was under military control. Towards the end of the war, the water was turned on, for the benefit of the residents, at certain points for a few hours every other day.

The monotony of the defense was broken by the arrival of new regiments, by occasional slight skirmishes, barren of results, and by sorties of the armored train.

On August 5, however, a reconnaissance in force was made towards King Osman. The official telegraphic report by Major-General Alison follows:

ALEXANDRIA, *August* 6—1.35 a. m.

Persistent native reports existing for the last two days that Arabi was retiring from Kafr Dowar upon Damanhour, I determined to make a reconnaissance which would ascertain clearly whether Arabi still held his original position strongly. For this purpose I directed a half battalion of the Duke of Cornwall Light Infantry and a half battalion of the South Staffordshire Regiment, with one 9-pdr. gun and the whole of the mounted infantry, to advance along the east bank of the Mahmoudieh Canal. The 60th Rifles, with one 9-pdr. gun, were to advance along the west bank. These constituted my left attack. They were to follow the line of the canal till they reached a house in a grove of trees towards the point where the railway coming from Cairo approaches nearest to the canal. Along this line of rail a strong battalion of marines was to come up in a train to Mellaha Junction, preceded by the naval armored train carrying one 40-pdr. and two 9-pdr. guns, a Nordenfeldt and two Gatlings. The train was to stop at the Mellaha Junction. The marines were to detrain there and advance by the railway line, accompanied by the two 9-pdrs. and covered by the fire of the 40-pdr. from the train. The left column commenced its advance at a quarter to 5 in the afternoon from the out-picket station of the Ramleh lines, moving by both banks of the canal. It soon came into action with the enemy, who were strongly posted in a group of palm trees on the eastern side and a strong defensible house and gardens upon the other. These positions were carried. At this time Lieutenant Howard Vyse, of the Rifles, attached to the mounted infantry, and a soldier of the corps, were killed. The enemy then took up a second position half a mile in rear of the first, upon the east bank of the canal, among high crops and houses and behind the irregular banks of the canal. From this position, also, the enemy was driven with great loss.

I accompanied the right column myself, which followed what was the chord of the arc upon which the left column was moving. I placed the marines and the 9-pdr. guns, dragged by blue-jackets, to the west of and under cover of the railway embankment, and moved them forward as rapidly as possible, and quite out of sight of the enemy engaged with Colonel Thackwell, with a view to cutting off their retreat. After a time our movement was perceived; the enemy opened upon us with artillery. I pushed on as rapidly as possible till I came to the point where the railway approaches nearest to the Mahmoudieh Canal. I then opened fire with musketry from the railway embankment upon the enemy lining the banks of the Mahmoudieh Canal. The two 9-pdrs. were dragged up onto the embankment and came into action against the enemy's guns, the 40-pdr. firing over our heads against the point where the enemy's forces were beginning to appear. Fixing my right upon both sides of the embankment, I now threw forward two companies to carry a house near the canal, and followed up this movement by throwing some four companies still more to my left upon the banks of and across the canal. I had now attained the position I wished, and formed a diagonal line across both the canal and the railway. The enemy fell back slowly before us. The fire of their 7-pdrs. and 9^{cm} guns, which they shortly after brought into action, was speedily got under by the fire of my artillery. The object of the reconnaissance on my part was attained. Desirous of inducing the enemy to develop his full power before withdrawing, I held my position for about three-quarters of an hour, until dusk was rapidly drawing on. I determined now to withdraw. This movement was carried out with the most perfect regularity and precision by the Marine Battalion under Colonel Tuson. They fell back by alternate companies with the regularity of a field day. Every attempt of the enemy to advance was crushed by the beautiful precision of the 40-pdr. and the steady fire of the 9-pdr. naval guns. The losses of the enemy seem to have been very great, and they were so dispirited that, contrary to the usual practice of Asiatics, they made no attempt to follow up our withdrawal. The guns and troops were quietly entrained at the Mellaha Junction and slowly steamed back to Alexandria. At the same time, the left column withdrew along the banks of the canal to the Ramleh lines unmolested.

As a reconnaissance, the success of the move was all I could wish.

I regret to state that our loss has been somewhat heavy. It was especially so in the marine battalion and seamen under my immediate direction, who, I fear, have lost one man killed and some twenty wounded. In the left attack, as far as I have yet heard, there have been one officer and one private killed and six or seven privates wounded. The officer, I grieve to state, is Lieutenant Howard Vyse of the Rifles. He was one of the most promising officers I have ever met. Detailed lists of the killed and wounded will be telegraphed as soon as received.

The following table gives the British loss in this engagement:

Corps.	Killed.		Wounded.
	Officers.	Men.	
3rd battalion King's Royal Rifle Corps............	1	1	2
1st battalion South Staffordshire Regiment.......			1
Naval Brigade...................................		1	4
Marine Battalion................................		1	20
Total.......................................	1	3	27

On the side of the defense, rumors were received afterwards that the losses had been very heavy. A Circassian, who made his way from Arabi's camp to Alexandria on August 9, stated that three officers and seventy-six men were killed and a large number wounded on this occasion.

Beyond Mellaha Junction (see Plate 144), the ground between the canal and railway is occupied by native houses and gardens and is traversed in all directions by small irrigation ditches. Here were the outposts of the Egyptians, the point of attack. It was a place admitting of very thorough defense, and it gained in practical value on August 5, by the fact that the attack was divided, by the Mahmoudieh Canal, into two parts, which could only pass from one side to the other with great difficulty and at great risk. An enemy, on the alert, could have routed the extreme left column before any assistance could have been rendered by its neighbors, the action taking place under the cover of the high canal banks.

Four companies of the South Staffordshire Regiment (late 38th foot) and four of the Duke of Cornwall's Light Infantry (late 46th foot), about 800 in all, and the mounted infantry, numbering 80, formed the left attack. The mounted infantry were in advance; and six companies of the King's Royal Rifle Corps, about 500 strong, formed the center. To each of these two columns was attached a 9-pdr. naval gun on a field carriage, manned and served by blue-jackets under Commander Morrison. The right attack fell to the combined marine battalions, 1,000 strong, commanded by Lieutenant-Colonel Tuson, R. M. A. The bluejackets numbered in all 200 men.

In unofficial accounts of the action, reference is made to the inaccurate fire of the Egyptians, the majority of whose bullets passed harmless overhead. This fault marks the Egyptian practice throughout the campaign.

There appear to have been at least two distinct charges; one by the advance of the Rifles and the other by the Marines. In both cases the Egyptians broke and ran, although enjoying excellent protection. In encounters with semi-civilized troops, cold steel has not yet lost its prestige.

The tactics employed were the usual British formation for attack—about a third of each battalion being deployed in line at intervals of three paces, a second third 300 yards in rear as a support, and the remainder about the same distance again behind in reserve.

The left wing had orders to seize a certain white house on the canal, but its commander, Lieutenant-Colonel Thackwell, of the 38th, mistook the first white house reached for the one designated. In consequence, the left of the marines was uncovered, and the substantial benefits of the fight lost. Had the two wings joined, many prisoners would have been secured and two guns, if not more, captured. Signals were made to the left wing to advance, but the smoke of the battle and the failing light prevented their being read.

The skill with which the blue-jackets did their part of the work is recorded in the official report quoted above. Their pluck is seen in the number of their losses, one being killed and four wounded out of 200 men engaged. Their 9-pdrs., it must be remembered, were worked on the canal banks and railway embankment, and was entirely unprotected.

It seems more than probable that Sir Archibald Alison could have continued the advance, headed by the marines, up to the main line at King Osman, had he been so desirous, for the Egyptians had refused to meet his men at short range, and had receded from point to point with alacrity. When the order was given to return, a battalion about 300 or 400 strong, in front of the marines, was seen holding up a white flag in token of submission, but no time was left to take them as prisoners.

Beyond the moral effect on the attacking force of a successful brush with the enemy, the reconnaissance in force was barren of results. The strength of the Egyptians was neither developed nor ascertained, nor was the position held from which they had been driven. The balance of advantages seems to be negative; valuable lives were sacrificed, and the enemy regained the ground he had lost without suffering severely enough to be seriously affected.

At this time, it is believed, the Egyptian force at Kafr Dowar and King Osman was made up of four regiments of infantry, one of cavalry and several batteries of artillery, between 12,000 and 15,000 men in all, outnumbering the garrison of Alexandria at least four to one.

To increase the defensive strength of the city an effort was made to flood Lake Mariout, whose bed is slightly below the level of the sea, by cutting a canal at Mex across the isthmus. The details are given in another report already made to the Department. The attempt resulted in failure.

In other parts of Egypt little was done during the six weeks following the bombardment, except to gather a strong naval force at each end of the Suez Canal. At Suez, Rear-Admiral Sir William Hewett, V. C., commander-in-chief of the British squadron in the East Indies, landed a force of 450 sailors and marines on August 2, seizing the town and protecting the valuable docks and the property of the Peninsular and Oriental Steam Navigation Company. He experienced no opposition, the place having been abandoned by the Egyptians, although in greatly superior force. His fleet there present comprised the Euryalus (flagship), a wooden-sheathed iron corvette of 18 guns and 400 men; the Eclipse, wooden corvette, 12 guns and 200 men; the Ruby, composite sloop, 12 guns and 282 men; the Dragon, sloop, 6 guns and 140 men; the Mosquito, gun-boat, 4 guns and 60 men.

The Penelope, on board of which Rear-Admiral Hoskins had hoisted his flag immediately after the bombardment, had gone to Port Said, where was also accumulating a considerable fleet. On August 5 the Agincourt, Monarch, and Northumberland, armored ships, the Tourmaline and Carysfort, wooden sloops, the Ready and Beacon, gun-vessels, &c., were at the northern end of the canal. The Don and Dee, iron river gun-boats, arrived a few days later. The powerful light-draught iron-clad, the Orion, mounting four 25-ton guns, was sent to Ismailia, on July 26, where she was joined subsequently by the Carysfort of 14 guns and 220 men, and the Cygnet, gun-boat.

The lake (Timsah) was patrolled at night by a steam launch with an armed crew, which moved about twice in every watch. The Orion's electric light was also used during the first and mid watches for a space of about a quarter of an hour, from July 28 to August 20. Her electric-light apparatus consists of two C Gramme machines, driven by a Brotherhood engine, and two Mangin projectors, one with a plain glass front, while the other is provided with a vertical diverging lens which spreads the beam of light horizontally.

The advance of the troops from England, the Guards brigade, commanded by Major-General H. R. H. the Duke of Connaught, arrived in Alexandria on August 10 and 12 in the hired transports Orient, Iberia, and Batavia. It was composed of the 2d battalions of the Grenadier and Coldstream Guards and the 1st battalion of the Scots Guards. The general commander-in-chief of the expeditionary force, Sir Garnet Wolseley, reached Egypt on August 15 in the Calabria. Other transports were coming in rapidly, and everything pointed to an immediate advance upon King Osman and Kafr Dowar. It had, however, been determined, long before, to seek a base in another quarter, and Alexandria soon reverted to its previous condition of quiet waiting, in which it was only disturbed by occasional night attempts by Bedouins to spike the British guns, and by infrequent and resultless skirmishes.

X.

THE COMPOSITION OF THE EXPEDITIONARY FORCE.

The troops dispatched to Egypt by England formed an army corps of two divisions.

Each division was composed of two brigades of infantry (four battalions each), besides certain other detachments from various corps which went under the general designation of "divisional troops." The divisional troops are under the immediate control of the division commander, and are intended to make the division an independent military unit in the event of separate action. In this case they included two squadrons of cavalry, a spare battalion of infantry, two field batteries of artillery, a company of royal engineers, a commissariat and transport company, one half of a bearer company (aids to the wounded), a field hospital, a field post-office, and a veterinary department.

Besides the two divisions, are various other bodies of men known collectively as "corps troops," under the direct orders of the commander-in-chief or his chief of staff. These consisted of a cavalry brigade, with its battery of horse artillery, its commissariat and transport company, its half of a bearer company, and its field post-office; of the corps artillery, two field and one horse batteries and the ammunition column; of the siege train, of the ordnance-store department, of the royal engineers, of the military police, of the veterinary department, of the commissariat and transport corps, of one-half of a bearer company, of four field hospitals, and of the general post-office.

Two additional battalions of infantry and a battery of artillery were sent out for garrison duty at Alexandria.

These troops were reinforced in the field by the Indian Contingent, by the two battalions of marines, and by various detachments of seamen from the fleet.

Convenient depots were established at Malta and Cyprus, where were assembled various bodies of the different corps to be drawn upon as occasion demanded.

At Gozo, the island adjoining Malta, and at Cyprus, large and commodious hospitals were formed.

The details of this disposition are shown in the accompanying tables.

It must be borne in mind, however, that the troops thus described were not used together in accordance with the plan given on paper, but were distributed according to circumstances by the commander-in-chief Thus, for instance, the 4th brigade, under Major-General Sir Evelyn Wood, was left at Alexandria when the base was changed to Ismailia, and its place filled at Tel-el-Kebir by a scratch brigade under Lieutenant Colonel Ashburnham.

It may be remarked, in explanation, that in the British army the supplying of forage and rations falls to the Commissariat and Transport Corps; that of all military stores to the Ordnance Store Department.

The following were the principal officers in the expeditionary force:

General commanding-in-chief.—General Sir Garnet J. Wolseley, G. C. B., G. C. M. G.

Chief of the Staff.—General Sir John M. Adye, K. C. B., R. A.

Officer commanding Royal Artillery.—Brigadier-General W. H. Goodenough, R. A.

Officer commanding Royal Engineers.—Brigadier-General C. B. P. N. H. Nugent, C. B., R. E.

Provost Marshal.—Colonel H. G. Moore, V. C.

Senior Commissariat Officer.—Commissary-General E. Morris, C. B.

Senior Ordnance Store Officer.—Commissary-General of Ordnance H. A. Russell.

Principal Medical Officer.—Surgeon-General J. A. Hanbury, M. B., C. B.

Command of base and lines of communication.—Major-General W. Earle, C. S. I.

1st Division.—Lieutenant-General G. H. S. Willis, C. B.

1st brigade.—Major-General H. R. H. the Duke of Connaught, &c., &c.

2d brigade.—Major-General G. Graham, V. C., C. B., R. E.

2d Division.—Lieutenant-General Sir Edward B. Hamley, K. C. M. G., C. B., R. A.

2d brigade.—Major-General Sir Archibald Alison, K. C. B.

4th brigade.—Major-General Sir H. Evelyn Wood, G. C. M. G., K. C. B.

Garrison of Alexandria.—Major-General G. B. Harman, C. B.

Cavalry Division.—Major-General D. C. Drury-Lowe, C. B.

1st Cavalry brigade.—Brigadier-General Sir Baker C. Russell, K. C. M. G., C. B., A. D. C.

Indian Contingent.—Commanding, Major-General Sir Herbert T. Macpherson, V. C., K. C. B.

2d Cavalry brigade.—Brigadier-General H. Williamson.

Infantry brigade.—Brigadier-General O. V. Tanner, C. B.

The accompanying table gives the details of the force sent from England and Malta. That of the Indian Contingent will be found under another head.

Table showing the details of the force sent from England and Malta.

Corps, &c.	Officer commanding.	Name of transport.	Date of arrival in Egypt.	General officers.	Officers.	Warrant officers.	Non-commissioned officers and men.	Animals.					Water-carts.	Two-wheeled carts.	Tents.			Miscellaneous.
								Officers' horses.	Troop horses.	Draught.	Pack.	Total.			Marquee.	Bell.	Indian.	
Staff		Capella	Aug. 17	6	23	2	94	87	3			87	2		6	45	43	
Base and line of communications				1	7		17	25				25			1	9	7	
Special employ					19		38	24				24				18	10	
1ST DIVISION.																		
Divisional staff		Orient	Aug. 10	1	15	1	41	40	1			41	2		1	27	10	
1st brigade:																		
1st brigade staff		do	Aug. 10		2		8	11				11				6	5	
1st battalion Grenadier Guards	Lieut. Colonel P. Smith.	Batavia	Aug. 12		30	1	761	4	4	26	21	55	2	10	1	95	54	
2d battalion Coldstream Guards	Lieut. Col. G. J. Wigram.	Iberia	Aug. 12		30		767	4	4	26	21	55	2	10		95	54	
1st battalion Scots Guards	Lieut. Col. G. W. Knox.	Orient	Aug. 10		30		767	4	4	26	21	55	2	10		96	55	
2d brigade:																		
2d brigade staff	Lieut. Col. ———			1	2		8	11				11				6	5	
2d battalion Royal Irish Regiment	Lieut. Col. C. F. Gregorie.	City of Paris	Aug. 21		30	1	761	4	4	26	21	55	2	10	1	95	54	
1st battalion West Kent Regiment	Lieut. Col. A. E. Fyler.	Catalonia	Aug. 15		30		767	4	4	26	21	55	2	10		105	59	
2d battalion York and Lancaster Regiment	Lieut. Col. F. E. E. Wilson.	Nevada	Aug. 17		30		761	4	4	26	21	55	2	10		95	54	
1st battalion Royal Irish Fusiliers.	Lieut. Col. J. N. Beasley.	Arab	Aug. 19		30		761	4	4	26	21	55	2	10		95	54	
Divisional troops:																		
Two squadrons 19th Hussars	Lieut. Col. K. J. W. Coghill.	Assyrian Monarch.	Aug. 22		18		286	31	222	14		267	1	3		41	25	1 small-arm ammunition and 1 forge cart.
2d battalion Duke of Cornwall's Light Infantry.	Lieut. Col. W. S. Richardson.				30	1	861	4	4	26	22	56	2	10		106	60	
A battery, 1st brigade, Royal Artillery.	Maj. P. T. H. Taylor.	Palmyra	Aug. 24		7		194	3	28	122		153	1	1		28	17	1 forge cart.
D battery, 1st brigade, Royal Artillery.	Maj. T. J. Jones.	British Prince	Aug. 19		7		194	3	28	122		153	1	1		28	17	
24th company Royal Engineers.	Captain C. De R. Carey.	Duke of Argyll	Aug. 21		6		185	1	12	24		37	1	9		25	16	

Table showing the details of the force sent from England and Malta—Continued.

Corps, &c.	Officer commanding.	Name of transport.	Date of arrival in Egypt.	General officers.	Officers.	Warrant officers.	Non-commissioned officers and men.	Officers' horses.	Troop horses.	Draught.	Pack.	Totals.	Water-carts.	Two-wheeled carts.	Marquee.	Bell.	Indian.	Miscellaneous.
1st DIVISION—Continued.																		
2nd brigade—Continued.																		
Veterinary department					4		4	8				8						
11th company commissariat and transport		Prussian and Lydian Monarch.	Sept. 5 Aug. 27		3	2	208	3	11	140		154	4	74		31	18	
One-half bearer company		Marathon	Aug. 17		6	2	71	2	3			5		3		14	10	
Two field hospitals		do	Aug. 17		16		90	14	4	2		18	4	40	1	124	64	
Postal department							3					2		1	1	1	1	
2ND DIVISION.																		
Divisional staff		Catalonia	Aug. 15	1	15		41	40	1			41			1	27	16	
3rd brigade:																		
3rd brigade staff	Lieut. Colonel D. Macpherson.			1	2		8	11	4	26	21	11	2	10	1	0	5	
1st battalion Royal Highlanders.	Lieut. Colonel A. Straghan.	Nepaul	Aug. 20		30	1	767	4	4	26	21	55	2	10	1	96	55	
2nd battalion Highland Light Infantry.	Lieut. Colonel D. Hammill.	France	Aug. 20		30	1	767	3	4	26	22	54	2	10	1	96	55	
1st battalion Gordon Highlanders.	Lieut. Col. J. M. Leith.	H. M. S. Orontes.	Aug. 12		30	1	767	4	4	26	22	56	2	10		96	55	
1st battalion Cameron Highlanders.					30	1	767	3	4	26	22	55	2	10		90	55	
4th brigade:																		
4th brigade staff	Lieut. Colonel S. Hackett.	Catalonia	Aug. 15	1	2		8	11	2	18	11	11	1	8	1	6	5	
1st battalion Sussex Regiment.	Lieut. Colonel W. Corban.	H. M. S.			13		350	2	4	26	21	33	1			44	25	
1st battalion Berkshire Regiment.	Lieut. Col. W. de W. Thackwell.	H. M. S. Northumberland.	July 17		30	1	861	4	4	26	21	55	2	10		106	60	2 ambulances.
1st battalion South Staffordshire Regiment.	Lieut. Col. G. N. Foadall.	Lusitania	Aug. 21		30	1	861	4	4	26	21	55	2	10		106	60	
1st battalion Shropshire Light Infantry.					30	1	861	4	4	26	21	55	2	10		106	60	

														1 S.A.A. cart 1 forge wagon.
Divisional troops: Two squadrons 19th Hussars.	Lieut. Col. A. G. Webster.	Montreal	Aug. 22	13	287	31	222	14		267	1	3	41	25
3rd battalion King's Royal Rifle Corps.	Lieut. Col. C. Ashburnham.	H. M. S. Agincourt.	July 18	30	961	4	4	26	22	56	2	10	89	51
1 battery, 2nd brigade, Royal Artillery.	Maj. W. Ward.	City of Lincoln.	July 22	7	194	3	28	122		153	1	1	26	17
N battery, 2nd brigade, Royal Artillery.	Major W. A. Bruncker.	Grecian	July 20	7	194	3	28	122		153	1	1	26	17
26th company Royal Engineers.	Maj. B. Blood	Californian	July 23	6	185	2	11	24		37	1	9	25	16
Veterinary department				4	4	8				8				
12th company commissariat and transport.		Bolivar, Viking, and Lydian Monarch.	July 25 July 18 July 27	3	211	3	11	140		154	4	74	31	16
One-half bearer company		Caspian	July 22	5	72	2	3			5		3	14	10
Two field hospitals		do	July 22	16	90	14	4		2	18	4	40	124	64
Postal department					3					2		1	1	1
CORPS TROOPS.														
Cavalry brigade: Staff		Calabria	Aug. 15	2	8	11				11			6	5
Three squadrons Household Cavalry.	Lieut. Col. H. P. Ewart.	Holland	Aug. 14	24	452	50	360	21		431	2	6	63	37
4th Dragoon Guards	Major G. R. A. Denne.	Greece, City of New York, Italy.	Aug. 21 Aug. 21 Aug. 18	31	573	62	444	20		526	2	6	77	45
7th Dragoon Guards	Lieut. Colonel C. Campbell.	Egyptian Monarch.	Aug. 17	31	573	62	444	20		526	2	6	77	45
N battery, A brigade, Royal Horse Artillery.	Major (†. W. Borrodaile.	Tower Hill	Aug. 16	7	175	13	63	100		176	1	1	26	16
12th company commissariat and transport.		Bolivar	Aug. 25	2	218	3	11	164		178	4	87	29	17
One-half bearer company		Lydian Monarch.	Aug. 27	6	71	2	3			5	3	3	14	10
Postal department					2			2		2		1	1	1
Corps artillery: Regimental staff		Capella	Aug. 17	3	6	5				5			4	3
G battery, B brigade, Royal Horse Artillery.	Maj. W. M. B. Walton.	Ludgate Hill	Aug. 21	7	175	13	63	100		176	1	1	26	16
C battery, 3rd brigade, Royal Artillery.	Maj. E. R. Cottingham.	Olympus	Aug. 22	7	168	3	28	96		127	1	1	25	17
J battery, 3rd brigade, Royal Artillery.	Maj. L. F. Perry	Ascalon	Aug. 22	7	168	3	28	96		127	1	1	25	17
F battery, 1st brigade (ammunition reserve).	Maj. W. S. Hebbert.	Texas Lydian Monarch.	Aug. 25 Aug. 27	7	178	3	22	182		207	1	1	28	18
Siege train: Regimental staff	Maj. G. A. Noyes			2	9	2				2			4	3
4th battery, London division, Royal Artillery.				4	138	1				1			20	13

4 gun-carriages and limbers spare.

2 ambulances.

Table showing the details of the force sent from England and Malta—Continued.

Corps, &c.	Officer commanding.	Name of transport.	Date of arrival in Egypt.	General officers.	Officers.	Warrant officers.	Non-commissioned officers and men.	Officers' horses.	Troop horses.	Draught.	Pack.	Total.	Water-carts.	Two-wheeled carts.	Marquee.	Bell.	Indian.	Miscellaneous.
CORPS TROOPS—Continued.																		
Siege train—Continued.																		
5th battery, London division, Royal Artillery.	Maj. W. H. Graham.				4		138	1				1	1			20	13	
5th battery, Scottish division, Royal Artillery.	Maj. G. B. Macdonell.	Iberia	Aug. 12		4		138	1				1	1	4		20	13	
6th battery, Scottish division, Royal Artillery.	Maj. F. T. Lloyd.				4		138	1				1	1			20	13	
Ordnance-Store Department.		Irthington	Sept. 4		10	5	150						2	18		27	16	
Corps Engineers:																		
Ponton troop	Maj. R. J. Bond.				7		194	2	13	46		61	2	18		27	17	10 ponton wagons.
Telegraph troop	Maj. Sir A. W. Mackworth.	Oxenholme	Aug. 26		7		184	3	13	50		66	4	14		26	16	12 telegraph wagons.
Field park	Capt. C. A. Rochfort-Boyd.				1		83	1	4	22		26	1	8		6	4	1 printing-wagon.
8th company Royal Engineers.	Capt. S. Smith.	Canadian	Aug. 23		5	1	103	1	5	4		5	1			18	12	
Railway staff		H. M. S. Northumberland.	July 17		2		3	2	1	4	10	12	1	10		16	10	
17th company Royal Engineers.	Capt. E. Wood.				4		85											
18th company Royal Engineers.	Maj. W. Salmond.	Viking	Aug. 18		6		99	3	4	4		7	1	1		16	9	
Military police, troop	Capt. C. E. Beckett.	Adjutant	Aug. 30		2		93	4	66			74	1	1		10	6	
Military police, foot	Maj. G. Barton.	do	Aug. 30		2		65	1	1	4		6	1			10	6	
Veterinary department					10		10	20				20	1			6	3	
Chaplain's department					13		8	10	8			8						
Commissariat and transport:																		
Staff					36	29		10				10	4	5		28	16	For the Cyprus depot.
2nd company commissariat and transport.		Courland			2	4	43						4	5		11	6	
7th company commissariat and transport.		do	Aug. 17				43										6	
8th company commissariat and transport.		Lydian Monarch. Caspian.	Aug. 22		2	1	238	2	23	246		272	1	32		31	16	

													For Cyprus
10th company commissariat and transport.				2					6	25		15	8
15th company commissariat and transport.			1	1	86	3				1			11
One-half bearer company			2	2								22	10
Four field hospitals	Pelican	Aug. 17		1	150	3	19	36	123	201	3		14	76
	do	Aug. 17	5		72	2	3		61	66		80	96	3
	Carthage	Aug. 21									8			
	Pelican	Aug. 17	32	4	180	16	2		4	22	1	33	2	
	Dacca	Aug. 10									1		5	
Postal department at headquarters.			2	1	13									
Postal department at base			1		22	1								
Garrison of Alexandria:														
2nd battalion Manchester Regiment.	H. M. S. Euphrates. Mail steamer	}	30	1	750	3	4	26	22	55	2	10	96	55
2nd battalion Derbyshire Regiment.	H. M. S. Orontes.	Aug. 12	30	1	750	3	4	26	22	55	2	10	96	55
Malta Fencible Artillery	H. M. S. Humber.		4		120	1				1			15	8
21st company Royal Engineers	Capt. Puxy	Aug. 17	1		54									
Totals			14 1,065	88	22,802			6,227	111	776	3,475	2,037

SUMMARY.

Troops.	First division.		Second division.	
	Officers.	Men.	Officers.	Men.
Infantry:				
1st (or 3rd) brigade	93	2,303	123	3,076
2nd (or 4th) brigade	123	3,058	106	2,938
Divisional troops:				
Cavalry	18	286	13	287
Infantry	30	861	30	961
Royal Artillery (12 guns)	14	398	14	398
Royal Engineers	6	185	6	185
Veterinary department	4	4	4	4
Commissariat and transport	3	208	3	211
Army Hospital Corps	6	71	5	72
Field hospitals	16	90	16	90
Post-office department		3		3
Divisional staff	16	41	16	41
Add warrant officers		13		14
Total	329	7,521	336	8,280

SUMMARY OF CORPS TROOPS.

Troops.	Officers.	Men.
Cavalry brigade:		
Cavalry brigade staff	3	8
Cavalry	86	1,598
Royal Horse Artillery (6 guns)	7	175
Commissariat and transport	2	213
Army Hospital Corps	6	71
Postal department		2
Add warrant officers		5
Total	104	1,877
Corps Artillery	31	605
Siege train	18	561
Ordnance-Store Department	10	150
Corps Engineers	32	751
Military police	4	138
Veterinary department	10	10
Chaplain's department	13	8
Commissariat and transport	45	560
Army Hospital Corps	5	72
Field hospitals	32	180
Post-office department	3	35
Add warrant officers		48
Total corps troops	307	—

ADDITIONAL BATTALIONS.

	Officers.	Men.
Royal Marine Light Infantry	37	1,006
Royal Marine Artillery	13	450
Total marines	50	1,456

The following are the totals of the principal corps. In the infantry is included the Royal Marine Artillery battalion, which was armed as a foot detachment.

	Officers and men.
Infantry	15,642
Cavalry	2,304
Artillery (including siege train)	2,435
Engineers	1,161
Commissariat and Transport Corps	1,294
Army Hospital Corps	313
Army Medical Department	429

If to these is added the reinforcement of the Indian Contingent, the whole number of men landed in Egypt is found to be in the neighborhood of 35,000, while about 6,000 more were on their way or in reserve at near points.

XI.

THE SEIZURE OF THE SUEZ CANAL AND THE CHANGE OF BASE.

The British operations in Egypt were formally legitimized through the passage by Parliament, on July 28, of the bill granting £2,300,000 sterling for the expense of the expedition. At the moment of which this report now treats the state of affairs may be briefly summarized as follows:

The British had a foothold at Alexandria and at Suez, besides strong naval forces at Port Said and Ismailia. The Suez Canal was still open to traffic, vessels coming and going through it as usual, unmolested. Egyptian detachments held Port Said and Ismailia, in the interest of Arabi Pasha, who had been declared a rebel by the Khedive. These two ports were the only maritime places of importance to the attack. With the exception of Suez and Alexandria, the whole of Egypt lay in the possession of Arabi and his followers. It was known that these amounted to between 50,000 and 60,000 regulars, including the reserves, besides numberless volunteers generally spoken of vaguely as Bedouins.

The ends which General Wolseley had to accomplish were three in number: first, to crush Arabi's forces; second, to seize Cairo and save it from the fate which had befallen Alexandria; third, to re-establish the Khedive's authority. The last, while politically embracing the two former, was, in a military sense, their necessary outcome.

Referring to the map of Lower Egypt, Plate 47, it will be seen that Cairo is at the apex of the delta, a district roughly 110 miles on each side of the triangle which it forms. Through this district run the two principal branches of the Nile, which separate a few miles below Cairo, and which serve as the main arteries of trade and of a vast system of irrigation canals and ditches. The banks of these canals and the railway embankments are the roads of this country, where wheeled vehicles are practically unknown outside of the larger towns. These embankments could have been readily utilized as formidable intrenchments. To engage Arabi in the delta would have been folly. Possessing an intimate knowledge of this network of dikes and water-courses, he could have avoided or sought battle at his own convenience, securing for himself the most advantageous conditions, and, if defeated, could have either retired to other and similar positions, or have carried on a prolonged and harassing guerrilla warfare, trusting to the high water in the Nile, now rapidly rising, to flood the ground in front of the British, and to defeat them by the malarial fevers which are the concomitant of the overflow. He could thus have retreated at comparative leisure, destroying all European property as he withdrew, and, if forced up the Nile Valley, leaving behind him a mass of smoking ruins to mark the site of Cairo.

The French under Bonaparte in 1798 had marched from Alexandria to Damanhour and up the left bank of the western or Rosetta branch of the Nile to Cairo; but this route could only have been followed by General Wolseley after taking or turning the fortified lines at Kafr Dowar, and it was open to the further objections that along it Arabi could not be forced to fight in the open, and that a wide, deep, and swift river, almost devoid of bridges, lay between it and Cairo.

The chances and probable results of a direct advance from Alexandria had been fully considered, and even before he left London General Wolseley had determined upon his plan of campaign, which involved the use of Ismailia, on the Suez Canal, as a base of operations. He hoped to be able to induce Arabi to fight a decisive battle at some point in the desert where the Egyptians could be absolutely crushed, and then to push on from that point, whatever it might be, and occupy Cairo. This probability of a fair fight in the open was in fact the main object to be subserved by the selection of this route. As secondary advantages, however, were, first, the relative proximity to Cairo of the base, 96 miles distant by rail over this line, as compared with 127 miles from Alexandria; second, the existence of a railway susceptible of easy defense, for the transportation of supplies from the base; third, the greater salubrity of the desert region; fourth, the possession of a well-sheltered inland harbor where the operation of disembarking could be conducted without interference from gales of wind or heavy surf.

The precautions taken to keep the plan a military secret were thoroughly successful. It was allowed to be understood that a combined attack on Aboukir and its forts was in course of preparation, and every facility was given to newspaper correspondents to obtain such details as might prudently be made public without exciting too much suspicion as being merely a *ruse de guerre*. In the mean time, General Wolseley and Admiral Seymour, in full accord, were busily employed in making all the necessary arrangements for the transportation of troops to Ismailia and the seizure of the Suez Canal.

On August 18, several transports, with troops on board, steamed outside the harbor of Alexandria and anchored off the Bogzha Pass. Detailed instructions were issued for bombarding the forts at Aboukir and for landing the soldiers, as well as for a simultaneous advance on Arabi's left at King Osman. The troops selected for embarkation were the 1st division under Lieutenant-General Willis, C. B. The 1st brigade of this division was composed of three battalions of the Guards. The 2nd brigade was incomplete at this time, only the 2nd battalion of the York and Lancaster Regiment (late 84th foot) and the 1st battalion of the West

Kent Regiment (late 50th foot) having arrived. This deficiency was made good by the marine battalions and the 3rd battalion of the Rifles. On Saturday, August 19, the various transports moved to the eastward in a fleet escorted by the Inflexible, Minotaur, Superb, and Temeraire, and anchored in regular lines, according to a prearranged plan, in Aboukir Bay, at 3.30 p. m., the men-of-war being nearest the beach. The troopship Euphrates, with the Duke of Cornwall's Light Infantry, the Rhosina, with the Royal Marine Light Infantry battalion, and the Nerissa, with the Rifles and the Royal Marine Artillery battalion, pushed on to Port Said. These transports experienced singularly bad luck, the last two breaking down *en route*. The delay resulting was not serious, for their escort, the Alexandra, towed the Nerissa at the reputed rate of twelve knots an hour, while the Euphrates helped the Rhosina. After dark these vessels were followed by the other transports, which left Arabi and Aboukir, in a military sense, *dans l'air*. On arriving at Port Said the next morning, they found the entire Maritime Canal in the hands of the British navy.

The official reports descriptive of this operation are quoted at length.

H. M. S. PENELOPE,
Port Said, August 23, 1882.

SIR: I have the honor to make the following report of my proceedings after I left Alexandria in the Iris, on the evening of the 16th instant, with the plan of operations agreed on between Sir Garnet Wolseley and yourself:

2. I arrived at Port Said the next morning (Thursday) at 10 o'clock, and immediately sent the Nyauza, condenser steamer, with tents, provisions, and 100 men of the Northumberland, to Ismailia, as a reinforcement to Captain Fitz Roy.

3. On Friday morning, the 18th instant, Captain Fitz Roy joined me from Ismailia, and after discussion with him I gave him the accompanying orders with reference to the occupation of that place.

4. I also arranged for the occupation of Port Said by Captain Henry Fairfax, of H. M. S. Monarch, to whom I gave the instructions appended.

5. On Friday evening I brought in two companies of the battalion of Marines from the Northumberland and placed them on board of the Monarch and Iris.

6. M. Victor de Lesseps, who is the working head of the canal company at Ismailia, came on board on the 17th instant and entered into a long discussion, presenting a series of arguments against any possible intention on our part to disembark in the canal, and disputing the grounds of my intimation that I considered Ismailia, both town and port, to be Egyptian. He left with the conviction, I feel sure, on his part, that we, sooner or later, should use the canal for a military purpose, while I had imbibed a conviction that no remonstrance on our part would induce Count Ferdinand de Lesseps to willingly accept the position and withdraw his opposition to our doing so.

7. I considered, therefore, that to insure the safe passage of our troops it was absolutely necessary that the barges and dredges, &c., should be occupied along the whole line of the canal to Ismailia; and, further, that it was most desirable that the Kantara telegraph station should be seized and our through telegraphic communication be restored, while Arabi's communication with Syria should be stopped.

8. For this duty I selected Commander H. H. Edwards, of H. M. S. Ready, as an officer thoroughly conversant with the canal, and in whose judgment I had confidence.

9. He started at 8 p. m. on Saturday evening, the 19th instant, taking the necessary telegraphists, and left the parties told off for each post as he passed up.

10. At the same time I brought in the remaining three companies of the battalion of Marines, under Lieutenant-Colonel Graham, from the Northumberland, and towards daylight transferred them to the Ready and Dee, with two launches from the Penelope, to facilitate their landing on arrival at Ismailia.

11. The Falcon, which had just arrived from Alexandria, was sent an hour before sunset on the 19th to an anchorage off the coast half way between Port Said and Ghemil, and the Northumberland anchored during the night off Ghemil Fort, the object being to check an exodus of the Arab coal-heavers from Port Said, and to create an impression that our intention was to attack that work.

12. About 4 o'clock a. m. on the 20th the movement was executed simultaneously along the line with complete success, the rebels being completely taken by surprise; telegraphic communication was restored between Ismailia, Kantara, and Port Said, and the Syrian telegraph was under our control. It was found, however, that the latter had been previously disconnected.

13. On your arrival in the Helicon, about 8 a. m. on the 20th, I had intended to proceed at once to Ismailia to reinforce Captain Fitz Roy who was exposed to the possibility of attack by a large force of enemy moving down on him by rail.

14. Circumstances, however, as you are aware, necessitated my remaining at Port Said to see the 1st Division of Transports into the canal, and by their entering I was precluded from going on for some time in my flagship. When night fell, therefore, I went up to Ismailia in a picket-boat, and arrived about 4 a. m.

15. I immediately landed and joined Captain Fitz Roy and inspected the position he had taken up. It appeared to me to have been admirably chosen, and the works thrown up for the protection of our men by Captain Stephenson's party, with the advantage of Major Fraser's, R. E., advice, to have been thoroughly satisfactory.

16. It is known that three trains full of soldiers were moved down by the rebel general from Tel-el-Kebir with the view to attempt to retake the place, but he was deterred from making an attack, probably by the shell-fire on the Nefiche station, and after some time spent in observation of our position, the trains ran back in the direction from whence they came.

17. I would here draw your particular attention to the effective fire maintained by the Orion and Carysfort on a position which could only be seen from the mast-head of the latter at over 4,000 yards' distance; a fire by which a train standing on the rails at the station was twice struck, and the carriages and trucks secured for our own uses.

18. I inclose reports from Captains Fairfax and Fitz Roy and Commander Edwards, of their respective share in the operation, and desire to express my sense of the judgment, zeal, and ability shown by them in the performance of the difficult and delicate duties which devolved on them.
I have, &c.,
A. H. HOSKINS,
Rear-Admiral.

To Admiral Sir F. BEAUCHAMP SEYMOUR, G. C. B., &c.,
Commander-in-Chief, Mediterranean.

P. S.—My report would not be complete without my mentioning that I employed Captain Seymour, of the Iris, on the delicate duty of securing the canal company's office at Port Said, and in preventing any information being conveyed through it to their other stations, or to the rebels, a duty which was performed, as have all others on which I have employed Captain Seymour, entirely to my satisfaction.

The following brief note contains the instructions from the Rear-Admiral to Captain Fitz Roy, of H. M. S. Orion, upon which the latter seized Ismailia:

H. M. S. PENELOPE,
Port Said, August 18, 1882.

Memorandum.

Some time before daylight on Sunday morning next you are to land the available force under your command at Ismailia, and proceed to occupy the town, which you are to hold until you are reinforced, which will probably be at the latest within twenty-four hours.

It is of the greatest importance that the telegraph office, both of the canal company and the Egyptian Government, should be seized at once and all telegrams prevented from passing.

The waste-weir to the westward of the upper lock should also be seized at once, and held, if possible, until the troops arrive. As this is under the fire of the guns at Nefiche, intrenchments should be thrown up as soon as possible to cover the men.

You are to use your own discretion as to supporting this movement with the fire of the ships, but you will bear in mind that it is most desirable that no injury whatever should be done to the town of Ismailia or its inhabitants by any measures which you adopt yourself, and you should use every means in your power to prevent it on the part of others.

The Staff Commander of the Orion should be ready to place any ship arriving with troops in the best berths for them to occupy, with a view to the disembarkation and their draught of water.

From the verbal communication we have had, the support you may expect from myself and Sir William Hewett is made fully known to you.

In the event of your being attacked by a superior force of the enemy, you are to use your own discretion as to falling back upon the ships.

Any persons attempting to set fire to the houses should be at once shot.

A. H. HOSKINS,
Rear-Admiral.

To Captain R. O'B. FITZ ROY,
H. M. S. Orion.

The orders to Captains Fairfax and Seymour, charged with similar work at Port Said, the execution of which would occur in the presence of Rear-Admiral Hoskins, were more detailed:

PENELOPE, AT PORT SAID,
August 19, 1882.

At 3.30 a.m. on Sunday next, the 20th instant, Port Said is to be occupied in the following manner:

2. The direction of operations will be under Captain Fairfax, of H. M. S. Monarch.
3. The landing party will consist of—

From H. M. S. Monarch, 100 seamen, small-arm men, 18 [*a*] Gatling gun's crew, 48 Royal Marines, 1 Gatling gun.

From H. M. S. Iris, 80 seamen, small-arm men, 18 [*a*] Gatling gun's crew, 28 Royal Marines, 1 Gatling gun.

From H. M. S. Northumberland, battalion 200 Royal Marines.

Total, 180 seamen, small-arm men, 36, Gatling-gun crews, 276 Royal Marines, 2 Gatling guns.

Total strength, 492 men and 2 Gatling guns.

4. The Iris' seamen and marines will at once proceed to the outskirts of the town by the Quay Eugenie (Plate LII), and take the right of the line, to extend from the sea to Lake Menzaleh, between the European and Arab towns, *i. e.*, from the right of the Rue du Nord to the beach.

5. They will be followed immediately by the company of the Battalion of Marines from the Iris, who will turn to the left at the Rue de l'Arsenal, and form round the north angle of the barracks.

6. The Monarch's seamen and marines will form on the wharf opposite the ship and march by the Rue du Nord to the Consulate, which the marines will take charge of, posting sentries. The blue-jackets will continue on the same line of street, and form on the left of the Iris men, extending to Lake Menzaleh, and detaching a party to guard the reservoir and its neighborhood.

7. The Battalion Company of the Royal Marines of the Monarch will form on the left of the above on the wharf and march after the advance to the south corner of the barracks, taking care not to extend into the Rue de l'Arsenal, so as not to be in the way of the fire of the Iris' detachment. The Egyptian troops are to be summoned to lay down their arms and then marched down to the wharf.

8. One Gatling gun will accompany the advance of the Iris, and the other the Marine Battalion Company of the Monarch to the entrance of the barracks.

9. A sergeant's party is to be kept on the wharf to prevent any attempt being made to fire the custom-house, round which sentries are to be posted.

10. The Khedive's Governor, now in the Poona, will be on board the Penelope, and land directly the occupation is effected, and aid in the maintenance of order with the police who are known to be loyal.

10 a. Arrangements are to be made to send the breakfasts on shore, with anything else that may be wanted, at about 7 a. m. The men are to have a meal of cocoa before landing.

11. Care is to be taken that men do not land with loaded rifles, or load without orders, and it is to be impressed on all the landing party that no firing is to take place without orders, and that it is of the greatest importance to preserve amicable relations both with the white inhabitants of all nations and also with the Arabs, on whom we are dependent for the coaling of the ships.

12. A guard must be placed by the Iris over the governor's house at the earliest opportunity. Arabi's Governor, Ronchdy Pasha, is to be received as a friend if he surrender himself.

13. It is very desirable to secure the Bimbashi,* if possible, and Major Tulloch,† with an interpreter and a small party of picked men, will endeavor to effect this. Prisoners should be put on board the Iris when the Governor has been consulted as to who should be released and who retained as such.

14. Marines will land in blue with helmets, seamen in blue with white cap-covers. As soon as possible, a change of white clothing and hats for the seamen should be sent on shore, and strict attention is to be paid to their appearance on parade and their general tone and bearing. All defaulters are to be sent at once on board the Monarch.

A patrol of trustworthy men under an officer is to be told off at once for the maintenance of discipline amongst our own men, and such patrols as may be necessary to support the Egyptian police must be forthcoming immediately the occupation has taken place. Major Tulloch will be good enough to attach himself to the Governor *pro tem.* in order to insure requirements for the maintenance of order being promptly made known to Captain Fairfax or the officer deputed by him.

Captain Seymour will carry out independently my private orders to him.

Captain Fairfax will act as Military Commandant of Port Said during my absence until the pleasure of the Commander-in-Chief is known.

A. H. HOSKINS,
Rear-Admiral.

To Captain HENRY FAIRFAX, C. B., A. D. C., *of H.M.S. Monarch*, and
Captain EDWARD H. SEYMOUR, *of H. M. S. Iris.*

For the work to be done in the canal itself, between Port Said and Ismailia, the following instructions were given to Commander Edwards by Rear-Admiral Hoskins:

PENELOPE, AT PORT SAID,
August 19, 1882.

Commander Edwards, of H. M. S. Ready, will start soon after dark this evening with boats containing one company of the Northumberland's landing party.

---

* Military commandant.   † Military A. D. C. to the commander-in-chief.

He is first to occupy the dredges, putting on board of each an officer and 15 men to prevent any communication with the shore; and to insure each dredge being kept close to the bank out of the way of passing ships. Four days' provisions are to be put on board with each party.

Having done this and given his orders to the officers, he is to proceed to Kantara and seize the telegraph office and both the Egyptian and Canal Company's wires, and allow no message to pass through till he is certain it is made either by us or in our interest.

Having done this, he is to take steps to insure all the ships in the canal between Port Said and Lake Timsah bound north, i. e., to Port Said, being gared.*

Sir William Hewett, at Suez, has been instructed to allow no ship to enter the canal on Saturday; therefore it may be assumed that there will be found no ships on the other side of Lake Timsah.

DETAILS OF OPERATION.

The following force will leave Port Said soon after nightfall, under Commander H. H. Edwards, who will have charge of the operations, viz: 3 officers and 35 men of H. M. S. Northumberland; 4 officers and 56 men of H. M. S. Penelope; total, 7 officers and 91 men.

On proceeding up the canal 1 officer and 15 men are to be placed on board of each dredge met with, with orders to get her in to the bank as close as possible, or, if close, not to allow her to be moved.

The officers and men of the Northumberland are to be landed at Kantara, with the telegraph clerks, who will accompany them and carry out the instructions given them.

The remaining officers and men of the Penelope are to be kept ready to occupy any gare which may require it.

All steamers met with bound northward, if gared, are to be ordered to remain so. If under way or secured to the bank of the canal, to make fast immediately in the next gare. At the same time a dispatch boat is to be sent back past the next gare to warn following vessels not to pass the gare. Until the vessel going north has gared they should make fast to the bank.

The party of 1 officer and 10 men to be sent in a boat to occupy the gare station until this has been done, returning in the boat.

For this service, a picket boat (Northumberland's), a torpedo boat (Iris), a steam cutter (Tourmaline's), and steam pinnace (Monarch's), will be appropriated.

A. H. HOSKINS,
Rear-Admiral.

In obedience to these orders just quoted, the whole length of the canal was secured by the British.

The occurrences at Port Said are thus described in an official report by Captain Fairfax, of the Monarch:

H. M. S. MONARCH,
Port Said, August 21, 1882.

SIR: In pursuance of your orders dated the 19th instant, that at 3.30 a. m. on the 20th I was with the force named in the margin † to occupy the town of Port Said, and if possible, to surprise and capture the soldiers, whilst in the barracks and before they had any time to commit any acts of incendiarism, I made the following disposition of the force under my command:

The canal is, so to speak, a single-tracked road. The *gares* are the turnouts or sidings, where the floor of the canal is widened so that ships may pass each other. Garing is the operation of hauling out of the fairway, which is thus left clear.

† Already detailed in Rear-Admiral Hoskins' orders.

1. Lieutenant A. Cook, R. N., with Iris' naval brigade, a Gatling gun and a company of the Royal Marine battalion, under the command of Captain R. P. Coffin, R. M. L. I., were to land abreast of the Iris and double down the beach, the company of marines turning down the street in which the barracks are situated, and halting immediately opposite them, the men from H. M. S. Iris advancing along the beach till they reached the narrow neck of land which separates the Europeau from the native town, there to place sentries across from the sea to the road that passes down the center of it.

2. Commander T. F. Hammill, with two companies of seamen from the Monarch, was ordered to land abreast of the ship, and doubling through the southern part of the town (leaving half a company to protect the block of buildings in which the British consulate is situated), to push on to the neck of land and form a line of sentries from Lake Menzaleh to the road, thus completing with the Iris men a chain of sentries right across from the lake to the sea, and barring escape from the town.

3. The company of the Marine battalion under Captain F. M. Eden, R. M. L. I., and a Gatling from the Monarch under Lieutenant Charles Windham, R. N., were to proceed up the center of the town and halt on the other side of the barracks to that occupied by the other company of marines.

4. Arrangements were made that the force should fall in with the least possible noise so as not to alarm the sentries on the quay. A lighter was planked over, and after dark placed alongside the ship; this a few minutes before landing was hauled to the shore, and with the launch formed a floating bridge over which the men were able to pass.

5. The Khedive's Governor, who had been living on board the P. & O. steamer, came on board the Monarch at 3 a. m. and landed with me.

6. Major Tulloch, of the Royal Welsh Fusiliers (who gave me much valuable information and assistance), landed with six marines and secured three out of four sentries on the quay.

7. At 3.30 commenced landing, and succeeded in getting on shore without observation, and all the arrangements made werecarried out in every particular. I was accompanied by Major James W. Scott, R. M. L. I., commanding the two companies of the Royal Marine battalion, who posted his men in such a way that escape from the barracks was impossible.

8. The soldiers, who when we arrived appeared to be asleep, were ordered to surrender. Shortly after 160 fell in and laid down their arms.

The Governor having addressed them, they swore allegiance to the Khedive, and his excellency then requested that I would permit them to return to their barracks, but two officers were arrested and sent on board H. M. S. Iris.

9. On Monday afternoon I received a request from the Governor that I should make prisoners of the soldiers, as he found that they were leaving the town, and some were trying to incite the Arabs against the English. I therefore ordered two companies to arrest them in barracks, where only 52 were found. They were marched down to the quay, where they were embarked and sent off to H. M. S. Northumberland.

10. I am much indebted to Commander T. F. Hammill and Major J. W. Scott, R. M. L. I., for the able way in which they executed my orders, the silent and orderly manner in which the work was done contributing very much to the success of the undertaking.

11. The conduct of the officers and men landed gave me entire satisfaction.

I have, &c.,

H. FAIRFAX,
Captain.

To Rear-Admiral ANTHONY H. HOSKINS, C. B., &c.,
Senior Officer.

It may be well to add here that the Monarch had been so moored in the canal, off the town, that her forward turret guns commanded the main street leading to the quay, while the Iris was to seaward of the Monarch where she could shell the beach and the Arab town. At 11

p. m. Saturday night the ship's company were called on deck and warned that they would be landed at 3 a. m. Strict silence was enjoined. This order was so carried out that the people on board of the French ironclad La Galissonière, moored astern of the Monarch and to the same buoy, knew nothing of what was going on.

Of the arms surrendered by the garrison of Port Said but one piece was loaded. The military commandant was absent and all the Egyptian sentries were asleep at their posts. The place was held by the ships' marines and blue-jackets until September 16, when they were relieved by 200 Royal Marine Light Infantry and 100 Royal Marine Artillery who came out from England.

The work done in the canal between Port Said and Lake Timsah is thus detailed by Commander Edwards:

H. M. S. READY, AT ISMAILIA,
August 22, 1882.

SIR: I have the honor to report my proceedings in carrying out your orders dated 19th August, in connection with the occupation of certain points on the Suez Canal. Learning that it was very important that the dredger stationed at the ninth mile should be secured, I placed Lieutenant Davies, of the Penelope, with 20 men in charge of her. Proceeding up the canal, I informed all vessels bound to Port Said, also the *gare* keepers, that it would be necessary for the ships to remain in *gare* until they received further instructions. I detached Sub-Lieutenant Blomfield in Tourmaline's steam-cutter with six additional hands, to insure the above instructions being complied with, having previously obtained a promise from the English shipmasters that they would obey them. After occupying Kantara as instructed, I detached Lieutenant Barnes-Laurence in Iris' torpedo boat to insure the canal being kept clear. He reports that on his return to the *gare* at Kilometer No. 34, he found the Messageries Maritimes steamer Melbourne leaving, and that on remonstrating with her captain he was informed that the steamer should only be stopped by armed force, and that the first man stepping on board would be the signal to let go the anchor and leave the ship in his hands.

Lieutenant Barnes-Laurence not considering that his instructions warranted the use of force, left to report to me, and sent the Tourmaline's steam cutter to warn ships coming up from Port Said.

Shortly after leaving, he observed the British steamers Ross-shire and Counsellor weigh and follow the Messageries steamer, upon which he chased them and compelled them to haul into the next *gare*, and having cautioned the masters, who reiterated their promise, he left to rejoin me. Mr. Blomfield informed me on his return that directly the Iris' torpedo boat was out of sight the English ships appear to have again left the *gare*, as he met them steaming down the canal at a point where it was useless to stop them. The other duties assigned to the party under my command were all punctually executed, and on Sunday, the 20th instant, all who could be spared were employed lightening the steamer Kaiteur, aground in the canal, but she could not be moved.

In conclusion, I beg to express my thanks to all the officers, especially Lieutenant Barnes-Laurence, of the Iris, Sub-Lieutenant R. G. H. Blomfield, of the Tourmaline, and Mr. A. H. Freeman, midshipman, of the Monarch, for their zealous attention to my orders, also my great satisfaction with the behavior of the men during nearly 48 hours of continuous hard work.

I have, &c.,
H. H. EDWARDS,
Commander.

To Rear-Admiral A. H. HOSKINS, C. B.,
Second in Command.

To the casual reader of Commander Edwards' report it would seem that Lieutenant Barnes-Laurence was less deserving of commendation than of a court-martial. His unwillingness to accept the responsibility of stopping the French steamer Melbourne might have frustrated, as it certainly did delay, the execution of a strategic plan upon which depended the success of the whole campaign.

The most important place to be seized was Ismailia, while the proximity of a large armed force of Egyptians rendered the task dangerous in the extreme. As elsewhere, the landing of the British was completely unexpected and almost unresisted. The operations at this point are given in Captain Fitz Roy's official report, as follows:

ORION, LAKE TIMSAH,
August 21, 1882.

SIR: I have the honor to report that in accordance with your secret orders of the 18th instant I took possession of Ismailia, the Arab town, and advanced sufficiently towards Neficho to cover the weir.

The force landed consisted of 565 officers and men, comprising 40 marines, one 9-pounder gun's crew, one Gatling, a torpedo engineer party, and 12 riflemen from Orion, one Gatling and one rifle company from Northumberland, and one 7-pounder gun, Coquette's landing party, with 21 Royal Marine Artillery of Northumberland and Carysfort, under Captain Stephenson, C. B., including a company of marines under Captain Gore; also 100 seamen and marines from the Nyanza, troop-ship, belonging to the Northumberland.

The enemy were known to have a strong picket at Arab town, several patrols, and a guard at Ismailia, about 2,000 men and six guns encamped at Nefiche, and a considerable number of Bedouins in the neighborhood.

At 3 a. m., in perfect silence, the Orion's and Coquette's men landed, the Carysfort's shortly following, and advanced. The silence was so perfect that Commander Kane surrounded the lock guard before we were discovered. The lock guard fired their rifles and so did our men, and here Commander Kane was wounded by a rifle bullet on the left cheek.

The governor's guard laid down their arms to Lieutenant Lenox Napier and the Royal Marine Artillery, under Lieutenant Swinburne. No further resistance was experienced in the town. Commander Kane seized the railway and telegraphs, the Orion's men the canal-lock bridge, town generally, and government house (with the governor), where I established my headquarters.

Captain Stephenson and his party had slight skirmishing in advancing, and in Arab town some of the enemy were killed. The ships, at 3.40 a. m., bombarded the guard-houses at Arab town, firing five rounds of shell each. By 4 a. m. the whole place was occupied as ordered. By intercepted telegrams and reports, I ascertained the enemy were making arrangements to forward a large force to Nefiche to at once attack Ismailia and the ships. Considering this, the small force at my disposal, and that the inhabitants were getting alarmed, I determined to dislodge the enemy from Nefiche and destroy their camp and any trains running; therefore Orion and Carysfort commenced a slow bombardment at 11 a. m., at a distance of 4,200 yards. By noon the camp was destroyed and enemy retreating towards Cairo; also one train running south severely hit and stopped for a time. The bombardment was stopped for a short time, but at 4 p. m., as another train was seen arriving and discharging men from Cairo way, it was continued, wrecking the train, jamming and apparently overturning trucks on the line, driving every one away, and from the position of the train on the Suez line, completely blocking Arabi's communications with his forces between Nefiche and Suez by railroad. This was most satisfactory. The squadron was in charge of Commander Moore, Lieutenant Royds having charge of the Carysfort and her guns, under Commander Moore's orders. Her mast-heads were the reconnoitering and lookout places. The bombardment then ceased until 10 p. m., after which shells were fired at Nefiche, at intervals of half an hour, until daylight, to prevent the railway being cleared and to check troops coming by train from the west. My position was still an anxious one. At 6 p. m. 340 marines arrived, 200 reinforced Commander Kane, 140 Captain Stephenson, who had, with the assistance of Major Fraser, intrenched himself in advance of Arab town. Lieutenant Napier had secured his admirable position in the Khedive's palace, and I reinforced him with 20 seamen of Northumberland and an officer. I have since heard that on this afternoon Arabi, with 3,000 men in three trains, did advance to within a few miles of Nefiche, but retired again. During the night the search lights were worked as necessary.

At 10.30 p. m. General Graham arrived with the advance guard of the army, reinforced the different positions, and assumed military command.

I was directed to retain command in Ismailia until 4 p. m. the 21st August, 1882, when Sir Garnet Wolseley relieved my guards.

At 8 a. m. to-day I sent a Gatling gun and crew, under Lieutenant Adair and Lieutenant King-Harman, torpedo engineer party, with General Graham, to occupy Nefiche, where they now remain. I have also a steam cutter and the jolly-boat working on the Fresh Water Canal to Nefiche.

The officers and men did their work perfectly. I have to thank Captain Stephenson, Commander Kane, Commander Moore, Major Fraser, R. E., Lieutenants Napier, Royds, and King-Harman (who destroyed the railway approaches to my west front in two advanced positions); also my first lieutenant, Cross, who had, with a gun, charge of the canal bridge and town approaches specially.

Seven prisoners, Arabi's soldiers, were taken near lock bridge and Arab town, sent on board Orion for two days, and, being disarmed, were allowed to proceed on shore.

I had every reason, on the evening of the 20th August, 1882, to expect a night attack in force, so I placed the Ready and the Lee, that had arrived with the marines, close inshore in position that would cover a retreat on our part through the town.

Captain Stephenson brings to my notice the services of Lieutenant Langley, the senior lieutenant of the Carysfort, with the landing party. I have great pleasure in also specially mentioning this officer to you. Captain Stephenson forwards a letter from Major Fraser, R. E.

I have the honor to inclose herewith a report from Captain Stephenson.

Major Fraser's report will follow.

I have, &c.,

ROBT. O'B. FITZ ROY,
Captain.

To Rear-Admiral ANTHONY H. HOSKINS, C. B.,
Senior Officer.

Captain Stephenson thus describes his particular share in the landing:

CARYSFORT, AT ISMAILIA,
August 22, 1882.

SIR: In accordance with your confidential memorandum, I landed with the force as per margin* at 3.30 a. m. of the 20th, leaving Lieutenant Thomas, H. M. S. Northumberland, with 13 small-arm men in charge of the telegraph station on the pier. I advanced with a strong advanced guard in skirmishing order, under Captain Gore, R. M. L. I., over the canal bridge, through European, native, and Arab towns, meeting no opposition.

---

*Seventy-four small-arm men; 1 field gun's crew, 12 men; 1 Gatling gun's crew 15 men; 24 pioneers, &c., 74 marines, 2 captains, and aid-de-camp; total 201.

2. Having taken possession of Arab town, I immediately loopholed it and threw up intrenchments under the guidance of Major Fraser, R. E.

The Egyptian picket retiring was fired upon by the Gatling and 9-pounder guns. Two of the picket were killed, one carrying a Remington rifle, but no ammunition.

3. About 8 a. m. three Egyptian mounted officers galloped towards our intrenchments from Nefiche, waving a flag of truce. They stated that they came to place themselves under my protection, and, receiving their swords and horses, I sent them under escort to you, and now forward their swords.

4. About 10 p. m. General Graham, C. B., V. C., arrived with 300 of the 50th Regiment under Colonel Tyler, whom he placed under my command for the defense of this outpost.

5. About 8 a. m. of the 21st, I advanced with the force under Major-General Graham, with two Gatling guns, on Nefiche, which was occupied without opposition, leaving the Gatlings for the defense of the railway bridge. I then returned to Ismailia, and embarked two small-arm companies and the 9-pounder field gun, in accordance with your orders.

6. In referring to this service it is my pleasing duty to report the satisfactory behavior of all under my command. Intrenching the outpost under a burning sun was most trying, and I regret the death of A. Wager, ordinary seaman, from sun-stroke. I would especially like to mention the name of Major Fraser, R. E., who was of great assistance in fortifying the Arab town; Captain Gore, R. M. L. I., belonging to H. M. S. Northumberland, and Lieutenant Langley, senior and gunnery lieutenant of this ship, whose untiring zeal and energy deserve my best thanks.

I inclose a report and sketch of the position from Major Fraser, R. E.

I have, &c.,

H. F. STEPHENSON,
Captain.

To Captain R. O'B. FITZ ROY,
Senior Officer, Ismailia.

The engineer officer who had been sent to act under the orders of Captain Fitz Roy was the brigade major of the Corps Engineers. His account is of value as further elucidating the situation, and as indicating the technical measures taken to improve the defenses of Ismailia. It is proper to state that where the town ends the desert of light sand begins at once. Major Fraser's report runs as follows:

ISMAILIA, *August* 26, 1882.

SIR: Having been detailed to accompany your force in taking Ismailia, I submit the following as to the part I took under your orders:

The enemy being at Nefiche with a force of all arms, it was to be expected that in the first instance he would resist us at the Arab village west of Ismailia.

Your force of 200 men, viz, 150 small-arm men, one 9-pounder and one Gatling, having reached the bridge at the water-works about 4 a. m., I took some skirmishers forward so as to gain and secure the front for the main body, which came up by the canal.

On moving into the open, a number of people appeared on our right front, and as a security I took, by your orders, a party of small-arm men and posted them on the bank in front of the bridge.

After a little firing we found we were not attacked, and then organized the defense of the village.

The village consists of low houses of sun-dried bricks, generally only one story high, with flat roofs and garden walls. There is a good east foreground towards Nefiche, but to the north and west it is more undulating.

The garden walls were cut down, houses loopholed, lateral gaps, and gaps to the rear formed where required. The upper rooms of the few two-storied houses were loopholed so as to give a double tier of fire, and the ends of streets were closed by shelter trenches. The gun and Gatling were intrenched with sand or sun-dried brick parapets, and platforms were made of doors. The spirit bottles were smashed in the grog shops, and the windows made defensible by filling up with boxes of wood containing sand. The sailors' cutlasses proved most useful for loopholing walls, and the shovels we took out enabled us in an hour or two to be in a state to resist serious attack. After some hours' labor we could let the men rest and feed.

Before sunrise, Arabi Pasha must have learned of our landing by telegraph from Nefiche.

Our information from all sources made it appear probable that an attack in force would be made before we could be reinforced; it was therefore desirable to induce the Arabs to postpone the attack.

Finding telegrams arriving from Cairo to the traffic manager, Ismailia, in ignorance of our arrival, I telegraphed in his name to the war minister at Cairo to say 5,000 English were already on shore and asked him to inform the authorities. He acknowledged receipt and said he had done so.

An officer, stating himself to be the chief of staff of Arabi's forces in the district, having come in to surrender, strongly advised the bombardment of Nefiche by the ships to prevent attack. This was done, and the effect was to cause the retreat of three trains of troops that approached Nefiche and the abandonment of a fort at Nefiche, a very remarkable result, considering the place was only seen from the tops, and the range was 4,000 yards.

In the afternoon I opened communication by placing two canal boats across the Sweet Water Canal, stern to stern.

In the fighting line itself a party of Royal Marine Light Infantry held the shelter trench by the canal, where also was the signaling station. The marines also held the group of houses by the railway, and the blue-jackets held the remainder.

In the evening, having been reinforced by some 140 marines (Royal Marine Artillery), they were posted along the high canal banks as a support for our fighting line.

At night we posted sentries 300 to 400 yards to our front and went rounds, and in the early morning Major-General Graham came in with part of his brigade and bivouacked in our rear.

In conclusion I would draw your attention to the very efficient and willing manner in which all of your party did the work of intrenching, and the aptitude they showed for such work.

I have, &c.,

T. FRASER,
Major, Brigade Major R. E.

To Capt. H. F. STEPHENSON, C. B.,
Commanding H. M. S. Carysfort.

It is well to add, as a matter of professional detail, that the eighteen men composing the Gatling gun's crew of the Orion were armed with the Martini-Henry rifle; that they carried two days' provisions in their haversacks, and 120 rounds of ammunition distributed as follows: One large pouch or ball bag, with 40 loose rounds, and two small pouches each containing 40 cartridges in package. The dress was blue serge with straw hats and regulation leggings. Later on, the men improvised *puggeries*. They had no tents. The other Gatling guns' crews were armed according to rule with cutlasses and revolvers. These and the 9-pdr. guns' crews (of eighteen men usually) carried 36 rounds of pistol ammunition. In the gun limbers were eight shell, twelve shrapnel, and four case-shot. This supply was subsequently increased to 75 rounds, of pistol cartridges, all told, by addition sent to the front, while the Gatlings had each 1,200 rounds with two spare cases of 680 cartridges each under the limbers. With each party went four stretcher-men armed with swords, eight spare-ammunition men similarly armed, two signal-men with kit, armed with swords and revolvers, an armorer with sword, pistol, and sack of tools, and two pioneers, one carrying a shovel slung over the left shoulder, a pick-ax in hand; the other, a saw, file, and hand-ax slung over the shoulder, and a felling-ax in hand. Each pioneer was armed with a bill-hook, saw-backed sword, and revolver.

The landing was effected at the central wharf. A large lighter had been secured and on it were placed the Northumberland's and a portion of the Orion's party, about 250 in all. They seized the wharf and main avenue up to the canal lock. The first lighter was followed by a smaller one with the balance of the Orion's men.

The "torpedo party," under Lieutenant King-Harman, was composed of ten blue-jackets and nine artificers. They carried with them gun-cotton disks and the necessary electrical apparatus for their detonation. This party pushed on in the darkness, covered by a company from the Northumberland, and blew up the railway just behind the "*canal de ceinture*," about 500 yards from the station, using two 9-ounce disks of gun-cotton fired by a platinum wire-bridge fuze (25 grains of fulminate of mercury), insulated wicks, and a portable battery of three Leclanché elements. This done, and railway access to Ismailia being prevented, they retired to the town again.

The shelling of Nefiche was a case of firing at a target invisible from the gun. As described by Lieutenant Langford, R. N., who directed the operation on board the Orion, under Commander Moore, the method appears to have been very simple. From the masthead an angle was taken between the ship's head and Nefiche station, just visible, and the gun was trained accordingly by the marks on the racer or training track. In this line of sight was a small bush on the low sand-hill to the westward of the lake, which gave the gun-captain a permanent point at which to aim. The distance was pricked off from the chart and the elevation subsequently corrected by watching the fall of the shot. The gun used was a 12-inch Armstrong M. L. R. of 25 tons, with common shell weighing 500 pounds, and time-fuzes cut to 14 seconds.

Fifteen rounds were fired from the Orion, the last being at 8 a. m. of August 21. The same methods were adopted on board the Carysfort with similar but lessened results, due to the smaller size of her guns, the largest being 7-inch M. L. R.

In the southern half of the canal from Lake Timsah to Suez the events of the day were on a smaller scale, but none the less interesting. It will be remembered that Suez had been in the possession of the British navy for nearly three weeks, and that the advance of the Indian Contingent, the 1st battalion of the Seaforth Highlanders (late 72d Foot), under Lieutenant-Colonel Stockwell, had come up from Aden where they had been previously quartered. The following is the report of Rear-Admiral Sir William Hewett, the commander-in-chief of H. M. naval forces in the East Indies, the bulk of whose squadron had rendezvoused at the southern end of the Maritime Canal:

EURYALUS, *at Suez, August* 21, 1882.

SIR: On Friday last, the 18th instant, I had the honor of receiving, through Rear-Admiral Hoskins, C. B., a copy of the plan of operations in the Suez Canal, agreed to between yourself and Sir Garnet Wolseley, and your telegram of the 17th instant gave me authority to act on it.

2. Immediately put in train the work to be carried out at Suez, and telegraphed to you that your instructions had been received and would be complied with.

3. In the course of the same afternoon the rebels were observed intrenching themselves in our front, and movements of Bedouins on our left flank also called for attention. I consulted with Brigadier-General Tanner, C. B., who commanded the troops, and we agreed that the Naval Brigade would be too weak to hold the place by itself if attacked by a large force, such as we knew to be in our vicinity. I therefore, with the concurrence of the brigadier-general, telegraphed to you that 100 of the Seaforth Highlanders would be detained at Suez until the arrival of the troops from India.

4. Later on, Captain Hastings, whom I had sent in the Seagull to reconnoiter the banks of the canal, returned with a report that showed the information sent me from time to time by Captain Fitz Roy of the movements of the enemy in our direction to be fairly correct; and the Brigadier-General then agreed with me that it would not be prudent to send any of the Highlanders away without previously reconnoitering the neighborhood, for, as I have already stated in my telegram, the collection of military stores at Suez represented a considerable value, and a matter of still more serious consequence was the fact that the town had recently become crowded with women and children, Copt Christians, who had sought refuge at Suez from the brutalities of the surrounding Bedouins.

5. On Friday night I caused the telegraph wires to be cut between Suez and the first canal station, and on Saturday morning notices were issued that from that date, the 19th instant, until the prohibition was formally removed, no ships or boats would be allowed to pass into the canal from the Suez side without my special permission. The damage to the wire on the above occasion was soon repaired, but on the following night I caused the poles which conveyed the line across the creek close to the company's offices to be cut down, and placed a guard over them to prevent their being restored.

At the time when it was decided to retain the Highlanders the regiment was already on board the Bancoora. This was on Saturday night, and their disembarkation on Sunday must have had a very puzzling effect upon the officials of the canal company and others who were interested in our movements. It must also have had the happy effect of qualifying any reports that may have reached the rebels that our troops were about to enter the canal.

6. On Sunday morning at daylight 400 Highlanders, under Lieutenant-Colonel Stockwell, were disembarked from the transport and marched 8 miles in the direction of Chalouf to make a feint attack in our front. Brigadier-General Tanner, C. B., accompanied this force, and at the same time I sent my flag captain, Captain A. P. Hastings, in the Seagull, with the Mosquito in company, and 200 of the Seaforth Highlanders, to Chalouf by the Maritime Canal.

7. The party under Lieutenant-Colonel Stockwell returned to Suez at about 4 p. m. without having touched the enemy; but later in the day Captain Hastings returned in a steam pinnace to report very successful operations from the gun-vessels. It appears that the first that was seen of the enemy along the canal was a small cavalry patrol about 3 miles this side of Chalouf, and on arrival at Chalouf his presence in force was only discovered by a few heads appearing over the railway embankment on the other

side of the Sweet Water Canal, this embankment forming a natural intrenchment behind which it was afterwards discovered there was some 600 infantry ready to resist our advance. These men were extremely well armed and accoutered, and had a plentiful supply of ammunition with them.

8. The manner in which the position was taken reflects the highest credit on Captain Hastings, and I recommend him to your favorable notice.

- 9. The coolness and dash of the Highlanders and the excellent fire from the ships' tops seem to have been the chief causes of success, and the conduct of all concerned appears to have been in every way creditable.

10. I consider that credit must be given to Lieutenant-Colonel H. Helsham Jones, R. E., for the fact of there now being fresh water at Suez. Opening the lock gates above the point occupied, kept the canal below full, notwithstanding the waste which took place through a breach made by the enemy in the banks of the canal, which has since, however, been repaired by a company of the Madras Sappers.

11. I am in hopes that the action taken at Chalouf will do much to secure the safety of the canal, and as the Indian forces are now arriving, the Highlanders will go to Serapeum to-morrow.

12. I beg to recommend to your favorable notice the officers mentioned by Captain Hastings in the accompanying letter.

I have, &c.,
W. HEWETT,
Rear-Admiral and Commander-in-Chief on the East Indies Station.

To Admiral Sir F. BEAUCHAMP SEYMOUR, G. C. B.,
Commander-in-Chief in the Mediterranean.

Captain Hastings' account of the occurrences in the Maritime Canal on the August 20, is as follows:

H. M. S. SEAGULL,
At Chalouf, August 20, 1882.

SIR: I have the honor to submit the following report of my proceedings in command of the force* (as per margin) dispatched this day from Suez to secure the Fresh Water lock at Chalouf.

2. On my arrival off the place, which is distant 15 miles from Suez, on the west bank of the Maritime Canal, there were at first but few signs of the enemy's presence; there was no camp visible, and the first indication we saw of them was a few men's heads showing over the embankment of the railway on the other side of the Sweet Water Canal, which lay between us and the position the enemy occupied. This embankment, forming as it did a natural intrenchment, concealed a force of about 600 infantry, and in the distance we saw from 40 to 50 cavalry patrolling in the direction of Suez.

3. I first landed the Highlanders and the landing parties of the Seagull and Mosquito without field guns, and then opened fire from the tops of the ships, which were armed as follows:

Seagull: In foretop, a 7-pounder boat-gun; in maintop, a Gatling gun. Mosquito: In foretop, a Gatling gun.

For some time there was no reply to our fire, but presently we got a volley from the left which left no doubt as to the enemy's position.

Previous to this, Captain Lendrum had occupied the lock with G company of the Seaforth Highlanders, and Lieutenant-Colonel H. Helsham Jones, R. E., to whom I am much indebted for his valuable advice and assistance throughout the day, finding the gates open closed them, and so kept the Suez end of the canal full of water.

---

*H. M. S. Seagull, Commander Mather Byles; H. M. S. Mosquito, Lieutenant and Commander the Honorable F. R. Sandilands, and 200 Seaforth Highlanders, commanded by Major Kelsey.

Had this not been done, it is needless to say that the canal would have soon emptied itself.

Major Garnett's company and the men of the Mosquito now searched the village between the Fresh Water and Maritime Canals, where the firing was coming from, the advance of this party being protected by the small-arm companies of the Seagull and the remaining companies of the Highlanders, under Brevet Major Fergusson and Captain Hughes-Hallet.

Previous to this the skiff of the Mosquito had been transported to the Fresh Water Canal, and I sent Lieutenant E. Rae, of H. M. S. Seagull, to the opposite bank in her to examine the enemy's movements.

By this time Major Garnett had passed the village, which was found to be deserted, and had pushed his men across the canal by means of a boat obtained by Lieutenant H. G. Lang, of the Highlanders, who in a very plucky manner swam the canal and in the face of a hot fire procured it from under the opposite embankment.

Sub-Lieutenant W. O. Story and the men of the Mosquito accompanied the Highlanders, and the fire from this party was now so hot that the enemy was soon dislodged from his position.

Another boat having been procured by Assistant Paymaster Thomas R. B. Rogers of H. M. S. Seagull, from the lock end of the canal, the remainder of the ships' landing party and the Highlanders were likewise crossed over the water and the enemy was soon in full retreat.

Lieutenant-Colonel Jones, R. E., accompanied me with his party.

Some of the fugitives took the line of the railway, others went straight into the desert, while a few fled to a hill to the rear of their line, where they were eventually surrounded by Captain Hughes-Hallet and made prisoners of.

At this point was captured a 7-pounder brass field piece of French make, from which two rounds had been fired before being seized. We now ceased firing and proceeded to embark our prisoners. The enemy's loss was about 100 killed (including three officers, one of whom was the officer in command) and 62 prisoners, out of which 27 are wounded, and we have captured a large number of Remington rifles, with quantities of ammunition and stores.

The enemy fought with bravery, but their shooting was most inferior, and, owing to this latter defect, I am happy to say there are only two casualties on our side, viz, Benjamin Davis, A. B., Euryalus, one of my boat's crew who accompanied me, slightly wounded, and Joseph Fernandez, wardroom steward of the Seagull, one of the stretcher party, severely wounded. Besides the above, I regret to say Corporal Hind and Private Reeves of the Highlanders were drowned in trying to cross the canal. The wounded men are receiving every possible attention from Surgeons A. McKinley, of the Mosquito, and L. W. Vasey, of the Seagull, who were attached to the landing parties of their respective ships.

The conduct of the seamen and marines under fire was everything that could be desired, and I would wish to express my admiration for the coolness and gallantry of the Highlanders, to which, with the excellent fire from the ships, the success of the day must be attributed.

I have to thank Commander Mather Byles of the Seagull, Lieutenant-Colonel H. Helsham Jones, R. E., Lieutenant and Commander the Honourable F. R. Sandilands, of H. M. S. Mosquito, and Major W. F. Kelsey, of the Seaforth Highlanders, for their valuable co-operation and assistance, and I beg to bring to favorable notice the services of Lieutenant E. Rae, who commanded the landing party from the Seagull; Sub-Lieutenant W. O. Story, who commanded the landing party from the Mosquito; Sub-Lieutenant E. J. Carus Wilson, who worked the Gatling gun in the maintop of the Seagull; Mr. George Peavitt, gunner, who worked the 7-pounder in foretop of the Seagull; Mr. G. Gore Browne, midshipman, my aid-de-camp, who was most useful to me; and Mr. T. R. B. Rogers, assistant paymaster in charge, of the Seagull, who rendered good service by bringing the boat from the lock.

I attach a plan of the position drawn by Navigating Lieutenant Richard J. Rogers, of H. M. S. Seagull.

I have, &c.,

ALICK P. HASTINGS,
Captain.

To Rear-Admiral Sir W. N. W. HEWETT, K. C. B., V. C.,
Commander-in-Chief, East Indies.

The next report is by Major Kelsey, commanding the detachment of the Seaforth Highlanders engaged in the action at Chalouf, and is rendered to Captain Hastings:

CHALOUF, *August* 20, 1882.

SIR: I have the honor to report for your information that on landing at Chalouf on the 20th August, 1882, I found two companies, each company 50 rifles, up in extended order, supported by two others, total 200 rifles.

On arriving on the bank of the Fresh Water Canal, the enemy showed, and I opened fire about 11.30 a. m.; at the same time I sent Captain Lendrum with one company, under the direction of Colonel Jones, R. E., to hold the lock about two miles to our right.

About twenty minutes after the action commenced, I sent a company under command of Major Garnett, to work round through some houses on our extreme left; this company was supported by a party of blue-jackets and marines from H. M. S. Mosquito, under command of Sub-Lieutenant Story, R. N., the houses were occupied by Major Garnett, and I reinforced him with half another company of Seaforth Highlanders, under command of Lieutenant Lang. The houses were passed through and the bank of the Fresh Water Canal lined. Major Garnett's party was here checked for some time until a boat was procured by Lieutenant Lang swimming over to the other side, under the enemy's fire, and bringing it back. Sub-Lieutenant Story, R. N., and a party of blue-jackets then crossed and held a house until reinforced by the Seaforth Highlanders, then advanced and took the enemy in flank, who then retreated rapidly.

About 4 p. m. Captain Hughes-Hallett took his company across the canal in a boat sent to me by Captain Lendrum from the lock he was occupying. This boat was towed up by a couple of men of his company under the direction of Paymaster Rogers, R. N., H. M. S. Seagull. As soon as Captain Hughes-Hallett's company had crossed, the remainder of our line was taken across, and advanced, driving the enemy before it.

A party of blue-jackets and marines from H. M. S. Seagull occupied a forward position in the center of our line during the action, and by their fire kept down the enemy's considerably.

The Gatlings in the tops of H. M. S. Seagull and Mosquito kept up a galling fire during the day and did great execution.

I beg to bring to your notice the name of Sub-Lieutenant Story, R. N., H. M. S. Mosquito. Major Garnett reports to me that he led his men in a forward and gallant manner.

I regret to have to report the loss of two men of Major Garnett's company by drowning; their names are Corporal David Hind and Private William Reeve. I inclose Major Garnett's report of the occurrence.

I have, &c.,

W. F. KELSEY,
Major Commanding Detachment First Battalion Seaforth Highlanders.

From the account of this affair given by an officer present, it is learned that the Egyptians engaged were mostly reserve men and old. So harsh had been the measures resorted to in recruiting that many had been brought down from the interior in chains. These chains were secured to anklets, were of iron and weighed about 10 pounds. With such troops it is hardly to be wondered at that the aim should have been indifferent. They held their pieces at arm's length above the head and discharged them vaguely over the embankments behind which they had taken shelter. Even chance shots are neither safe nor welcome, so that the operation was not free from danger, especially in the rear of the lines. To this shooting over may be attributed the slight damage done to the standing and running rigging of the gun-boats in the Maritime Canal. The crossing of the Fresh Water Canal should have been almost impossible, the boats being so small as to convey but seven or eight at a time, and the canal being so full of reeds as to render swimming difficult and perilous. The dash of the British more than counterbalanced the disadvantages of numbers and of an attack on a position of much natural strength.

With the exception of the Serapeum stretch, between Lake Timsah and the Bitter Lakes, where no great annoyance or interruption of traffic was expected, the whole of the Maritime Canal was in the possession of the British navy by nightfall of August 20.

On the following day, the Tourmaline and the Don moored permanently at Kantara, where the caravan road to Syria crosses the canal, and there established a strongly defended post, while the gun-boats in the southern half completed the link which perfected the chain from Port Said to Suez.

Having seized the canal, the navy prepared to protect it. Between Ismailia and Suez this was effected by the Mosquito and Seagull, which patrolled it constantly, no force being permanently landed. In the northern half, the Tourmaline and Don held Kantara and the *gares* adjoining on either side. Strong detachments of sailors from the fleet at Port Said, with Gatlings, were landed at the other *gares*, breastworks were thrown up and regular camps established, each in command of a lieutenant. At Port Said a camp was pitched between the European and Arab towns, where never less than 500 blue-jackets and marines were kept. Intrenchments were thrown up across the isthmus from Lake Menzaleh to the Mediterranean, and field pieces mounted. In the canal itself, steam picket-boats, launches, &c., with armed crews, were used as patrols. The fast Thorneycroft torpedo launches of the Iris and Hecla were employed as dispatch-boats, making the passage between Port Said and Ismailia in about four hours and a half, their speed not being allowed to exceed ten knots.

Sunday, August 20, was a busy day. The transport fleet arrived at Port Said from Alexandria and Aboukir early in the forenoon. Had it not been for the action of the master of the French steamer Melbourne, mentioned in the report of Commander Edwards, the transports could have pushed on at once into the canal and towards Ismailia. As it was they were obliged to wait until the way was clear. During this delay, and in anticipation of possible trouble, 300 of the York and Lancaster

Regiment were put on board H. M. S. Falcon (light-draught gun-boat), and a similar number of the West Kent Regiment on board H. M. S. Beacon, to form the advance. These vessels arrived at Ismailia in the evening of the same day.

The Nerissa led the transport fleet, followed by the Rhosina, the troop-ship Euphrates, and others. Ismailia was reached that night and the next morning, the only accident being the grounding of the Catalonia, with the balance of the West Kent Regiment on board. She took against the west bank at the distance of 7 miles from Lake Timsah, but did not seriously interrupt the passage of other vessels.

The administration of the Suez Canal was in the hands of the British during Sunday, Monday, and part of Tuesday, the company's employés having orders from Count Ferdinand de Lesseps, the president, to abandon their work. When it was found that the British could manage the traffic without the assistance of the French servants of the company— *the large fleet that went through to Ismailia at this time being piloted by English naval officers*—the company became anxious to resume its functions. Every obstacle had been thrown in the way of the use of the canal on the part of the British, its neutrality had been invoked, and Count de Lesseps had attempted to carry off all the employés from Ismailia, deserting the administration completely. This move was frustrated by a refusal by the British senior naval officer to permit them to leave Lake Timsah, a fast torpedo launch barring their entrance into the canal. Count de Lesseps finally yielded to the convincing argument of facts, and a *modus vivendi* was agreed to. Prior to this time, his expressions had been characterized by the most open hostility to the English; he had entertained Arabi at Ismailia, and had imbued that Oriental with his own notion that they would not dare to make use of the canal as a base of military action on account of the inviolability which it was supposed to enjoy. There is little doubt that his influence led Arabi to neglect the precaution of blocking the channel, and that practically, although not designedly, M. de Lesseps proved the strongest possible ally that England could have desired or secured. In this connection it may be allowable to quote a telegram from M. de Lesseps dated at Ismailia August 19:

The English Admiral at Suez informs the company's chief traffic agent that in consequence of orders from his Government he forbids, until the receipt of further orders, any ship, large or small, even the company's boats, to enter the canal, and he will resort to force to prevent any attempt to contravene these orders. The Admiral moreover has placed a gun-boat at the mouth of the canal. I have protested against this act of violence and spoliation.

In a circular of protest, the canal company from its principal office in Paris says, among other things:

The company is obliged to * * * object to any military action by the English Government.

And again:

The company is obliged to protest against the claim of the English Government, which calls itself the Khedive's agent, to carry out any enterprise on the whole or a part of the canal or its dependencies, no one, even with the Sultan's authorization, and, à fortiori, without that authorization, having a right to disturb the company in the free and peaceful enjoyment of its concession.

The inference to Americans is obvious that the neutrality of any canal joining the waters of the Atlantic and Pacific Oceans will be maintained, if at all, by the nation which can place and keep the strongest ships at each extremity.

The exact footing of the British is defined by the following proclamations, the first by the senior naval officer present in that part of Egypt, the second by the commander-in-chief of the expeditionary force:

PROCLAMATION.

His Highness the Khedive having given the Admiral commanding the British fleet authority to take charge of all places in or near the Maritime Canal as may be necessary for operations against the rebels, Rear-Admiral Hoskins, commanding the British vessels in the Maritime Canal, now takes possession of Port Said for the purpose indicated, and trusts that all the inhabitants will assist him, as far as lies in their power, in maintaining order and protecting life and property.

The Governor, Ismael Pasha Hamdy, appointed by His Highness the Khedive, will resume his office and conduct his duties as formerly.

The Captain of H. B. M. S. Monarch will act as military commandant of the garrison, and be responsible for the defense of the town against the rebels, and the support of the Khedive's civil authorities against any attempt that may be made against life or property.

The police patrols, which will consist of English soldiers and Egyptian police, will at once arrest all persons causing disturbances, more serious crimes being dealt with by martial law.

The Rear-Admiral trusts that all business will be conducted and the affairs of the town go on in the ordinary course, under the rule of His Excellency the Governor.

A. H. HOSKINS,
Rear-Admiral Commanding H. B. M. Ships in the Maritime Canal.

Also,

BY AUTHORITY OF THE KHEDIVE.

PROCLAMATION TO THE EGYPTIANS.

The General in Command of the British forces wishes to make known that the object of Her Majesty's Government in sending troops to this country is to re-establish the authority of the Khedive. The army is, therefore, only fighting against those who are in arms against His Highness.

All peaceable inhabitants will be treated with kindness, and no violence will be offered to them; their religion, mosques, families, and property will be respected. Any supplies which will be required will be paid for, and the inhabitants are invited to bring them.

The General in Command will be glad to receive visits from the chiefs who are willing to assist in repressing the rebellion against the Khedive, the lawful ruler of Egypt appointed by the Sultan.

XII.

THE CAMPAIGN.

The country between Ismailia and the delta is so monotonous that but few words of description are needed to give a notion of its character·

It is a desert of sand, across which run the Fresh (or Sweet) Water Canal and the railway, side by side. To the northward of these lines the ground is, as a rule, somewhat higher, sloping in a southerly direction past the canal. The surface is slightly diversified by occasional low hummocks and mounds, and is dotted at great intervals by tufts of "camel grass." The soil is a deep, light, shifting sand near Ismailia, but it gradually increases in firmness towards the westward, and at Tel-el-Kebir, especially on the upper crests of the hills, is a fairly compact gravel, over which progress is comparatively easy. The sky here is rarely cloudy, so that the sun beats down with full force during the day, while at night the radiation is so great that the air becomes cool and almost chilly. Shelter is needed against the sun in the day-time. At night a good blanket is indispensable, both on account of the lower temperature and the dews.

On account of the absence of rain and the dryness of the soil, stores of all kinds were freely piled up, uncovered, wherever needed, without fear of injury. The Sweet Water Canal furnished the necessary water, usually of good quality after filtering to get rid of the mud held in suspension. The extreme heat from about 9 a. m. to 4 p. m. rendered work of all kinds imprudent.

The Egyptian flies, the worst of their species, make life almost unbearable through their countless swarms and their loathsome stickiness. They disappear with the sun, being relieved by an equally energetic and numerous pest, the mosquito.

No time was lost in pushing on the work begun at Ismailia. The advance was instituted on the day following the occupation. At 11 a. m. Major-General Graham started from the town with 800 men and a small naval contingent, under Captain Stephenson of the Carysfort, and marched across the heavy sand, arriving at 1.30 p. m. The Egyptian camp was found to be deserted, the enemy* having retired up the Sweet Water Canal. A few tents were left behind and about thirty railway trucks full of provisions and ammunition. The entire force bivouacked here.

The naval detachment was composed of two Gatling guns' crews from the Orion and Carysfort, a torpedo party from the Orion, and 104 marines from the Northumberland.

The position was at once placed in an efficient state of defense, shelter trenches were thrown up, one Gatling was placed to command the railway from Suez, the other that from Zagazig. Later in the day, a reconnaissance was made towards the westward, revealing the presence of the enemy about four miles distant.

The troops had carried with them two days' rations. It was necessary to accumulate at least a small stock of stores before continuing the advance. In consequence, August 22 and 23 were devoted to preparation.

---

*This term is used throughout as a convenient means of avoiding the too frequent repetition of the word "Egyptians."

The operations of the 24th are best described in the official report quoted at length below.

ISMAILIA, *August* 26, 1882.

SIR: I have the honor to supplement my telegraphic dispatch of the 24th instant with a detailed report of the events which took place on that date in the neighborhood of Abu Suer, and of Tel-el-Mahuta, on the Sweet Water Canal, about 9 miles west of Ismailia.

A gradual but continuous decrease of level in the canal determined me to push forward my available cavalry and artillery (very little of which had landed as yet), together with the two infantry battalions, which I had advanced to Nefiche Junction on the 21st instant with the object of seizing and occupying a position on the canal and railway which would secure possession of that part of the water supply of the desert lying between Ismailia and the first cultivated portion of the delta, which I had reason to believe was the most vulnerable to damage at the hands of the enemy.

The paramount importance of this object, as affecting all my future operations, induced me to risk a cavalry movement with horses which had been less than two days on shore after a long sea voyage, and also neutralized the objections, which I must otherwise have entertained, to placing the strain of a forward movement upon the recent and partially organized supply service.

Accordingly, at 4 a. m. on the 24th, I advanced with the troops marginally noted,* whom I placed for the day under the command of Lieutenant-General Willis, C. B., commanding 1st division, reached Nefiche at daybreak, and, following the general line of the railway, arrived at 7.30 a. m. on the north side of the canal, at a point about midway between the spot marked El-Magfar on the map and the village of Tel-el-Mahuta.

At this point the enemy had constructed his first dam across the canal, and after some skirmishing with his scouts and light troops, in which two squadrons of Household Cavalry charged very gallantly, I took possession of it.

From this point the enemy could be observed in force about one and a half miles further on, his vedettes holding a line extending across the canal, lining the crest of a ridge which curved round to my right flank at a general distance of about 2,000 yards from my front. The canal and railway at Tel-el-Mahuta are close together, and both are there carried through deep cuttings, with mounds of sand and earth on both sides of them. These were strongly intrenched, and crowds of men could be seen at work there. At Mahuta the enemy had constructed a very large embankment across the railway and a wide and solid dam across the canal, which afforded him easy communication from one side to the other.

From the statement of some prisoners taken by the mounted troops, as well as by the length of front covered by the enemy, it was apparent that he was in force at Mahuta, and I could see by the smoke of his locomotives, which kept constantly reaching his position throughout the forenoon, that he was being largely reinforced from Tel-el-Kebir. I could perceive that the enemy's force in my immediate front was large; I estimated it at 10,000 men and ten guns, but I have since found that it consisted of one regiment of cavalry, nine battalions of infantry (about 7,000 men), twelve guns, and a large but indefinite number of Bedouins. Although I had but three squadrons of cavalry, two guns, and about 1,000 infantry, I felt it would not be in consonance with the traditions of Her Majesty's army that we should retire, even temporarily, before Egyptian troops, no matter what their numbers might be. I decided, therefore, upon holding my ground until evening, by which time I knew that the reinforcements I had sent for to Nefiche and Ismailia would reach me. I consequently took up a position, suited to the numbers at my disposal, with my left resting on the

---

*Household Cavalry; Mounted Infantry; 2 guns battery N-A (N battery, A brigade), R. H. A.; York and Lancaster; Marines.

captured dam over the canal, and the cavalry and mounted infantry covering the right.

It was now 9 o'clock a. m. The enemy had kept gradually reinforcing his left, showing considerable skill in the method with which he swung round his left, moving along the reverse slope of his position, and showing only his light troops upon the sky line.

The two guns of N battery, A brigade, Royal Horse Artillery, only reached me at 9 a. m., although the officer in command had made every effort to push his way as rapidly as possible through the deep sand over which our route lay. They took up a good position on a sandy hillock near the railway embankment, from which a good view of the enemy's position was to be obtained. By this time the enemy had opened a heavy artillery fire upon us, and his infantry advanced in very regular attack formation, halting and forming a line of shelter trenches about 1,000 yards from our position. On my left he had pushed his infantry along the canal to within about 900 yards of the dam held by the York and Lancaster Regiment, but the steady and welldirected fire of this battalion easily checked his movement upon that side.

From 10 to 11 o'clock the enemy continued to develop his attack upon my center and right. His guns were served with considerable skill, the shells bursting well among us. Fortunately they were common shells with percussion fuzes, which sank so deep in the very soft sand before bursting that few splinters flew upwards; when he did use shrapnel the time-fuzes were badly cut.

Feeling complete confidence in my ability to drive back any close attack the enemy might make, I did not allow our guns to open fire for some time after they were placed in position, hoping he might thereby be the more readily induced to advance to close quarters, under the notion that we had no artillery with us. When, however, he brought twelve guns into action, to relieve the Household Cavalry, into whose ranks and those of the Mounted Infantry he was throwing his shell with great accuracy, our two guns opened upon his twelve guns with marked effect, our practice being very good.

The Household Cavalry and Mounted Infantry were skillfully maneuvered by Major-General Drury-Lowe on the extreme right, to check the enemy's advance on that side, but the horses, just landed from a long sea voyage and fatigued by their march across a desert deep in sand, were in no condition to charge.

Major-General Drury-Lowe spoke in the highest terms of the manner in which the Mounted Infantry were handled throughout the arduous fighting that fell to their lot during the day. No troops could have behaved with greater dash or steadiness. I regret to say that Captain Parr was severely wounded, and also Lord Melgund slightly wounded, who was doing duty with the Mounted Infantry. The heat at this period of the day was very great.

About noon two Gatlings, with a party of sailors under command of Lieutenant King-Harman, and belonging to H. M. S. Orion, arrived and took up a position for action. The manner in which the sailors brought these Gatlings into position, and the energy shown by them and by the Marine Artillery, deserve the highest commendation.

The fire opened by the enemy on my right was as accurate as that which he had already directed against my front; but although many shells continued to drop in and around the hillock where our two guns were in action, causing loss to the overworked men of N battery, A brigade, Royal Horse Artillery, they continued to work their two guns with great steadiness during many hours, exposed to a concentrated fire from twelve guns and under very trying conditions of heat, glare, and sunshine.

I desire to bring to notice the manner in which Lieutenant Hickman, Royal Horse Artillery, the officer commanding the division, performed his duty, and the spirit and resolution displayed by all ranks under him. Later on in the day, when these men were extremely tired, the men of the Royal Marine Artillery requested permission to help them, and did so until the close of the action.

At 3.30 p. m., the Household Cavalry, under General Lowe, and the Mounted Infantry again moved forward on my right, causing the enemy to partially withdraw his attack on that flank.

At 1 p. m., the 2d battalion of the Duke of Cornwall's Light Infantry had arrived from Nefiche.

About 5.15 p. m., the enemy again advanced his left, pushing four guns across the ridge and moving his cavalry with a considerable force of infantry some distance down the slope, but not near enough to come within effective infantry or Gatling fire.

At this time our reinforcements began to arrive rapidly. Colonel Sir Baker Russell with 350 sabers of the 4th and 7th Dragoon Guards reached the field, and at 6 p. m. the brigade of Guards, under His Royal Highness the Duke of Connaught, arrived. It was now too late to begin an offensive movement; the troops I had with me were tired by their exertions during the early part of the day, and the brigade of Guards which had moved from Ismailia at 1.30 p. m., had suffered much from the great heat of the desert march.

Shortly after sunset, the entire force bivouacked on the field which they had so tenaciously held all day, and the enemy withdrew across the ridge to his position at Mahuta.

I have every reason to be satisfied with the conduct of the men engaged and with the exertions made by the Cornwall Light Infantry and the brigade of Guards to reach the field in time to share in our operations.

I have, &c.,

G. J. WOLSELEY,
General.

At nightfall the dam across the canal was strongly held by the York and Lancaster Regiment. From this point the line extended to the northward, the right being refused. The troops rested in their places.

During the night reinforcements continued arriving, and at daybreak line of battle was formed in the following manner:

Beginning on the left was Graham's brigade, or rather such of its component parts as had reached the front. It consisted then of the York and Lancaster Regiment, the Duke of Cornwall's Light Infantry, and the Marine Battalion. Then came four guns of battery A. 1, then the Guards brigade, then six guns N. A., then the cavalry, 4th and 7th Dragoon Guards, then two guns of battery A. 1, then the Household Cavalry, and lastly the Mounted Infantry.

Battery N. A was strengthened by two guns each of N. 2, R. A., and battery G. B, R. H. A., that came up during the advance.

On August 25 another short advance was made and Tel-el-Mahuta occupied. The following is the official report:

ISMAILIA, *August* 27, 1882.

SIR: In continuation of my dispatch No. 2 of yesterday's date, I have the honor to inform you of the events which took place on the 25th instant in the neighborhood of Tel-el-Mahuta, and further along the line of the canal and railway as far as the station of Mahsameh.

The attack on the enemy's intrenched post at Tel-el-Mahuta, which was deferred on the 24th instant in consequence of the lateness of the hour at which the reinforcements could arrive, and also because of the fatigue undergone by the troops in action, was successfully carried out shortly after daybreak on the 25th instant.

Accompanied by General Sir J. Adye and the headquarters staff, I left Ismailia at 3 a. m. and reached the scene of yesterday's fighting at 5.30 o'clock. I took with me the remaining squadron of the 1st cavalry brigade, most of whom had only landed the previous day. The 1st division, including the troops marginally noted,* had by that hour quitted their bivouack and had advanced towards the enemy's position in the following order: The cavalry and mounted infantry formed the extreme right, thrown well forward upon the desert ridges over which the enemy had on the previous day carried out his flank movement. The artillery moved on the left of the cavalry, towards the summit of the high ground overlooking the line of railway between Ramses and the Mahsameh station. The infantry, on the left of the artillery, advanced in *echelon* from the right upon Mahuta, the brigade of Guards leading.

When the summit of the ridge was gained, the enemy was observed to be abandoning his earthworks at the last-named place, and to be retiring his forces along the canal banks and the railway line towards Mahsameh. His railway trains were also to be seen in motion towards the same place.

At 6.25 a. m. our artillery came into action against the enemy's infantry, and guns which were posted on the canal bank to the west of Mahuta.

As it was of great importance to obtain possession, if possible, of some of the enemy's locomotives, I ordered the cavalry to push forward with all speed and attempt to cut off the retreating trains. The cavalry and eight guns moved as rapidly as their horses, which were in no condition for hard work, would permit. The ground was much better and harder than that moved over yesterday.

The enemy offered considerable resistance in the neighborhood of Mahsameh, but nothing could stop the advance of our mounted troops, tired even as their horses were. Mahsameh with its very extensive camp, left standing by the enemy, was soon in our possession. Seven Krupp guns, great quantities of ammunition, two large trains of railway wagons loaded with provisions, and vast supplies of various kinds fell into our hands. The enemy fled along the railway and canal banks, throwing away their arms and equipments and showing every sign of demoralization. Unfortunately there was not at this time in the whole cavalry brigade a troop that could gallop; their long march and rapid advance having completely exhausted the horses, who were not yet fit for hard work after their long voyage from England.

The results of the operations, extending over two days, have been most satisfactory. The enemy has been completely driven from the position at Tel-el-Mahuta, which he had taken such pains to fortify, and upon which he had, by force, compelled 7,000 peasants to labor.

The canal has been cleared for more than half the distance intervening between Ismailia and the delta; and the water supply completely secured to us.

The railway line is in our possession for more than 20 miles from this place, and the vigor, dash, and energy displayed by the troops in the sudden forward movement, made with horses out of condition and from a base hastily organized, and where we are still contending with all the difficulties incidental to rapid disembarkations, have assured to the army an important strategic position, the possession of which cannot fail to influence the future operations of the campaign.

Amongst the prisoners taken was Mahmoud Ferni Pasha, who was Chief Engineer to Arabi Pasha, a very important personage among the rebel chiefs.

The enemy were commanded by Rashid Pasha, and the force he had collected at Mahuta and Mahsameh consisted of ten battalions of infantry (at least 8,000 men), of six squadrons of cavalry, and twenty guns, besides a large force of Bedouins.

Owing to the result of the action of the previous day (24th instant) many of his troops had retreated during the night, and upon our guns opening on his works early on the morning of the 25th instant the 7,000 laborers ran away. Rashid Pasha then issued orders for a general retreat.

Military operations in Egypt at this season of the year are very trying to the soldiers engaged, and the complete absence of anything approaching the nature of a road renders all movements most difficult and fatiguing.

Owing to the fact of this advance being made before the railway or the telegraph

---

* Household Cavalry; 4th and 7th Dragoon Guards; battery N. A, R. H. A.; 3rd battalion Royal Rifles.

lines had been repaired, or the canal cleared of obstructions, or any regular system of transport had been effectively organized, considerable exposure without tents, and severe privations as regards food, have been imposed upon all ranks. These hardships have, however, been cheerfully borne, and the conduct of the troops has been everything I could wish.

The troops engaged were, upon both the 24th and 25th instant, under the immediate command of Lieutenant-General Willis, C. B., who carried out my views in a most satisfactory manner. My advanced troops, under Major-General Graham, now hold the Kassassin lock.

I cannot praise too highly the manner in which the cavalry, horse artillery, and mounted infantry were handled by Major-General Drury-Lowe, who speaks in the highest terms of the assistance rendered him by Brigadier-General Sir Baker Russell, Lieutenant-Colonel Stewart, assistant adjutant-general, and Lieutenant-Colonel McCalmont, brigade major of the 1st cavalry brigade. He also begs me to mention his appreciation of the dash and skill with which the mounted infantry were commanded by Captain Pigott, of the King's Royal Rifles.

I am, &c.,

G. J. WOLSELEY,
General.

To the foregoing account it may be well to add that a small naval detachment took part in the operations of the day. It was composed of two Gatlings and 70 marines from the Carysfort and Orion, and was commanded by Captain Fitz Roy of the latter vessel.

The Marine Infantry battalion, under Lieutenant-Colonel Howard S. Jones, had left Ismailia at 4 p. m. the day previous, and had reached El Magfar at 1.30 a. m. of the 25th. It started again at 4 a. m. with the general advance, and at 5 p. m. was able to march into the Egyptian camp at Mahsameh, which had been seized by the cavalry in the morning. So good a piece of work deserves record.

The extreme right of the British line was on a ridge about a mile and a half from the center. When Mahsameh station was in plain sight, the two guns of battery A. 1, came into action and shelled the fugitives, the cavalry and mounted infantry dashing in and capturing the camp, which they occupied permanently until the advance on Tel-el-Kebir.

The stock of provisions captured was a most welcome addition to the stores in hand, and, in particular, the grain left on the ground in large quantities was invaluable, for the horses had been for several days on an extremely short allowance of forage.

It will be perceived that the operations of the day did not reach the dignity of an engagement, the Egyptians offering practically no resistance, but falling back on Tel-el-Kebir, where a large camp had been established north of the railway, and where extensive intrenchments were begun along the crest of a range of hills running north and south.

On August 26 a small force of the 7th Dragoons occupied the lock in the Fresh Water Canal at Kassassin without opposition. This was a most important step, since the possession of the lock gave General Wolseley control of the water in the upper reach of the canal. That it could have been accomplished so readily is but another indication of the ignorance or habitual carelessness of the Egyptians.

Later in the day the Duke of Cornwall's Light Infantry, the York and

Lancaster Regiment, and the Royal Marine Artillery marched up and established themselves at this point, the cavalry withdrawing to Mahsameh, a mile and a half to the eastward.

The force had now completely outrun its commissariat, and for two days the men had lived from hand to mouth. On the third day the navy succeeded in getting a few stores to the front by the Sweet Water Canal, but the prospects were, to say the least, gloomy.

On August 27, the distribution of the troops was approximately as follows:

At Kassassin lock were a squadron of the 19th Hussars, the York and Lancaster Regiment, the Duke of Cornwall's Light Infantry, the Royal Marine Artillery battalion, and two guns of battery N. A.

At Mahsameh, the Household Cavalry, the 4th and 7th Dragoon Guards, the 2nd Bengal Cavalry and 13th Bengal Lancers, the Mounted Infantry, and the Royal Marine Light Infantry battalion.

At Tel-el-Mahuta, the 1st brigade (Guards), the Rifles, the 24th company Royal Engineers, and battery A. 1, R. A.

At Nefiche, the West Kent Regiment.

At Ismailia, the 7th, 8th, and 18th companies of Royal Engineers, besides many other corps landing from the transports.

On August 28 the Egyptians made an effort to regain their lost ground by a serious attack on General Graham's force at Kassassin, as narrated in the official reports given herewith. The first is from Major-General Graham to General Wolseley:

KASSASSIN, *August* 29, 1882.

SIR: I have the honor to report that an important engagement with the enemy took place here yesterday, the 28th instant, in which, though attacked by a vastly superior force numerically, tried seriously by exposure to the sun and previous privations, the troops I have the honor to command finally drove back the enemy at all points; and, with the aid of the cavalry under Major-General Drury-Lowe, C. B., inflicted severe chastisement.

The position, the advanced brigade occupied at Kassassin, is not the best for defense. We are astride the canal (which runs nearly east and west), and hold the bridge and locks. Taking the west as our proper front, on our right the desert rises to a ridge, with an elevation of from 100 to 160 feet; at a distance of from 2,000 to 3,000 yards there is the millet and palm covered plain of the Ouady, intersected by a disused branch of the canal. This ridge, on our right, is obviously a source of danger to a force too weak to occupy it, as I have already observed in a previous report.

About 9.30 a. m. on the 28th instant the enemy's cavalry appeared in force on our left front on the north side of the Fresh Water Canal, and I at once heliographed to Major-General Drury-Lowe at Mahsameh. The force under my command, consisting of 57 cavalry, 70 mounted infantry, 1,728 infantry, and 40 artillery, with two 13-pdrs. as detailed in margin,* were at once posted by me under cover, fronting to the

---

* Royal Horse Artillery, two guns, officers, non-commissioned officers, and men. 40
4th Dragoon Guards, officers, non-commissioned officers, and men 15
7th Dragoon Guards, officers, non-commissioned officers, and men 42
Duke of Cornwall's Light Infantry, officers, non-commissioned officers, and men. 611
York and Lancaster Regiment, officers, non-commissioned officers, and men... 690
Mounted Infantry, officers, non-commissioned officers, and men 70
Royal Marine Artillery, officers, non commissioned officers, and men 427

Total 1,895

north and west, the cavalry and mounted infantry (50) being thrown out on the flanks to observe the enemy's movements while I awaited the development of his attack. About 11 a. m. it was reported that a large force of cavalry, infantry, and artillery were being moved round towards our right, behind the ridge. At 12 the enemy opened from two heavy guns on our left front, at least 4,000 yards off, the shot from which fell short.

The enemy's attack seemed to languish, and about 3 p. m. the officer commanding the Mounted Infantry reported the enemy retiring.

The men had been suffering very much from their long exposure to the heat of the sun without food, so I ordered them back to their camps. Major-General Drury-Lowe brought a brigade of cavalry within 2 or 3 miles of the camp, and about 3 p. m. withdrew them to Mahsameh, as I had previously requested him not to engage them unnecessarily.

At 4.30 p. m. the enemy advanced his infantry in great force, displaying a line of skirmishers at least a mile in length, with which he sought to overlap my front on the left, supported by a heavy and well-directed fire of artillery, with which he searched the camp, wounding a sick officer in the house where I had established my headquarters, but which, as the best building, was now given up as a hospital. My dispositions to meet this attack were as follows: On the left the Marine Artillery were directed to take up a position on the south bank of the canal, where (secure from being turned themselves, the canal being 5 to 6 feet deep) they could check the enemy's advance by a flank fire (the Royal Marine Artillery, therefore, gave fire to west and northwest).

In the center the 2d battalion, Duke of Cornwall's Light Infantry, extended a fighting line of three companies, facing west by north, about 800 yards to the right rear (east northeast) of the Royal Marine Artillery. The supports and reserves of the Duke of Cornwall's Light Infantry were under cover of the railway embankment, facing north. The 2d battalion York and Lancaster extended the fighting line of the Duke of Cornwall's Light Infantry with two and a half companies, keeping the remainder in support and reserve.

The position of the infantry was, therefore, an irregular *echelon*, right thrown back. The troop of the 7th Dragoon Guards was kept on this flank, and the two 13-pdrs., now reinforced by two others, took up a position on the ridge. Unfortunately, these guns had only got their ammunition in their limbers, and had soon to cease firing for want of a further supply, though they did good service while it lasted. The Mounted Infantry and detachment of 4th Dragoon Guards occupied a portion of the gap between the Royal Marine Artillery and Duke of Cornwall's Light Infantry, and all the persistent efforts of the enemy to break through at this point were unavailing, owing to the steady fire of the Royal Marine Artillery and the gallant resistance of the little band of Mounted Infantry and detachment of 4th Dragoon Guards dismounted and employed as infantry. The enemy made great efforts to overcome this resistance, putting a number of men across the canal; and three times his guns were kept from advancing by their horses and men being shot when trying to press past. In order to support the left, the companies on the left of the Duke of Cornwall's Light Infantry, acing north, were spread out along the line of the railway embankment, and a fresh company from the right half battalion was moved to the left to prolong the line.

Feeling secure on my left, I turned my attention to the right flank. On the first notice of the attack (4.30 p. m.) I sent a message to Major-General Lowe, by heliograph, and by a mounted officer to Mahsameh, 3 and 4 miles distant, requesting him to move up the cavalry brigade to cover my right flank, and to send forward the Royal Marine Light Infantry.

At 5 p. m., thinking I saw the cavalry advancing, I sent an order to Major-General Drury-Lowe to bring round his cavalry, under cover of the hill, fall upon the left flank of the enemy's skirmishers, and roll up his line. This order was received and gallantly executed. For an account of this part of the action, I beg to refer to Major-General Drury-Lowe's own report.

At 5 p. m. I observed reinforcements coming to the enemy by train, and fearing a charge of cavalry on our exposed right, directed the officer commanding the reserve company of the York and Lancaster to prepare to receive them in line. Near the right of our position, on the line of railway, a Krupp gun, taken from the enemy at Mahsameh, had been mounted on a railway truck and was being worked by a gun detachment of the Royal Marine Artillery, under Captain Tucker. This gun was admirably served, and did great execution among the enemy. As the other guns had to cease firing for want of ammunition, Captain Tucker's gun became the target for the enemy's artillery, and I counted salvoes of four guns opening on him at once with shell and shrapnel; but although everything around or in line was hit, not a man of the gun detachment was touched, and this gun continued to fire to the end, expending 93 rounds.

At 6.45 p. m. I ordered an advance, with the object of closing on the enemy's infantry about the time of the expected cavalry charge. The advance was made very steadily, by the fighting line, in *echelon* from the left, about 600 yards to our west front, when the line fired volleys by companies, the reserves following in rear of the railway embankment.

On arriving at the point held by the Mounted Infantry, a message reached me that the Royal Marine Light Infantry had come on to the ground on our right, and, galloping back, I at once directed them to advance in order of attack. This advance was continued for about 2 or 3 miles, supported by the Duke of Cornwall's Light Infantry on the left, the York and Lancaster being left behind in reserve, the enemy falling back, only one attempt being made at a stand on our left, which broke at the first volley of the Royal Marines.

At about 8.15 p. m. I first heard of the cavalry charge from an officer of the 1st Life Guards who had lost his way.

We had now been advancing, for an hour and a half, in the moonlight, and my two aids-de-camp had had narrow escapes in mistaking detached bodies of the enemy for our own troops. Fearing some mistake might be made, and seeing no further chance of co-operation with the cavalry, I ordered the marines and Duke of Cornwall's Light Infantry to retire at 8.45 p. m. On approaching the camp, I called in the other troops.

The accompanying rough sketch shows approximately the position held by the infantry during the action.

During the night the enemy made no sign, and this morning at daybreak I rode out over the battle-field, and have had all wounded that were found brought in.

I append a detailed list of killed and wounded, an abstract of which is given in the margin.* The corps which suffered most heavily was the Royal Marine Artillery, under Lieutenant-Colonel Tuson, whom I would beg to bring especially to your notice. Lieutenant-Colonel Tuson speaks in high terms of the conduct of Major Ogle, Captain

---

* List of killed and wounded.

Organizations.	Killed or dangerously wounded.	Wounded.
Cavalry (with General Graham's force)	1	
Royal Marine Artillery	7	25
Mounted Infantry		7
Duke of Cornwall's Light Infantry	1	24
York and Lancaster Regiment	1	11
Army medical department	1	
Total	11	67

Rawstorne, Lieutenants Pym and Talbot, and of Captain and Adjutant Noble, whose horse was killed under him. The Mounted Infantry also suffered heavily, and, early in the action, were deprived of the service of their gallant leader, Lieutenant Piggott, an officer who deserves especial mention. Another valuable officer of this corps, Lieutenant Edwards, was also wounded. The services of the Mounted Infantry have been invaluable to me in the absence of a sufficient force of cavalry. I have also to bring to your notice the admirable steadiness of the 2d battalion Duke of Cornwall's Light Infantry under fire, and during their advance under Colonel Richardson. This officer mentions Lieutenant-Colonel John, Major Grieve, Lieutenant and Adjutant Ashby, and Lieutenant Falls as being indefatigable in their exertions. The 2d Duke of Cornwall's Light Infantry were effectively supported by the 2d York and Lancaster under Colonel Wilson, to whose careful personal leading, ably supported by the officers under him, much credit is due. The Royal Marine Light Infantry, although they arrived too late to take any decisive share in the action, showed by the promptitude of their march to the field, and the steadiness of their advance, under Colonel Jones, that they are well capable of sustaining the high character of their corps.

In general, I cannot too highly express my opinion of the steadiness of the troops under fire, and the ready alacrity with which they carried out my orders. Although exposed for two hours to a heavy fire of artillery the lines I advanced were full of cheerful confidence and eager to close with the enemy. I may also mention that the five hours' exposure to the sun in the morning, expecting an attack, had been most trying to the men, and that the Duke of Cornwall's Light Infantry had not had time to eat their dinners before they were ordered out to meet the enemy.

I estimate the enemy's force at 1,000 cavalry, 8,000 infantry, and twelve guns.

I beg to bring to your notice Major Hart, V. C., R. E., who showed the utmost devotion on this as on other occasions.

Lieutenant Pirie, 4th Dragoon Guards, was attached to me as extra aid-de-camp, and rendered invaluable service in carrying my orders to Major-General Drury-Lowe to charge. At the time I imagined the brigade to be near at hand, and Lieutenant Pirie galloped on until his horse dropped, fortunately near to a battery of Royal Artillery, where he got another horse and continued his gallop till he reached General Drury-Lowe.

Captain Hare, my Brigade Major, also rendered good service in carrying messages and by his cheerful readiness to do any service required in the fighting line.

I have, &c.,
GERALD GRAHAM,
Major-General Commanding Advanced Brigade.

The next report is on the special operations of the Cavalry Division, under Major-General Drury-Lowe, and is submitted by that officer to Lieutenant-General Willis, C. B. Its text is as follows:

MAHSAMEH, *August* 29, 1882.

SIR: Having received information from Major-General Graham, at Kassassin, that the enemy were advancing on his position, and having been told by Colonel Keyser that his signalers had been withdrawn, I turned out the following troops of the 1st cavalry brigade, under Brigadier-General Sir Baker Russell, viz, Household Cavalry, 7th Dragoon Guards, and four guns N battery, A brigade, Royal Horse Artillery, and advanced towards the enemy's left. A distant and ineffective artillery fire was being directed against General Graham's position, but beyond this nothing was taking place. I remained some hours, communicated with General Graham, and withdrew my brigade about 4.30 p. m.

At about 5.30 Major Molyneux arrived from Kassassin and gave me a message from General Graham that the enemy were advancing in force; I again, at 5.30 p. m., turned out the brigade, and moved to the sound of the heavy firing that was now taking place. *En route,* a galloper reached me from General Graham, who stated that the general desired him to say that "he was only just able to hold his own, and that he wished me to attack the left of the enemy's infantry skirmishers." The sun had now set, and a bright moon was shining. The light, however, was not good, owing to the haze, and we were guided by the flash of guns and musketry. I made a wide circuit to turn the enemy's left, and the brigade arrived without being noticed near this portion of their line. As we approached, a heavy fire of shells and musketry was opened upon us, which was practically harmless as it was very high. I cleared the front of our guns by a retirement of the first line, whilst the Household Cavalry, on their right, formed line.

After a few rounds from our guns, Sir Baker Russell led a charge of the Household Cavalry, under Colonel Evart, against the enemy's infantry, which had commenced to advance. Moving most steadily towards the flash of the rifles the charge was right gallantly led and executed. The enemy's infantry was completely scattered and our cavalry swept through a battery of seven or nine guns which in daylight must have been captured, but, unfortunately, their exact position could not be found afterwards, and they were no doubt removed during the night, after our retirement. The enemy's loss was heavy, the ground being thickly strewn with their killed, and quantities of ammunition, &c. I beg to attach a list of casualties* sustained by the brigade, which, considering the nature of the attack, was not heavy. The greatest praise is due to the Household Cavalry for their behavior throughout, and I have to thank Brigadier-General Sir Baker Russell and the officers and men of the brigade for their gallant conduct.

I have, &c.,

DRURY-LOWE,
Major-General Commanding Cavalry Division.

The reason of the lack of ammunition for the British artillery was the heaviness of the road from the base to the advanced brigade. Efforts were made to get up a proper supply, but the wagons stuck in the sand and were late in arriving.

The immunity of the detachment of Royal Marine Artillery, working the 8^{cm} Krupp gun on the railway wagon, was thought by Captain Tucker to be due to constant shifting of its position on the rails. The gun itself was protected by a breastwork of sand-bags.

The Egyptian attack is described by officers present as heavy and direct, and their fire rapid. The British troops, although greatly outnumbered, stood to their ground with coolness, expending their ammunition effectively and deliberately, for there appears to have been but a slight reserve supply at hand, holding the enemy in check for two hours, when his retreat began. This movement appears to have been accompanied by very little fighting, and to have been conducted in good order.

Two batteries of field artillery, A 1 and D 1, arrived from Mahuta, but too late to take part in the engagement. They had been obliged to drop their ammunition wagons in order to get their guns and limbers up.

In spite of the wording of General Graham's report, it seems certain that the cavalry charge took place after the enemy had retreated several miles, and at about 9 p. m. From an account of an officer, a witness to the charge, it appears that at this time some of the enemy were observed making a movement on General Drury-Lowe's right. The cav-

---

*Three killed and sixteen wounded.

alry advanced, the 4th Dragoon Guards on the left, the Household Cavalry on the right, and the four guns of battery N. A., Royal Horse Artillery, in rear of the former. Approaching within 500 or 600 yards of the Egyptians, the guns were unmasked by the cavalry and brought quickly into action, ceasing fire when the Household Cavalry crossed in front to ride down the enemy. This moonlight charge was the most dramatic as it was one of the most gallant episodes of the campaign. It ended the battle in a brilliant and novel manner.

The following telegrams from Arabi Pasha, published in the then official paper, give his view of this action. The translation is taken from the London Times newspaper:

August 28.—Our victorious troops have worsted the enemy and made him retreat to Mahsameh, by the strength and power of God. At the present moment the two armies are facing each other at a distance of about 5,000 meters from Al-Mahsameh, and after a little rest, and when the horses have been watered, there will be a charge, please God. Give us the aid of your pure prayers in asking for succor from the Lord Almighty.

August 28, 7.40 p. m.—The fighting has begun again. Cannon have been firing since 4 p. m. till 7.30 p. m., and still continue. I pray God for help against His enemies. Pray God to help His true believers.

Till this hour the fighting continues with cannon and musketry. I thank God for the endurance He has given us, and pray for perfect help and victory. Pray to Him that He may help His servants, the true believers, and disappoint our treacherous enemies. It is now twenty minutes past eight in the evening.

August 28, 11.15 p. m.—Thanks be to God, the fighting has ceased on both sides, after a serious engagement with musketry and cannon, followed by a charge by our cavalry on that of the enemy, when they were in a *mêlée* and used their swords against each other, after which they separated. God is the best protector.

The results of this fight were of the greatest possible importance, small as was the force employed. It became evident, in the first place, that Arabi felt himself to be strong enough to assume the offensive and thus attempt to regain the prestige which he had lost at Magfar and Tel-el-Mahuta. In the second place, it showed the British that the task they had undertaken was likely to prove more than a parade across the desert, and that their enemy was willing to come within range and hold his own for hours together; but it also showed that he would not stand an attack at close quarters, and that, unless in greatly superior numbers, he might be expected to give way if resolutely assailed.

The value of the action in its influence on the *morale* of the British troops, and especially of the younger recruits, was incalculable. It gave them that self-reliance which can only be obtained through actual and successful contact with the enemy.

The British left being well supported by the canal and its banks, the most obvious move on the part of the attack was to double up their right and force them back into the canal, cutting off communication with their rear. The Egyptians had no commander capable of realizing the importance of this object, and in consequence the main attack was in front, and the flanking movement half-hearted and unsuccessful.

The burying parties next morning found that many of the bodies had been shockingly mutilated during the night. The circumcised had all been spared. The persons committing these outrages followed a fixed plan which they applied to the uncircumcised corpses of both armies. Of these they had lopped off the feet, hands, and genitals, and had deeply gashed the abdomen and the upper part of the forehead.

With this battle ends the first part of the campaign. On August 20 Ismailia was seized, on the 26th Kassassin Lock occupied, and on the 28th its possession secured to the British advance after an earnest effort at dislodgment by the Egyptians.

The actual distance covered, a matter of 20 miles, is no measure of the result achieved. It must be borne in mind that in spite of certain favorable conditions, of which absence of rain was the principal, the advance was beset with many real difficulties. The railway was broken in several places and blocked at others. There were no locomotives to haul the trucks conveying stores from the base to the front, and the army transport had completely broken down. The draught animals were few and in poor condition, pack-mules were lacking in sufficient numbers, and camels were, practically, entirely wanting. The strong army carts, suitable for use on hard European roads, were so heavy as to stick hopelessly in the sand by their own weight. To each wagon designed for two horses not less than six were imperatively needed, and the more that could be hitched on the better. The navy was doing all it could to assist in getting supplies forward by the Sweet Water Canal (and its aid was of vital importance at this juncture). For the moment it seemed doubtful whether even the few troops already pushed ahead could be maintained, and every effort was made towards keeping them furnished with the food requisite to enable them to pull through the crisis. To their excellent behavior, under the trying circumstances, all bear witness. They bore their privation, which was but one degree removed from being perilous, and their discomforts cheerfully and almost good-naturedly, but they suffered severely until the arrival of the locomotives from Suez made it possible to supply them properly.

The canal water was practically their sole supply (wells being rare, scant, and bad), and frequently this was loathsome. It is of light coffee color, due to the mud it contains. Filtration or decantation renders it clear, while its flavor is, normally, extremely sweet and good; but the soldiers, having frequently no means of filtering or settling the water, had to drink it thick and tepid. Its excellent taste had been spoiled by the presence in the canal of the putrefying dead bodies of camels, horses, and human beings, and its innocuousness, in consequence, seriously questioned. Latterly it became too bad to support the fish that usually live in it, but that now died in large numbers, contributing their share to its offensiveness. Much labor was expended in cleaning out this reservoir of water, but the damage could not be entirely remedied.

In addition to this discomfort was the ever-present possibility of cutting the railway in rear, or of interrupting the canal traffic by strong raiding parties. Either of these contingencies would have seriously imperiled the troops at the front.

Fears that these contingencies might be realized, combined with short rations, bad water, excessive heat, flies, mosquitoes, hard work, inadequate shelter, sun-stroke, dysentery, and fever, rendered the advance more honorable than either safe or pleasant.

The exertions made to meet the exigencies of the case are detailed under their appropriate heads. It is sufficient here to remark that the fight during the second part of the campaign was for adequate transport and for a sufficiency of the bare necessaries of life for the troops already thrown to the front.

In the mean time the 3d brigade, 2d division, composed of Highlanders, had arrived at Ismailia. It was not landed at first, but was retained on the transports in the harbor, pending the solution of the transportation problem.

On September 1 General Wolseley telegraphs to the Secretary of State for War, in London:

ISMAILIA, *September* 1.

In reply to your inquiry of 29th ultimo, circumstances have forced me ahead of transport, but it is rapidly becoming efficient.

The necessity of securing a sufficient supply of fresh water in the canal rendered it imperative to push on as quickly as possible.

My successes on the 24th and 25th, and retreat of the enemy, have enabled me to seize [the] two important positions on the canal of El Magfar and Kassassin Lock, the latter about 20 miles from this place. I am, therefore, in a more forward and favorable position generally than I had anticipated, and am only now waiting till my transport arrangements are more complete, to enable me to make a further movement.

In the absence of roads I had always calculated on partially using the canal and railway in sending supplies to the front, but the enemy having blocked the former by two large dams, and the latter by an embankment, and the partial removal of rails, it has been necessary to get these obstructions removed. I have one engine on the line, and expect a second from Suez to-night, and am preparing the land transport companies, some of which are now landing, to supplement the other means above indicated.

A supply of mules has arrived from Cyprus. I expect 400 more from Malta and Italy to-morrow; and the large supply collected at Smyrna and Beyrout, at last released by Ottoman Government, are on their way.

In a desert country like this part of Egypt, it takes time to organize the lines of communication.

The above telegram will make abundantly clear the state of affairs during this phase of the campaign.

By September 2 the whole of the Indian Contingent had reached Suez except the 6th Bengal Cavalry, and many of its troops had gone to the front.

Except for an occasional reconnaissance, bringing about the interchange of a few shots, and for one real assault, this period was one of quiet preparation for a further advance, stores first, and then men, being slowly accumulated at Kassassin.

On September 6 the distribution of the forces was as is shown in the following table:

Corps.	Officers.	Men.	Horses.
ISMAILIA.			
Cavalry:			
19th Hussars	7	130	140
Infantry:			
Royal Irish Fusiliers	31	760	54
Royal Marine Light Infantry	3	101	
Royal Artillery:			
C battery, 3d brigade (C. 3)	6	167	125
J battery, 3d brigade (J. 3)	6	168	121
F battery, 1st brigade (F. 1)	5	132	117
5 battery, 1st brigade, Scottish division	3	129	6
Royal Engineers:			
8th and 18th companies	12	235	12
Half of A troop	2	75	31
Half of C troop	2	76	23
Commissariat and Transport:			
2d, 8th, 11th, and 17th companies	21	744	824
Ordnance Store Department	5	78	
Army Hospital Corps	24	200	
Indian Contingent:			
20th (Punjaub) Native Infantry	9	490	202
Madras Sappers	7	251	
29th (Beloochees) Native Infantry	10	485	193
NEFICHE.			
1st battalion Seaforth Highlanders	32	749	64
7th Bengal Native Infantry	6	512	175
TEL-EL-MAHUTA.			
Cavalry:			
4th Dragoon Guards	20	292	288
Infantry:			
2d battalion Grenadier Guards	27	668	48
2d battalion Coldstream Guards	26	712	55
1st battalion Scots Guards	28	700	55
Royal Artillery:			
J battery, 3d brigade (one-half) (J. 3)			
N battery, 2d brigade (N. 2)	5	186	143
I battery, 2d brigade (I. 2)	5	190	149
5 battery, 1st brigade, Scottish division	2	65	
Royal Engineers:			
17th and 24th companies	5	113	73
Detachment C troop			
Commissariat and Transport:			
12th company	2	130	186
Army Hospital Corps:			
Field Hospital No. 2	8	37	24
Half of No. 1 Bearer company	3	73	
Indian Contingent:			
13th Bengal Lancers	3	70	73
MAHSAMEH.			
Cavalry:			
Household Cavalry	25	430	360
7th Dragoon Guards	29	500	460
Royal Horse Artillery:			
N battery, A brigade (N. A)	7	174	172
Army Hospital Corps:			
No. 2 Bearer company	4	98	
KASSASSIN.			
Cavalry:			
19th Hussars	7	130	140
4th Dragoon Guards	1	38	39
Mounted Infantry	4	76	73
Infantry:			
Duke of Cornwall's Light Infantry	26	680	56
Royal Marine Light Infantry	37	850	61
Royal West Kent	30	800	56
King's Royal Rifles	21	601	60
York and Lancaster Regiment	28	680	55
Royal Irish	30	735	55
Royal Artillery:			
Royal Marine Artillery (armed as infantry)	15	424	21
G battery, 3d brigade (horse) (G. 3)	7	174	172
A battery, 1st brigade (field) (A. 2)	7	194	153
D battery, 1st brigade (field) (D. 1)	6	189	144

Corps.	Officers.	Men.	Horses.
KASSASSIN—Continued.			
Royal Engineers:			
Half of A troop	4	105	32
Half of C troop	5	82	41
17th and 24th companies	4	138	....
Commissariat and Transport:			
12th and 15th companies	4	260	305
Army Hospital Corps:			
Field hospital No. 3	8	37	25
One-half No. 1 Bearer company	4	73	19
Indian Contingent:			
2d Regiment, Bengal Cavalry	6	180	198
6th Regiment, Bengal Cavalry	2	120	128
13th Regiment, Bengal Lancers	4	250	275
7th battery, 1st brigade, Northern division	5	247	10

(This last battery carried 7-pdr. screw-jointed guns on the backs of mules.)

On September 9 the Egyptians made a desperate effort to crush the British force at Kassassin. The following is the official report of the engagement:

CAMP KASSASSIN, *September 10, 1882.*

SIR: I have the honor to acquaint you that the enemy made a combined attack yesterday morning upon this position, one column advancing from the north from the Salihieh direction, the other from Tel-el-Kebir. Arabi Pasha was on the ground, but the attacking troops were commanded by Ali Fehmi Pasha, Rashid Pasha being, it is asserted by prisoners, in disgrace for having lost his camp and guns in the fight of the 25th ultimo, at Mahsameh station. The enemy's force was about thirty guns, of which we took four, and seventeen battalions of infantry, several squadrons of cavalry, and a few thousand Bedouins.

From the information I have obtained from prisoners, it would seem that the enemy expected an easy victory, thinking the force here was only a weak advance guard.

The troops in camp, when the attack began, were, as below, under the command of Lieutenant-General Willis, commanding 1st division. With these he immediately moved out, attacked and drove back the enemy, who retreated with loss within their line of works at Tel-el-Kebir, from which they opened an angry but harmless fire upon our troops, which had been halted beyond the range of their guns.

Our troops moved with great steadiness, and Major-General Graham has especially brought to my notice the dashing manner in which two Krupp guns were taken by the battalion of Royal Marine Light Infantry, and the excellent manner in which that battalion was handled by its commanding officer, Lieutenant-Colonel Jones.

Our casualties were 3 men killed and 2 officers and 78 men wounded. Lieutenant Purvis, of H. M. S. Penelope, is amongst those who were severely wounded. He was in command of the naval detachment that was serving the 40-pdr., which is mounted on a railway truck. He is a very good officer, and I have to regret very much the loss of his valuable services with this army. With the exception of five, who were too severely injured to be moved by railway, all the wounded were sent to Ismailia last night, and those five were sent there this evening by the Fresh Water Canal.

I have, &c.,

G. J. WOLSELEY,
General,
Commander-in-Chief of the British Forces in Egypt.

The troops engaged were those enumerated in table (p. 140), as at Kassassin, with certain changes. Thus the detachment of 4th Dragoon Guards and the Mounted Infantry had joined the cavalry at Mah-samseh; of the Engineers, A and C troops and the 17th company are not included among those that took part in the action, nor are the Commissariat and Transport companies. Battery N.A, Royal Horse Artillery, worked with the Indian cavalry, while half of Battery 5.1 Scottish division, had come up and established three 25-pdrs. for the permanent defense of the position. These were behind breastworks on the south side of the canal, close to the lock.

The camp was situated near this lock, between the railway embankment and the canal, in a plain surrounded by hills on the west, north, and east.

Two batteries of field artillery, A and D.1, were in gun-pits north of the camp, facing to the westward, the left of D.1 resting on the railway. Upon the latter were the captured Krupp 8^{cm} gun, worked by Captain Tucker's detachment of Royal Marine Artillery, already mentioned, and a B. L. R. 40-pdr. on an armored truck manned by bluejackets from H. M. S. Penelope, described elsewhere.

The Egyptian attack was meant to be from two sides—on the west by a sortie of the Tel-el-Kebir garrison, and on the north by a body from Salihieh, variously estimated at from 1,500 to 5,000 men.

There appears to be little doubt that the British came near being surprised. Early in the morning Colonel Pennington, of the 13th Bengal Lancers, going out to the westward to post vedettes, found the Egyptians advancing in force. Although but 50 men were with him, he dismounted them behind a ridge, and deliberately opened fire on the advancing enemy, and, when hard pushed, charged five squadrons of cavalry, killing ten men and capturing five horses. Immediate and timely warning of the impending danger was thus given to those in camp, enabling the line of battle to be formed, as shown in the accompanying diagram, not drawn to scale:

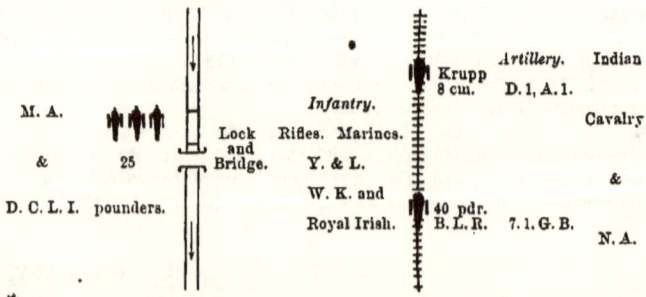

The cavalry and battery N. A., Royal Horse Artillery, were kept back in anticipation of a move from the direction of Salihieh.

By about 7 a. m. Arabi had succeeded in posting most of his guns on an eminence known as Ninth Hill, 2,000 yards to the British right front, while his infantry deployed for attack, with the right resting on the canal, and then advanced to within 1,200 yards. A few of his troops were south of the canal.

The testimony to the accuracy of the Egyptian artillery practice is very general, shot after shot falling admirably into the camp and lines. The shells, however, burst so indifferently as to neutralize the excellence of the aim.

Batteries A.1 and D.1, partly on account of the enemy's fire, and partly because of some uneven ground in their front, soon left the pits and advanced slightly. These batteries, aided by G.B. and 7.1 on the right, and the railway guns on the left, replied vigorously with shell and shrapnel. The 25-pdrs. did excellent work on the enemy's right on both sides of the canal, sending their projectiles over the heads of the British infantry until the advance was begun. Batteries A.1 and D.1 shot down the detachments of two of the captured guns, which were seized by the line as it advanced. The other two were carried by a charge of the marines in their forward march. The battalion, in regular formation for attack, came upon a battery of four guns which was playing briskly upon it at the distance of 1,400 yards. Without returning a shot, the marines kept on until they were 400 yards away, when they began firing volleys by half companies, still continuing the march. This steady work proved too severe for the Egyptians, who broke and ran, leaving two of the four guns behind.

The infantry, also engaged, held its ground for an hour and a half, a forward movement not being permitted until it should be definitely known that no danger was to be apprehended from the north. At 8.30 it was deemed prudent to assume the offensive, and the line was ordered to advance, the extreme right being, however, kept refused. The infantry and the four batteries of artillery on its right moved forward about a thousand yards, and re-engaged the enemy, who had retired. At 9.30 the advance was resumed, and the Egyptians were slowly driven back into their intrenchments at Tel-el-Kebir. These fortifications were approached to within 5,000 or 6,000 yards, more for the purpose of observation than of assault. At 12.30 the British started to return to Kassassin.

In this action the British artillery proved its value, and received credit for the manner in which it was handled. The infantry had less opportunity of distinguishing itself, for the Egyptians were unwilling to engage at short range.

The repulse did not take the form of a rout, although little doubt can be entertained that the retreating army would not have stopped at Tel-el-Kebir had a vigorous assault been attempted. In fact, the British troops, both officers and men, were extremely anxious to continue the advance; General Wolseley, however, would not give his consent, but ordered the withdrawal to Kassassin, merely observing that he was not ready.

The Salihieh contingent was late in arriving on the scene of action.

It failed to unite with the troops from Tel-el-Kebir, and it was met by the cavalry division, under Major General Drury-Lowe, in the desert north of the lines. Seeing the impossibility of joining Arabi, in the face of the force unexpectedly found ready to receive him, its commander withdrew before General Drury-Lowe's advance, losing a field gun in his retreat. There was no fighting at this point.

The failure of the movement was attributed by the Egyptians to their having kept too far to the eastward.

The Egyptian version of the affair is worth reading. It runs as follows, and is from a telegram sent by Arabi to the ministry of war at Cairo:

September 9.—Last night some mounted Arabs of the province of Sharkiyeh, belonging to the tribes of Nakiat, Tamailat, Ayad, and Haim, rode out towards the enemy at 2 a. m., under the command of Ali Bey Ismet, superintendent of the Arabs, and with them Captain Abdul Hamid Effendi Hamdy and 40 cavalry soldiers. They went forward as far as the enemy's outposts, rode at them, and fired a volley, which made them retire, and then the Arabs found forty-five oxen grazing [*sic*] which they drove off, while some of the party remained to keep back the enemy. At sunrise the enemy came out with infantry, cavalry, and artillery, and firing began, and continued on both sides for about an hour. Then the Arabs charged like lions, displaying a courage and bravery which enabled them to drive back the enemy, who were much more numerous than themselves. Then they followed the enemy, driving them until they had killed about 100 of them, and dispersed the rest, driving them back into their tents. The Arabs captured the oxen, about 500 meters of torpedo wire, and other military stores, and they returned to their posts victorious. This engagement, including the attack and pursuit, lasted about six hours. * * * Thanks be to God, not one of the Arabs nor of the soldiers was wounded. Give this news to those under your administration.

Also, a second telegram, dated September 10 (Arabic):

On this day, September 9, an engagement took place with the enemy at 5 a. m. Our force was composed of infantry, cavalry, and artillery, in the two directions of Ras-el-Ouady and of Salihieh. After the enemy had hidden himself behind his intrenchments at the bridge of Al-Kassassin, our troops retired to their posts in perfect order, and when there was a considerable distance between them the enemy came out of his intrenchments and endeavored to cut off our troops. The engagement lasted till 5 p. m., when the enemy retreated, defeated with great loss, to Al-Kassassin. Thanks be to God, our losses were very small in comparison with those of the enemy. We and our officers and the conquering army, his excellency Mahmoud Pasha Samy,* and his officers and soldiers, are all in perfect health, our two divisions being at their post in perfect condition of readiness; and we pray God to give us the victory over our enemies and to strengthen our courageous men against them, for the sake of the Lord of the beginning and of the end. Amen. O Lord of the Universe.

A more minute account is rendered three days later:

September 12.—I give you good news, which will cause you joy and will delight each individual of the people—namely, that the engagement of Saturday (9th September) was the most serious battle that has yet taken place between us and the English, for the force of both armies was very great, and the fighting lasted for twelve hours, with impetuosity and daring, while the cannonade and the discharge of musketry were unceasing, pouring down like rain on the field of battle. Still we lost only

---

* The commandant at Salihieh.

31 men, martyrized, and 150 were slightly, not dangerously, wounded, according to the official returns presented by the various regiments, with great exactness and precision. It had been thought that our casualties would have been double that number owing to the seriousness of the engagement and its long duration. Moreover, from true observation it has been proved to us that the number of the enemy killed and remaining on the field of battle is about 2,500, and their carts were insufficient for carrying off the wounded. * * *

In the writing of dispatches, if in nothing else, Arabi was truly Napoleonic.

On September 9 the Highland brigade, under Major-General Alison, K. C. B., started from Ismailia for the front.

The 10th, 11th, and 12th were occupied in bringing up the troops to Kassassin and in making preparations for a general advance.

During the latter part of this second or quiescent period of the campaign, reconnaissances were made daily in the direction of Tel-el-Kebir, but serious engagements were strictly forbidden. The military habits of the Egyptians were carefully studied. On one occasion Colonel Buller, V. C., C. B., C. M. G., of the Intelligence Department, managed to get around the enemy's flank as far as Karaini, and to ascertain that his outposts at night were withdrawn to very near the trenches.

The transport question, the only obstacle in the way of further offensive operations on the part of General Wolseley, had received a solution which, if not complete, was measurably satisfactory. The railway service had been developed to an extent sufficient to permit the accumulation of supplies beyond the needs of daily consumption, and the anxiety which had been experienced in the earlier stages of the campaign had given place to impatience to resume the march to Cairo. The war now passes into its last period.

The following table gives the disposition and a fairly trustworthy enumeration of the Egyptian forces at this time.

Place.	In command.	Infantry		Artillery		Cavalry		Irregulars and Bedouins	Total.
		Regiments.	Men.	Guns.	Men.	Regiments.	Men.		
Tel-el-Kebir	Arabi Pasha, Ali Ruby Pasha.	8	24,000	60	1,000	2	1,000	2,500	38,500
Kafr Dowar	Toulba Pasha	2	6,000	40	800			6,000	12,800
Mariout	Halil Khamil			18	350		200	5,000	5,550
Aboukir and Rosetta	Khoutshid Pasha	3	9,000	18	350		200	5,000	14,550
Salihieh	Mahmoud Samy Pasha			12	200			5,000	5,200
Damietta	Abdul Al Pasha	2	5,500						5,500
Cairo		4	12,000						12,000

Total regulars, say 60,000; total irregulars, say 34,000; grand total, about 94,000 men.

XIII.

THE BATTLE OF TEL-EL-KEBIR AND THE CONCLUSION OF THE WAR.

To remain behind and guard the line of communication during the forward movement now to be undertaken, the following detail of men was made:

Place.	British troops.	Indian Contingent.	19th Hussars.
Ismailia	800 of the Manchester Regiment	500 native infantry	
Nefiche	50 of the West Kent Regiment	150 native infantry	1 troop.
Mahuta	100 of the West Kent Regiment	50 native infantry	1 troop.
Mahsameh	100 of the West Kent Regiment	100 native infantry	
Kassassin	200 of the West Kent Regiment 24th and 26th companies Royal Engineers		1 troop.

At 2 p. m. on September 12, the army having concentrated at Kassassin, the Royal Irish Fusiliers being the last battalion to arrive, two days' rations were served out for man and beast. At 5 p. m. the men's valises (new pattern of knapsack), blankets, and all baggage were stacked beside the railway, and a non-commissioned officer and two men detailed from each company to stay by them. After sunset no bugles were allowed to be sounded. The camp was to be left under the command of General Nugent, R. E.

The regimental transport was ordered to carry cooking utensils, two days' rations, one day's fuel, butchers' tools and signaling instruments, together with as many overcoats or blankets as could be taken without overloading; to be brigaded at daylight of the next day, and to follow along the northern side of the canal. With each battalion were to go the usual water-carts and stretchermen (four to each company). The men were to carry two days' provisions in their haversacks, and, before starting, were to fill their water-bottles with tea. Each man had on his person 100 rounds of ammunition, and 30 additional rounds per man were to follow in rear on mules.

After dark all tents were struck and piled near the railway, and the camp fires were left burning. The troops formed in order of battle as shown on Plate 49. In the 1st division the formation was by half battalions in columns of companies; in the 2d division, by half battalions in double company columns at deploying intervals, thus:

2d division.   1st division.

The batteries of artillery were all placed by 10 p. m., and the other corps formed on them. The men then rested on their arms waiting for the word to advance. The right of the Highland brigade, the guiding point, was to follow a line of telegraph poles, 100 yards apart, which had been planted the evening before by the Telegraph Troop, and when these ended was to be directed by Lieutenant Wyatt Rawson, R. N., naval aid-de-camp to General Wolseley. The vacant space in the front line was covered by a succession of infantry files at intervals of ten paces. Similar files maintained the distance and communication between the leading and supporting brigades in each division, while the intervals between the artillery and the neighboring infantry brigades were bridged over by mounted non-commissioned officers. The attack on the intrenchments of Tel-el-Kebir was to be made at the point of the bayonet, in the same formation, without change except in deploying the rear companies.

During the march several halts were made to rest the troops, one, towards 3 a. m., being nearly an hour in length. Daybreak was the time fixed for arrival at the fortified lines, and it would have been as undesirable to reach them too soon as too late.

The position selected by the Egyptians for a final stand was by nature the strongest it was possible to find in that flat section of country. Near the station of Tel-el-Kebir there is a general and gradual rise of the ground towards the west, culminating in a range of hills that stretch from a point on the railway, about a mile and a half east of the station, northward to Salihieh. Roughly parallel to the Sweet Water Canal is a second series of hills intersecting the first about two miles distant from the railway (at Q on Plate 50). Viewed from the railway this east and west range appears as a moderate hill. Its real character, however, is that of a table-land sloping away to the northward, with a rather steeper descent towards the south. The generally even nature of the ground is seen in Plate 51, together with its extreme barrenness, amounting to desolation.

The Egyptian intrenchments were laid out along the crests of these two ranges, the north and south lines being prolonged over two miles beyond the intersection.

The plan included an ample dry ditch, from 8 to 12 feet wide, and from 5 to 9 feet deep, in front of a breastwork from 4 to 6 feet high, with a banquette in rear. The trace was broken by occasional salients where were placed well-designed redoubts possessing a wide command on either flank. The sides of these redoubts are marked on Plate 50. In rear were frequent shelter trenches irregularly spaced. Passages through the parapet for field pieces and vehicles were provided in various places, and were guarded by outlying traverses and breastworks. The revetment differed mainly in the care which had been bestowed upon it, and consisted mostly of reeds, grass, &c. The interior slopes were the only ones thus treated. (See Plate 52.)

The southern portion of the defenses was practically completed at the time of the battle. Here the revetment was neatly finished, as in Plate 54. Work was in progress on the northern and western lines, their extremities being scarcely more than laid out.

The extent of these defensive works, which is enormous in comparison with the number of troops at Arabi's disposal, would seem to imply an inordinate reliance upon mere ditches and breastworks to keep out an enemy, however vigorous. It led, as a necessary consequence, to the excessive spreading-out of the defenders, and the fatal weakening of the force which could be gathered at any given point. Had the same amount of labor been expended in several concentric lines, it would have resulted in a position of great strength, permitting the retiring, if necessary, from one line to the next, and an almost indefinite prolonging of the fight.

At the southern end of the line (see Plate 50) there were two well-built redoubts, one on each bank of the canal, mounting three guns. A view of these redoubts is given on Plate 54, while sections and the plan of that on the northern bank are seen on Plate 55. Connecting the two, and stopping the flow of water in the Sweet Water Canal, was a stout dam.

The section of the parapet between the canal and the railway is shown at B, Plate 55. In rear of this line were various shelters, some of which are given in section at C, D, and F of the same plate.

On each side of the railway was one gun. The form of the gun emplacement is shown at E.

Plate 56, A^1 H is a section through the gap and its defenses; I J K are sections of the parapet and shelters adjoining. A view of L is given on Plate 62.

In front of this portion of the lines, and distant about 1,100 yards, was a formidable outwork marked M on Plate 50, and given in plan and section on Plate 56. This was a polygonally-shaped redoubt, entirely lacking in protection against reverse fire. It was provided with an envelope in front and on either flank. It mounted eight guns. From an inspection of the section, it is seen that the battery itself had no banquette between the embrasures, and hence was ill-adapted to defense by musketry. Once the men were driven out of the envelope, the battery itself would surely fall. It may be pointed out that this defect exists in all the batteries at Tel-el-Kebir.

N is a four-gun battery, in rear of which, on the highest point of the inclosure, was a lookout and telegraph station, the wire running back to Arabi's headquarters, near the railway station, and in the midst of a large camp. The diminished size of the ditch from this part of the lines northward is very noticeable. The attack was evidently hoped for at and near the railway.

At Q the junction of the two series of intrenchments was the most elaborately finished of all the redoubts. It mounted five guns, as shown on Plate 15. It had no envelope, but was amply provided with traverses and expense magazines. This battery was the left of the attack, being struck fairly by the Highland Light Infantry, the extreme left battalion of the line. It is on the second of a succession of knolls, on each of which a battery was constructed.

The lines adjoining as far as V were carried by the Highland brigade. The forms of the parapet are given in Plate 57, where they are marked R S, S T, T V, respectively. They are much less effective as defenses than those to the southward, and, as the event proved, were incapable of acting as serious obstacles to resolute men.

Battery V, Plate 58, was a formidable work within a spacious envelope, and mounted five guns. The work itself was completed, but parts of the accessory defenses were still unfinished. It was turned by the Highlanders, who passed to the southward.

The attack of the 2d brigade took place in next line of trenches as far as W. The ditch, as seen by the section at V, Plate 59, was of the same general character as that encountered by the Highlanders, but was a trifle larger in its dimensions. It varied, however, not being a completed work.

The redoubts W and Y are shown both in plan and section on the same plate. As indicated, this part of the line was hardly begun.

As regards the east and west line, from A' and E' to O', enough of the details are shown on Plate 60 to make its character clear. It was absolutely useless in the battle, being taken by the Highlanders in rear and by the second brigade in the flank.

The soil at Tel-el-Kebir is sand and gravel, easily worked, but as easily displaced. The interior slopes were revetted with tufts of grass, &c., while the exterior slopes were allowed to assume their natural talus. The ground is hard enough to retain, approximately, the shape indicated in the ditch sections, but the passage of the first few men invariably broke down the sides of the ditch, making a causeway for those who came behind.

A defect of design in the redoubts is the lack of sufficient depression to the soles of the embrasures. In consequence, the projectiles were harmless at close quarters, passing well over the heads of the British.

The account of the battle of Tel-el-Kebir, contained in General Wolseley's report, is given below at full length. The omitted paragraphs relate to events subsequent to the action, and are quoted elsewhere:

CAIRO, *September* 16, 1882.

SIR: I have already had the honor of reporting to you by telegraph that I attacked the intrenched position of Tel-el-Kebir a little before sunrise on the morning of the 13th instant, completely defeating the enemy, with very great loss, and capturing fifty-nine field guns, vast quantities of ammunition, military stores, and supplies of all sorts.

* * * * * * *

From the daily reconnaissance of the position at Tel-el-Kebir made from our camp at Kassassin, especially from the good view I obtained of the enemy's works on the 9th instant, when our troops drove back within the intrenchments the force of thirteen battalions, five squadrons, and eighteen guns that had attacked our camp in the morning, it was evident that their works were of great extent and of a formidable character. All the information obtained from spies and prisoners led me to believe that the enemy's force at Tel-el-Kebir consisted of from sixty to seventy horsed guns, which were mostly distributed along their line of works, of two infantry divisions (twenty-four battalions) of about 20,000 men, and three regiments of cavalry, together with about 6,000 Bedouins and irregulars, besides a force of about 5,000 men, with twenty-four guns, at Salihieh, all under the immediate command of Arabi Pasha. I have since been able to verify these numbers, which are certainly not overstated, except as regards the number of guns at Tel-el-Kebir, which I believe to have been fifty-nine, the number we took in the works and during the pursuit.

Owing to the numerous detachments I was obliged to make for the defense of my long line of communications from Suez to Ismailia, and thence on to Kassassin, and owing to the losses incurred in previous actions, I could only place in line about 11,000 bayonets, 2,000 sabers, and sixty field guns.

The enemy's position was a strong one. There was no cover of any kind in the desert lying between my camp at Kassassin and the enemy's works north of the canal. These works extended from a point on the canal 1¼ miles east of the railway station of Tel-el-Kebir for a distance almost due north of about 3½ miles.

The general character of the ground which forms the northern boundary of the valley through which the Ismailia Canal and railway run is that of gently undulating and rounded slopes, which rise gradually to a fine open plateau from 90 to 100 feet above the valley. The southern extremity of this plateau is about a mile from the railway, and is nearly parallel to it. To have marched over this plateau upon the enemy's position by daylight our troops would have had to advance over a glacis-like slope in full view of the enemy, and under the fire of his well-served artillery, for about 5 miles. Such an operation would have entailed enormous losses from an enemy with guns and men well protected by intrenchments from any artillery fire we could have brought to bear upon them. To have turned the enemy's position either by the right or left was an operation that would have entailed a very wide turning movement, and therefore a long, difficult, and fatiguing march, and what is of more importance, it would not have accomplished the object I had in view, namely, to grapple with the enemy at such close quarters that he should not be able to shake himself free from our clutches except by a general fight of all his army. I wished to make the battle a final one; whereas a wide turning movement would probably have only forced him to retreat, and would have left him free to have moved his troops in good order to some other position further back. My desire was to fight him decisively where he was in the open desert before he could retire to take up fresh positions more difficult of access in the cultivated country in his rear. That cultivated country is practically impassable to a regular army, being irrigated and cut up in every direction by deep canals.

I had ascertained by frequent reconnaissances, that the enemy did not push his outposts far beyond his works at night, and I had good reason for believing that he then kept a very bad look-out. These circumstances, and the very great reliance I had in the steadiness of our splendid infantry, determined me to resort to the extremely difficult operation of a night march, to be followed by an attack before daylight, on the enemy's position. The result was all I could have wished for.

At dawn on the morning of the 12th instant, accompanied by all the generals and brigadiers, I inspected the enemy's works and explained to them my intended plan of attack, and gave to each a sketch showing the formation in which it was to be effected.

As soon as it was dark, on the evening of the 12th instant, I struck my camp at Kassassin, and the troops moved into position, the left being at near the point marked "Ninth Hill" on sketch A, where they bivouacked.

No fires were allowed, and even smoking was prohibited, and all were ordered to maintain the utmost silence throughout the night's operation. At 1.30 a. m. on the morning of the 13th instant, I gave the order for the advance of the 1st and 2d divisions simultaneously. The night was very dark, and it was difficult to maintain the desired formation, but, by means of connecting files between the battalions and brigades, and between the first and second lines, and through the untiring exertions of the generals and the officers of the staff generally, this difficulty was effectually overcome.

The Indian Contingent—7. 1, R. A. (mountain battery), 1st battalion Seaforth Highlanders, 3d battalion Native Infantry, made up of detachments of 7th Bengal Native Infantry, 20th Punjaub Infantry, and 29th (Beloochees)—under Major-General Sir H. Macpherson, and the Naval Brigade, under Captain Fitz Roy, R. N., did not move until 2.30 a. m. To have moved them earlier would have given the alarm to the enemy, owing to the number of villages in the cultivated land south of the canal.

Telegraphic communication by means of an insulated cable was kept up through Kassasslu all through the night between the Indian Contingent, on the south of the canal, and the Royal Marine Artillery, with which I moved, in rear of the 2d division.

In moving over the desert at night there are no landmarks to guide one's movements. We had, consequently, to direct our course by the stars. This was well and correctly effected, and the leading brigades of each division both reached the enemy's works within a couple of minutes of each other.

The enemy were completely surprised, and it was not until one or two of their advanced sentries fired their rifles that they realized our close proximity to their works. These were, however, very quickly lined with infantry, who opened a deafening musketry fire, and their guns came into action immediately. Our troops advanced steadily without firing a shot, in obedience to the orders they had received, and when close to the works, went straight for them, charging with a ringing cheer.

Major-General Graham reports: "The steadiness of the advance of the 2d brigade gade (2d Royal Irish Regiment, Royal Marine Light Infantry, 2d battalion York and Lancaster Regiment, 1st battalion Royal Irish Fusiliers), under what appeared to be an overwhelming fire of musketry and artillery, will remain a proud remembrance."

The 2d brigade was well supported by the brigade of Guards under His Royal Highness the Duke of Connaught.

On the left, the Highland brigade (1st battalion Royal Highlanders, 1st battalion Gordon Highlanders, 1st battalion Cameron Highlanders, 2d battalion Highland Light Infantry), under Major-General Sir A. Alison, had reached the works a few minutes before the 2d brigade had done so, and in a dashing manner stormed them at the point of the bayonet, without firing a shot nutil within the enemy's lines. They were well supported by the Duke of Cornwall's Light Infantry and the 3d Royal Rifles, both under the command of Colonel Ashburnham of the last-named corps.

In the center, between these two attacks, marched seven batteries of artillery, deployed into one line, under the command of Brigadier-General Goodenough, and after the capture of the enemy's works several of these batteries did good service, and inflicted considerable loss upon the enemy, in some instances firing canister at short ranges.

On the extreme left the Indian Contingent and the Naval Brigade, under the command of Major-General Sir H. Macpherson, V. C., advanced steadily and in silence, the Seaforth Highlanders leading until an advanced battery of the enemy was reached (it is not shown in sketch A), when it was most gallantly stormed by the Highlanders, supported by the Native Infantry battalions.

The squadron of the 6th Bengal Cavalry, attached temporarily to General Macpherson, did good service in pursuing the enemy through the village of Tel-el-Kebir.

The Indian Contingent scarcely lost a man, a happy circumstance, which I attribute to the excellent arrangements made by General Macpherson, and to the fact that, starting one hour later than the 1st and 2d divisions, the resistance of the enemy was so shaken by the earlier attacks north of the canal that he soon gave way before the impetuous onslaught of the Seaforth Highlanders.

The Cavalry division, on the extreme right of the line, swept round the northern extremity of the enemy's works, charging the enemy's troops as they endeavored to escape. Most of the enemy, however, threw away their arms, and, begging for mercy, were unmolested by our men. To have made them prisoners would have taken up too much time, the cavalry being required for the more important work of pushing on to Cairo.

Such is a general outline of the battle of Tel-el-Kebir. All the previous actions of this short campaign were chiefly cavalry and artillery affairs; but that of the 13th instant was essentially an infantry battle, and was one that, from the time we started, at 1.30 a. m., until nearly 6 a. m., when it was practically over, was peculiarly calculated to test, in the most crucial manner, the quality and the fighting discipline of our infantry.

I do not believe that at any previous period of our military history has the British infantry distinguished itself more than upon this occasion.

I have heard it said of our present infantry regiments that the men are too young, and their training for maneuvering and for fighting and their powers of endurance are not sufficient for the requirements of modern war. After a trial of an exceptionally severe kind, both in movement and attack, I can say emphatically that I never wish to have under my orders better infantry battalions than those whom I am proud to have commanded at Tel-el-Kebir.

Our casualties have been numerous, but not so many as I had anticipated. Her Majesty has to deplore the loss of many gallant men, who died as became the soldiers of an army that is proud of the glorious traditions it has inherited.

It would be impossible in this dispatch to bring to your notice the services of those officers whom I consider especially worthy of mention. I shall do so in a subsequent dispatch, but I cannot close this without placing on record how much I am indebted to the following officers who took part in the battle of Tel-el-Kebir, and who, by their zeal and ability, contributed so largely to its success:

General Sir John Adye, K. C. B., chief of the staff; Lieutenant-Generals Willis and Sir E. Hamley, Major-Generals Sir A. Alison, His Royal Highness the Duke of Connaught, Drury-Lowe, Sir H. Macpherson, and Graham; Brigadier-Generals Goodenough, R. A., Sir Baker Russell, the Honorable J. Dormer; Deputy Adjutant-General Tanner, and Colonel Ashburnham, who temporarily commanded a brigade during the action; and to Captain Fitz Roy, who commanded the Naval Brigade.

Brigadier-General Nugent, R. E., remained during the action in command of the camp left at Kassassin to cover the rear of the army operating in his immediate front and to protect that position, with all its stores and depots, from any possible attack from the enemy's force at Salihieh. He rejoined me in the evening at Tel-el-Kebir, having carried out the orders he had received.

The medical arrangements were all they should have been, and reflect the highest credit upon Surgeon-General Hanbury.

In the removal of the wounded on the 13th and 14th instant to Ismailia, the canal-boat service, worked by the Royal Navy, under Commander Moore, R. N., did most excellent work, and the army is deeply indebted to that officer and to those under his command for the aid he afforded the wounded, and for the satisfactory manner in which he moved a large number of them by water to Ismailia.

No exertion has been spared on the part of Major-General Earle, commanding the line of communications, and of Commissary-General Morris, to supply all the wants of this army during its advance from Ismailia.

To the headquarters staff, and to officers composing the staff of each division, my best thanks are due for the able manner in which they performed their duty.

In conclusion I wish to express my deep sense of the high military spirit displayed throughout the battle of Tel-el-Kebir, and during all our previous engagements, by commanding officers, by all regimental officers, and by every non-commissioned officer and private now serving in Egypt. I have also the honor to inclose a roll of the casualties which occurred at the battle of Tel-el-Kebir.

Major George Fitz George, 20th Hussars, the senior member of my personal staff, is the bearer of this dispatch, and I have the honor to recommend him to your favorable consideration.

I have, &c.,

G. J. WOLSELEY, *General*,
Commander-in-Chief of Her Majesty's Forces in Egypt.

Summary of the killed, wounded, and missing in the battle of Tel-el-Kebir.

Corps.	Killed.		Wounded.		Missing.	
	Officers.	Non-commissioned officers and men.	Officers.	Non-commissioned officers and men.	Officers.	Non-commissioned officers and men.
Staff, army corps			*1			
Staff, 1st division				1		
2d battalion Grenadier Guards		1	1	9		
2d battalion Coldstream Guards			1	7		
1st battalion Scots Guards				4		
2d battalion Royal Irish	1	1	2	17		
Royal Marine Light Infantry	2	3	1	53		
2d battalion York and Lancaster				12		
1st battalion Royal Irish Fusiliers		2		34		3
10th Hussars			1			
2d battalion Duke of Cornwall's Light Infantry			1	5		
Royal Artillery			2	17		
1st battalion Royal Highlanders	2	7	†6	37		4
1st battalion Gordon Highlanders	1	5	1	29		4
1st batt'lion Cameron Highlanders		13	3	45		
2d battalion Highland Light Infantry	3	14	5	32		11
3rd battalion King's Royal Rifles				20		
1st battalion Seaforth Highlanders		1		3		
Native troops		1		9		
Chaplains			1			
	9	48	27	353		22

* Since dead.   † One since dead.

The fullness of General Wolseley's official report renders extensive comment unnecessary; nevertheless a few words may be added to make the individual parts of the battle more distinct.

It may be observed, *passim*, that the night march offered two great advantages: avoidance of the heat of day-time and a period of fourteen hours' light for pursuit of the Egyptians if defeated.

Practically there were three separate but nearly simultaneous infantry attacks: by the 1st division, under General Willis; by the 2d division, under General Hamley; and away on the extreme left, south of the canal, by the Indian Contingent, under General Macpherson. In point of time, General Hamley's was somewhat earlier than the others, and General Macpherson's the last of the three.

When the action began, at early dawn, General Willis' leading brigade, commanded by Major-General Graham, was about 900 yards from the intrenchments. Partly owing to the difficulty of keeping a proper alignment during the night march, partly to the fact that the line of march was not normal to the line of the earthworks, and partly to the confusion created by an Egyptian scout who galloped into his lines, General Willis was obliged to form again under heavy fire, changing front forward on the left company before assaulting, adopting the regular attack formation. At 300 yards' distance a volley was fired by the British, after which they rushed up to 150 yards' distance, fired a second volley, and then reached the ditch. Here the fighting line was joined by the supports, a last volley delivered, the ditch jumped, and the works cleared at the point of the bayonet. As soon as the brigade reached the parapet, the Egyptians broke and ran, some stopping occasionally to fire back at their pursners, who chased them for upwards of a mile, only halting when the artillery had gotten inside the works and had begun shelling the fugitives.

This brigade struck the trenches not 100 yards from the point aimed at. It was longer exposed to the Egyptian fire than were the Highlanders, whose attack had begun a few minutes previous and had fully aroused the whole line of the defense, which had been sleeping on their arms behind the parapets.

To the Highland brigade, led by Major-General Alison, fell the task of carrying the lines to the left. The first shots were fired at them at 4.55 a. m. from a picket of about 30 men posted 150 yards in front of the intrenchments, then 300 yards distant from the Highlanders. Immediately afterwards the enemy opened with artillery and then with musketry. Without returning this fire the brigade advanced steadily for about 100 yards further, when the fire became a perfect blaze. At 150 yards bayonets were ordered to be fixed, and the bugle sounded the advance, when, with a yell, the men charged in the dim light through the smoke, carrying the lines in fine style in the face of determined opposition. The enemy did not run far, but halted at about 60 yards in rear and delivered a heavy cross-fire. The left battalion, the Highland Light Infantry, struck the strong redoubt (Q, Plate 50) with a high scarp, which held the center companies for a moment, but the flank companies got around it and took it. The rest of the brigade pushed steadily on, driving the enemy before it, and capturing three batteries of field guns. The advance was continued, and Arabi's headquarters and the canal bridge seized at 6.45 a. m. The Highland Light Infantry, which had suffered severely, soon afterwards joined the rest of the brigade.

The force under the command of General Macpherson was the Naval Light Battery and the Indian Contingent, less the latter's cavalry, one of its two batteries of artillery, and a considerable number of its infantry detailed as guards along the line of communication.

The advance of this division was by the south bank of the canal, the Naval Light Battery of 6 Gatlings accompanying it on the northern side along the railway embankment.

General Macpherson started an hour later than the main army, but was within gunshot when the action was begun by the Highland brigade. The Egyptian artillery at once opened fire down the line of the canal, although it was still too dark to see the approaching troops plainly, while the infantry lost no time in opening a heavy fusilade. The Contingent immediately left the exposed canal bank by which it had been proceeding, and took to a more sheltered roadway beside it. The Seaforth Highlanders, who were leading, deployed for attack. The first obstacle encountered was in the shape of a battery of 7-pdr. Lahitte howitzers in gun-pits, barring the way. This was first opened on with case by the mule battery, and then carried gallantly by the Seaforth Highlanders with a rush at the point of the bayonet. In continuation of this line of gun-pits was a long shelter trench, which was at once evacuated, the Egyptians retreating into some villages near by, whence they were driven by the native Indian troops.

On the other side of the canal the Naval Gatlings were busily employed firing on the Egyptian lines in front and on either hand.

The British advance was not checked for an instant, but was continued rapidly into and past the intrenchments and on to the bridge and railway station. One squadron of the 6th Bengal Cavalry, which had remained with General Macpherson, charged the fugitives on the extreme left across the cultivated ground.

The operations of the Artillery brigade are given in the following note, by Captain Martin, R. A., aid-de-camp to the general commanding:

Seven batteries were formed up in line at full intervals between the 4th brigade and the Guards brigade. There were intervals of 150 yards on either flank between the guns and the infantry. General Goodenough commanded the forty-two guns in person, and directed their march from the left of the line, keeping up the touch to either flank during the night march.

At 4.55 a. m. the first shot was fired by the enemy. About two minutes afterwards the enemy opened fire all along the intrenchments and from his guns. At this time the line of guns was some 800 yards from the intrenchments. It was too dark to lay guns, and, moreover, the Highland brigade overlapped the front of four batteries, so General Goodenough awaited the development of the attack and halted. In five or six minutes, seeing from the flashes that the attack was gaining ground, he ordered an advance from the center in *échelon*, thus:

N.2 and I.2.

H.1, J.3; C.3.   A.1 and D.1.

In this order, favored by the darkness, and on the left by smoke, the leading division, N.2, and I.2, approached the trenches to about 300 yards. General Goodenough then halted the guns, rode forward into the intrenchments, and finding the attack successful, directed the leading division to enter. N.2 led the way in column of route. The first gun cantered into the ditch and over the parapet somehow, bringing down some of the earthwork and making some sort of a way for the other guns. N.2, followed by I.2, rushed through the infantry and came into action beyond them, firing west and northwest at groups of the enemy, who were falling back, fighting. It became daylight suddenly, just before the guns entered the works—time about 5.10 a. m. About 5.15 (as I judge it) Graham's attack approached, and about 5.20 a swarm of fugitives came rushing back from his direction (the right attack). About 5.25, N.2 was ordered to cease firing, and work down the ridge running southwest to the camp and railway station. This was done, the battery coming into action frequently at close ranges, and keeping the masses of fugitives on the move. I.2 was directed, a few minutes later, to follow N.2. The ridge ended some five or six hundred yards from the station. N.2 reached this point and opened fire at trains moving off and the fugitives retiring by the railway embankment. I.2 arrived here just as the firing ended, at 6.40 a. m.

A.1 and D.1, seeing the leading division enter the works, and their front not being covered by infantry, trotted forward and came into action at 200 yards from the intrenchments and opened fire with case and shrapnel. When the parapet in their immediate front was silenced, they again advanced, swung forward the left and enfiladed the line of parapets northwards. This was to assist General Graham's attack. On this succeeding, they were ordered southward to silence the outwork (M, Plate LIV), which had been missed by the Highland brigade in the dark. Finding the gorge open, they went for it and settled the matter with a few rounds of case. The Egyptians got a gun or two round to meet them, but before they could do much harm were shot down. A.1 and D.1 then made for the camp, bringing in the six guns in the outwork with them.

C.3, J.3, and H.1, finding the Highland attack successful, advanced to the parapet, cleared a way through it, and entered. They came into action successively, beyond the infantry, and fired a few rounds at the enemy falling back. Seeing N.2 working down the ridge towards the camp and station, C.3, and subsequently J.3 and H.1, followed in that direction. C.3 came into action at the end of the ridge and fired at the trains moving off and the fugitives near the bridge and station. It ceased fire at 6.40 a. m. J.3 and H.1 were arriving at this time. H.1 was halted a few minutes until the Indian Contingent came up to the bridge over the canal. It was then directed to join that body, and went on to Zazazig.

On the extreme right, the Cavalry division, under Major-General Drury-Lowe, was designedly late in arriving, being fully 2 miles distant when the first shot was fired at the Highlanders. Hearing the sound it quickened its pace, reaching the intrenchments in time to permit its two horse batteries N.A. and G.B. to take in reverse and enfilade the lines north of General Graham's assault, while the cavalry took up the pursuit of the runaways, as described in the official report, and galloped to the railway station, capturing several trains and locomotives. The whole division, cavalry and artillery, united shortly afterwards at the bridge over the canal prior to advancing towards Cairo.

The Egyptians were sleeping in the trenches when the attack was made, and although, in one sense, surprised, were nevertheless quite ready. General Hamley thinks the alarm was given by mounted scouts who were met on the march. Yet Arabi and his second in command were both aroused by the noise of the fight, and both, without a moment's hesitation, ran away. The warning could not have been of very great value at the best.

The supply of ammunition was practically inexhaustible. At intervals of three or four yards were open boxes, each containing 1,050 cartridges. The fire was for the most part ill-directed and too high. It appeared to the British as though they merely rested their pieces on the parapet, loading and firing as rapidly as possible without stopping to take aim. The fusillade was tremendous while it lasted, but it could only be really effective when the attacking troops were actually on the parapet. By that time the result of the action was beyond doubt. Their artillerists made, as usual, *the mistake of using shell instead of shrapnel and canister.* The former bury themselves in the soft ground to a considerable depth before the percussion fuzes act, and, in consequence, the explosion is muffled and comparatively innocuous. Many of the shells actually passed over the heads of the supporting brigades.

The trenches, after the battle, were found to be filled with dead, mostly bayoneted, and the ground in rear, as far as the railway station, was dotted with the bodies of those shot down in retreat. The British cavalry sweeping around the northern end of the intrenchments cut down the fugitives by scores, until it became evident that the rout was complete. After that all were spared who had thrown away their arms and who offered no resistance. Most of the bodies were observed to be lying on their backs facing the trenches as if the men had stopped to have a parting shot at their pursuers.

The Egyptian loss in killed alone was not far from 2,000. There was no return of their wounded, the army organization having disappeared, but 534 were treated at Tel-el-Kebir during the four days succeeding the battle, 27 capital operations being performed. Of these wounded 202 were soon able to go to their own homes, while the balance were sent to Cairo in charge of Egyptian surgeons. The British medical authorities did all in their power to alleviate the sufferings of these poor wretches, and furnished tins of meat, bottles of brandy, and skins of water to the railway trucks conveying them away. Many more who were slightly wounded must have managed to get to the neighboring villages and eventually to their homes, and thus have escaped enumeration. It may be remarked, *àpropos*, that the Egyptian hospital arrangements were of the most meager description.

It is stated, and the statement bears the stamp of credibility, that extremely few superior officers were killed or wounded, and, as has been already mentioned, the two in chief command were the first to escape. Arabi himself mounted his horse and rode rapidly towards Belbeis. There appears to be no doubt that proper leaders in every sense of the word were wanting on the Egyptian side, and that the officers set a shocking example to the men. It has been humorously, and more or less truthfully, remarked that each officer knew that he would run but hoped his *neighbor* would stay.

The men displayed real courage at Tel-el-Kebir, as the desperate struggle in the trenches and their heavy loss in killed abundantly prove. The black regiments, composed of negroes from the Soudan, were especially noticeable for their pluck, fighting bravely, hand to hand, with the British. More intelligence and less downright cowardice in the upper grades might have converted these men into a formidable army.

So many cases are authenticated of the virulence displayed by the Egyptian wounded, that it is demonstrated beyond question that many of these fellows not only shot at the stretchermen engaged in carrying off the injured, but in some cases actually killed the very Englishmen who had stopped to give them water or to bind their wounds.

The Egyptian guns were 8^{cm} and 9^{cm} Krupp steel B. L. R. of the old pattern (1868), all mounted on field carriages. The small-arms were of the well-known Remington make. *These showed a defect in design, breaking readily at the small of the stock.*

In the previous encounters between the British and the Egyptians, the artillery and cavalry had borne the brunt of the fighting and had carried off the honors, but the battle of Tel-el-Kebir was, as General Wolseley states, an infantry action. The tactics employed, a direct assault without flank movements of any kind, were of the simplest description. The object to get at close quarters with the enemy and crush him, was accomplished. After the attack, Arabi's army ceased to exist. In scattered groups it might be found all over Egypt, but as an organization it may be said to have been annihilated.

In view of the decisiveness of the victory, comment appears unnecessary. It may be alleged that the mode of attack adopted was hazardous to the degree of imprudence: that no commander would dare to employ such tactics on European territory; that a night march of 9 miles could only be followed by a properly disposed and immediate assault under circumstances so exceptional as to be providential. It must, however, be remembered that General Wolseley understood his enemy, knew his military habits and numbers, as well as the ground intervening, had a fairly good idea of his intrenchments, a just appreciation of his *morale*, a strong conviction as to the proper manner of engaging him, and confidence in the officers and men of his own command. What he would have done, had the enemy been of a different character, is another question, whose consideration does not come within the province of this report. It seems a sufficient answer to such criticisms as are briefly referred to above to remark that the means were adjusted to the end to be reached, and that the justification (if any be needed) of the risks incurred lies in the success which attended them, a success as rare as it was complete.

No time was lost in reaping the fruits of the morning's work. Advances were at once ordered in two directions, the one along the railway to the important railway center of Zagazig, whence a double-tracked road proceeds to Cairo via Benha and a single tracked road via Belbeis, the other along the Ismailieh or Sweet Water Canal to Cairo. Of these movements General Wolseley speaks in his report of September 16 in the following terms:

The enemy were pursued to Zagazig, 25 miles from our camp at Kassassin, by the Indian Contingent, the leading detachment of which reached that place, under Major-General Sir H. Macpherson, V. C., a little after 4 p. m., and by the Cavalry division, under General Lowe, to Belbeis, which was occupied in the evening. Major-General Lowe was ordered to push on with all possible speed to Cairo, as I was most anxious to save that city from the fate which befell Alexandria in July last.

These orders were ably carried out, General Lowe reaching the great barracks of Abbassieh, just outside of Cairo, at 4.45 p. m. on the 14th instant. The cavalry marched 65 miles in these two days. The garrison of about 10,000 men, summoned, by Lieutenant-Colonel H. Stewart, assistant adjutant-general to the Cavalry division, to surrender, laid down their arms, and our troops took possession of the citadel. A message was sent to Arabi Pasha through the prefect of the city, calling upon him to surrender forthwith, which he did unconditionally. He was accompanied by Toulba Pasha, who was also one of the leading rebels in arms against the Khedive.

The Guards, under His Royal Highness the Duke of Connaught, reached Cairo early on the 15th instant.

The result of the battle of Tel-el-Kebir has been the entire collapse of the rebellion. The only place that has not, as yet, surrendered, is Damietta, and its capture or surrender can be easily effected at our leisure.

The men of the rebel army having laid down or thrown away their arms in their flight, have now dispersed to their homes, and the country is so rapidly returning to its ordinary condition of peace that I am able to report the war to be at an end, and that the object for which this portion of Her Majesty's army was sent to Egypt has been fully accomplished.

The seizure of Zagazig was effected in the dashing manner peculiar to all the incidents of the day, and shows what may be done by a few bold men.

The squadron of the 6th Bengal Cavalry left with the Indian Contingent led the way, and when within about 5 miles of the town broke into a gallop. The horses being somewhat fatigued by the hard work of the preceding twenty hours, were not in a condition to keep together, and, as a consequence, the best got to the front and the others dropped to the rear. The advance of the squadron was, therefore, composed of Major R. M. Jennings, Lieutenant Burns-Murdock, R. E., and not above half a dozen troopers. These pushed right into the railway station where were five trains filled with soldiers, and seven locomotives. At the sight of this handful of men, the engine drivers either surrendered or ran away, except one who began opening his throttle, and was shot by Lieutenant Burns-Murdoch, while the Egyptian soldiers, hundreds in number and too demoralized to think of resistance, threw away their arms, left the cars, and ran off as rapidly as possible. By 9 p. m. the entire force under General Macpherson had reached Zagazig, not a man having fallen out by the way.

In the other direction, similar energy was displayed. The Cavalry division crossed the Sweet Water Canal at Tel-el-Kebir, and following the canal bank proceeded with all practicable speed, keeping up a running fight with Arabi's rear guard. It reached Belbeis that night and bivouacked. Making an early start the next morning (September 14), and leaving the cultivated ground a few miles south of Khankah, to strike across the desert intervening, it reached Cairo at 4.45 p. m.

The garrison of the city was divided into two parts: one, from 6,000 to 7,000 strong, at Abbasieh; the other, of from 3,000 to 4,000 men, at the citadel on a high hill within the city. The former having surrendered at once to General Drury-Lowe, the Mounted Infantry and two squadrons of the 4th Dragoon Guards were immediately sent to demand the surrender of the latter. The Egyptians here, without hesitation, submitted to a force not one-tenth of their own number. Both garrisons were merely called upon to lay down their arms and accouterments, to go to their homes and keep the peace, conditions which they accepted with cheerful promptness.

The leader of the rebellion had caught a train at Belbeis the day before and had gone to Cairo, where he quickly began preparations for the destruction of the city, drawing up an elaborate plan for a repetition of the Alexandria outrage. According to this scheme, the place was divided into a number of districts, and fire was to be simultaneously applied, on signal, to certain houses indicated.

The vigor displayed by General Drury-Lowe in this march, and his audacity in exacting the yielding of a force, securely placed in positions of immense natural and artificial strength, and many times his own in number, were attended by results of inestimable value. Arabi's plan of revenge was defeated, and Cairo saved from ruin, while he himself was lodged in prison, and the only body of his followers from whom serious harm could have been anticipated were hurrying to their villages in all possible directions, glad of a return to peaceful and congenial occupations.

With the successful issue of the attack on Tel-el-Kebir, the British Commander-in-Chief accomplished the first of his aims, the crushing of the force in armed rebellion against the Khedive. Through the agency of his lieutenant, General Drury-Lowe, the second was achieved in the salvation of Cairo from destruction.

So carefully had General Wolseley matured his plans before quitting England, that he had predicted his arrival in Cairo on September 16. Under the circumstances, an error of one day on his part may be pardoned; he entered the city with the Guards brigade, by rail, on the morning of the 15th.

The submission of the Egyptian troops in various other quarters, Kafr Dowar, Aboukir, Rosetta, Tantah, &c., followed in rapid succession. Damietta, the last fortress to hold out, was evacuated without a struggle on the approach of a British force dispatched from Alexandria, for its subjection, under Major-General Sir Evelyn Wood, on the 23d of the month, when its commander, Abdul Al, from whom resistance had been expected, gave himself up unconditionally.

The last military object of the war was now reached in the restoration of the Khedive's authority over the whole of Lower Egypt.

Steps were immediately taken to send away all the troops, except a small contingent, which it was decided to retain in the country until the government could be effectively re-established. The base was changed back again to Alexandria, various corps re-embarked for England, and the Indian Contingent started from Suez. By November 1, the force left in Egypt for the support of the Khedive was about 11,000 men under Major-General Sir Archibald Alison, K. C. B., and comprised the 2d division of the Army Corps, the 7th Dragoon Guards, 19th Hussars, batteries G.B and C.3, the 17th and 21st companies of Royal Engineers, with two battalions of infantry, the 2d Royal Irish and 2d Duke of Cornwall's Light Infantry, which, together with two batteries of garrison artillery, were to constitute the garrison of Alexandria. The brigade commanders were changed and stood as follows: 1st brigade, Major-General W. Earle, C. B., C. S. I.; 2d brigade, Major-General G. Graham, V. C., K. C. B., R. E.; Cavalry brigade, Brigadier-General W.

Arbuthnot; in command at Alexandria, Major-General G. B. Harman, C. B.

The troubles with which the Khedive had now to contend were purely political. Their solution bids fair, in point of time, to contrast strongly with that of the military difficulties so resolutely grappled by the British expeditionary force.

From the first gun of the bombardment until the occupation of Cairo but sixty-six days were consumed, the campaign proper taking twenty-five in all. The rapidity with which the blow was prepared was the outcome of England's maritime supremacy, but the force with which it was delivered was drawn from skill in plan joined to vigor, courage, and self-confidence in execution.

PART III.

MISCELLANEOUS.

XIV.

THE WORKING OF THE NAVAL TRANSPORT SERVICE.

The entire British sea transport is managed by the Royal Navy, and is presided over by a naval officer at the Admiralty, entitled the Director of Transports. The present incumbent is Admiral W. R. Mends At each principal port at home and abroad, in the colonies, is a Transport Officer, in charge of the transport operations at that point. To him all Masters of transports are directly responsible, reporting to him on arrival and every morning afterwards for instructions.

The army is represented in this connection by a Military Landing Officer, through whom the commanding military officer transacts all business relating to the sea transport of troops, animals, and material. Practically, the Army states the number or quantity of the latter to be moved and the Navy furnishes the means. The responsibility of the Navy begins at the water-line on embarking or loading, and ends at the water-line on disembarking or unloading.

A naval officer may be or may not be sent in each hired transport as Transport Officer. His duties are mainly those of superintendence, the Master not being relieved of his responsibility in any way. He examines and signs all the Master's reports, and ascertains the latitude and longitude daily by observation. It would appear as though the Transport Officer is only really needed on board of a ship commanded by a stupid or malicious Master.

The ships employed by Great Britain to convey troops and munitions of war, fall under three categories: First, private vessels, belonging to established lines, making regular trips over a fixed route, on board of which passage and freight are secured; second, Her Majesty's troopers; third, hired transports.

The steamers of the Peninsular and Oriental Steam Navigation Company were, during the campaign, the principal representatives of the first category. In addition to their usual accommodations, these steamers were obliged to provide fittings, according to the Government regulations, in proportion to the troops carried.

The vessels of the second category suffice for the ordinary needs of the army, in times of peace, in exchanging battalions, bringing home invalided soldiers, &c.

The following table is sufficiently descriptive of them:

Transport.	Displacement.	Indicated horse-power.	Capacity.			
			Officers.	Women.	Men.	Horses.
	Tons.					
Crocodile	6,211	4,180	200	90	1,097	58
Euphrates	6,211	3,900	200	90	1,097	58
Jumna	6,211	3,040	200	90	1,097	58
Malabar	6,211	4,890	200	90	1,097	58
Serapis	6,211	4,030	200	90	1,097	58
Orontes	5,920	2,570			1,097	58
Assistance	2,500	1,440			800	8
Himalaya	4,690	2,500			1,097	10
Tamar	4,050	2,500			1,097	10

The five first named are of one class, large "Indian troopers," the cost of their maintenance being at the charge of the Indian Government. The soldiers' wives live apart at the forward end of the main deck, where they are bulkheaded off. Their quarters include a spacious hospital and a wash-room, &c. The bunks here are in two tiers of galvanized-iron frames.

The accompanying series of deck plans of the Jumna (Plates 61, 62, 63, 64, 65) exhibit the internal arrangements of this type more clearly than a written description.

The entire equipment of hammocks and mess gear is maintained on board, so that the troops have everything ready on their arrival. They keep clean and in order the parts of the ship devoted to them. Twenty men go to a mess.

These steamers can make from 10 to 12 knots continuously. One peculiarity of their construction is not evident from the plans. Between the quarter-deck and forecastle a tier of rooms runs along the ship's side, but within these limits the "saloon deck" is a well. Attention is called to the pontons these ships carry. Mess-tables for the troops rest on a cleat at the side and the other end is suspended from the beam overhead.

The ships are of iron and are provided with water-tight bulkheads and ample pumps for emptying the bilge as well as for extinguishing fire. They are an integral part of the Royal Navy, and are subject to the same discipline. Their routine, however, is adapted to the peculiar service they perform.

In all cases involving the moving of any considerable number of men at a time it is upon the third category, hired transports, that the bulk of the labor must fall. A list of vessels available for this work is always kept at the Admiralty, but in case of need, as when the Egyptian expedition was resolved upon, bids are invited by advertisements. The hired transports are all iron screw vessels provided with an adequate number of water-tight compartments, and it is required that they must have made at least one long voyage. When not intended exclusively as freight ships they must be not less than 6 feet high between decks, measuring from deck to beam, and the higher the better. If it is contemplated to carry horses in the hold, the height of the latter must be 12 feet or over. The charter is based upon the gross tonnage, so much per ton per month being paid. For the campaign just ended, the prices paid varied according to circumstances, the size, nature, and condition of the ship, the amount of internal fitting needed, &c. For the imperial transports, those bringing troops out from England, the average was 20s. 8d. per ton. The Indian transports were more expensive, costing about half as much again, a fact due to the scarcity, at the time, of suitable steamers in the ports of India.

The steamer offered for hire is subjected to a rigid inspection inside and out by Naval Transport Officers, who may cause the owner to dock her at his own expense. The engines and boilers are examined by Naval Engineers. A trial trip at the dock or under way may be exacted. When accepted, the rate of hire represents the charge for her use as a ship, complete in all respects and ready for sea. She can be employed in any manner that may be ordered, to carry troops, animals, or stores, or to serve as a hospital ship. She carries a blue pendant and the blue or naval reserve ensign, with a yellow anchor in the fly. She is given a number, by which she is known and registered. The number is painted on each bow and quarter in figures 3 feet long. The British transports in the Egyptian campaign were all painted black, and carried their numbers in black on a white rectangular ground. Those which brought the Indian Contingent were lead-colored, and had their numbers painted in red figures. On each a war risk is assumed by the Government equal to her value. The owners must cut the decks for increased ventilation and hatchway accommodation where ordered, take down or rearrange cabins or bulkheads, and they have no claim for compensation for any such alteration or for any restoration at the termination of the service. All special fittings required for the particular duty on which the ship may be employed are put in at the expense of the Government. These fittings are Government property and can be altered or removed at the pleasure of the Admiralty during the charter, but all left standing at its expiration become the property of the ship-owner.

The Government furnishes all provisions, medical comforts, forage, and bedding needed for the troops and animals, or else they are provided by the owners according to a fixed scale of compensation. The owners also provide, on an established schedule, table utensils and other articles for use on troop decks, for cooking, distilling, baking, &c., tools and other articles employed about horses and mules, receiving a money allowance per man or animal of the number fitted for, and a per diem sum for the number actually carried.

Pay begins the day the fittings are completed, provided the ship is in all respects ready for sea. Should the Government elect to put up the fittings, it has the right to ten days without payment.

The Government supplies all coal, except that burned in the ship's galley for her own crew and for first and second class passengers.

The entire charge for wages, food, or other expenses of any sort for officers, crew, or other civilian persons, is borne by the owners. The latter must keep the vessel in repair and in readiness to move when desired. If through derangement of hull or machinery she is unable to sail when ordered, the owner forfeits a certain proportion of the hire.

The crew must be at least three men to every 100 tons up to 1,000 tons, and three to every 200 additional tons. They must be physically satisfactory, and may if desired be inspected by a medical officer of the navy.

The carrying capacity is determined by a competent inspector, and is based upon the following conditions:

First-class passengers (officers, &c.) have separate cabins of at least 30 superficial feet of floor; if two are in one room, then of 42 superficial feet.

Second-class passengers have such standing berths or other second-class accommodations as the ship affords. These passengers are warrant officers and their families, staff sergeants, and the like.

Third-class passengers (troops) are apportioned to the available berthing space, each hammock occupying 6 feet by 16 inches. One-fourth more than the number which can be swung in hammocks at a time may be embarked.

The number of horse-stalls that can be erected is equal to the running length of the space chosen, in inches, divided by 27, the width of each stall.

It may be fairly estimated that each man occupies 52 and each horse 126 cubic feet. Roughly speaking, each man conveyed requires from 3 to 4 tons, and each horse, from 8 to 10 tons of gross tonnage. This mode of looking at the question gives a notion of the magnitude of the task of transporting any large body of troops.

The transport is thoroughly inspected before the embarkation of the troops by a board composed of two naval officers, one military staff officer, and one military officer not under the rank of captain. The senior military medical officer of the station and the surgeon in medical charge of the troops to be embarked accompany the board and express their opinion as to the sanitary arrangements. The embarkation form is given on page 173.

After the soldiers are on board a final inspection is held before the ship puts to sea, by two naval officers, one army field officer (not belonging to the corps embarked), and one army officer not under the rank of captain. An army medical officer, not in medical charge of the troops embarked, expresses his opinion as to the sanitary arrangements.

The standard of messing for first-class passengers and the number of meals served are the same as on board first-class passenger steamers. Ale, beer, wine, and spirits are only furnished on payment. The second-class passengers have "a good, respectable table," and receive a pint of beer or ale daily. Third-class passengers (troops) have the army ration.

When more than 50 men disembark a report is made out by the military commanding officer upon the mess and other arrangements, the cleanliness of the ship, &c. This report is evidence of the way in which the contract has been discharged.

The Transport Officer furnishes the Master of the hired transport with a monthly certificate of efficiency, which forms the basis of claim for compensation. For short terms, one month's hire is paid in advance. The final account is not settled until all possible bills have been audited. The document required to obtain a first advance is the embarkation return. The balance of hire is not paid until the report by the military commanding officer has been received. The claim for allowance on the score of mess is based on the mess certificate, and in the case of troops supplied, on a similar certificate.

The following notes are relative to the fittings necessary to the conversion of a vessel into a transport:

Non-commissioned officers are allowed 20 inches hammock drift. All billets are clearly numbered and assigned. The head and foot hooks are 9 feet apart, and the hammocks overlap 18 inches at each end. When the height from deck to beam exceeds 7 feet, hammock beams are run athwartships at 6 feet 6 inches above the deck.

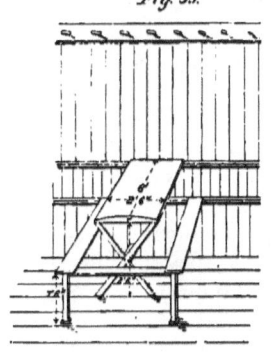

Fig. 55.

Fig. 55 shows the mess table and benches as arranged along the ship's side. A batten is run fore and aft at the side. Upon this the outboard end is placed, the inner resting on a trestle. Underneath the table is a shelf 9 inches broad.

Along the side of the troop-deck and over the mess tables a long batten is run, with pegs for clothing and accouterments, three for each man.

Arm racks of the common pattern are placed as needed. Two broad horizontal pieces are secured to a bulkhead, the upper perforated for the muzzles of the rifles, the lower scored to receive the butts.

Temporary latrines are built on deck, at the rate of 3 per cent. of the force fitted for, in covered houses 6 feet high in the clear, Fig. 56. The trough is lined with lead, and a sheet-iron soil-pipe is carried down outside of the ship. Ample water supply for flushing is insisted upon. A comfortable step, a hinged seat and a grating bottom are exacted. In addition, as many urinals, as may be deemed necessary, are built of wood lined with lead, and having a proper discharge-pipe overboard.

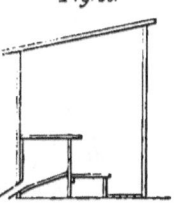

Fig. 56.

A house, usually beside the latrines, is built on deck for water-proof coats and caps, and must be large enough to contain one-third of those belonging to the troops to be embarked. The sides are fitted with pegs and the ceiling with hooks. This "coat room" is in charge of a non-commissioned officer.

The troop hospital is a proper space below, screened off by canvas. These screens can be rolled and stopped up. Standing bunks 6 feet long and 27 inches wide, in one or two tiers, as directed, are built. The frame is of wood, but the bottom of iron netting, 4-inch mesh. Inside the hospital is a dispensary with drawers or cupboards, work-table, bottle-racks, washstand, &c., all simply but solidly constructed.

The ventilation is carefully attended to, the decks being cut, and air-pipes put in where ordered. A simple plan for exhausting the foul air was fitted to the transports during this campaign. A steam jet is introduced into an iron ventilator. Tubes and wooden trunks run through, and from all the horse and troop decks, to connect with the ventilator, and are perforated where they are designed to be effective. The steam jet draws the foul air from below through the air trunks and discharges it overboard. When not in use as an aspirator, the steam being shut off, the ventilator cowl is turned to the wind, and the apparatus answers the purpose of an inspirator.

The magazine is built of two tiers of crossed deal boards, fastened with copper nails. It must be large enough to hold one hundred rounds per rifle.

Other special rooms are also built, including bread rooms, an issuing room, a helmet room, a baggage room, &c., all provided with proper locks or bolts and padlocks.

The hammocks are stowed in temporary bins built where ordered, preferably in covered houses on the upper deck.

The prison is designed for four men, is 6 feet 6 inches wide, and 12 feet 6 inches long in the clear. It is fitted with three inside removable bulkheads, so as to be divided into four separate cells. The frames are 4 inches square and 2 feet apart, well cleated, top and bottom. The ends and sides are of two layers of $\frac{3}{4}$-inch boards crossed and nailed. A 6-inch space is left at the bottom of the bulkhead and another 18 inches wide at the top, for ventilation. Iron bars $\frac{7}{8}$ inch in diameter and 3 inches apart fill up the space. Each of the four cells into which the inclosure may be divided has a bench, and a stout iron jackstay in the deck, to which violent men may be shackled.

The troop galley and bakery are always built on the upper deck. They are simply stout wooden houses of the necessary capacity. The sides and deck are lined with tin or sheet-iron. The floor is paved with tiles laid in cement. The coppers must hold three pints per man and be fitted with proper apparatus.

The fittings for the accommodation of troops are such as would naturally suggest themselves to an intelligent officer, and therefore have been rather referred to than minutely described. The horse-stalls, however, are especially the outcome of long experience.

The series of plates, 66 to 70, give the details of the present plan. The stalls are so designed that by lowering the breast rail, parting bars, and haunch rail, they may be used for pack horses and mules. To shorten up the stall an extra piece 4 inches thick is provided and fastened to the inside of the regular haunch rail. Each deck or compartment is furnished with one pump (or more if required), to bring fresh water from the hold. When not practicable to have scuppers to convey the urine overboard, it is first collected in tanks below and then pumped into the sea. One or two loose box-stalls are provided for sick horses, and 5 per cent. of the stalls are 6 inches longer and 2 inches wider than the others. But nine-tenths of the stalls are ever occupied, the other tenth being for shifting the horses. A large number of these stalls are always kept on hand, ready for use. The animals are usually hoisted on board by a steam winch, in stout slings, and are discharged in the same manner. But few of the transports had loading ports large enough to admit a horse.

It is one of the rules in all hired transports that there shall be no smoking below the spar deck. This rule is most imperative.

The discipline of the troops embarked is in the hands of the military commanding officer.

For sanitary purposes, sawdust (for use about horses particularly) MacDougall's disinfecting powder, chloride of lime, and carbolic acid are freely used. The men are only allowed below during meal hours and at night.

The Master of the transport must obey the orders of the Transport Officer on board, the Transport Officer ashore, or of the Senior Naval Officer present. Should there be no naval officer at hand he must obey the orders of the military or other Government authority.

Either the Master or the first officer must sleep on board. The crew must be exercised in lowering and getting boats out and in. In the logbook must be kept a complete record of all that relates to the troops or Government property on board. The log is inspected daily by the Transport Officer in Charge.

As in the Government service, the Master is liable to punishment for misconduct, the Senior Naval Officer at the first port touched having the power to suspend him from his duties. The Flag Officer of the station can, if necessary, remove him from his ship.

For the Master's guidance a set of instructions is furnished him which defines his duties and responsibilities very minutely, especially in regard to the expenditure of the Government stores with which he is intrusted. The rationing of the troops and animals embarked is his particular charge, and he always keeps or should keep on hand a sufficient amount of forage, provisions, bedding, &c. He is subjected to a very rigid system of accounts, quarterly and other returns. By the terms of the charter party the owners are pecuniarily responsible for any loss of or damage to the Government stores arising out of incapacity or negligence on the part of the *personnel* of the transport. He is responsible for the general good order and condition of the ship, although the troops keep clean the horse and troop decks, &c. The Master is therefore ordered to co-operate to the full extent of his power with the military commanding officer on board to secure this end. The precautions to be taken against fire are very clearly set forth in orders, and the Master held to a strict observance. These precautions are of the usual nature common to all naval vessels.

The crew of the transport and her boats are at all times available for the public service in any desired way. The men are not expected to work more than ten hours in this connection any day in port, nor to do exceptional duty on Sunday. If so exceptionally employed they receive extra compensation according to a fixed scale as shown below.

The landing of troops or stores is simple and effective. A petty officer is sent in charge with every lighter or boat load and is provided with a list of the troops, animals, or stores contained therein. This list, called the "landing note" (see page 174), is signed by the master, and is handed by the petty officer in charge of the lighter to the Military Landing Officer. A stub copy is retained on board the transport. From these stubs a report is made the following day to the Transport Officer on shore. The appended form is not in the "Regulations for Her Majesty's Transport," and the other following it is a new form substituted for the old one.

TRANSPORT NO. —, 1882. } *Application for extra pay to merchant seamen for working over time.*

Dates employed (Sundays in red ink).	No.	Rank or rating.	No. of hours.	How employed.	Amount.			Remarks.
					£	s.	d.	

Approved for payment at the undermentioned rates.

Officer in charge of working party.

Captain R. N., Prin. Tran. Officer.

Per day of 10 hours:
(1) When employed on exceptional duties away from their own ships during working hours on week days ....Petty officers, 1s. 3d. per day; others, 1s. per day.
For every extra hour beyond 10 hours:
(2) When employed on exceptional duties on working days beyond 10 hours, exclusive of meals either in their own ships or elsewhere..Petty officers, 7d. per hour; others, 5d. per hour.
For every hour thus employed on Sundays:
(3) When employed on exceptional duties on Sundays, whether in their own ships or on duties unconnected therewith ....Petty officers, 10d. per hour; others, 7d. per hour.

Admira'ty letter AG No. 11, 12½7, of 11th August, 1882.

EMBARKATION RETURN.

[Ship's name ―――.]

Return of officers, troops, or others embarked on the ―――, 18—, at ―――, for conveyance to *―――.

Regiment or corps.	†Officers, first-class passengers, and their families.			Second-class passengers and their families.			Staff sergeants and their families.			Troops, third-class passengers, and their families.			Officers' servants.		Horses.	Dogs.	On what day first messed, victualled, or foraged on board.	Remarks.
	Officers, &c.	Wives, or daughters of 16 and upwards.	Children under 16.	Men, of 16 and upwards.	Women, of 16 and upwards.	Children under 16.	Men.	Women.	Children under 17.	Men.	Women.	Children under 17.	Male (not being soldiers).	Female (not being soldiers' wives).				

Total ....

* Separate returns are to be furnished when troops, &c., are embarked for more than one port.
† The names of officers and the particulars of their families are to be inserted on the other side.

Approved, ―――, *Transport Officer.*

――――――, *Military Commanding Officer.*
――――――, *Master of the Ship.*

T. ¹⁴⁴.
G & S [908] 1000 7182

[On the reverse side.]

Nominal list of officers and their families.

Regiment or corps.	Officers.		Wives, or daughters of 16 or upwards.	Children under 16.	Servants.	
	Rank.	Name.			Male (not being soldiers).	Female (not being soldiers' wives).

LANDING NOTE—TRANSPORT NO. —.

[Number of lighter. —. Date, ——— —, 1882. Hour left ship or shore, — m. Hour cleared, — m. Name of petty officer in charge, ——— ———.

PASSENGERS OR HORSES.

Regiment or department.	Officers.	Men.	Horses.	Office column not to be filled up on board.

CARGO.

Description.	No. of packages.	To whom addressed.	Office column not to be filled up on board.

Master.

The foregoing paragraphs give a general idea of the hired transport service. Like all organizations, however perfect in theory, it depends ultimately for its successful working upon the intelligence and vigor of those to whom its administration is intrusted.

For the campaign in Egypt the entire local control of the transports was given to Captain Harry H. Rawson, R. N., with the title of "Principal Transport Officer." This officer had, four years previously, been in charge of the disembarkation of troops and stores at Cyprus, where his skill and executive ability won him commendation. Profiting by his experience, he matured his plans before leaving England, and had elaborated them so thoroughly that, as far as he was concerned, it may be said that no point was neglected and no precaution omitted which could facilitate the important duty that fell to his lot.

Foreseeing the difficulty he might have to encounter, if dependent on the naval vessels in port for assistance in the shape of men and boats, he succeeded in obtaining H. M. S. Thalia for the special needs of disembarkation. The commanding officer of this vessel, Captain J. W. Brackenbury, was, so to speak, Captain Rawson's second in command. He assumed the title and functions of "Disembarkation Officer."

The Thalia, 2,240 tons displacement, and 1,600 indicated horse-power, technically known as an "armed trooper," is an old wooden corvette with a light spar deck added. On this deck are a few 64-pdrs., with Gatlings, Nordenfeldts, and 7-pdr. and 9-pdr. boat-guns. The main deck is usually devoted to troops, of whom she can readily carry a few hundred. In this case she brought out no soldiers. She was given an abnormally large crew, 430 in number, particularly strong in mechanics of all sorts, and an extra supply of boats, one 37-foot steam-pinnace, two 25-foot steam-cutters, besides three pulling cutters and five gigs. She was subject to the immediate orders of the Principal Transport Officer. An electric light for night operations was placed on board of her.

At Ismailia, where the greater part of the work was done, Captain Rawson established his office on board the hired transport Nevada (of the Williams and Guion Line), close to the Central Wharf, maintaining communication with the Thalia, the Central Wharf, and the Military Headquarters on shore, by means of semaphore and flag signals.

Every transport that came out from England brought horse boats and "flats," so that as the troops arrived at Ismailia the means of landing them were always on hand in more than adequate quantity. In all, at this place, there were no less than 60 horse-boats and flats, and 20 open lighters of various sizes and patterns. The lighters were gotten at Malta, Alexandria, Port Said, and elsewhere, and were collected at Ismailia.

Fig. 57 represents a horse-boat. The bow may be either square or sharp. These boats could land ten animals, or two field guns with their limbers. The cross braces are hinged and pinned. The flap at the stern lowers to form a gangplank which is useful in landing vehicles as well as animals. The "flats" are square-ended lighters decked over.

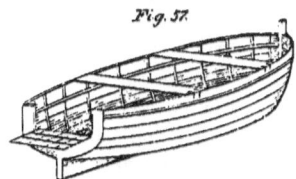

Fig. 57.

The pontoon-rafts carried by the Indian troopers (Jumna and class), to which reference has been already made, were most useful at Ismailia on account of their great capacity, each carrying as many as 35 horses at a time. Figs. 58 and 59 represent roughly these rafts as seen when put together. In the top of each pontoon are jogs for receiving four cross-pieces, which are lashed in place to ring-bolts. Upon the chesses or cross-pieces is laid a suitable platform. Each pontoon is of iron, 36 feet long and 5 feet in diameter.

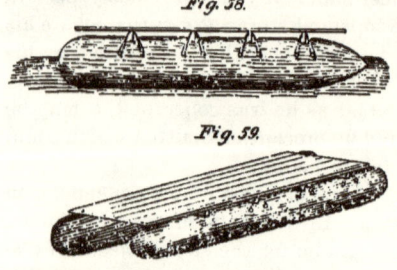

Fig. 58.

Fig. 59.

Powerful tugs, nine in number, five screw and four paddle, were bought or hired and sent to Lake Timsah.. The largest was the Storm Cock, included in the list of hired transports. The lighters were handled mainly by working parties from the Thalia, who were busy day and night. As a rule, a steam-launch was placed between two lighters. The disembarkation of the troops being conducted on both sides of the ship at once, was rapidly effected without confusion. By putting the men directly on the large tugs, and using both gangways at once, a battalion of infantry could be landed in a very short time. The two Irish regiments, the Royal Irish and the Royal Irish Fusiliers, were landed at night with their baggage in two hours, and the Highland brigade, between 3,000 and 4,000 strong, in three hours, but without baggage.

When the articles to be landed were heavy and the tugs very busy the lighters were placed alongside the transport, and after receiving the freight, the Thalia's men in charge laid out lines, and assisted by the soldiers warped themselves ashore. The artillery was chiefly landed in this way on the beach, which is of shelving sand. The other naval vessels in port aided to some extent, mainly in furnishing steam cutters and launches.

On board the Thalia the working gangs were detailed from "each part of the ship" so as to keep the men under the petty officers to whom they were accustomed. Although the labor was arduous and incessant, the men enjoyed excellent health throughout. This is attributed by Captain Brackenbury to his rule never to permit a party to begin work at any hour of the day or night without first having had at least a biscuit and a cup of hot cocoa. This beverage was ready in the galley at all times. As soon as the men returned to the ship another ration was served out.

To attend to the work ashore, a naval officer was kept at each pier, who worked in conjunction with the "Military Landing Officer." It may be remarked that wherever the army and navy came in contact during this campaign they pulled together with great harmony and effect. While this circumstance is largely due to the fact that the duties of each are *sharply and clearly defined, so that no doubt can exist as to where the province of the one begins and the other ends*, the spirit of mutual accommodation and good will which marked the relations of the two services was the ultimate cause of this satisfactory result.

The task of landing at the base at Ismailia was accomplished rapidly, without a hitch of any sort, and without damage to a man or an animal. The conditions were most favorable—smooth water, no rain, and an unvarying breeze; but to profit by these favorable conditions, energy and forethought were indispensable.

The speed and ease with which large bodies of men can be conveyed in these days of steam, render possible to a great maritime power like England the landing of an army at a great distance from home in comparatively little time. *The attack is vastly more independent now than formerly, and can select its point of debarkation without regard to contrary winds and perverse currents.* These considerations entail the necessity of efficient defense, no matter how remote the coast may be from powers that are to be dreaded, and are of especial value in connection with our own isolated but not unattackable position.

The transports which brought the British troops from England to Egypt accomplished their journey, on the average, in a little more than one-third of the time consumed by Bonaparte's flotilla in 1798 in the passage from Toulon to Alexandria over a distance less than half as great.

The details of the imperial transports are given in the accompanying table, together with the duty they performed.

948 EG——12

Details of the

Number.	Name.	Tonnage.			Nominal horse-power.	Days' coal carried.	Consumption per diem.	No. of months' charter.	Date of entry into pay.	Place or port at which to be discharged.	Owners, line, or company.
		Registered.	Engine room.	Gross.							
1	Nyanza	1,216	653	1,869	200	26	21		2 July 12	United Kingdom	Pen. & Orient.
2	Osprey	557	538	1,094	250	6	25		1 July 21	London	Gen. St. Nav. Co.
3	Calabria	2,031	1,290	3,221	220	22	27		2 July 22	United Kingdom.....	....
4	Holland	2,462	1,385	3,847	300	20	34		2 July 22	River Thames	National ....
5	Empusa	732	421	1,153	120	14	12		2 July 23	United Kingdom	Collins, London
6	Viking	1,680	902	2,588	350	25	28		2 July 25	....do	Thistle ....
7	Tower Hill	2,616	1,405	4,020	600	31	48		3 July 26	....do	Hill............
8	Pelican	1,089	897	2,585	270	22	...		2 July 25	... do	Bird ....
9	Nevada	2,355	1,261	3,616	400	12	50		2 July 24	... do............	Williams & Guion.
10	City of New York	2,286	1,245	3,521	500	20	60		2 July 24	....do............	Inman ....
11	Grecian............	2,374	1,236	3,612	400	15	41		2 July 25	....do............	Allen ....
12	Caspian...........	1,718	1,010	2,727	400	24	48		2 July 24	....do............	....do ....
13	Prussian..........	1,940	1,069	3,029	400	17	38		2 July 25	....do............	....do..........
14	Palmyra	1,382	762	2,144	212	17	27		2 July 24	....do............	Cunard ....
15	Batavia	1,628	925	2,553	450	16	30		2 July 24	....do............	....do ....
16	Greece............	3,242	1,067	4,309	400	15	30		2 July 25	....do............	National ......
17	Canadian	1,869	1,036	2,905	280	22	29		2 July 25	....do............	Allen ....
18	Montreal	2,160	1,148	3,307	375	21	40		2 July 24	....do............	....do ....
19	City of Paris.......	1,993	1,093	3,085	450	20	42		2 July 24	....do............	Inman ....
20	Orient	3,440	1,945	5,385	1,000	25	70		2 July 23	....do............	Orient ....
21	Iberia	2,982	1,689	4,670	750	30	50		2 July 24	....do............	....do ....
22	Egyptian Monarch.	2,552	1,364	3,915	500	17	44		2 July 25	....do............	Monarch ......
23	Olympus..........	1,585	830	2,415	270	20	30		2 July 26	....do............	Union ....
24	City of Lincoln	2,601	584	3,185	350	15	31		2 July 25	....do............	Thistle ....
25	Texas..............	1,839	978	2,817	350	23	30		2 July 24	....do............	Dominion .....
26	Ludgate Hill	2,702	1,460	4,162	600	40	42		3 July 20	River Thames........	Hill............
27	Whitley	736	403	1,139	120	13	9		2 July 24	United Kingdom	D. N. Shields...
28	France............	3,238	1,043	4,281	400	20	38		2 July 30	River Thames........	National ......
29	Italy..............	2,059	1,510	4,169	500	17	38		2 July 28	Liverpool Docks	....do ....
30	Tagus	1,250	658	1,912	*200	26	47		2 July 25	United Kingdom.....	Pen. & Orient..
31	Oxenholme	1,714	951	2,665	350	35	29		2 Aug. 1	....do............	....
32	Carthage	2,588	2,424	5,012	850	{15 25	a65 b39}		2 July 25	....do............	Pen. & Orient..
33	Catalonia.........	3,093	1,748	4,841	400	16	60		2 July 24	....do............	Cunard ....
34	Bolivar	1,577	487	2,064	400	42	22		2 July 28	....do............	West Indian...

a At 14 knots; *b* at 11½ to 12 knots.

Imperial Transports.

Accommodation				Troops carried			Corps	Port of embarkation	Date		Remarks	Number
Officers	W. O.	N. C. O. and men	Horses	Officers	W. O.	N. C. O. and men	Horses			Sailing	Arrival in Egypt		
..	..	..	..	..	..	..	..					Fitted as condenser.	1
..	..	..	..	..	..	..	..	Commissariat stores				12 knots	2
16	..	250	220	18	..	214	219	Household Cavalry	London	Aug. 2	Aug. 15		3
20	1	300	240	14	..	252	239	do	do	Aug. 1	Aug. 14		4
..	..	..	..	..	..	..	..	Commissariat stores					5
8	2	250	132	8	2	213	117	18th Co. Royal Engineers					6
								12th Co. Commissariat & Transport	London	Aug. 4	Aug. 18		
16	..	180	176	14	..	178	173	N. A, Royal Horse Artillery	Southampton	Aug. 4	Aug. 16	Twin screw	7
7	..	210	210	7	..	180	204	Bearer Company; 1 field hospital; 15th Co. Com. & Trans.	London	Aug. 5	Aug. 17		8
44	1	870	66	31	1	077	58	2d Brigade staff; 2d Batt. York and Lancaster.	Liverpool, Kingstown	Aug. 4, Aug. 5	} ..do		9
22	1	360	286	17	1	391	280	Part of 4th Dragoon Guards.	Southampton	Aug. 0	Aug. 21		10
7	..	200	153	0	..	196	150	N. 2, Royal Artillery	do	Aug. 9	Aug. 20		11
22	3	162	92	5	3	133	92	Signalers; detachment of 8th Co. Commissariat & Transport.	London	Aug. 11	Aug. 22		12
8	..	156	106	9	1	102	103	11th Co. Commissariat & Transport.	do	Aug. 12	Aug. 25		13
10	..	200	153	10	..	197	153	A. 1, Royal Artillery	Portsmouth	Aug. 3	Aug. 14		14
30	1	770	55	29	..	761	55	2d Batt. Grenadier Guards.	Queenstown	July 31	Aug. 12		15
25	1	250	242	18	..	226	242	Part of 4th Dragoon Guards.	Southampton	Aug. 9	Aug. 21		16
7	6	108	7	6	6	108	7	8th Company Royal Engineers; railway staff and material.	London	Aug. 9	Aug. 23		17
13	1	300	270	13	..	305	268	2 squadrons 19th Hussars.	Southampton	Aug. 10	Aug. 22		18
39	1	664	6	36	1	812	3	2d Batt. Royal Irish and 100 men 2d Bearer Company.	Portsmouth	Aug. 11	Aug. 21		19
51	1	850	110	50	1	824	103	Staffs 1st Div. & 1st Brigade Scots Guards.	London	July 30	Aug. 10		20
50	..	785	55	45	..	767	55	2d Batt. Coldstream Guards	Kingstown	Aug. 1	Aug. 12	Charter extended.	21
15	..	300	266	15	..	290	264	Part of 7th Dragoon Guards.	London	Aug. 5	Aug. 17	Charter extended 2 months.	22
10	..	170	127	6	..	170	125	C. 3, Royal Artillery	Southampton	Aug. 9	Aug. 22		23
9	..	240	163	8	..	202	150	I. 2, Royal Artillery	London	Aug. 8	Aug. 22		24
13	2	200	220	7	..	202	205	Ammunition reserve, I. 1, R A.	Portsmouth	Aug. 12	Aug. 25		25
16	..	180	176	9	..	177	175	G. Royal Horse Artillery	London	Aug. 8	Aug. 21		26
													27
30	1	800	66	30	2	774	59	2d Battalion Highland Light Infantry; staff 3d Brigade.	Portsmouth	Aug. 8	Aug. 20		28
26	..	300	274	29	1	293	266	Part of 7th Dragoon Guards.	Southampton	Aug. 7	Aug. 18		29
													30
15	..	400	152	16	..	404	152	Ponton and Telegraph Troops and field park.	London	Aug. 9	Aug. 26		31
30	5	220	..	30	2	211	..	{ 5 field hospitals; staff or Carthage as hospital ship. }	London	Aug. 10	Aug. 21		32
51	1	920	107	48	1	824	100	1st Batt. West Kent, 4th Brigade staff.	Portsmouth	Aug. 4	Aug. 15		33
17	6	300	98	6	3	300	98	12th and 15th Companies, and part of 17th Company Commissariat & Transport; 42 men of 2d Bearer Company.	Portsmouth	Aug. 11	Aug. 25		34

* Four ladies as nurses.

Details of the Imperial

Number	Name	Tonnage			Nominal horse-power	Days' coal carried	Consumption per diem	No. of months' charter	Date of entry into pay	Place or port at which to be discharged	Owners, line, or company
		Registered	Engine-room	Gross							
35	Ascalon	1,950	401	2,351	300	25	16	2	Aug. 4	United Kingdom	
36	Assyrian Monarch	2,008	1,362	3,970	500	19	43	2	July 31	....do............	Monarch......
37	Lusitania	2,425	1,407	3,832	550	20	64	2	Aug. 1	....do............	Orient......
38	Teviot	1,349	708	2,057	250	21	20	2	Aug. 1	....do............	A. Norwood, London.
39	Courland	438	803	1,240	130	30	15	2	July 27	....do............	D. Currie......
40	Arab	2,044	1,126	3,169	500	23	41	2	Aug. 4	Southampton	Union......
41	Capella			3,359	450	15	33	3	July 31	United Kingdom	Star......
42	Nepaul	1,088	1,548	3,536	600	19	50	2	Aug. 1	....do............	Pen. & Orient.
43	Marathon	1,553	850	2,403	300	17	30	3	July 28	....do............	Cunard......
44	Duke of Argyll	2,037	1,078	3,114	400	35	30	2	July 30	United Kingdom or Bombay.	Ducal......
45	Irthington	1,290	671	1,961	200	20	13	2	July 31	United Kingdom	
46	British Prince	2,548	1,425	3,973	350	28	44	3	July 31	....do............	Princes......
47	Californian	1,267	544	1,831	250	40	17	2	July 31	....do............	West Indian...
48	Storm Cock	91	238	329	250			2	July 27	....do............	
49	Recovery	255	230	484	150		11		July 28	....do............	
50	Notting Hill	2,616	1,405	4,021	600				July 28	United Kingdom or Aden, Bombay, or Calcutta.	Hill......
51	Lisbon	860	474	1,334	120		12		Aug. 2	Gibraltar	
52	Neera	1,397	770	2,167	300		25		Aug. 3	Alexandria, Malta, Portsmouth or the River Thames.	
53	Rhosina	1,774	932	2,706	250			*	June 16	Malta, Alexandria, or Port Said.	
54	Nerissa	1,299	701	2,000	260			*	June 16	Malta or United Kingdom.	
55	Maulkins Tower	1,803	947	2,750	300			*	June 16	Malta or Alexandria	
56	North Britain	1,118	611	1,729	175			*	June 21	Malta	
57	Lydian Monarch	2,546	1,370	3,915	500	30	30	2	Aug. 9	United Kingdom	Monarch......
58	Stelling	565	324	889	100	39	9	2	Aug. 7	....do............	
59	Leechmere	724	396	1,120	100	10	10	2	Aug. 7	....do............	
60	Adjutant	1,478	797	2,275	230		24	2	Aug. 11	....do............	Bird......
61	Amethyst	872	485	1,357	110		10	2	Aug. 12	....do............	
62	Dalbeattie			1,395	120		10	1	Aug. 12	Malta	
63	Osiris	1,224	655	1,879	200		16	2	Aug. 15	Alexandria	
64	Libra	557	477	1,034	250		27	2	Aug. 15	United Kingdom	
65	Kent	666	379	1,045	99	15	11	2	Aug. 16	Malta or United Kingdom.	
66	Thursby	321	176	497	71	12	7	1	Aug. 9	Gibraltar	
67	Persian Monarch										
68	Medway										
69	Tana										
70	Helen Newton										
71											
72	Magdala										
73	Ely Rice										

Transports—Continued.

Accommodation			Troops carried			Corps.	Port of embarkation.	Date		Remarks.	Number.
Officers. W. O.	N. C. O. and men.	Horses.	Officers. W. O.	N. C. O. and men.	Horses.			Sailing.	Arrival in Egypt.		
7	170	127	6	170	125	J.3, Royal Artillery	Portsmouth	Aug. 12	Aug. 25		35
18	1,300	268	18	1,281	263	2 squadrons 19th Hussars.	Southampton	Aug. 10	Aug. 22	Charter renewed.	36
39	1,870	55	29	1,659	54	1st Batt. Shropshire Regiment.	Kingstown	Aug. 10	Aug. 21		37
20	1,250	...	11	1,285	3	Ordnance stores and garrison artillery (2 batt.).	Woolwich	Aug. 15	Sept. 5	Stopped at Mal-Cyprus ta 6 days	38
13	10,100	...	12	9	91	6 2d and 7th C. & T. Cos. for Cyprus.	Woolwich	Aug. 2	Aug. 15	Hospital ship.	39
33	1,770	6	32	1,729	4	1st Batt. Roy. Irish Fusiliers.	Southampton	Aug. 8	Aug. 19	Charter renewed.	40
35	2	90	90	36	1	81 65 Headquarter and artillery staffs.	Liverpool	Aug. 5	Aug. 17		41
30	1,780	55	31	1,772	55	1st Batt. Royal Highlanders.	London	Aug. 8	Aug. 20	Charter extended.	42
13	2,200	147	13	1,211	51	½ Bearer Company; 2 field hospitals; horses of R. Irish Regiment.	Portsmouth	Aug. 8	Aug. 21		43
14	4,320	196	9	4,323	187	24th Co. Royal Engineers; part of 17th Co. C. & T.; horses of R. I. Fus.	Southampton	Aug. 8	Aug. 21		44
1	2,100	...	2	2	40	Ordnance-Store Department.	Woolwich	Aug. 19	Sept. 4		45
23	350	153	13	310	150	D.1, Royal Artillery	Portsmouth	Aug. 8	Aug. 19		46
17	200	50	6	183	37	26th Co. Royal Engineers	Southampton	Aug. 9	Aug. 23		47
										Tug	48
										Salvage tug	49
						Mules from Natal (turned back at Aden).					50
						Mules					51
						Mules					52
	1,400										53
	200										54
										Condensing ship.	55
										do	56
18	1,300	26	10	5,310	268	Parts of 8th, 11th, and 12th Cos. C. & T.	London / Portsmouth	Aug. 14 / Aug. 16	Aug. 27		57
						Ordnance-Store Dep't					58
						do					59
8	2,350	104	8	4,297	95	(3 off., 3 W. O., 143 men & 6 horses for Malta); Military police, &c.	London	Aug. 17	Aug. 30		60
						Commissariat stores					61
						do					62
						Railway material from Alexandria.					63
						Commissariat stores					64
						do					65
						do					66
											67
											68
											69
											70
											71
											72
											73

*No final period.

It may be pointed out that the embarkation of troops was carried on simultaneously at Liverpool, London, Portsmouth, Woolwich, and Southampton in England, and at Kingstown and Queenstown in Ireland. The first body of troops to sail from England in the hired transport fleet was the Scots Guards in the Orient, and the last of the fighting line, J battery, 3rd brigade, Royal Artillery, followed two weeks later.

The gross tonnage of the fleet was thus distributed:

Troops, &c.	Number of ships.	Tonnage.
Cavalry	8	30,269
Artillery	10	30,736
Infantry	10	38,968
Royal Engineers	*5	10,252
Ordnance-store Department	3	3,971
Commissariat and Transpor	19	31,276
Army Hospital Corps	†1	....
Hospital ships	2	7,615
Miscellaneous	11	....

* Two were shared with the Commissariat and Transport Corps.
† Shared with the Commissariat and Transport Corps.

XV.

THE ARMED TRAINS.

Two armed railway trains were employed during the late campaign in Egypt, one at Alexandria and the other on the Ismailia and Tel-el-Kebir Line. Both were rigged and operated by seamen from the British fleet. The former has been described by Lieutenant Barnes of the U. S. S. Nipsic in a report already made public. The accuracy of this report is sufficient excuse for quoting it at length. Plates 71 and 72 give general views of the train.

U. S. S. NIPSIC (THIRD RATE),
Alexandria, Egypt, September 8, 1882.

SIR: I have the honor to report that I have visited and examined the armored train used by the English forces in their operations against the Egyptian insurgents under Arabi Pasha. I found Lieutenant Poor, R. N., of H. M. S. Inconstant, in charge, who kindly pointed out and explained to me its details and the mode of operation.

Its components vary somewhat at different times, according to the force it carries, but may be regarded as consisting of six different parts, as follows:

First. One or more vacant platform cars, intended to feel the way and give notice of any obstructions upon the track before they are reached by the more important parts of the train, or to take the shock of torpedoes.

Second. A platform car carrying one gun, a 40-pdr. Armstrong of old pattern, so arranged as to admit of training about four points upon either side. It rests upon a solid platform of wood 4 inches thick, in which is fitted a pivot which holds the slide, and with a breeching hitched to a bolt on each side of the car checks the recoil. This car is unarmored, except at the front end, where, inside the wooden end wall, is an iron plate $\frac{3}{16}$ of an inch in thickness, inclosing on three sides a wooden box 3 feet in thickness, and as high as will permit the free working of the gun, the box being filled with bags of sand and a few others hanging from the plates on the sides. At the rear end of the car is a wooden wall some 3 feet high, on which are hung the implements for serving the gun. On the floor near by are carried a few rounds of ammunition.

Third. The locomotive. This is protected on each side by three bars of railroad iron hung with wire partly covering the boiler, and an inch plate of iron about 2 feet by 4 covering the cylinder, the piston rod and its connections. The caboose is protected by iron plates $\frac{3}{16}$ of an inch in thickness, backed with bags of sand. Although the most vital, this is the weakest part of the train. A large part of the boiler and considerable machinery are exposed, but can hardly be better protected, as the springs will hardly sustain any additional weight. Its armor is the heaviest, but it is not complete. I think lighter armor more completely shielding the locomotive would be preferable, for the train can hardly expect to withstand even the fire of field guns unless at long range, and the rest of the train is designed to be proof only against musketry.

Fourth. A platform car protected on all sides by a movable wooden wall 2 inches thick, backed with iron plates $\frac{3}{16}$ of an inch thick, and sand-bags, the sides of a height convenient for firing over by men kneeling upon the lower tier of sand-bags. Around the walls hang a supply of intrenching tools, such as picks and shovels, and at one end lies a pile of a dozen stretchers. On each side outside is lashed a small spar, a handspike, and several looms of oars or similar small pieces of wood, with short pieces lashed across their ends. These are designed for carrying the gun in case of need. By lashing one of the spars on top of the gun and crossing the other pieces under it, the latter with the short pieces at their ends, will permit fifty men to get a good hold without crowding. This car is intended to carry a force armed with rifles.

Fifth. A car similar to the one just described and protected in the same way, armed with a Gatling in front and a Nordenfeldt in rear, between which is carried a supply of ammunition—5,000 rounds for the former and 12,000 for the latter. This car also carries intrenching tools.

Sixth. A platform car protected in the same way as the last two, carrying two 9-pdr. R. H. with a small supply of ammunition. They are intended principally for service off the train, and heavy skids are carried for convenience in putting them off or taking them on the car.

At times another car is carried protected like the rest, except that the rear wall is higher and has a port where a Gatling is mounted.

A number of drag ropes are carried so that in case of any accident disabling the locomotive the men may man them on the side away from the enemy and thus draw the train while retreating.

One of the cars usually carries a tripod of small spars surmounted by a platform, forming a lookout elevated 20 feet above the train, which commands a good view of the country and makes it difficult for the enemy to conceal his men behind small irregularities of the ground.

A second train closely follows the first as a supply and relief train.

The front end of its advance car carries a steam derrick intended for use in clearing away wrecks. If a car of the fighting train should be demolished by the enemy's fire, or from any cause, the relief train would draw away the cars in rear of it to the nearest switch (and there is one near the point of operations), then return, and, with the derrick, dump the wreck clear of the track, after which it would draw away the rest of the train.

This train carries tools and materials for repairing the track or even laying a new one should it be cut or torn up in their rear; also gun-cotton, torpedoes, and an electric battery and wires for destroying by explosives whatever it may be advisable thus to get out of the way.

A most interesting and elaborate feature of the supply train is a magazine car—a platform car protected by wooden walls and iron plates like those in the fighting train. The magazine is in front and further protected by a solid wooden backing of 12 inches on all sides, except in rear, where it is open. Leaving a space high enough for a powder tank it is covered with a half-inch iron plate, bars of railroad iron laid close together, and above all bags of sand. The rear half of the car is divided by pieces of plank laid across into compartments, in which are stowed shell, shrapnel, and canister for both 40-pdr. and the 9-pdrs. The ammunition is carried by hand from the magazine car to the fighting train, the men running along the railroad under the shelter of its embankment.

The supply train also carries a few passenger cars, used as quarters for officers and men, and two box cars for their cooking and messing arrangements; but they are never taken beyond the junction near the English lines, at Ramleh.

At present these trains pass the day at the freight depot in this city but at 8 p. m. go out, pass the night reconnoitering between the English and Egyptian lines, and at 6 a. m. return to the city.

For a time it was claimed that the armored train did excellent work, but I cannot learn that it was used except as auxiliary to reconnoitering parties. I do not regard it as of much military value, for its operations are limited to one track, and it can be easily avoided or successfully opposed by heavy guns mounted near the track. Arabi Pasha has adopted the latter means, and with his 7-inch rifles has made it dangerous for the train to approach nearer than 6,000 yards to his fortifications, which is about the distance of the English lines. The train is armored only sufficiently to withstand rifle fire, nor can it well be protected against the fire of any guns as heavy as it carries. As Arabi's guns are effective at 6,000 yards, and the heaviest in the train at not more than 3,500, it is obvious that at present it is of little use, but it is intended to increase its efficiency by mounting upon it a 9-inch rifle.

It was at first intended to advance to the attack supported by a skirmish line, but that plan has been abandoned, and the force, originally two hundred men, is now reduced to fifty. Its first use was attended with considerable fighting, and it went through one prolonged engagement, but its operations are now limited to an occasional shot with its heaviest gun, which accomplishes little. The train has been manned and operated entirely by blue-jackets from the English fleet.

I am, sir, very respectfully, your obedient servant,

N. H. BARNES,
Lieutenant, United States Navy.

To Commander H. B. SEELY, U. S. N.,
Commanding U. S. S. Nipsic.

The "7-inch rifles" spoken of in the foregoing were, in reality, the 15^{cm} Krupp so frequently referred to in the paragraphs relating to the operations about Alexandria.

The first trip of the train took place on the of July 27. It was composed as shown in the following diagram:

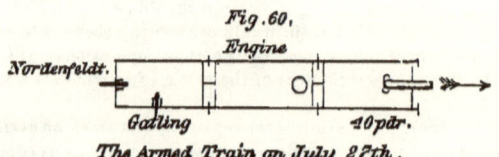

The Armed Train on July 27th.

So satisfactory were the results of the trip and so promising was this mode of warfare, that on the next day the train was made up on a larger scale, as shown below.

In the gun-truck were rails and pot sleepers for repairing the line where necessary.

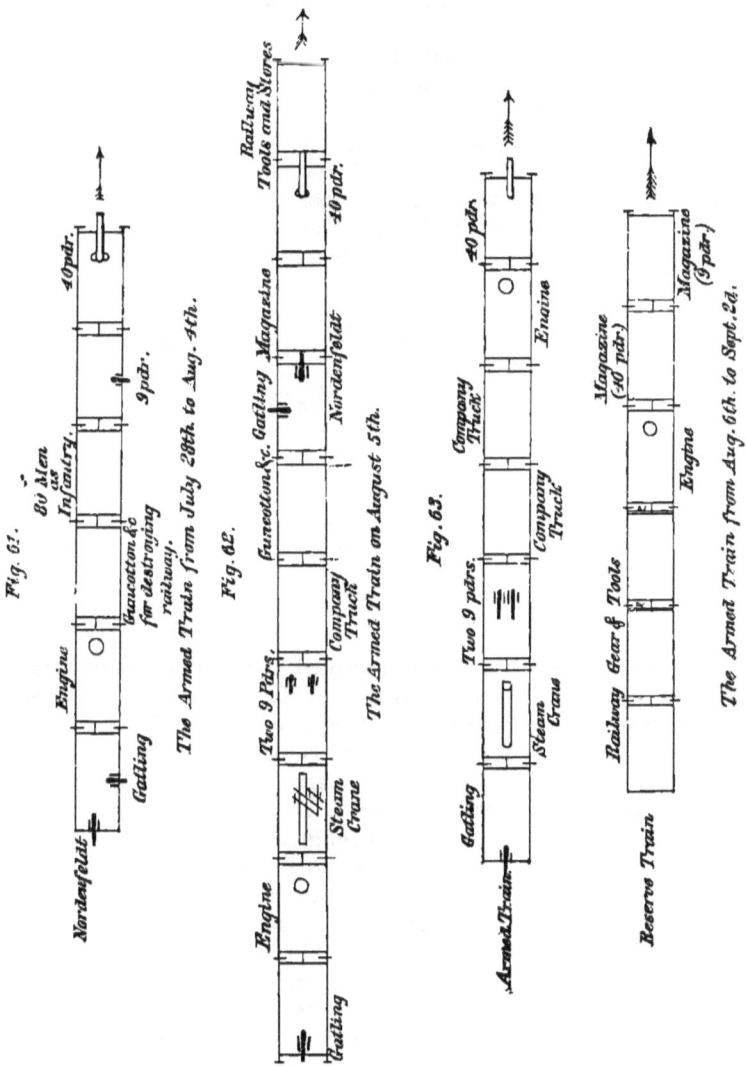

Even this extension seemed inadequate, and, on August 4 the train was composed of no less than nine trucks besides the locomotive, and was arranged as seen in Fig. 62.

The train as thus formed took part in the reconnaissance in force of that day, described on page 166.

The cars in front of the steam crane were pushed forward and uncoupled, the locomotive then backing down out of range, with the balance of the train. General Alison bears witness to the excellent practice of the 40-pdrs. thus mounted on that occasion.

The armed train, which had reached the unwieldy development of a movable citadel, was after this divided into two parts—a fighting line and a reserve, so to speak. The composition of these parts is shown in the accompanying diagram.

The reserve train was to be kept out of range. In this shape the train did service during the remainder of the month of August. On September 3 it was definitely devoted to outpost duty, as described by Lieutenant Barnes, the reserve train being left at Gabarri. The working train after this date was made up as shown in Fig. 64.

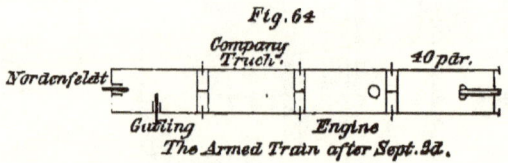

Fig. 64

The Armed Train after Sept. 3d.

The *personnel* was distributed as follows:

	Men
To the 40-pdr	12
To the Gatling	4
To the Nordenfeldt	4
To the Infantry Company	40
Total fighting men	60

This last development may be accepted as the result of five weeks' experience, and as indicating what those in charge thought the best composition for patrol and outpost work over a short line and from a fixed base. To put Lieutenant Barnes' verdict in another form, *it may be fairly stated that the sphere of real usefulness of such an armed train lies without the limit of effective range of the enemy's guns.* For serious attack, therefore, it must mount pieces of greater range than the enemy's, while it will rarely enjoy such freedom from mines and malicious tampering with the rails as characterized the operations at Alexandria.

The detachment lived in comparative luxury, being quartered in first-class railway carriages on the dock at Gabarri. The rations were supplied by the army commissariat. The health of officers and men was fair. At the outset the drinking water was taken from the same well as that which furnished the locomotive, but as its use was followed by attacks of diarrhœa and dysentery, recourse was had to distilled water. Each man had his blanket and a shift of clothes, both blue and white. The arms were rifles and cutlasses.

The value of this train was impaired by the superior range and power of the Krupp gun which the Egyptians mounted, after a short while, in the King Osman lines. Its gunners succeeded in obtaining great accuracy of practice and in frequently placing its 84-pound shell in dangerous proximity to the armed train.

The 9-inch 12-ton M. L. R. which Lieutenant Barnes speaks of as about to be mounted on a railway truck and used against the Krupp just mentioned, was only ready for service the day after the battle of Tel-el-Kebir. A few experiments were made, first with 15 pounds of powder and no shot, then with 30 pounds of powder and a common shell weighing 230 pounds, and, lastly, with 50 pounds of powder and a 255-pound chilled shell. The truck was left free on the rails, the recoil of the gun being thus converted into retrograde motion of the truck. The results of these trials were considered to be satisfactory. It is, however, open to grave doubt, whether so heavy a gun could be permanently or even frequently used on an ordinary line and on a car not specially constructed to carry so great a weight and to resist so violent a shock.

The other armed train employed in Egypt was prepared and manned from H. M. S. Penelope.

Upon a four-wheeled open truck a platform was laid of 3-inch planks fore and aft. These planks were bolted through the floor of the truck. On the sides of the truck were placed half-inch steel plates, riveted to the angle-iron frame of the truck. These plates being 6 feet long by 3 wide and standing on their edges formed a low breastwork that was

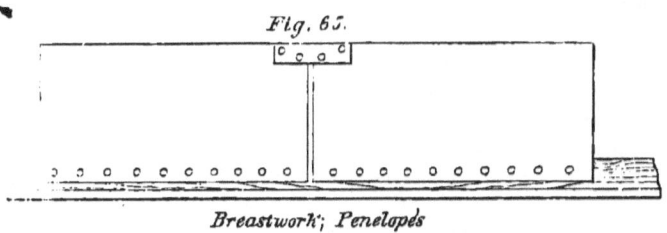

Breastwork; Penelope's Train.

fairly bullet proof. The top edges of these plates were connected by small lap plates, 6 by 3 inches, bolted with half-inch bolts.

Outside of all were awning stanchions bolted to the side of the truck. An awning was fitted to the cars, and from the ridge-rope were suspended the belts of the gun's crew. Sandbags were hung around the car outside of the steel plates.

A breast-piece was built up at the front end of the truck of timber, 8 inches square, and was secured firmly to the bottom frame by five 2½-inch stay-bolts, as seen in the accompanying sketch, Fig. 66.

Breast piece, Armed Train.

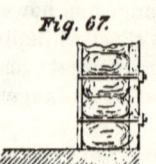

Fig. 67.

Magazine

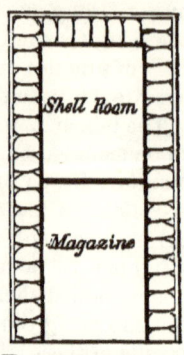

Fig. 68.

Plan of Ammunition Car. Penelope's Armed Train.

The magazine was built in an open box-car. Just within the wooden sides of the car was stacked a tier of sand-bags, extending around the front and sides. Figs. 67 and 68. Inside the sand-bags were thin steel plates, held in place by long bolts passing between the bags and through the side of the car. The space inclosed within was divided by a transverse steel plate into two compartments, the forward one for shells, the rear for charges. The roof was of loose boards, on which were laid, first, ⅜-inch iron plates, and then sand-bags. The entrances to the magazine and shell room were openings in the roof.

The provisions for the men were carried in the gun truck, and the tents, three in number, were slung underneath.

The detachment was composed of twenty-four men in all, equipped with rifle and sword-bayonet and carrying 60 rounds of ammunition. A gunner's mate and an armorer were in the party. The 40-pdr. ammunition consisted of 230 rounds, mostly shrapnel.

In action the gun, having reached its position, was left alone, and the magazine truck run 50 or 60 yards to the rear. The supply of ammunition was maintained by hand.

The first start of the armed train was made on August 26, when it was dragged from Ismailia to Nefiche by sixteen horses, four abreast. A few days later, it returned to Ismailia for certain repairs and improvements.

On September 1 it went to Kassassin. The part it took in the action of September 9 is described in a verbal account by Sub-Lieutenant Erskine, R. N., upon whom the command devolved after the wounding of Lieutenant Purvis.

When the infantry was called out under arms, trains were clearly seen coming up from Tel-el-Kebir to within 5,000 yards, where they discharged their cargoes of troops and retired. The 40-pdr. opened on the artillery posted on the enemy's right, engaging at about 4,000 yards, but not firing often for fear of *inflicting damage on the British infantry in front through the stripping of the shell, a not infrequent occurrence.* The Egyptian fire was very hot, their shell falling all about the camp and among the troops. Early in the engagement, Lieutenant Purvis was wounded, losing his left foot.

The enemy's advance being checked and his retirement begun, the 40-pdr. was pushed forward by hand to keep within range. Parts of the train were hit several times. One shell burst under a truck which had been placed in front of the gun to explode any mine which might have been laid under the rails, and a second burst near the magazine.

No real damage was sustained. Having succeeded in securing a pair of horses, Sub-Lieutenant Erskine chased the Egyptians upwards of two miles.

The 40-pdr. expended about 40 rounds in all, and did good execution. The moral effect of its comparatively large projectiles was, perhaps, of even more influence than its practice. The lack of an engine prevented easy change of position, and the fire was embarrassed by the presence of another gun, the captured 8^{cm} Krupp, worked by the Royal Marine Artillery, immediately ahead of it on the rails.

This was the only engagement in which the Ismailia armed train took part. It shared in the advance on Tel-el-Kebir, where it was not fired. It went on to Zagazig, Benha, and to Tantah, when that town surrendered to General Alison and the Highlanders. It finally returned to Ismailia for re-embarkation on September 23.

At no time during the four weeks spent on shore was the detachment without ample supplies of all kinds. Its sanitary condition was excellent. The men were always in good spirits and looked upon the unusual service which they were called upon to perform as partaking of the nature of a pic-nic. They expressed themselves to the writer as anxious to prolong their stay with the army. They had managed to make themselves very comfortable in their train, and even to provide themselves with certain luxuries occasionally. Their cheerfulness and well-being were but another example of the general rule of the war—everywhere the seamen operating on shore were well sheltered, well fed, and glad to remain on duty with the land forces.

The value of a gun permanently mounted on a railway carriage depends mainly upon its *size*. On the one hand, *it must be heavier than the ordinary field piece*, to justify the sacrifice of mobility entailed, and, on the other hand, a limit to its weight is reached when it becomes impossible to give the gun the maximum train its mounting permits without incurring an imprudent risk. It is doubtful whether guns weighing more than *four or five tons* can be advantageously employed in this manner. *It finds its most favorable use in defending a long stretch of straight road, near or along which the enemy must advance*, attacking with infantry and field pieces. These conditions were fulfilled at Kassassin, where the armed train did its best work. *Against a flank attack such a gun is powerless*, and hence is not adapted to independent operations on any scale.

XVI.

THE BOAT TRANSPORT IN THE SWEET WATER CANAL.

The selection of the line of the railway from Ismailia to Zagazig along the Fresh Water Canal for the advance, secured to the British expeditionary force in Egypt the additional advantage of water transport between the base and the front. The importance of this particular transportation is shown by the fact that it was the first established.

On of August 21, the day after the seizure of Ismailia, Major-General Graham was at Nefiche with the advance. To retain possession of the railway junction and canal lock at that point was a military necessity, unless the campaign was to be conducted on the defensive. Graham had to be supported both by reinforcements and material. To get the latter to him was no easy matter, for the railway was broken down and wheeled transport absolutely useless. There remained only the Sweet Water Canal as an available channel.

Admiral Seymour, who had come around from Alexandria in the Helicon to Lake Timsah, when addressed on the subject, at once, as was to have been expected, put the thing on a permanent footing. The service was inaugurated that afternoon, when two steam pinnaces and two cutters, from H. M. S. Orion, entered the canal through the locks at Ismailia (Plate 48) and took provisions to Nefiche. Returning at once to Ismailia, their trips were then continued day and night, as rapidly as possible, for the next seventy-two hours, following up the army in its march to Magfar. Here was encountered an obstacle of the most serious nature, a dam across the canal, which effectually stopped for the moment all further progress by boat to the westward. It had been constructed with the hope of cutting off this practically sole supply of water from the attacking force. There were distillers on board all the steamers in the harbor, which could be employed as a last resource, but to burden the feeble transport service with the maintenance of the water ration, would have insured perhaps not the failure, but at least the inordinate prolonging of the campaign.

The dam at El Magfar gave immense trouble, for it was skillfully built of crossed layers of rushes packed in with mud. It is but scant justice to say of the Egyptians that if they thoroughly understand construction in any material, that material is mud. Vain efforts were made to blow it up. It had finally to be picked to pieces and removed by handfuls. Even when destroyed as a dam, parts of it still remained as a bar and gave much subsequent trouble.

The boat transport had developed into a definite service under Commander A. W. Moore, R. N., the second in command of the Orion. As assistants, he had one lieutenant at Ismailia, and a second at the front, wherever that might chance to be. A naval engineer was stationed at each end of the route to inspect the machinery of all boats propelled by steam, and at Ismailia a small repair shop was established with a working equipment of tools, material, and artificers.

In addition to the boats' crews, Commander Moore had a working party of 30 men from the Orion and Penelope, divided between the stations as finally fixed at Kassassin, Tel-el-Mahuta, El Magfar, and Ismailia, at each of which tents were pitched and a camp routine initiated. These tents were drawn from the army, were six in all, four Bell and two Indian.

The boats employed varied in number, size, and kind. The water in the canal grew steadily shallower, the supply above being shut off by the Egyptians, who were able to control its flow past the lock at Abou Hamed beyond Tel-el-Kebir, the leakage into the British lines through the dams at Tel-el-Kebir not being sufficient to replace the loss by leakage into Lake Timsah, by actual consumption, and by evaporation. Nothing could have been better than a canal transport service if at all permanent or certain, but the decreasing depth of water caused the service to change from day to day, as the heavier boats were gradually withdrawn.

The original force was augmented, on August 25 and afterwards, by the purchase of twelve native boats of different sizes. Their capacities ranged from 3 to 10 tons. The rough sketch, Fig. 69, will suffice to give

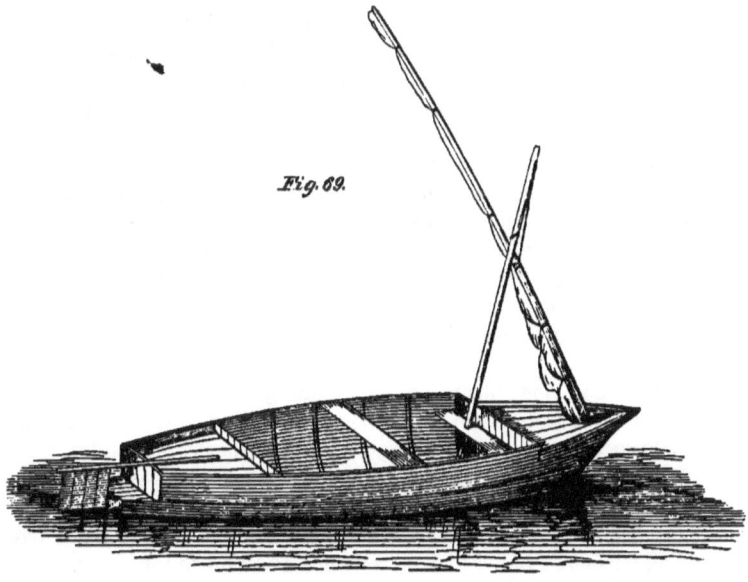

Fig. 69.

an idea of their general build and appearance. They were deficient in thwart-ship bracing, and would open out when heavily laden. The larger ones could not be loaded to their full capacity on account of lack of water.

Six horse-boats belonging to the naval transport service, and all the steam launches which the fleet could spare, were also admitted into the canal. The latter boats comprised six steam pinnaces, each from 35 to 37 feet long, and a 42-foot picket-boat from the Alexandra, which, however, drew too much water to be of any use. These were employed to tow the other boats, lighters, &c., and were in charge of sub-lieutenants or other junior officers.

The larger steamers drew 39 inches of water and the smaller 33. Commander Moore asked for a minimum depth of 42 inches throughout, after the lock at Kassassin had passed into the possession of the advance. The reach of the canal above this lock was tolerably well filled to the depth of 5 feet 6 inches. It was not, however, deemed prudent to draw upon this supply of water, so greatly needed at the front, by allowing enough of it to flow into the Kassassin-Ismailia reach to secure the depth Commander Moore desired.

The first two steam pinnaces had been thoroughly equipped for contingent action with the enemy, one carrying a Nordenfeldt, with its musketry shield, the other a Gatling gun. The subsequent necessity of reducing the draught as much as possible caused Commander Moore to remove this armament as well as such other weights as could be dispensed with from all the boats in his little fleet.

The crews were composed of one coxswain, two seamen, two leading stokers or artificers, and two stokers. The coxswain was armed with a revolver, the rest with rifles. Each man carried 60 rounds of ammunition. The kits consisted of one spare suit of blue, a blanket, a water-bottle, haversack, and the usual pot, pannikin, &c.

There were many drawbacks and hitches, owing for the most part to insufficient water in the canal, but no serious injury or avoidable interruption of the traffic. Among the petty sources of inconvenience and discomfort was the frequent fouling of the screws by clothing and other articles which had been thrown into the canal. Near Mahsameh the bed of the canal seemed to be quite covered with rush bags, doubtless used for conveying earth and sand in the construction of trenches, dams, &c. It was no unusual experience to have the screws fouled by these baskets as often as a dozen times in a mile. Again, the shallowness of the water prevented the attainment of satisfactory speed, while the fine mud it contained clogged up the boilers and gave great trouble.

A special advantage enjoyed by the men engaged in this service was the catching of fish, particularly an excellent species of mullet, from 5 to 6 pounds in weight, which abounds in the Sweet Water Canal. Large numbers of these mullet jumped into the boats while under way, being frightened by the noise of the screw. It was rarely that a trip was made without a catch and its welcome addition to the ration.

The night work between the army posts was conducted with extreme caution, as the Bedouins might easily have made a raid upon a tow while outside of the defended points of the canal, and have inflicted severe damage. In this respect the newer type of boats was preferable, being comparatively noiseless, while the older made a noise which could be heard miles away.*

Commander Moore established a species of headquarters at El Magfar, where he kept a full stock of rations for his men. Three days' supplies were drawn at a time from the Orion and taken for issue to this place

The crews of these boats, with but few exceptions, were unchanged throughout the operations, yet this work was severe in the extreme, while life was rendered almost intolerable by the swarms of flies during the day and the mosquitoes at night. To do justi e to these pests requires a fund of objurgation not at the command of the average mortal. Of the men sent back to the ship all were on account of sickness, four of the number being disabled by mosquito bites.

Each boat carried a light in the bow, which was effectually screened from observation from the land by the high canal banks on either hand.

Until September 2 the larger boats did the towing up to El Magfar, the smaller ones beyond. Practically the actual towing never extended past Tel-el-Mahuta, on account of the lack of water in the upper part of the reach. From Tel-el-Mahuta to Kassassin the lighters and cargo boats were hauled by mules or horses.

It was on this section that Commander Moore's service was supplemented by the Royal Engineers with their pontoons and special rafts, freight being shifted to them at Tel-el-Mahuta when necessary.

A second dam was found at Tel-el-Mahuta, larger but less carefully constructed than that at El Magfar.

The continued lowering of water in the canal rendered useless the heavy native boats and the lighters, the former requiring 3 feet of water to carry a paying load. It had now come to a point when every inch lost was of vast importance. As a substitute for the heavier craft, Commander Moore obtained eight ship's pulling-boats belonging to the hired transports in Lake Timsah. Being of lighter draught and carrying small loads, these boats were handier than the lighters and more easily gotten afloat after grounding. Their employment began on September 5. By exercising great care they could be worked to within a mile of the cavalry camp near Kassassin.

Between Ismailia and Kassassin the water shoals 3 feet and 4 inches. Thus, on August 28 there was a depth of 5 feet 2 inches at the former, and on September 2 but 4 feet 8 inches, with corresponding depths of 1 foot 10 inches and 1 foot 6 inches at the latter place. The average depth between Kassassin and Tel-el-Mahuta was 2 feet 4 inches, and below Tel-el-Mahuta 3 feet 4 inches. This loss of 6 inches threw out the heavier boats, as before mentioned, and materially reduced the traffic. Before then from 60 to 70 tons of supplies went daily by the canal, and the boats in returning brought back sick and wounded, for whom this mode of transit was especially desirable.

---

*The old engines were similar to those used in our service.

By September 6 there had been sent by the canal from Ismailia to Tel-el-Mahuta 550 tons of provisions. The boat service then stood as follows: Steam launch and pinnace of the Orient; steam pinnaces of the Orion, Falcon, Carysfort, Thalia, and Euphrates. Three large boats were thrown out of use by the lack of water.

With this diminished fleet, aided by the pontoons of the Royal Engineers, the work was urged ahead, in the feeling that the more done the quicker ended. The result reached may be gauged by the fact of the delivery at Kassassin of 48 tons of stores on September 7 and 45 tons on September 8—a great falling off from the original 60 to 70 tons daily, but still yielding an addition of supplies to the reserve depot well worth the trouble and vexation incurred. In this way the canal service was maintained, the army co-operating with the navy until the march on Tel-el-Kebir.

On September 10 Commander Moore began to prepare some of his boats for the special transportation of the wounded from the field of the impending battle.

Water transport for men suffering either from painful wounds or diseases involving local inflammations or ulcerated tissues is far preferable, there being no noise or jolting; on the contrary, steady, absolute motion, with relative rest. It was presumed that the losses in the next encounter with the Egyptians would be heavy, and it was determined that there should be no ground for complaint as to the treatment of the wounded in particular or any branch of the army medical department in general. In consequence the arrangements were on a liberal scale and the details carefully worked out.

The boats selected for the purpose were two horse and seven ship's boats, ordinary clinker-built cutters, belonging to the hired-transport fleet. These were taken through the lock at Kassassin into the upper reach of the canal, where they were fitted. Pine boards 1 inch thick and 12 inches wide were laid fore and aft upon the thwarts, to form an even platform the whole length of the boat. Upon this platform a thick bedding of loose hay was spread. Awnings were rigged and awning curtains were gotten up. Each boat was provided with two breakers of water and tin cups, and had a blue-jacket to steer it. A nurse was detailed for the care of the wounded.

On September 13 the boats were divided into four sections, three of two boats each and one of three boats, each section being an independent tow, with a naval lieutenant in charge of every two sections. The tracking was done by sixteen mules, accompanied by the necessary drivers. The boats followed in rear of the Indian Contingent, laden with the appliances for the establishment of field stations for the temporary dressing of wounds. The latter were located on the canal bank near the Egyptian intrenchments. The work began at 9 a. m. From the dressing stations the wounded were put into the boats. As soon as a section was filled it was sent off to Kassassin, to deliver the patients to the general field hospital. These disposed of, the section would return as rapidly as possible to Tel-el-Kebir for another load.

At first it might appear that nine boats were insufficient for the work, but it must be remembered that each case had to be examined and the wound bound before the sufferer could be safely transported over even so slight a distance as that which intervened between Tel-el-Kebir and Kassassin. Owing to this circumstance, and to Commander Moore's organization and superintendence, the provision proved ample. Deputy Surgeon-General Marston, who had charge of the work at the dressing station, states that "the transport down the canal was excellent."

The lightest cases were, as a rule, most quickly disposed of, the more serious needing longer time and greater attention; and in the first trips of the boats the majority of the wounded conveyed were but slightly hurt. The two horse-boats alone took down no less than fifty-seven. After this the number in each boat was decreased to about nine severe and six mild cases.

Two trips were made by each section during the day of the battle at Tel-el-Kebir. Commander Moore says that upwards of 200 men were brought down to Kassassin. The last embarked at 9 p. m., twelve hours after the beginning of the work. The embarking and landing of these sufferers was very distressing, the steep muddy banks of the canal rendering the operation most painful in spite of every care.

The military events of this day, resulting in the completion of the campaign and the distribution of the British troops over new lines, rendered the breaking up of all stations in the desert possible and desirable. The emptying of the field hospital at Kassassin was therefore immediately begun. During the two days following, Commander Moore's fleet was employed in removing the wounded from Kassassin. The serious cases, for whom water transport was so essential, were all moved in this way. The boats were passed through the Ismailia locks into Lake Timsah and taken alongside the hospital ship Carthage without change. Twenty-six cases on September 14 and twenty on the 15th profited by this comfortable mode of conveyance.

The water had not yet come down from above to raise the level in the canal. There were still but 14 inches at Kassassin. To obtain a start at this point, when everything was in readiness, the lock-gates were slightly opened, giving a rush of the water into the lower reach, which carried the boats into deeper water, where the animals could tow them to Mahuta. At Mahuta the steam launches were in waiting to take them to Ismailia.

This sad labor completed, the canal service, no longer embarrassed by deficiency of water, was continued for the purpose of aiding in clearing out the stations between Ismailia and Tel-el-Kebir, the two points at which the stores hitherto spread over the line across the desert were now being collected. This object was accomplished on September 22, when the men and boats were returned to their respective ships.

The Sweet Water Canal Service commanded the sympathy of those who were in a position to watch its hard and successful struggle against disheartening circumstances. It received the commendation of those in authority for having achieved all that was humanly possible at a time when *comparatively small achievements were of great value.*

XVII.

THE NAVAL BRIGADE AT TEL-EL-KEBIR.

The equipment of men landed from British ships of war for military operations is not a matter of individual taste or caprice, but is uniform and efficient. As a consequence it is possible to assemble squads, companies, or guns' crews from a number of vessels, meeting for even the first time, into a homogeneous military organization which is not open to criticism as a laughable combination of heterogeneous elements.

The dress is always understood to be blue, unless otherwise directed. The white cap-cover is fitted behind, in warm climates, with a havelock or cape falling upon the shoulders and extending to the temple on each side. The men themselves prefer the straw hat, as lighter and cooler and *affording shade to the eyes.* In Egypt, after the occupation of Alexandria, this was the head dress habitually worn.

To carry his kit each man uses his blanket, which is made into a long roll of uniform pattern, containing shifts of clothes (as ordered), soap, towel, &c., and is carried with the bight over the left shoulder, the ends meeting under the right arm. The leggins *are provided by Government.* They are represented in Figs. 70, 71, and 72. They are of stout tanned

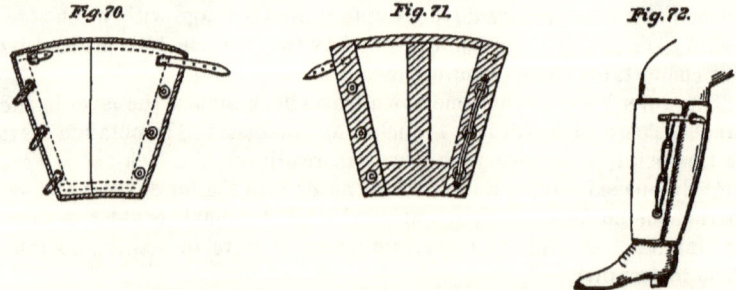

canvas, bound with leather, and are strong and serviceable. The shaded parts are of leather. The holes for the loops are guarded by brass eyelets. The loops slip each over the one next above, the topmost being passed over the retaining strap, which is buckled.

The belt is of uncolored leather, and well designed for work. The workmanship is an honest specimen of the saddler's art. The metal parts are of brass. It may be best described as a waist-belt supported by straps which go over the shoulder and cross behind. Figs. 73 and 74 give front and rear views of the belt in use. It appears at first

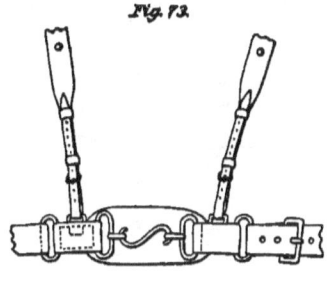
Fig. 73.

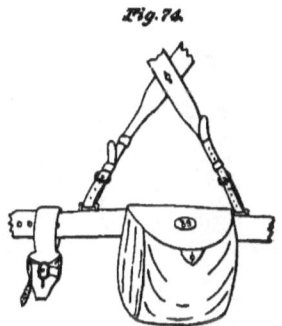
Fig. 74.

sight to have an enormous number of buckles, but these serve the purpose of adjustment in all directions, so that when once fitted the man may wear it with great comfort. The S hook in front permits ready unclasping. When even momentarily halted, the wearer may relieve the strain on the waist, the entire weight then swinging clear of the side by the shoulder-straps. On the latter, in front, are two studs to which the haversack may be attached, while behind they button together at the cross.

The ball-pouch is of soft black leather, carried behind, Fig. 74. Other stiff cartridge-boxes, similar to those in our own service, are strung on the belt as needed.

The bayonet-frog is on the left side, as usual. Its only peculiarity is a short strap by which the bayonet may be *buckled in*.*

Fig. 75.

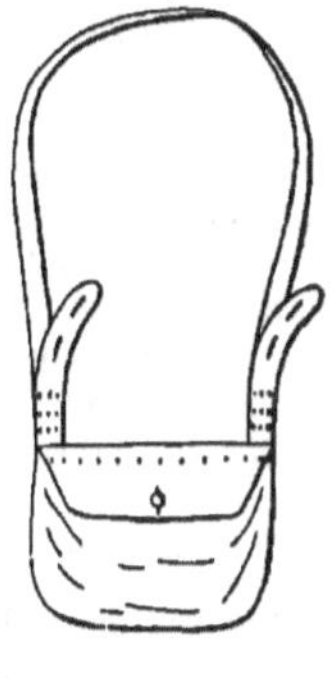

The haversack, Fig. 75, is a simple flax canvas bag with a canvas strap to go over the shoulder. Two loops are stitched to the strap near the haversack. When worn by riflemen this is carried at the back, the loops passing over the shoulders and buttoning to the studs already mentioned on the supports of the waist-belt. If worn by a cutlass man, the haversack is under the left arm.

The water-bottle is a small coopered barrel, shown in Figs. 77, 78, and 79. It is of Italian manufacture, supplied by Guglielminetti Brothers, Turin, and is carried by both branches of the military service. In the navy, riflemen carry it on the belt and cutlassmen under the right arm. The latest

---

* This arrangement would hardly cost as much as the bayonets we lose annually overboard in manning boats.

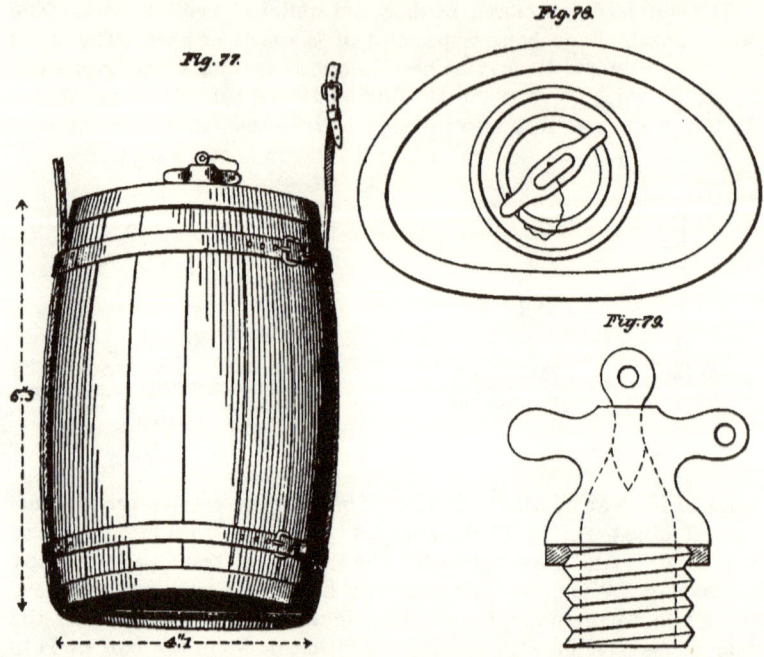

pattern is covered with gray felt. Its capacity is one quart. It is stout, withstands rough usage, and is cheap, but it is heavy in comparison with the water it contains. The bands and stopper are of galvanized iron. The top view, Fig. 78, gives the shape of the section. The stopper is only removed for filling, the drinking-hole being in it and closed by a wooden plug. The sling is of soft brown leather, as shown in Fig. 77.

The weight of a rifleman's equipment in full marching order is as follows:

	Lbs.	oz.
Martini-Henry rifle	9	0
Bayonet	2	8
Haversack, with 2 days' rations	4	8
Water-bottle	2	8
Belt, 3 cartridge-pouches, and bayonet-frog	6	0
120 rounds of ammunition	13	0
Blanket and kit from 3 pounds upwards, say as a maximum	7	8
(Maximum) total	45	0

It was decided to send a Naval Light Battery of six Gatling-guns to aid in the assault on Tel-el-Kebir. The organization and command were intrusted to Captain Fitz Roy, R. N., of H. M. S. Orion, the same officer who had occupied Ismailia. Commander Kane, of the Alexandra, was second in command.

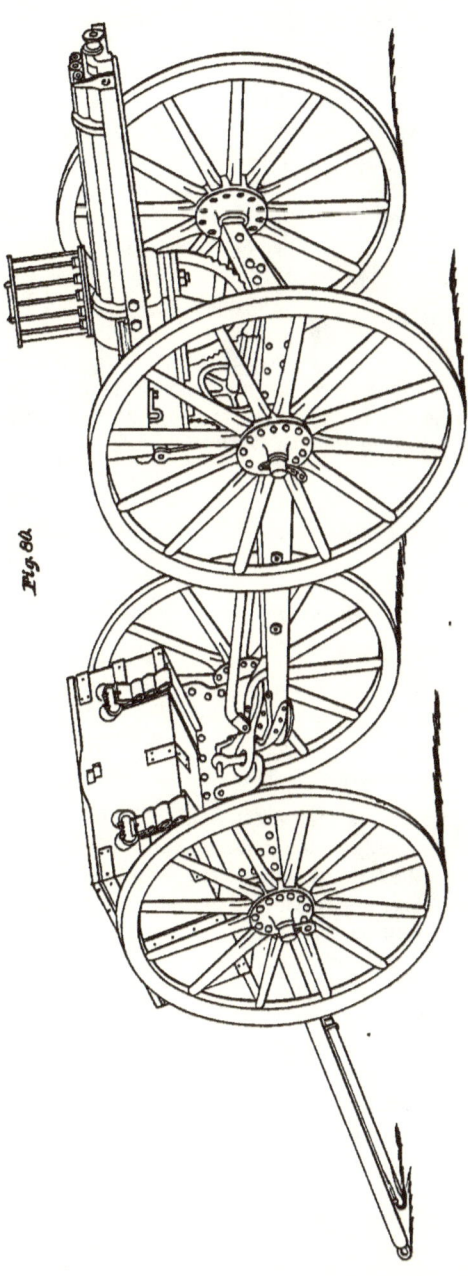

Fig. 86.

On September 8, two Gatling-gun limbers were taken ashore at Ismailia and fitted for mule draught. It may be remarked here that the howitzers and machine guns in the British navy which are sent on board ship for contingent use on shore are all *provided with limbers.* Fig. 80 is a view of the Gatling gun and its limber as ordinarily furnished, while Fig. 81 shows how single-trees, &c., were adapted to the ones in question to enable four mules to be hitched to each gun.

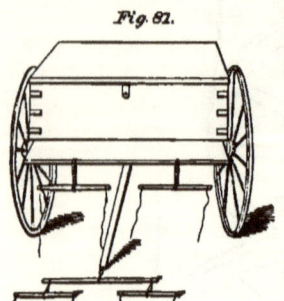

Fig. 81.

Arrangements were made for the necessary animals and the transport for the battery.

On September 9 the Humber arrived in Lake Timsah with four more Gatlings and their crews, drawn from the Mediterranean fleet. The folowing table gives the composition of the battery; each ship sent its own Gatling:

Ships.	Officer commanding.	Other officers.	No. of men.	Tents.*	
				Men.	Officers.
Alexandra	Lieut. J. E. Bloxland	1 surgeon, 1 midshipman.	30	3	1
Carysfort	Lieut. G. C. Langley		36	4	1
Monarch	Lieut. W. C. Reid	1 sub-lieutenant	30	3	1
Orion	Lieut. G. King-Harman		39	4	1
Superb	Lieut. T. G. Fraser	1 sub-lieutenant	30	3	1
Temeraire	Lieut. J. Gibbings	1 sub-lieutenant	30	3	1
Total			195	26	6

*Also 1 hospital tent and 1 tent for headquarters; total, 28.

The actual crews were each of 24 men. The remainder were stretchermen, mule and baggage guards, &c., usually four of the former and two of the latter. In the Orion's detachment were four men as a body-guard to Captain Fitz Roy, his servant, a gunner's mate, and a signal man. The Carysfort's additional men were artificers.

Fourteen of the men in the gun's crew were armed with rifles, the rest of each detachment with cutlasses and revolvers. The small-arm men carried 90 rounds of ammunition, the others 36 rounds. Each man carried his own tin pot and spoon. A mess-kettle was sent for every ten men, and one of the crew detailed as cook. To each gun were attached two mule-drivers from the army Commissariat and Transport Corps. The mules were 54 in number, distributed thus:

4 gun-mules to each Gatling	24
3 spare-ammunition mules for each gun	18
2 pack-mules to carry officers' luggage, mess-kettles, &c., to each gun	12
Total	54

In addition to these pack and draught animals were three horses, one for the commanding officer, one for Commander Kane, and one for the adjutant.

The guns and men were landed at 6.15 a. m. on September 10 at Ismailia. Proceeding to the railway station they were conveyed by train to Kassassin, arriving at 6 p. m. Here the tents, mules, &c., which had been supplied by the army were in readiness. Camp was at once pitched between the railway and the canal, according to the plan in the accompanying diagram, Fig. 82:

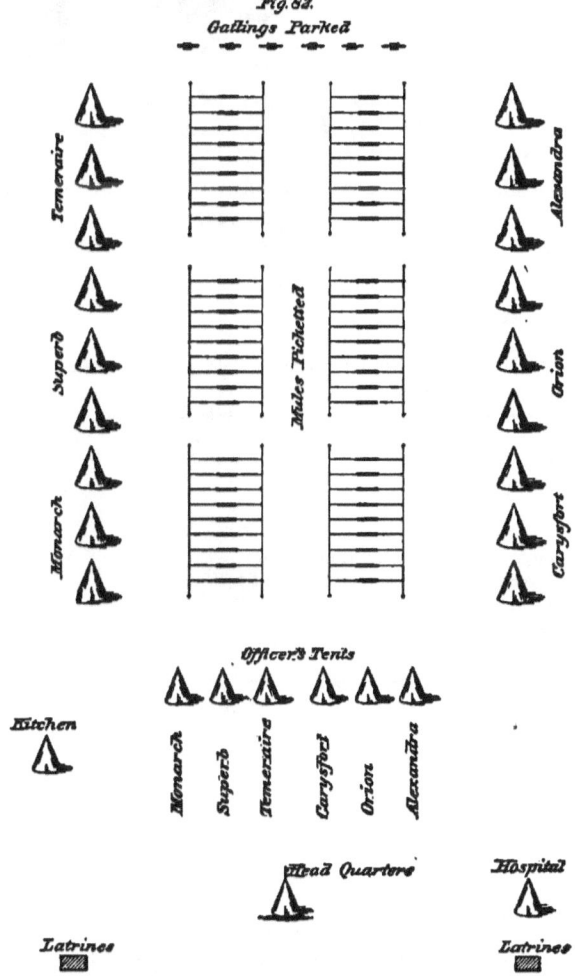

Plan of encampment of naval battery at Kassassin.

The latrines were simple trenches 12 feet long and 3 feet deep, 3 feet wide at the top and 18 inches wide at the bottom, Fig. 76 *a* and *b*.

For the officers the more elaborate accommodation was supplied which is sketched in Fig. 76 c. Into these latrines loose earth and sand were shoveled twice a day by men detailed for the purpose.

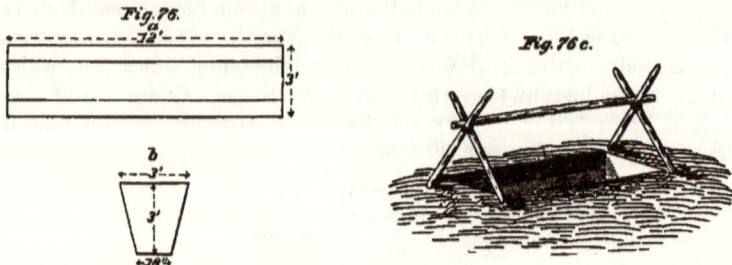

The guns' crews took turns in forming guard and in doing fatigue duty, one crew being told off every day for each of these tasks. They were thus, so to speak, in three watches.

The following routine was established:

ROUTINE OF THE NAVAL BATTERY.

3.30 a. m. Cooks called by the camp-sentry; fires lighted.
4.30 a. m. Reveille by bugle.
4.45 a. m. Bugle-call "cooks."
5.00 a. m. Breakfast.
5.45 a m. Latrine party fall in.
7.30 a. m. Relief guard; fall in fatigue party; old guard wash and clean up.
8.00 a. m. Clean arms and guns.
8.30 a. m. Dress bugle; clean up camp; trice up tent curtains; put on belts.
9.00 a. m. Bugle-call "advance;" parade; crews fall in in front of guns; arms are inspected; prayers; dismiss.
11.45 a. m. Bugle-call "cooks."
12. m. Dinner.
3.15 p. m. Fatigue party to draw provisions.
5.00 p. m. Supper; shift into night clothing.
6.00 p. m. Evening parade; exercise as mule artillery.
6.30 p. m. Latrine party fall in.
7.00 p. m. Bugle-call "grog."
8.15 p. m. First bugle.
8.30 p. m. Second bugle; out all lights in camp.

A packing-drill was improvised, as shown in the next paragraph.

Gun numbers.	Duty.
1 to 5	Harness the mules and hitch them to the limbers.
6 to 8	Prepare the limbers.
9 to 14	Pack the ammunition-mules.
15	Provide and pack three picketing-poles.
16	Provide and pack one picketing-pole.
17, 18	Provide an 8-gallon breaker of water and lash it in rear of limber.
24	Pack sand-bags on top of limber.

Stretchermen provide their stretchers and then assist generally in packing the mules.

On September 11 the battery was inspected by Major-General Macpherson, the commander of the Indian Contingent, who expressed himself as much pleased with the good order of the camp and the condition of the battery and men.

On September 12 camp was struck at 6.30 p. m., and all preparations made for the march. Four men were detailed to look out for the tents and baggage that were to be left behind at Kassassin. Two days' rations were carried in the haversacks, and 90 rounds of small-arm ammunition in the pouches. Everything not essential to actual fighting was discarded.

On the 13th, at 1.30 a. m., the battery limbered up and formed on the canal bank in column of sections. At 2 a. m. it started towards Tel-el-Kebir. The Egyptians opened fire at 4.55 a. m. with shell all along the line, followed by heavy musketry fire on the right of the battery. The rear Gatlings were deployed and a brisk fire begun at once; first, on some Egyptian cavalry who were in front of the works, and then on the intrenchments themselves. On reaching the lines they were found deserted; the enemy had fled.

The Gatlings' crews suffered no losses, being, in fact, little exposed, except to shell-fire, which was ordinarily in this campaign comparatively harmless. The enemy seemed to have concentrated his guns on certain predetermined points on the line of the advance, for in places the shells fell thick and fast. By exercising a little care in avoiding these zones of danger much loss was spared.

The Naval Battery spent the day at Tel-el-Kebir bringing in the wounded and burying the dead. Late in the afternoon it started for Zagazig, bivouacking on the road. On the 17th it returned by rail to Ismailia, where it re-embarked.

The commissariat was particularly well cared for. It must be borne in mind that when the battery joined the army this branch of the service had assumed such a development as to enable Captain Fitz Roy to draw upon it for supplies. A change was made in the hour for serving out grog, habitual on board ship. The earlier parties had adhered to the naval practice, and had received their tot at noon. The men under Captain Fitz Roy drew it after supper, when the work of the day was entirely completed. The wisdom of this arrangement was evident in the increased enjoyment it yielded the men, as well as in a marked improvement in the afternoon's work.

The health of the battery during their short term of service on shore was excellent. But one serious case of illness occurred. On the march only three men were obliged to fall out.

The wheels of the Gatling carriage and limber were *too small* and the tread *too narrow* for efficient use in such a sandy country. In many places the entire gun's crew had to assist the draught mules.

The organization and the morale of the battery were more than satisfactory. Its work at Tel-el-Kebir was of little real importance, as its attack followed after that of the Highlanders at a sufficiently great interval to allow it to profit by the general demoralization of the defense. No doubt can be entertained that it would have rendered a good account of itself had the defense been more stubborn.

XVIII.

THE MARINE BATTALIONS.

1. THE ROYAL MARINE LIGHT INFANTRY.

Several reasons combined to attract special attention to this body of men, the largest single battalion in the expeditionary force. They were "long-service" men; they were neither of the army entirely nor yet were they sailors. Their record during the campaign was not only irreproachable but in every way honorable, and it was known that a royal duke had asked to have them placed under his command with the Guards brigade. Their connection with the naval branch of the service is sufficient warrant for the separate mention they receive in this report.

The minimum stature of recruits is 5 feet $6\frac{1}{2}$ inches, and the term of enlistment twelve years. At the expiration of this period, the marine, if a desirable person, is offered the opportunity of re-engaging for nine years more. In the majority of instances this opportunity is accepted, the full length of twenty-one years completed, and the good-service pension secured. The men who served in Egypt averaged between eight and nine years' service and twenty-seven years of age.

The battalion was composed, at the outset, of five companies taken from the principal barracks in England. Portsmouth and Chatham each furnished 150 privates, and Plymouth 250. These men were not formed into a battalion at home, but were hastily collected on board H. M. transport Orontes, which took on board the first two detachments at Portsmouth on June 27, and sailed at once for Plymouth, where she stopped two hours to receive the remainder. She then went to Gibraltar. The command of the battalion (now about 600 of all ranks) was given to Lieutenant-Colonel Ley.

The haste which characterized the setting out therefore was in unison with the necessities of the case. It is greatly to be regretted that its subsequent movements were so much more deliberate, and that it was not on hand to seize Alexandria the day following the bombardment.

At Gibraltar the battalion was shifted into another transport, the Tamar, for the passage to Malta, where it arrived on July 6. It was not even yet too late to reach Alexandria in time, and prudence would, it seems, have dictated their presence there, if merely as a precautionary measure. Several days were lost in waiting at Malta. The Tamar then started under easy steam, not exceeding 6 knots speed, with orders to join the Channel squadron at Limasol in the island of Cyprus.

On reaching her destination, the Tamar found pressing orders to come at once to Alexandria, where she arrived at 2 a. m. of July 7. At daylight she went alongside the mole in the inner harbor, and, after noon, the marines were disembarked. The latter marched on immediately to Gabarri (see Plate 1), broke open some warehouses, in which the men were billeted, and, without delay, began the guarding of that portion of the city where the existing defenses were weakest.

The combined marine battalions, the Royal Marine Light Infantry and the Royal Marine Artillery, under Lieutenant-Colonel Tuson of the latter corps, took a prominent and honorable part in the reconnaissance in force of August 5, described on page 93 *et seq.*, their behavior receiving official praise.

A second detachment of four companies came out in the Dacca, which touched at Alexandria on August 8, landing Lieutenant-Colonel Howard S. Jones, who relieved Lieutenant-Colonel Ley, invalided. The Dacca then kept on to Port Said, the detachment under the command of Lieutenant-Colonel S. J. Graham being there transferred to H. M. S. Northumberland. Two of these companies were landed at Port Said on August 20, under Major J. W. Scott, to seize the place as described on page 107, while the balance, under Colonel Graham, were sent to Ismailia in H. M. S. Ready and Dace, and were the first troops to arrive at the new base, by that time in the possession of the navy. The following day the main body, under Colonel Jones, reached Ismailia from Alexandria in the Rhosina, and later Major Scott's detachment was brought up from Port Said, making a strong battalion of nine companies.

On August 25 Company D, under Captain R. W. Heathcote, was detailed as General Wolseley's body-guard.

The Royal Marine Light Infantry battalion did good work in the action of August 25, at Tel-el-Mahuta and Mahsameh, after a hard night march. In this engagement the two marine battalions were the only corps that kept up with the cavalry and reached the Egyptian camp at Mahsameh.

On the 28th the Royal Marine Light Infantry battalion was called up to Kassassin from its camp at Mahsameh, but too late to be of real service. It was actively engaged on September 9, capturing two Egyptian field pieces by a brilliant charge. In this affair it lost 27 men wounded, some mortally.

At Tel-el-Kebir the battalion was on the left of Graham's brigade, in the front line of the attack. Its behavior on this occasion, characterized by its accustomed coolness and steadiness, received well-earned praise. Its loss in this battle was only exceeded by those of two other battalions (see page 153).

The following table exhibits the strength of the two detachments as originally sent out:

Rank, &c.	First detachment.	Second detachment.
Steamer or transport	Orontes, Tamar.	Dacca.
Date of sailing	June 26	July 27
Date of arrival in Egypt	July 17	Aug. 8
Lieutenant-colonels	1	2
Majors	2	1
Captains (of companies)	5	4
Adjutant (captain)	1	0
Paymaster	1	0
Quartermaster (captain)	1	0
Staff (captain)	0	1
Lieutenants	10	8
Surgeons	2	1
Staff sergeants	9	0
Color (orderly) sergeants	5	4
Sergeants	20	16
Corporals	25	20
Buglers	20	8
Privates	500	386
Total rank and file	592	451
Grand total sent		1,043

The entire loss during the campaign from all causes, death, wounds, and disease, up to October 14, was 13 officers and 220 men. The invalided are stated by the adjutant, Captain A. St. Leger Burrowes, to have been chiefly from among the younger members of the battalion, both officers and men.

No regular transport was furnished the marines, but 67 mules and 8 Maltese carts were "picked up" at Ismailia. These were not enough to carry one-quarter of the equipment. The water-carts were lost in the sand near Nefiche early in the march, but this mishap was remedied to some extent by the fortunate capture of seven camels each carrying two large tin water-tanks.

So much has been said in commendation of this battalion that it is impossible not to believe it to have been second to no other body of troops in the field in organization, discipline, and performance. The greater average age of its members, as compared with that of the army proper, doubtless gave them the steadiness often urged in their praise, while to their experience afloat is due that "handiness" which is the characteristic of the sailor, and a most desirable habit on the part of the soldier. In physique, bearing, and military qualities generally the marines ranked very high, and they may point to the favorable notices of their work in official dispatches with honest pride.

2. THE ROYAL MARINE ARTILLERY.

This detachment was drawn from a corps of trained artillerymen who man a portion of the batteries of Her Majesty's ships of war. They date back in organization to the time when the *sailor* had nothing to do with the fighting of the ship. They have been gradually replaced by *seamen*, whose increased intelligence and careful training have rendered them competent to handle with skill the various kinds of ordnance in the British fleet. That the Royal Marine Artillery is not yet a thing of the past is seen in the fact that to-day it mans one-half of the Inflexible's 81-ton guns. These artillerists are, in addition, thoroughly drilled as infantry.

In the same transports with the Royal Marine Light Infantry battalion, the Orontes and Tamar, a detachment of Royal Marine Artillery, 300 in number, was sent to Egypt. It was organized as an infantry battalion and was commanded by Lieutenant-Colonel H. B. Tuson. At Alexandria it was associated with the Royal Marine Light Infantry. On August 5 the two battalions were combined under Lieutenant-Colonel Tuson, and did the extremely good service already narrated.

On August 19, when the base was changed, this battalion was embarked in the Nerissa, the first of the hired transports to arrive at Ismailia. The force was strengthened at Port Said by 100 men who had been sent from England in the Dacca to fill vacancies. Landing at Ismailia at 2 a. m. of August 21, the battalion, now numbering between 300 and 400 men, took part in the first advance, that in which Nefiche was occupied, marching out with two days' rations in their haversacks and 100 rounds of ammunition in their pouches. It took part in the affair of the of August 24 at El Magfar, when a small party relieved the worn-out Royal Artillerymen at their 13-pdrs., rendering highly efficient and welcome assistance. The following day it did further good service, advancing with the whole line. At 4 p. m. it pushed on to Mahsameh, where it occupied the enemy's deserted camp, and found much-needed provisions. The battalion had been without food all day.

The few days immediately succeeding were marked rather by inadequacy of rations than by the perilous nature of the work on hand. The men lived, for the time being, mostly on biscuits and such provender as the Egyptians had left behind in their retreat.

On the 26th the battalion reached Kassassin. It took an honorable part in the engagement of August 28, and was complimented by the general in command, Major-General Graham, for its gallant behavior under simultaneous direct and enfilading fire. It operated on the southern bank of the Sweet Water Canal in an exposed and important position. As has been already mentioned, a detachment under Captain Tucker had mounted a captured 8^{cm} Krupp gun on a railway truck and they worked it skillfully throughout the day. This gun subsequently pushed on with the naval 40-pdr. to Tel-el-Kebir, and then to Zagazig, Benha, and Tantah.

On September 9 the Royal Marine Artillery was again on the extreme left. It repelled a slight attack on the southern side of the canal, defending the bridge at Kassassin.

At Tel-el-Kebir the battalion started off 600 yards in rear of the Rifles (in the 4th brigade), but during the night was ordered to form General Wolseley's escort. It took, therefore, no active part in the assault, although subjected to distant shell-fire, principally from the advanced redoubt. (M, Plate 50.)

The Royal Marine Artillery, being less numerous, was less subjected to comment than the Royal Marine Light Infantry battalion; indeed, the majority of casual readers of accounts of the campaign hardly knew of the existence of such a corps, but its work was characterized by the same quiet efficiency, and it received a proportionate and gratifying meed of praise.

XIX.

THE LINES OF COMMUNICATION.

The British army has been so often engaged in operations conducted "beyond the seas" that its practice has developed a regular system, governing every step of the work of embarking, transporting to the base, disembarking, and forwarding to the front of troops, and animals and supplies of every sort. An important link in this chain is termed officially the "Base and Lines of Communication," which are united and made a separate command, under an officer clothed with ample authority. The proper performance of this arduous and unremunerative service, as may be presupposed, calls for great energy and force of character, coupled with administrative ability of a very high order.

The province of this officer includes the base and what is called the "advanced depot," together with all the means of transportation and exchange of intelligence employed between the two. Thus he controls the immediate disposition of arriving troops and stores, exercises military command over the base depot and garrison, directs the starting and other movements of convoys of men and of supply wagons, establishes the train service on the railways, if there be any within his department, regulates the use of the telegraph, provides for the defense of the base and the lines for all transport, including that of the wounded; in a word, is responsible for everything that reaches the base until it passes out of his care into the camp at the front or is re-embarked on board the transports.

The Base and Lines of Communication during the late campaign in Egypt were commanded by Major-General W. Earle, C. S. I., and no officer in the expedition was more unremittingly occupied or had greater difficulties to contend against.

The preliminary work at Alexandria, which General Earle reached on August 9, was of no particular moment. The troops from England began arriving on the following day, the Orient leading the van of the hired-transport fleet with the Scots Guards on board. The handling of these bodies of men, their outfits and supplies, was very simple. The spacious docks at Alexandria were an admirable landing place, whence the troops were marched at once over good roads to their camps, the most remote of which was only a few miles distant. For the men's kits and camp equipage and the officers' baggage the regimental and other army transport either sufficed or found ready supplement in hired carts and the local railways. The principal of the latter has a branch leading to the wharves, while another, the Ramleh Railway (owned by a private corporation), leads directly to the position of the main camp at Ramleh. The latter railway was used for the conveyance of both troops and stores.

General Earle's labors began in earnest with the change of base from Alexandria to Ismailia. He reached the latter place at 10 p. m. of August 20, and instituted his preparations and arrangements at once. On the day following, August 21, Major-General Graham was at Nefiche, in command of the advance of the army, a small body of about 800 men. Although very near Ismailia in point of distance, the break in the railway prevented the use of trucks for hauling stores to Nefiche, while the sand of the desert intervening, heavier here than anywhere else on the whole line of march, rendered the very small amount of transport then at hand totally inadequate. To supply this deficiency a boat service on the Sweet Water Canal was immediately started by Admiral Seymour, four boat-loads of provisions being sent to General Graham on the first or opening trip. This organization, which is detailed in Section XVI, worked in conjunction with the other means of transport as developed, all being subject to the control of the General commanding the Line of Communications.

During this and the next two days, August 21, 22, and 23, the base assumed its characteristic appearance. The different battalions and corps, now landing with all practicable speed, were assigned their respective camping grounds, and were given a place to store such articles of their kits, baggage, and stores as would not be immediately required on the march across the desert. The best methods of landing horses, mules, men, and materials were being worked out practically, and means sought to increase the landing facilities. The post and telegraph offices were established (operated by volunteers until the regular army troops charged with these duties could arrive), and preparations were made for working the railway by means of horsed trucks. The Khedive's palace, a large airy building, was occupied as the base hospital, and the Governor's house as the headquarters of the Commander-in-Chief. The various base stores of supplies, the sick-horse hospital, and remount depot were organized under the Royal Engineer, Ordnance-Store, and Commissariat Officers, the Surgeon and Veterinary Surgeon on the staff of the "Commandant of the Bases."

The plan of Ismailia, Plate 48, gives the general features of the base. When first seized the only landing facilities it possessed were at the

Central Wharf, a rectangular pier-head, with about 60 feet of water front, and 25 feet wide, built on piles out into 2 fathoms of water. A short, narrow gangway connected this pier-head with a stone wharf, the continuation of the broad avenue which leads directly from the railway station. This avenue is a fine specimen of macadam. It withstood the continued heavy traffic thrown upon it by its selection as the terminus of a military route without signs of deterioration, and it proved a real blessing to the British.

The harbor of Ismailia was formed, as is well known, by dredging out the shallow bed of Lake Timsah, and navigable water approach to the town was only secured at this one point, the Central Wharf. In consequence, the greater part of all heavy articles and stores, men and horses, were landed from here from lighters or from tugs, which the depth of water permitted alongside the pier. To relieve the strain on this sole place of disembarkation, additional accommodation was obtained west of the Central Wharf. The South Wharf, on piles, is low and well built. The pier-head is 22 feet long and 14 feet wide, and the pier itself a straight jetty 156 feet long and 9 feet wide. The water here is too shallow to allow the presence of tugs, but native boats, ships' cutters, and lighters can run alongside with ease. On the beach near by the greater part of the field pieces were landed.

At the South Wharf, the commissariat began also the work of disembarking their stores until the branch railway from the station to the mouth of the Sweet Water Canal was sufficiently advanced. They shifted their operations to this more convenient locality on September 9. The dock they made use of was a platform about 2 feet above the level of the water, 6 feet wide, and 75 feet long, built of wood and resting on piles, in two parts, separated by a balcony, which had been erected here long before by the Suez Canal Company. The railway was laid on the embankment 12 feet above the landing stage, the slope being mounted by steps and inclined planes, the latter for parbuckling heavy packages, and very useful in breaking up the base. Fig. 83. While the con-

Fig. 83.

venience of this wharf was of much importance, a further and very great advantage was found in the transfer of such large quantities of bulky stores, all coming under one department, to a place by themselves, leaving the other landing facilities to be undisturbed possession of other corps.

When the Indian Contingent arrived, it began at once, with that independence of action which marked all its operations to provide for its own disembarkation, the Madras Sappers constructing a separate pier. The spot selected was between the Central and South Wharves. A number of low four-wheeled trucks were used as the support of a superstructure, shown in plan in the accompanying diagram, Fig. 84.

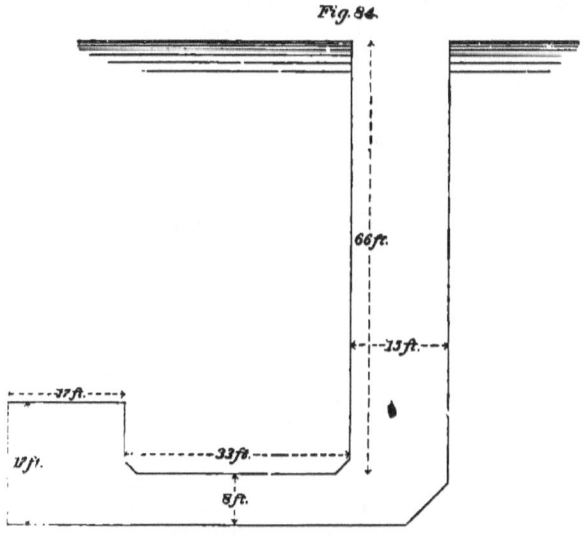

Temporary landing pier of the Indian Contingent at Ismailia.

The platform was roughly made of planks, resting on fore-and-aft scantling. The depth of water secured was only a little less than 3 feet. The pier was certainly light; indeed, everything connected with the Indian Contingent was light, but it served the purpose of its design, dry footing.

Each wharf was under the charge of an officer of General Earle's staff, whose duty it was to superintend the work and start everything in the right direction as soon as landed. This officer bore the title of "Military Landing Officer." That this duty was well performed is shown by the fact that blocks never occurred, even on the Central Wharf, which was always the most crowded. A regular system was adopted and adhered to, so that the disembarkation was effected with a minimum of confusion. The cattle and many of the mules were put into the water from the transports and made to swim ashore, while the horses were all landed in the boats described on page 175, or on flats, each horse being accompanied by his own harness or saddlery and other equipments. The latter being landed first and carried well up the wharf by fatigue parties, the horses were run ashore to their trappings, were harnessed or saddled, and led at once to their appropriate places in camp.

The value of making haste slowly was shown in the matter of getting wheeled vehicles ashore. These, at the outset, were put together on board of the transports, and were often loaded in the lighters alongside, but it was quickly found that the speed sought was really lost, and the process resorted to of landing the carts and wagons empty, or even in cases taken to pieces.

The work at the Central Wharf was superintended by Major H. G. MacGregor until September 1, when he was relieved by Major E. H. Sartorius, of the East Lancashire Regiment. The diligence and ability of these officers received well-merited commendation in official dispatches.

To help matters at the main landing place, a branch railway was laid to it direct from the railway station, so that the stores needed at the front could be put at once into cars and sent off, thus saving one handling, much time, and what was at least as important, avoiding the piling up of material in the very restricted space on the wharf.

The scarcity, amounting almost to a dearth, of native labor threw, practically, the entire work of moving the stores upon fatigue parties detailed from the different battalions. These fatigue parties were many and large, and kept every one busily employed, with little rest or intermission. It is satisfactory to hear, in the words of General Earle, the officer most interested, that "the troops worked well."

The base at Ismailia was under the immediate command of Colonel Sir W. O. Lanyon, K. C. M. G., C. B., 2d West India Regiment, with the title of "Commandant of the Base." The order which prevailed here after affairs had had a chance to settle down to a somewhat permanent status was admirable. The 1st battalion of the Manchester Regiment (late 63d foot) had come from India, and had been detailed for duty at the base, where it remained until the end of the campaign. That some should remain and guard the rear while others push ahead to fight is inevitable, but none the less is staying behind a fate hard to bear. It is a duty to testify to the soldierly bearing, neat appearance, and cheerfulness of this body of men. To see a fatigue party of them returning to camp at night after many hours' hard work landing and shipping stores was to realize the value of discipline and *esprit de corps*. One could not avoid the regret that this battalion had no chance to distinguish itself in a more martial way.

At the other extremity of the Line of Communication was the "Advanced Depot," under Captain J. H. Sandwith, R. M. L. I., where were kept the stores needed for present consumption. At first this depot was established at Tel-el-Mahuta, but afterwards it was moved to Kassassin. Other stations were at intermediate points, each being in charge of a "Station Commandant," responsible for the transmission of everything going to or coming from the army, and for the security of the roads and telegraphs within his district. The Station Commandant is never interfered with by his seniors except in case of actual attack.

He keeps the Station Commandants next to him on either side informed of the movements of troops and convoys, so that men, animals, and material cannot arrive without finding everything in readiness for their reception. He has a staff to aid him in executing his duty, as, for instance, a Railway Officer, an Engineer Officer, a Commissariat and Transport Officer, an Ordnance-Store Officer, a Surgeon, and a Veterinary Surgeon, or as many of them as the circumstances of the case may require. He must prevent disorders and excesses in his district, and hear and investigate all complaints made by natives. He regulates the departure of all convoys or detachments, giving written orders to the officer or non-commissioned officer in charge.

The work at these stations, and particularly at the advanced depot, was very heavy. The manual part was performed, as at the base, by fatigue parties of soldiers, often numbering upwards of 200. The limited amount of rolling stock and the rarity of railway sidings rendered it necessary to lose no time in unloading stores sent by train. The quantity and nature of the shipment being telegraphed ahead in every instance, men and animals in sufficient numbers were always in waiting to clear the cars without delay. The cars with stores for the cavalry were uncoupled at Mahsameh and left by the trains on their way out to Kassassin, to be picked up on the return trip.

The push of the advance along the railway to the westward, which began immediately after the seizure of Ismailia, continued, with insignificant halts, until Kassassin was occupied, on August 26. Each move, increasing the distance from the base and involving the establishment of additional camps to be maintained, rendered the distribution of supplies more complex. General Earle, speaking of affairs at this period, says: "The transport of provisions was the difficulty of the moment." The regimental transport had completely broken down. The railway lacked locomotives. The boat service in the Sweet Water Canal was the main dependence, and that was threatened by the steady lowering of the water-level. Luckily, the capture of a large stock of provisions at Mahsameh gave the sadly strained lines of communication a slight respite, and relieved temporarily the pressing needs of the troops of the advance. The telegraph was repaired and operated by volunteers as far as Tel-el Mahuta. The tide did not fairly turn, however, until regular trains were established on the railway, after the receipt of the first engine, on August 27. It was a critical time, for the rapid falling of the water in the Sweet Water Canal had reduced the boat traffic by nearly one-half, the slower process of tracking having to be resorted to, and rafts and pontoons substituted for the quicker but deeper boats, while it was not until September 3 that the Commissariat and Transport Corps scored its first piece of work on the Lines of Communication. At 5 p. m. of that date, 150 mules, with oats, badly loaded from want of experience, started from Ismailia, reaching Tel-el-Mahut the following day.

The steady increase in the railway service after August 28 began to encourage the hopes of those in authority, and on September 5 General Earle caused calculations to be made of the supplies needed to form a working reserve at Kassassin for 16,000 men and 7,000 animals. It was found that at least forty railway trucks daily would be required, each truck carrying five tons net. The distribution of these trucks would be as follows:

	Trucks.
Imperial troops:	
To provide for daily consumption	13
To create a reserve	16
Indian Contingent:	
To provide for daily consumption	3
To create a reserve	3
Ordnance-Store Department	1
Army Medical Department	1
Royal Artillery	1
Royal Engineers	1
Regimental and staff luggage, &c	1
Total	40

On September 6 General Earle issued an order to his staff covering the point. He directed that "the canal traffic and all transport by animals will be exclusively devoted to the reserve, and the railway will supply the current wants and do as much as it can for the reserve as well."

The object of these calculations and instructions was to accumulate at Kassassin rations for 10,000 men for thirty days.

A second estimate was made of the carriage required for tents and other camp equipage, men's valises, officers' light baggage, &c., when the force should move forward. As throwing light on the liberal scale of transport allowed in the British army, this estimate is given at length:

	Trucks.
15 battalions of infantry, 3 each	45
4 regiments of cavalry, 2 each	8
9 batteries of artillery, 1 each	9
4 companies and troops Royal Engineers, 1 each	4
Field hospital and bearer companies	8
Staff, &c	3
Total	77

That is to say, seven railway trains, averaging eleven cars each. In addition to these, provision would have to be made for replacing the ammunition expended in action.

The end aimed at began to be approached immediately, but it was only on September 9 that it seemed to be reasonably close at hand. On that day no less than 230 tons of stores went by rail to Kassassin, an excess of 30 tons over the desired amount estimated for on the 5th, and in addition to the delivery by the canal and by pack animals. The work, thus pushed ahead, bore speedy fruit, rendering possible the advance of September 13, which terminated the campaign. At that time 70,000 of the 300,000 reserve rations had been collected at Kassassin for the Imperial Troops, and the Indian Contingent had built up at about the same rate.

The seizure of Cairo and the intervening railway systems extended the scope of the Line of Communications without materially increasing the labor. The whole Egyptian equipment of rolling stock now became available, so that the supply of stores and provisions for the various garrisons could be readily maintained unmolested by rail.

The base was changed as rapidly as possible to Alexandria, and by October 1 hardly any signs of its temporary warlike importance were visible at Ismailia.

XX.

THE COMMISSARIAT AND TRANSPORT CORPS.

The important question, in the military art, of land transport, has received in England a solution which must be regarded as abnormal. The furnishing of food and transportation is the duty of the Commissariat and the Transport Corps, a civil branch of the army. The latter service is planned, to all appearances, for contemplated operations in Europe or in other highly civilized parts of the world which are traversed by ample roads of excellent construction.

If this anticipation had been realized, the value of the transport scheme would have been tested long ago, under the conditions for which it was devised, but as England has had no troops on the Continent either during the forty years intervening between Waterloo and Sebastopol or the thirty years, nearly, that have elapsed since the Crimean War, and, with this one exception, has conducted her military operations of the last three-quarters of a century in remote and generally savage countries, the inference is inevitable that the wish to be prepared for a serious although remote contingency has involved the sacrifice of many important and ever-present considerations, and has prevented her army from having a suitable transport service ready at the outset of her numerous and varied expeditions.

The organization of the corps is good. The plan of its equipment is, however, entirely lacking in elasticity, in adaptability to the different conditions under which it is constantly called upon to work; while its parts are heavy and cumbersome to such an extent as to seriously impair its efficiency.

For convenience the wagons are considered first.

The general-service wagon is strong and solidly constructed; it weighs, empty, about a ton. When carrying its full allowance of a ton and a half of load it requires an extremely good road and six powerful horses in excellent condition for its locomotion. Yet upon these wagons depend the carefully worked out system of regimental transport and the important packing drill. The moment other modes of conveyance are resorted to, a new distribution of the mess equipment, &c., must be devised, introducing general confusion and discontent. In spite of the lessons of the campaign just concluded, it may be safely predicted that the transport corps will continue to adhere to this impracticable and imperishable vehicle.

The two-wheeled carts upon which most reliance was placed were of the Maltese pattern, Fig. 84. The principal dimensions are as follows: Diameter of wheels, 5 feet; length of shaft, 10 feet; size of shaft, 2½ inches square; width of platform at back, 3 feet; width between shafts, 18 inches; net load, about 8 cwt.

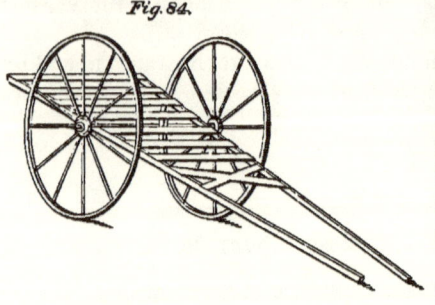

Fig. 84.

Somewhat different from the foregoing, was a small hand-cart which could be fitted for mule or donkey draught by the addition of removable shafts of bamboo. The ends and sides of this cart can be lifted off either for stowage or use. The principal peculiarity was the wheel, the spokes being ⅜-inch iron rods radiating from a heavy cylindrical hub terminating in iron plates. The spokes pass through these plates and are set up with a nut inside. Fig. 85 gives one spoke and shows the hub of this wheel.

Fig. 85.

Tip-cart, hub and spoke.

The water-cart is simply a large cask capable of holding 109 gallons, mounted on wheels, and drawn ordinarily by one horse. It may be broadly stated that none of these wagons were of use except for the local distribution of supplies.

In general terms, the transport of the British force in Egypt was as follows:

Each battalion had the Maltese carts, two water-carts, 26 draught horses, and 21 pack animals, with a driver to every two horses. Each cavalry regiment had six carts, an ammunition-wagon, a forge-wagon, and two water-carts. All this on starting; but what amount of transport each corps possessed at the close of the campaign it is impossible to say; the greater part had been lost in the sand or left behind at the base.

This transport, as thus detailed, was a part of the permanent organization of the battalion, and was intended on the march to carry rations for one day, together with all the regimental baggage except the tents. It was known as the "regimental transport," a term applied to the regular transport equipment supplied to every battalion of infantry or regiment of cavalry when mobilized. The equipment adopted in Egypt differed mainly from the regulation equipment in the substitution of small carts for large wagons.

To each division of the army corps was attached a company of the Commissariat and Transport Corps, consisting of 4 officers and 210 non-commissioned officers and men (see details, page 100 and 101). The standard equipment comprised 14 riding horses, 180 draught horses, 74 wagons and carts, 4 water-carts, and 3 forge-carts. This, technically known as the "Divisional or Departmental Transport," was designed to carry the equipage of the divisional and brigade staffs, the butcheries and bakeries of the two brigades, and one day's supply of groceries, provisions, and oats for the whole division. With the exception of certain modifications intended to better suit the needs of this particular case, this is the transport habitually assigned to a division on a war footing. A similar company was attached to the Cavalry brigade.

Except during an advance, the Departmental Transport is supposed to be employed in bringing up supplies from the base to the advance depot.

Besides these Commissariat and Transport Companies there were three "Auxiliary Companies," whose duty during an advance was to carry the tents, kits, &c., of the two divisions, and during a halt to operate along the line of communications. As a permanent force engaged on the latter special work two strong companies were sent out, supplemented by hired teams and pack animals. The majority of the teamsters were Maltese, and are described as "a very bad lot."

The composition of an Auxiliary Company, as authorized for the campaign in Egypt, is given below.

Rank, &c.	One section.	Total four sections.	Staff.	Total for company.
Commissariat and Transport Corps:				
Captain	......	......	1	1
Quartermaster	......	......	1	1
Subalterns	1	4	......	4
Staff sergeants	......	......	2	2
Sergeants	1	4	1	5
Corporals	1	4	1	5
Wheelers	1	4	1	5
Collar-maker	......	......	1	1
Farrier and carriage smith	......	......	1	1
Buglers	1	4	......	4
Privates	4	16	4	20
Artificers:				
Saddlers	1	4	......	4
Shoeing and carriage smiths	3	12	......	12
Natives:				
Interpreters	1	4	1	5
Superintendents	2	8	......	8
Drivers	54	216	6	222
Total all ranks	......	......	......	300
Animals:				
Riding	*6	24	†8	32
Pack	40	160	......	160
Draught	60	240	4	244
Spare	10	40	......	40
Total	116	464	12	476

*One riding horse each for the subaltern, sergeant, corporal, and interpreter; two riding horses for the superintendents; total, six.

†Two riding horses for the captain; one each for the quartermaster, sergeant-major, quartermaster sergeant, farrier sergeant, and interpreter, and one spare horse; total, eight.

The company equipment was as follows:

Equipments.	One section.	Total four sections.	Staff.	Total for company.
Vehicles:				
Carts	28	112	2	114
Forge carts	1	4		4
Water carts	1	4		4
Saddlery:				
Riding	6	24	6	30
Pack	40	160		160
Breast harness (single sets)	65	260	4	264
Tool-chests:				
Shoeing and carriage smiths	3	12	1	13
Collar and harness makers	1	4	1	5
Wheelers	1	4	1	5
Implements for carts:				
Axes	6	24		24
Spades	6	24		24
Picks	6	24		24
Lifting-jacks	3	12		12

The forge and water carts and one cart were for the use of the section to which they were assigned, leaving, as the working strength of each section, 40 pack animals and 27 two-wheeled carts, and of the entire company 160 pack animals and 108 two-wheeled carts. It is to these Auxiliary Companies that the bulk of the work on the Line of Communications should have fallen until the establishment of the railway service.

As will be seen from the above table the company was divided into four parts, each of which could be used as an independent unit, and this rule, it may be observed, characterizes the composition of all the commissariat and Transport Companies.

The foregoing indicates the theoretical plan. In practice it was found that even the small Maltese cart was immovable with less than four draught animals, so that one-half of the regimental wheeled transport was ineffective at the outset, while the pack animals supplied failed to make up the deficiency. In consequence, the troops were dependent for shelter upon captured Egyptian camps until the railway could bring the tents up. The Commissariat and Transport Corps was utterly unable to perform this portion of its duty.

In anticipation of difficulty in connection with wheeled transport, 700 mules had been bought in Smyrna and 800 in Beyrout, in ample time to meet the troops at Ismailia, but the Turkish Government had refused to allow them to be shipped. Others were purchased elsewhere, in Italy, Spain, South Africa, the United States, &c., but the three weeks' delay occasioned by the latent hostility of Turkey, and the inability to procure camels, or other substitutes, on the spot, were fatal to the successful working of the army transport over the desert that borders on Ismailia. The wagons and carts were discarded and the draught animals utilized by the Royal Engineers in hauling trucks on the railway and pontoons and boats on the Sweet Water Canal. Although the army began landing at Ismailia on August 21, it was not until September 3 that the Commissariat and Transport began conveying supplies to the front (see page 213), and it only assumed its legitimate functions after the battle of Tel-el-Kebir.

To this department ordinarily falls the task of handling the stores landed at the base, in order that the troops may be fresh for active military operations. Here again it failed. Numbering in all about 1,400 men, distributed wherever there were camps, from Alexandria to Kassassin, too small a force remained at Ismailia to execute this part of its work. Commissary-General Morris, the Senior Commissariat Officer of the expedition, having in vain asked in advance for a corps of hired laborers, 400 strong, to supply this deficiency, was obliged to seek relief in large fatigue parties of soldiers, who were thus diverted from their proper sphere of usefulness.

Another responsibility of this department is the feeding of the army.

The following table is of interest as giving the composition of the daily ration at three different periods. The first column contains the ration as usually supplied; the second, that ordered after reaching Ismailia; and the third, that issued after reaching Cairo.

Ration.	I.		II.		III.	
	Lb.	Oz.	Lb.	Oz.	Lb.	Oz.
Bread	4		1	4	0	12
Biscuit	1	0	1	0	0	12
Fresh meat	1	0	1	0	1	00
Preserved meat	1	0	1	0	1	00
Tea	0	0$\frac{1}{3}$	0	0$\frac{1}{2}$	0	0$\frac{1}{2}$
Coffee	0	0$\frac{1}{2}$	0	0$\frac{1}{2}$	0	0$\frac{1}{2}$
Sugar	0	2	0	2$\frac{1}{2}$	0	2$\frac{1}{2}$
Salt	0	0$\frac{1}{2}$	0	0$\frac{1}{2}$	0	0$\frac{1}{2}$
Pepper	0	0$\frac{1}{36}$	0	0$\frac{1}{36}$	0	0$\frac{1}{36}$
Lime-juice	*0	0$\frac{1}{2}$	0	0$\frac{1}{2}$	0	0$\frac{1}{2}$
Fresh vegetables	0	8	0	8	0	4
Compressed vegetables	0	1	0	1	0	1
Soap, on payment						
Tobacco, on payment						
Rice					0	4
Potatoes					0	8
Rum	$\frac{1}{2}$ gill.		†$\frac{1}{2}$ gill.		None.	

* Issued with $\frac{1}{4}$ ounce sugar when fresh vegetables cannot be cured. In II and III the lime-juice formed a part of the daily ration, irrespective of the issue of vegetables.
† Issued but twice a week.

The principal changes are in the amount of bread or the equivalent biscuit, less being required after the hard work of the campaign was over; in the tea, of which the allowance was trebled; in the lime-juice, which was made a steady instead of an alternative issue; in the fresh vegetables, of which half was curtailed and liberal weights of rice and potatoes substituted; and in the rum, the ration being first greatly reduced and then stopped entirely.

The hygienic value of these modifications is self-evident. In the case of the grog, it was found that the troops not only needed no stimulant in that hot climate, but were actually better off without it.

The ration was changed by the Commander-in-Chief's order, based on the recommendation of the Principal Medical Officer.

The component parts of the ration are put up as follows, viz: The preserved meat in boxes of 50 pounds; the bread in bags of 100 pounds; the tea in 14-pound tin canisters; the coffee in square tins, two in a box, whose gross weight is 100 pounds; the sugar, packed like the coffee, in 60-pound cases; the salt in 13-pound canisters; the rum in 10-gallon kegs, weighing 119 pounds; the pepper in cases of six 20-pound canisters, weighing 133 pounds gross.

The packages vary immensely in weight, and hence introduce great complexity in the operation of packing for transport on the backs of animals, whose loads on both sides must, of course, balance. Two uniform gross weights for all commissariat parcels, one of 50 and the other of 100 pounds, would yield much convenience and save time and labor in the field.

The commissariat animals stood the work very well in the main, very few being used up by the heat and heavy labor, and no special diseases being developed. This result is attributed to liberal feeding, the usual ration being supplemented by extra allowances. Roughly speaking, when actively employed these animals were given all the forage they could consume. It must be remembered, however, that, unlike the cavalry, they were never beyond the reach of abundant supplies, and the campaign was very short.

Not only was the transport service the weakest point in the expeditionary force, but it is not an exaggeration to say that it failed completely. In the rapid advance to Kassassin the troops were on several occasions entirely without adequate supplies. The opportune capture of a stock of provisions at Mahsameh alone enabled them to hold the ground they had seized, and saved the cavalry and artillery horses from actual want. The army is stated by its commander to have entirely "outrun its transport," but such a state of affairs ought not to have existed at 20 miles from the base. Upon the proper placing of the responsibility for this failure depends the chance of guarding against its recurrence in the future. For a report of this nature it is impossible to obtain the facts necessary to a complete determination of the causes that produced so lamentable a result. Certain considerations, however, are not out of place.

The wagon must be light and strong, and be fitted with brakes. Commissary-General Morris prefers the American type, which, with eight mules, can haul a load of from one to two tons. This wagon was much used at the Cape of Good Hope, and gave satisfaction. Teamsters should never ride, but should walk beside their horses.

As to harness, General Wolseley advocates the use of both breast straps and collars, so that a chafed animal may be shifted from one to the other, and his services not lost during convalescence.

The possibility that wheeled transport may be impracticable should be met, proper forms of pack-saddles should be adopted, and a well-digested packing drill devised in connection with their use.

The chief reason for the break-down in the transport was undoubtedly the attempted adherence to a rigid system, absolutely unsuited to the country in which the operations were to be conducted. The native inhabitants may be generally assumed to understand fairly well their own needs in this particular. In Egypt from time immemorial they have used pack animals exclusively. Had the British transport corps landed at Ismailia with an adequate and well-organized mule train, the heavy desert and the interruptions in the railways would have failed to check the flow of supplies to the front, and the army would have been spared the annoyance of seeming to suffer almost within sight of the base.

When the frequency of England's wars is remembered, it seems hard to believe that the outbreak of each should find this important department without the animals and drivers necessary to the proper placing of at least one army corps in the field.

The railways in England are so much more economical carriers of stores that the transport companies exist during peace mainly as *cadres*. The call to active military preparation means the hurried purchase of thousands of animals at exorbitant prices, and the engaging of hundreds of unknown teamsters at high wages. The money which would be needed for the maintenance, on a war footing, of the eight Commissariat and Transport Companies that ordinarily accompany an army corps, is consumed in the enforced haste of mobilization, while the result is seen in an undrilled mob, often quite as capable of harm as good.

During the Egyptian campaign, the Government purchased 10,000 mules. A large proportion of these animals were sold immediately afterwards at but a fraction of their cost. The loss incurred by the difference between the selling and the buying prices would have maintained the beasts for many months, and in some cases years.

War is expensive at the best, and nations that are liable to be called upon to take part in it find it cheapest in the end, as it is wisest, to be well prepared.

XXI.

THE TROOPS.

I.—THE CAVALRY.

A squadron from each of the three regiments, the 1st Life Guards, the 2d Life Guards, and the Royal Horse Guards ("the Blues"), which together comprise the Household Cavalry, was sent to Egypt and formed into a regiment about 450 strong.

At home, these men, none less than six feet in height, wear a steel cuirass and steel helmet, long cavalry boots, &c., but the exigencies of the climate caused the abandoning of this heavy equipment, to the great comfort of the wearers. The cuirass was laid aside, a cork helmet was substituted for the steel helmet, and, instead of boots, strips of serge (technically known by the Indian name of *puttees*) were wrapped about the calves of the legs.

The other cavalry regiments, the 4th Dragoon Guards, the 7th Dragoon Guards, and the 19th Hussars, each about 600 strong, were similarly dressed.

The organization of a British cavalry regiment on a war footing is given in the following table:

Officers, non-commissioned officers and men.	Numbers.	Horses.		
		Chargers.*	Troop.	Draught.
Lieutenant-colonels	2	8		
Majors	3	12		
Captains	5	15		
Subalterns	16	48		
Adjutant	1	3		
Paymaster	1	2		
Quartermaster	1	2		
Medical Officer	1	2		
Veterinary Surgeon	1	2		
Total	31	94		
Sergeant major	1			
Quartermaster sergeant	1			
Band sergeant	1			
Paymaster sergeant	1			
Armor sergeant	1			
Saddler sergeant	1			
Farrier sergeant	1			
Sergeant cook	1			
Trumpet major	1			
Orderly room clerk	1			
Transport sergeant	1			
Troop sergeant-majors	8		480	
Sergeants	24			
Farriers	8			
Saddlers	4			
Shoeing smiths	8			
Wheelers and saddletree maker	2			
Trumpeters	8			
Corporals	32			
Bandsmen	15			
Privates	480			
Drivers (transport)	22			44
Total	622	94	480	44

* Officers' private horses.

The ammunition carried by a regiment of cavalry is as follows:

Carbine:

                                                                                Rounds.

    30 rounds per carbine 16,500

    In reserve 10,080

        Total carbine ammunition 26,580

Pistol:

    36 rounds per pistol 936

    In reserve 1,200

        Total pistol ammunition 2,136

The regiment is divided into four squadrons, three of which are commanded by majors, the fourth by a captain. The establishment of the squadron is given in the following table:

Rank.	Numbers.	Horses. Chargers.	Troop.	Draught.
Major	1	4	......	......
Captain	1	3	......	......
Subalterns	4	12	......	......
Troop, sergeant-majors	2	}	120	......
Sergeants	6			
Corporals	8			
Artificers	4			
Trumpeters	2			
Privates'	120			
Drivers	2	......	......	4
Total	150	19	120	4

The equipment of the trooper consisted of sword and Martini-Henry carbine. The latter is carried in a leather bucket at the right side of the saddle. The Household Cavalry carried revolvers in addition and a heavier pattern of sword. All the metal trappings were allowed to rust, in order to avoid reflecting the sunlight.

The following tables give the weights carried by the cavalry soldier in marching order:

ARTICLES WORN.

	Lbs.	Oz.
Helmet	0	15
Tunic	3	0
Flannel shirt	1	1½
Drawers	0	12½
Trousers	2	6
Braces	0	4
Socks	0	4½
Shoes	3	3
Spurs	0	13½
Puttees	0	6
Gloves	0	3½
Total	13	5½

SADDLERY.

	Lbs.	Oz.
Saddle	22	0
Bridle	4	0
Breast-plate	1	3
Crupper	0	12
Pair of saddle-bags	2	12½
Head rope	0	15
2 shoe-cases and 4 shoes	5	13
Saddle cloth	2	12
Total	40	3½

ON THE SADDLE.

	Lbs.	Oz.
Hoof-pick	0	2
Nose-bag	1	1
Heel rope and shackle	1	2
Picketing peg	0	12½
Mess-tin	1	3½
Carbine bucket	2	0
Total	6	5

IN FRONT OF THE SADDLE.

	Lbs.	Oz.
Pair ankle boots	4	0
Forage cap	0	5
Cape	2	12
Total	7	1

ARMS, ETC.

	Lbs.	Oz.
Sword and belt, &c.	5	12
Haversack	0	9½
Water bottle	2	9
Pocket-knife	0	5
Pouch-belt	0	9

ARMS, ETC.—Continued.	Lbs.	Oz.	IN SADDLE-BAGS—Continued.	Lbs.	Oz.
Pouch and 30 rounds	3	13½	1 tin of grease	0	10
Carbine	7	8	1 horse-brush	0	9
			1 curry-comb	0	12
	21	2	1 horse-rubber	0	9
Add revolver for Household Cavalry			1 stable-sponge	0	1
	2	4	1 oil-bottle	0	4
			Pipeclay, &c	0	9
Total	23	6			
			Total	7	4½

IN SADDLE-BAGS.	Lbs.	Oz.	BEHIND THE SADDLE.	Lbs.	Oz.
1 flannel shirt	1	1½	Cloak	7	1
1 pair drawers	0	12¼	Trousers	1	9
1 hold-all, containing spoon, comb, &c	1	0	Corn-sack	1	13
			Picketing peg	0	12½
1 pair socks	0	4½			
1 towel	0	8	Total	11	3½
1 brush	0	4			

	Lbs.	Oz.
Weight of trooper's entire equipment	106	9
If in Household Cavalry	108	13

The equipment of camp utensils, &c., intrenching tools and implements, signaling instruments, &c, varied from the regular establishment in but insignificant particulars, occasioned by the exigencies of the climate and the desire to have no more impedimenta than was necessary.

The helmets, ordinarily white, *were stained a light brown with tea or umber to render them less visible in the bright light.* Blue goggles and veils were issued for the men and eye-fringes for the horses. The latter were most useful on account of the flies that swarm in Egypt, but the former were very generally discarded by the men, the veils only being habitually used during sleep.

The forage ration is 12 pounds of hay and 12 pounds of oats. It was not very strictly adhered to, the supply being too scant at first. Afterwards forage was issued very liberally and the horses allowed as much as they could eat.

A compressed grain cake, composed mainly of oats, with small proportions of beans, hay, and crushed linseed, was tried and found to answer the purpose very well.

It is proper to state that the veterinary arrangements were carefully ordered and the veterinary staff efficient, everything being done for the animals which the circumstances permitted.

The cavalry did excellent service all through the campaign, as detailed elsewhere in official reports. The horses stood the work well, only 210 being lost from all causes up to the end of September, notwithstanding that they were sent out from Ismailia immediately after landing from a long sea voyage, and that they were at times almost starved. Major-General Drury-Lowe attributes this record to the fact that the horses were all very carefully selected and none were underbred. He thinks underbred horses would not have pulled through.

The relative value of light and heavy cavalry was not tested during the war. The country was not adapted to rapid movements, and the Egyptians were always indisposed to allow the British to approach near enough to charge. On the other hand, the Household Cavalry, in spite of their weight, held their own in all combined movements, and lost nothing in comparison with their lighter colleagues.

This arm of the service achieved the two most brilliant and dramatic strokes of the campaign—the moonlight charge of August 28, and the seizure of Cairo. As to the first episode, it may be fairly doubted whether the Egyptians would have stood to their guns in broad daylight. The value of their presence on September 9, on the extreme right of the British line was shown in the failure of Arabi to attempt a turning movement by the Tel-el-Kebir force. After the experience of the preceding engagement his men conceived a real dread of the British cavalry, whose physical efficiency was proportionately enhanced by this increased moral prestige.

Judged by its record, the efficiency of the British cavalry in Egypt seems to leave little to be desired. That the result was reached by a general departure, in some cases, from the standard equipment is a fact which should be full of meaning.

II.—THE MOUNTED INFANTRY.

This corps was organized by Captain H. Hallam-Parr, C. M. G., Somersetshire Light Infantry, from volunteers from different regiments, mostly those in the field. It was actively employed at Alexandria, where no regular cavalry was present, and in all the engagements of the campaign from Ismailia to Cairo.

At the outset it was composed of 100 men selected mainly with reference to their skill as marksmen. The other conditions were good conduct and fair horsemanship. These men were provided with horses, and whatever was necessary to their maintenance as a mounted corps, but great exactness of cavalry drill was avoided, and they were strictly kept to the original idea of being mobile sharpshooters. They were engaged in the reconnaissance in force of August 5, leading the left attack with vigor, being honorably mentioned by General Alison in his official dispatch on that occasion.

They were brigaded with the cavalry after reaching Ismailia. By wounds or disease they had fallen off to about 40 in number at El Magfar and Tel-el-Mahuta. Prior to Tel-el-Kebir their ranks were increased to 150.

Their services throughout the campaign are constantly spoken of in reports in terms of commendation. Their riding was criticised to their disadvantage, for the average Englishman is exacting in this respect, but the fact that they managed to keep up at all with the cavalry in the two days' forced march from Mahsameh to Cairo proved their endurance on horseback, although it must be confessed they arrived somewhat the worse for the journey.

The sharpness of their work is seen in the disproportionately heavy loss they sustained. As an instance it may be noted that every officer, with one exception, was either killed or wounded before September 12.

Their value was conceded on every hand, and the desirability of such a force in all military operations universally acknowledged. As discussed by those interested, the question assumed the following shape: Is it advisable to crystallize the corps into a permanent organization? The opinion seemed to be general that it would best serve the purpose of its creation by retaining its quasi volunteer character, and by offering to men in regiments serving at home, as a species of reward for good conduct and marksmanship, the opportunity of active service in the field. The friends of the troop were very positive in the expression of their belief that the main object of its formation would be lost if permanently organized, and that it would inevitably grow into a cavalry company, peculiarly armed, to be sure, but still a cavalry company strictly speaking, the time and thought of the men being diverted from sharpshooting to precision of mounted maneuvers and over-careful maintenance of horse trappings.

It may be safely taken for granted that, in her next war, England will not fail to have a comparatively large force of mounted infantry to supplement her cavalry, its general plan being as simple as that of the hundred or so who did such satisfactory work in Egypt.

III.—THE INFANTRY.

The basis of organization in this branch is the battalion, and, in general terms, the scheme is as follows:

The battalions are assembled into regiments, bearing, as a rule, some name peculiar to the county where the headquarters are established and from which recruits are meant to be drawn. Two battalions are regulars, and two belong to the county militia. In addition are such volunteer infantry corps as the district possesses. The whole is under one or more titular colonels, who never serve in the capacity of regimental commanders, but whose position is ordinarily that of a general officer. A colonelcy, by the way, is a substantial reward for a distinguished military record or an honor accorded to persons high in court circles. That the honor is considered mutual is shown by the fact that H. R.H. the Duke of Cambridge, the Field Marshal Commander-in-Chief, is titular colonel of two cavalry regiments, of three infantry regiments, and of the regiments of Royal Artillery and the corps of Royal Engineers, while H. R. H. the Prince of Wales is colonel of the three regiments of the Household Cavalry, of the Tenth Hussars, and the Rifle brigade.

Of the regular infantry battalions one is supposed to serve at home, while the other is abroad. The introduction of this plan with its "territorial designations," some twelve years since, was attended by the breaking up of the old regimental system, and the suppression of numerical titles.

Each battalion, the practical working unit (for the regiment as a whole is never united), is under a lieutenant-colonel. The war establishment is as follows:

Rank.	Number.	Number.	Horses. Chargers.	Horses. Public riding.	Horses. Draught.
Lieutenant-colonels	2	30	4	......	......
Majors	4		4	......	......
Captains	4		....	......	......
Lieutenants, &c	16		....	1	......
Adjutant	1		1	......	......
Paymaster	1		....	1	......
Quartermaster	1		....	1	......
Surgeon	1		....	1	......
Sergeant-major	1	10	....	......	......
Quartermaster sergeant	1		....	......	......
Band sergeant	1		....	......	......
Drum-major	1		....	......	......
Orderly room-clerk	1		....	......	......
Armorer sergeant	1		....	......	......
Paymaster sergeant	1		....	......	......
Transport sergeant	1		....	1	......
Sergeant cook	1		....	......	......
Pioneer sergeant	1		....	......	......
Color sergeants (orderly)	8	40	......	......	......
Sergeants	32				
Buglers	16	16	......	......	......
Corporals	41	1,000	....	......	......
Pioneers and artificers	13		....	......	......
Band	20		....	......	......
Privates	904		....	......	......
Drivers	22		....	......	44
Total	......	1,096	9	5	44

The personal equipment of the foot soldier is shown in the table subjoined:

Arms and accouterments.	Weight. Lb.	Weight. Oz.	Articles worn by the soldier.	Weight. Lb.	Weight. Oz.	Valise, and articles carried in it.	Weight. Lb.	Weight. Oz.
Pouches	1	00	Helmet	0	15	Overcoat and cape	6	10
Waist-belt and frog	0	13	Frock	2	6	Shirt	1	2
70 rounds of ammunition	7	13	Flannel shirt	1	2	Socks	0	4½
Rifle	8	14	Trousers	2	4	Towel	0	8
Bayonet	1	8	Braces	0	3½	Comb	0	0½
Scabbard	0	9	Socks	0	4¼	Spoon	0	1½
Knife and lanyard	0	6	Leggings	0	13	Polishing brush	0	4½
Water-bottle, full	2	9	Boots	3	3	Tin of grease	0	6½
Mess-tin	1	6½				Housewife	0	4½
Haversack	0	8½	Total	11	2¾	Sponge	0	0
Total	25	7				Trousers	2	4
						Boots	3	3
						Glengarry cap	0	4
						Pocket ledger	0	2
						Valise and straps	4	4
						Total	20	11¾

The waist-belt and braces of the foot soldier differ materially from those of seamen landed for operations ashore. In appearance they seem an unnecessarily complicated arrangement of straps and buckles, but upon analysis they are found to be a well-considered scheme having for its aim the attaching of the weights carried in marching so as to throw the strain upon the shoulders and to relieve the hips. The old-fashioned knapsack has given place to a soft leather "valise," which is worn at the back below the waist.

All parts of the belt and suspension are provided with buckles for the purpose of adjustment to the size and shape of the man. The metal fittings are of brass, and the leather is undressed. In garrison the latter is pipeclayed.

The waist-belt, Fig. 86, has staples on either side of the clasp, to which

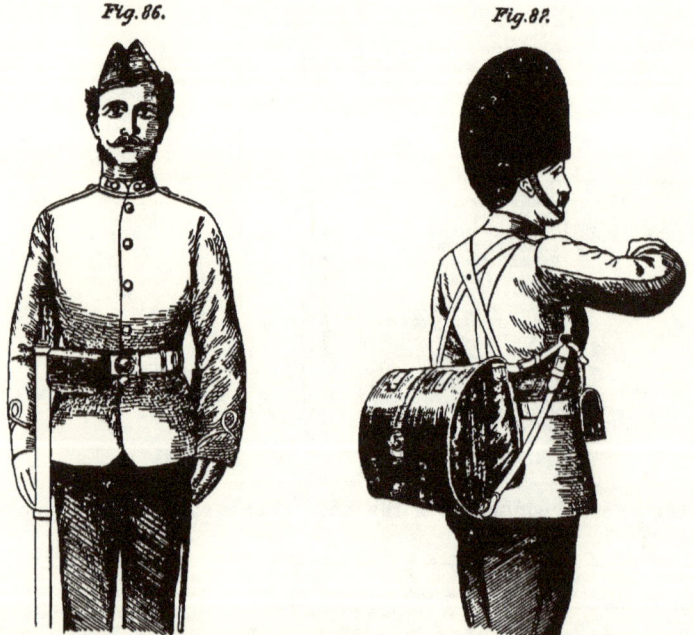

Fig. 86.   Fig. 87.

Front of a private in drill order; one pouch only.   *Valise without the overcoat.*

may be buckled the suspension straps from the shoulder-braces. On this are slipped the ball-bag and cartridge-pouch.

The braces are broad straps passing over each shoulder from the opposite upper corner of the valise. From the ring at the front end of each brace are three straps, Fig. 87, one going to the bottom and one to the top of the valise, which is thus prevented from flapping. The third takes the weight of the articles strung on the belt. The front and back loads are thus made to balance, roughly. Another strap is attached at will to each brace by a loop, and is for the purpose of carrying the overcoat, properly rolled up, between the shoulders.

229

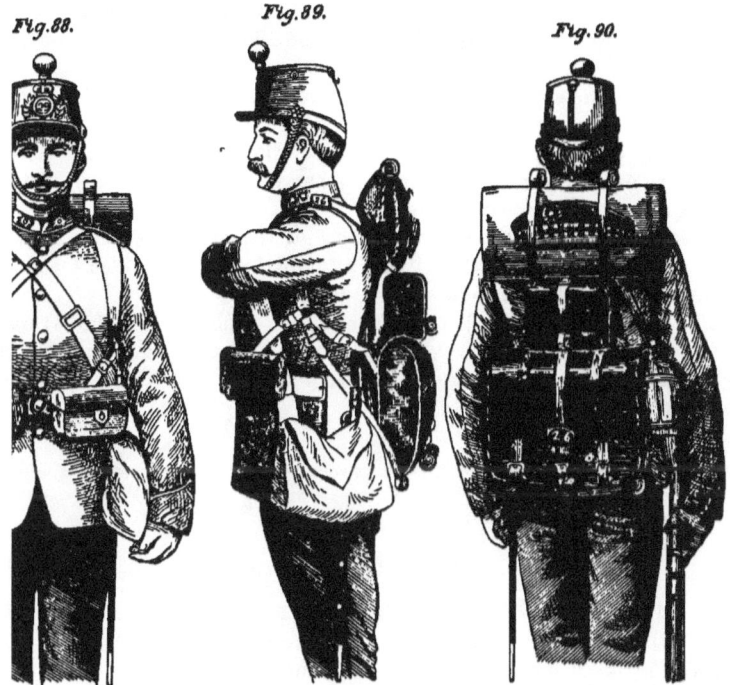

British foot soldier in heavy order.

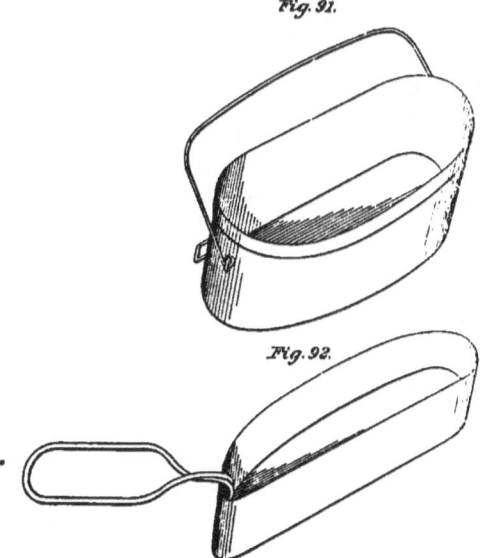

The mess equipment is worn on top of the valise in a water-proof cover. When in heavy marching order the soldier presents the appearance indicated in Figs. 88, 89, 90.

In Egypt, the cork helmet was the head dress for all corps.

The mess-tin is shown in Fig. 91. .Its principal dimensions are 6½ inches by 4 inches by 4 inches. The handle is of brass. The cover serves as a coffee-pot, and has a brass handle which folds down inside of the cover. Its appearance is given in Fig. 92.

It may be remarked that, practically, all the battalions were armed and equipped alike, the designations " light infantry," " rifles," " fusiliers," &c., being distinctions without differences.

The service arm is the Martini-Henry rifle, caliber 0.45 inch. It has seven grooves. The ball weighs 480 grains, and the powder charge is 85 grains. The piece is sighted up to 1,450 yards, but has an effective range twice as great.

XXII.

THE ROYAL ARTILLERY.

The field artillery of the British army is known as " Mountain Artillery " when the pieces and carriages are transported on the backs of pack animals; as " Field Artillery " when the pieces are hauled by horses, the crew being for the most part on foot; and as " Horse Artillery " when the pieces are hauled by horses and none of the crew are on foot.

All three classes of this branch of the service were represented in the Egyptian campaign, as will be seen from inspection of the following table, which gives the general details of each battery of six guns.

The nature of any battery is sufficiently indicated by its abbreviated title, the brigades of horse artillery being lettered, and those of field and garrison artillery being numbered, while the individual batteries of both horse and field artillery are lettered, and those of garrison artillery are numbered. (Garrison artillery is also distributed territorially into Northern, Scottish, London, &c., divisions.) In consequence, a battery spoken of by two letters, as N.A, is of horse artillery; by a letter and a number, as J.3, is of field artillery; and by two numbers, as 5.1, Scottish, is of garrison artillery. No matter the corps to which temporarily assigned, the batteries always retain their designations as such a battery of such an artillery brigade.

Corps to which assigned	Nature of battery	Title (Battery)	Title (Brigade)	Kind of gun	Major	Captain	Lieutenant	Surgeon	Veterinary surgeon	Non-commissioned officers and others	Troop and draught horses	Small-arm ammunition wagons	Water-carts	Two-wheeled carts	Forge wagon	Ammunition wagon and store	Ammunition wagon	Bell tents	Indian tents
1st division	Field artillery	A	1	M.l.R. 16-pdr.	1	3	1		1	194	153			1	1	1	6	2	28 17
Do	do	D	1	...do	1	3	1		1	194	153			1	1	1	6	2	28 17
2d division	do	I	2	...do	1	3	1		1	194	153			1	1	1	6	2	28 17
Do	do	N	2	..do	1	3	1		1	194	153			1	1	1	6	2	28 17
Cavalry	Horse artillery	N	A	M.L.R. 13-pdr.	1	3	1		1	175	176			1	1	1	6	2	26 16
Corps troops	do	G	B	...do	1	3	1		1	175	176			1	1	1	6	2	26 16
Do	Field artillery	C	3	...do	1	3	1		1	168	127			1	1	1	6	2	25 17
Do	do	J	3	do	1	3	1		1	168	127			1	1	1	6	2	25 17
Do	Ammunition reserve	F	1	None	1	3	1		1	178	207	42		1	1	1	4	6	28 18

The foregoing are "Imperial Troops." There came from India with the Indian Contingent two batteries, viz, H.1, field artillery, with the now obsolete 9-pdr. gun; and the 7.1, Northern division of garrison artillery, equipped as a mountain battery and carrying the 7-pdr. screw-jointed guns which will be found described at length in the section treating of the Indian Contingent.

It will be observed that here were four distinct calibers to be supplied. It may also be remarked that all the pieces, without exception, were of the muzzle-loading type.

In addition to the batteries mentioned above, a siege train, based on what is known as the "light unit," was sent to Ismailia, arriving on the September 6. It was partially landed but not used. Its composition was ten 40-pdr. M. L. R. of 35 cwt.; ten 25-pdr. M. L. R. of 18 cwt.; ten 6.3 inch M. L. R. howitzers of 18 cwt. With it, to work the guns, were four batteries, numbering 16 officers and 550 men, drawn from the 1st London and 1st Scottish divisions of garrison artillery, and enumerated in the table on p. 102. It was brought out for contingent use against Cairo. The gunners, however, remained on board the transport Teviot, at Ismailia, returning to England after the issue of the war was decided, their services happily not being required in Egypt.

Six 25-pdr. siege guns, sent from Malta, were planted on the Ismailia line: three at Kassassin, one at Tel-el-Mahuta, one at Mahsameh, and one at Nefiche, for the defense of the camps at these points. Those at Kassassin were the only ones used, and they to but a slight extent, on September 9, when they were manned by the 5.1 Scottish division.

It is thought well to describe briefly the 16 and 13-pdr. guns, as they were chiefly employed during the campaign, and represent the standard arm of the British field batteries of to-day. The former is represented in Figs. 93, 94, 95, and 96.

232

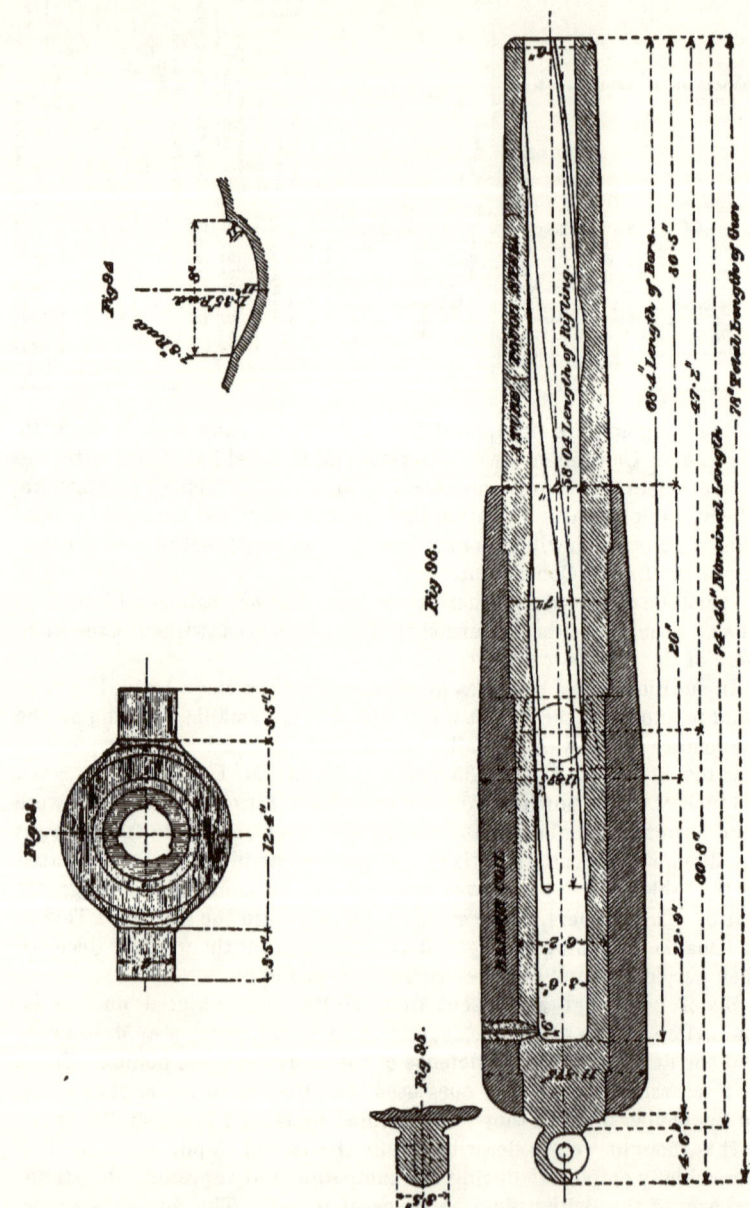

Its technical description is as follows:

Material:
- Exterior .... Wrought iron.
- Tube .... Steel.
- Length, total .... Inches, 78.
- Weight .... Pounds, 1,344.
- Preponderance .... Pounds, 7.5.
- Bore:
  - Caliber .... Inches, 3.6.
  - Length .... Inches, 68.4.
  - Capacity .... Cubic inches, 706.
- Rifling:
  - System .... Woolwich.
  - Length .... Inches, 58.04.
  - Grooves:
    - Number .... 3.
    - Depth .... Inch, 0.11.
    - Width .... Inch, 0.80
- Vent, hardened copper .... Inch, 0.6 from the bottom of the bore.

The gun is side-sighted only. The sights are set at a permanent angle of 1° 50' to the left to correct drift. The tangent scale is four sided and has a sliding leaf for deflection arising from the wind or other irregularity. The sides are marked as follows: 1st, in degrees; 2d, in tenths of fuze at corresponding ranges; 3d, in yards; 4th, blank. A table containing the same data is attached to the top of the right carriage bracket.

The projectiles used with the 16-pdr. are shell, shrapnel, and canister. The shell weighs 15 pounds empty, and 16 pounds 3 ounces when filled and fuzed. It is shown in section in Figs. 97 and 98.

The shrapnel contain 72 iron bullets of 18 to the pound, and 56 of 84 to the pound; 128 in all. The bursting charge is 1½ ounces of powder, and the total weight of the projectile when ready for firing is 17 pounds 14½ ounces. Figs. 99 and 100.

The canister contains 176 iron balls of 16½ to the pound, filled in with clay and sand. It weighs 15 pounds 3 ounces. Figs. 101 and 102.

The service charge for the gun is three pounds R. L. G. powder, giving an initial velocity of 1,355 feet per second.

The fuzes are either R. L. percussion or the usual Boxer time-fuze. The two types of the former are shown in Figs. 103 and 104, and require no explanation.

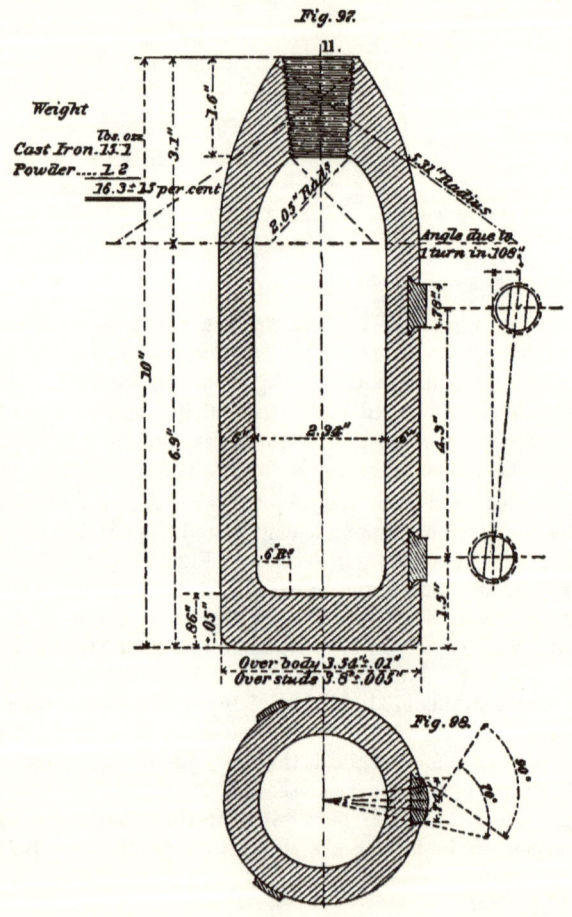

Fig. 97.
Fig. 98.

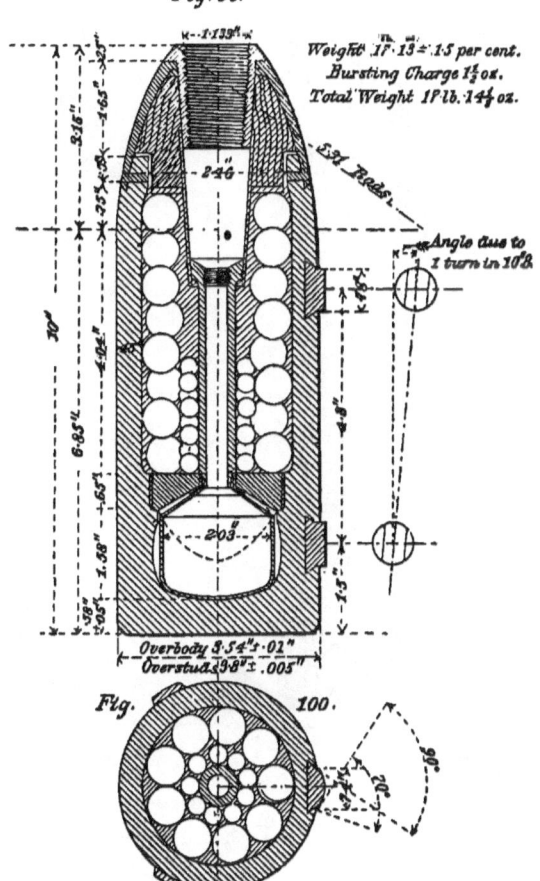

Fig. 99.

Fig. 100.

16 pdr. Shrapnel.

The Boxer fuze is now always supplied of the 15-seconds length, shown in Fig. 105, and, like the percussion fuzes, is too well known to need description.

These time and percussion fuzes are common to all calibers, the shells being tapped to a uniform gauge.

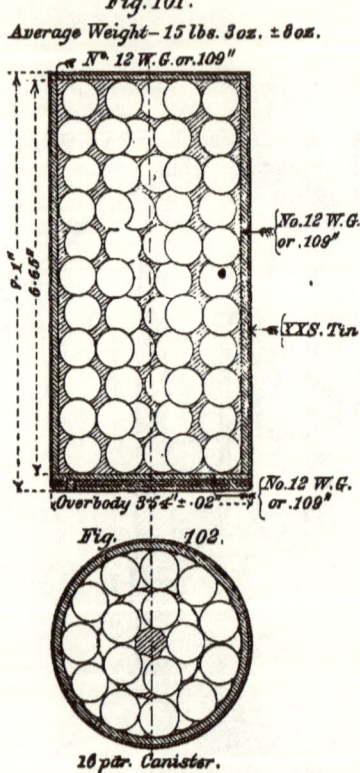

Fig. 101.
Average Weight—15 lbs. 3oz. ± 8oz.

Fig. 102.

16 pdr. Canister.

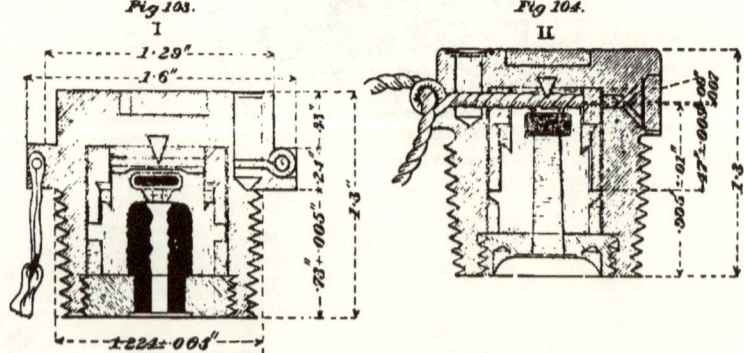

Royal laboratory percussion fuzes I and II.

The carriage of the 16-pdr. is of iron, mounted on composite wheels. The axletree boxes have guard-irons and foot-rests, so that they may serve for seats. Each box contains two rounds of ammunition.

The limber is also of iron and of the usual form. The shafts are "near and off;" (that is, the near shaft is in the center of the limber), and are fitted for single, double, treble, or bullock draught. There are three limber-boxes, the near and off, each carrying 12 projectiles and as many cartridges. The projectiles are packed on end around the

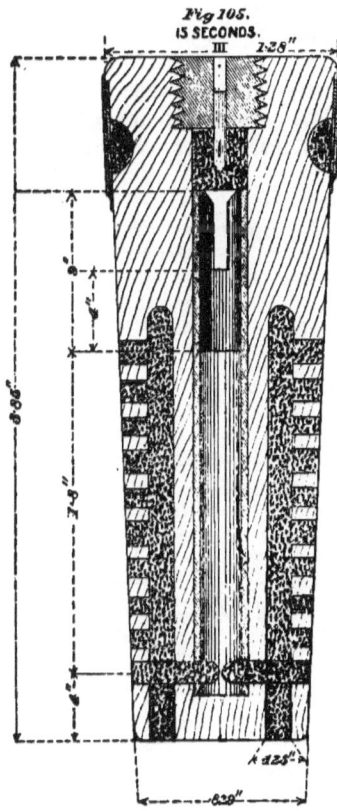

Boxer 15-seconds time-fuze.

sides of the box, the space within being reserved for the cartridges, an arrangement designed to protect the latter in the event of the limber being hit in action.

The center box, which is smaller than the others, contains an assortment of fuzes, friction primers, tools, grease, &c.

The working limit of this gun is at about 4,000 yards. At that range the projectile has an angle of descent of 15° 40′ and a remaining velocity of 693 feet per second. The time of flight is 14 seconds.

The 16-pdr. presents some points well worthy of analysis. Its weight is 84 times that of the projectile, its length of bore 19 calibers, its system of rifling is antiquated, its powder charge less than one-fifth the weight of the shell, its range small, and its remaining velocity low. These particulars are not in accord with the tendency of modern ordnance, and in consequence the gun is being replaced by the newer 13-pdr., an excellent weapon of its type. On account of its being the latest outcome of British experience and thought, a rather detailed account of the gun and its appurtenances is deemed in place.

The general appearance of the 13-pdr., Plate 73, is not unlike that of its predecessor, and its mode of construction is the same—a steel tube and wrought-iron breech coil. It varies, however, mainly in the rifling, in being longer and narrower, and in having a chamber.

The principal dimensions, &c., are as follows:

Material:
    Exterior... Wrought iron.
    Tube... Steel.
Length, total.. Inches, 92.
Weight.. Pounds, 896.
Bore:
    Caliber.. Inches, 3.
    Length.. Inches, 84.
    Total capacity... Cubic inches, 617.8.
    Total area of section... Square inches, 7.29.
    Diameter.. Inches, 3.15.
Chamber:
    Length.. Inches, 14.13.
    Capacity.. Cubic inches, 110.38.
Rifling:
    System.. Modern polygroove.
    Twist....Uniformly increasing from one turn in 100 calibers to one turn in 30 calibers at 9 inches from the muzzle, thence uniform.
    Length.. Inches, 69.
    Grooves:
        Number... 10.
        Depth.. Inch, 0.05.
        Width.. Inch, 0.509.
Means of rotation...Copper base expansion ring.
Vent, hardened copper..............................7 inches from the bottom of the bore.

The gun is center-sighted only. The sights are set at a permanent angle of 1° 30′ to the left to correct drift. The breech sight has a sliding leaf. In the upper edge of this leaf is a notch 0.06 inch deep and below it a hole 0.05 inch in diameter. Figs. 106 and 107. These correspond to the conical point and the sighting window, fitted with cross-hairs of the muzzle sight, and are used for rough and fine sighting respectively. The front sight is a removable block of bronze retained in its seat (a sight mass on the muzzle) by means of a key.

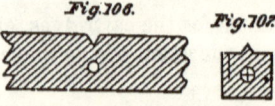

Rear and front sights, 13-pounder M. L. R.

Fig. 106. Fig. 107.

The breech sight is marked to degrees only, a brass range table on the bracket giving other information as desired.

In front of the chamber the bore of the gun is reduced by a choke to a diameter of 2.93 inches. This choke prevents the projectiles from entering the chamber and seats them all uniformly.

The projectiles used w th this gun are of the usual three types, shell, shrapnel, and canister. In design they are similar to those for the 16-pdr. shown in Figs. 90 to 95, but differ from them in the substitution of a base ring called the "gas check," which is made of 100 parts of copper to 3 of zinc, and which presents no peculiarity. The service charge is 3 pounds 2 ounces of R. L. G. 2 powder, giving an initial velocity of 1,595 feet per second. The fuzes are identical with those described already. The shell is of cast iron. The base for half an inch is reduced to 1.87 inches in diameter and cast with a circular groove for attaching the gas check, and with twenty radial grooves by which the ring imparts rotation to the shell. The head is struck with a radius of one and a half diameters, the point truncated, bored out, and tapped to receive the fuze. The interior is lacquered with a composition of 12 parts of resin, 2 of Spanish brown, and 1 of plaster of Paris thinned with turpentine. The length of the shell is 10.57 inches. The bursting charge is 10 ounces. When empty the shell weighs 12 pounds, and when filled and fuzed 13 pounds 6 ounces.

The shrapnel is in two parts, the body and the head. The former is a cylinder of cast iron, fitted like the shell with a base ring. The head is of thin charcoal iron 0.148 inch thick, struck with a radius of 1.2 diameters, the point being truncated to receive a gun-metal bouching tapped to the fuze-gauge and soldered to the head. Within the head is a wooden block or former. The head is attached to the body by four steel screws. It contains 116 bullets at 34 to the pound, the interstices being filled in with resin. The total weight when ready for use is 13 pounds 2 ounces. A reference to Fig. 94 will make this description clear.

The side of the case-shot is made of heavy tin. The top is of sheet-iron, No. 18 B. W. G., and is fixed to the case by turning over and soldering the notched ends of the case. A base ring of sheet-iron, No. 12 B. W. G., is riveted to the bottom of the case. There is an inside lining of sheet-iron, No. 14 B. W. G. The contents are 340 mixed metal bullets of 34 to the pound. The length is 9 inches, and the total weight 13 pounds 7 ounces. (See Fig. 92.)

The carriage is of steel. Its general design is made evident in Plate 73. The elevating apparatus (see Plates 73 and 77), Fig. 109, is worthy of especial attention. There are no axletree boxes. The bed on each side is fitted as a seat (see Plate 77, Fig. 108), mounted on springs and having guard-irons and a sliding foot-rest. Leather cases (see Plate 73) are fitted outside each bracket to carry two case-shot and two cartridges. An especial feature is the grease chamber in the front flange of the wheel. (See Plate 79, Figs. 107, 108.)

Both steel and iron enter into the construction of the limber (see Plate 75), which has but two boxes. The projectiles, assorted, are carried in steel trays (see Plate 78), which are placed at the sides of the boxes, near the wheels, the inside compartment of each box serving as a receptacle for cartridges. These trays are too light. They have a tendency to pound out of shape in a hard march, and give much trouble in withdrawal. The artillery officers prefer the old plan adopted in the limber-boxes of the 16-pdrs.

The shafts are "near and off," and the limber is fitted for single, double, or treble draught.

The general dimensions of the carriage and limber are as follows:

Height of center of gun.. 43 inches.
Length:
   Carriage:
      With wheels .... 8 feet 4 inches.
      Without wheels .... 7 feet 3 inches.
   Axletrees.. 6 feet 2¼ inches.
Angle of trail... 30°.
Maximum elevation .... 16°.
Maximum depression .... 5°.
Wheels:
   Track.. 5 feet 2 inches.
   Diameter... 5 feet.

Plate 76 represents the ammunition wagon. The front boxes carry seventeen assorted projectiles stowed vertically about a canvas pocket containing as many filled cartridges. The other wagon boxes hold eighteen projectiles and their charges.

The following diagrams give the distribution of the ammunition which habitually accompanies the guns, together with the tools and stores.

1st GUN AND LIMBER.

LIMBER.

ON FOOTBOARD.
1 cartouche, leather, large. 1 pair drag ropes.
1 swingletree, short traces.
traces for breast harness. hames‡
2 mallets.

1 shovel, under.
    1 felling axe.   1 spade.
    1 pickaxe, under.   1 bill hook.   } under.
                              1 water carriage brush.

NEAR BOX   OFF BOX
2 swords and 2 carbines ‡ ; (in cases) in front of boxes.

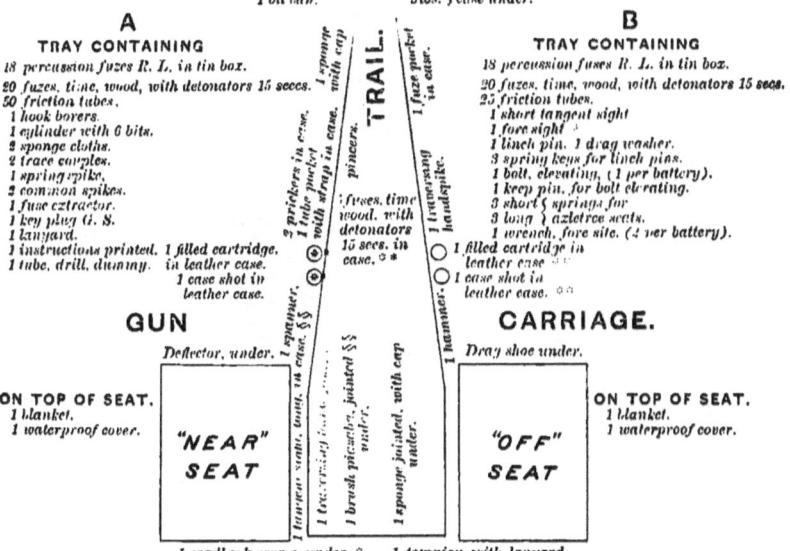

	A	18	18	B	
on top of lid of box. 1 blanket. 1 corn sack 1 waterproof cover.	8 shrapnel, 15 fuzes, time, wood with detonators15secs.	filled cartridges in cartouch.	filled cartridges in cartouch.	3 shrapnel, 15 fuzes, time, wood with detonators15secs.	on top of lid of box. 1 blanket. 1 corn sack 1 waterproof cover.
	5 shrapnel			5 shrapnel	
	4 shells. 1 case shot.	5 shrapnel.	5 shrapnel.	4 shells. 1 case shot.	

1 camp kettle, under. Knapsack   Knapsack.   2 leather buckets, under.
                       1 half round tin grease box) in leather
                       1 oil can.   3lbs.) case under.

A
TRAY CONTAINING
18 percussion fuzes R. L. in tin box.
20 fuzes, time, wood, with detonators 15 secs.
50 friction tubes.
1 hook borers.
1 cylinder with 6 bits.
2 sponge cloths.
2 trace couples.
1 spring spike.
2 common spikes.
1 fuse extractor.
1 key plug G. S.
1 lanyard.
1 instructions printed. 1 filled cartridge.
1 tube, drill, dummy.   in leather case.
                         1 case shot in
                         leather case.

GUN
Deflector, under.

ON TOP OF SEAT.
1 blanket.
1 waterproof cover.

"NEAR" SEAT

1 wadhook worm under. ⁂

B
TRAY CONTAINING
18 percussion fuzes R. L. in tin box.
20 fuzes, time, wood, with detonators 15 secs.
25 friction tubes.
1 short tangent sight
1 fore sight
1 linch pin. 1 drag washer.
3 spring keys for linch pins.
1 bolt, elevating, (1 per battery).
1 keep pin, for bolt elevating.
3 short (springs for
3 long) azletree seats.
1 wrench, fore site. (1 per battery).
1 filled cartridge in
  leather case
1 case shot in
  leather case.

CARRIAGE.
Drag shoe under.

ON TOP OF SEAT.
1 blanket.
1 waterproof cover.

"OFF" SEAT

1 tompion with lanyard.

† 1 pair on Nos. 1 3 & 5 gun limbers.   1 per division.   § with No. 1 gun.
‡ M. H. carbines are carried in leather buckets attached to the boxes.
** Carried on the carriage only when going into action. §§ when not in use in gun.

NOTE. The packing of the gun and wagon limbers is made nearly identical to facilitate the supply of ammunition in action by replacing one by the other.
Valises are carried on two of the ammunition boxes of horse batteries, attached to the guard irons.
Water-proof covers are issued additional for camp equipment, and for batteries on a war establishment.

	cwts.	qrs.
Weight packed, without personal equipment, { Carriage and gun	26	0
{ Limber	17	3
Total	37	3

948 EG——16

2d WAGON AND LIMBER.
LIMBER.
ON FOOTBOARD.

1 pair drag ropes.   1 lifting jack.   1 picket rope.
1 swingletree.   1 marline.   kicking straps.
1 shovel, under.   1 spade.
                1 bill hook.
1 felling axe.   1 water carriage brush } under.

NEAR BOX   1 pick axe, under.   **OFF BOX**
2 swords in front of boxes.

	C	18	18	D	
on top of lid of box. 1 blanket. 1 corn sack. 1 waterproof cover.	3 shrapnel. 15 fuzes, time, wood with detonators 15 secs.	filled cartridges in cartouch.	filled cartridges in cartouch.	3 shrapnel. 15 fuzes, time, wood with detonators 15 secs.	on top of lid of box. 1 blanket. 1 corn sack. 1 waterproof cover.
	5 shrapnel.			5 shrapnel.	
	4 shells. 1 case shot.	5 shrapnel.	5 shrapnel.	4 shells. 1 case shot.	

1 camp kettle, under.   Knapsack.   Knapsack.   2 leather buckets, (under).
1 half round tin grease box, 3 lbs.
in leather case under.

C   **D**
TRAY CONTAINING   TRAY CONTAINING

18 percussion fuzes R. L. in tin boxes.   18 percussion fuzes R. L. in tin box.
20 fuzes, time, wood, with detonators, 15 secs.   20 fuzes, time, wood, detonators, 15 secs.
50 friction tubes.   drag shoe   50 friction tubes.
1 hook borer, 1 cylinder with 6 bits.   spare wheel.   1 short tangent sight.
2 sponge cloths. 2 lanyards.   1 linch pin. 1 drag washer.
2 trace couples. 1 key plug, G. S.   3 spring keys for linch pins.
1 instructions, printed.   1 keep pin, elevating bolt.
                                     1 water carriage brush (under).

WAGON BODY

2 port-fires on inside of lid.   2 port-fires on inside of lid.
Knapsack and 2 swords.   Knapsack and 2 swords.

		7 shrapnel.	7 shrapnel.		
on top of lid of box. 1 blanket. 1 waterproof cover.	3 picket posts. 1 hand saw, in case under. / 3 shells.	17 filled cartridges in cartouch.	17 filled cartridges in cartouch.	3 shells. / 3 picket posts under.	on top of lid of box. 1 blanket. 1 waterproof cover.
		7 shrapnel.	7 shrapnel.		

1 camp kettle under.   4 reaping hooks.   1 camp kettle under.
2 spare lashings under.

	E	18	18	F	
on top of lid of box. 1 blanket. 1 waterproof cover.	3 shrapnel.	filled cartridges in cartouch.	filled cartridges in cartouch.	3 shrapnel.	on top of lid of box. 1 blanket. 1 waterproof cover.
	5 shrapnel.			5 shrapnel.	
1 port-fire stick.	4 shells. 1 shrapnel.	5 shrapnel.	5 shrapnel.	4 shells. 1 shrapnel.	

Knapsack.   Knapsack.
28 lbs. of grease, in two tin magazine boxes under.   1 cartridge and 1 shell with lanyard (drill).
1 maul under.   1 lb. tow, 1 tin for horseshoe nails,
shafts, spare, under { "near" with No. 1 wagon.   in box under.
                  { "off" with No. 2 wagon.

E   **F**
TRAY CONTAINING   TRAY CONTAINING

1 lb. slow match. 1 skein Hambro line.   1 funnel, leather. 1 knife, clasp, 1 port-fire clipper.
1 tube pocket with strap. 1 fuze pocket with hook borer.   1 screw driver, 1 drift, wood. 1 pair scissors.
                                     1 hold-all with 2 needles and 2 ozs. of silk.

* 1 per division, with 1, 3, and 5 wagons.

		cwts.	qrs.
Weight packed without personal equipment.	Wagon	26	2
	Limber	18	1
	Total	44	3

The total supply of ammunition with each gun is therefore—

Shrapnel	108
Shell	30
Canister	4
Total	142
Cartridges	142
Friction tubes	175
Total	317
Time fuzes	140
Percussion fuzes	72
Total	212

The carriages of C.3 were of a different design and had longer trails, while the ammunition was carried on end in top-lid boxes as with the 16-pdr.

The other batteries found that the short trail and its great angle were attended by the disadvantage that in soft soil the trail buries itself at each discharge, necessitating constant change of elevations, and threatening accident in some cases by excessive jumping.

The 13-pdr. has a working range of about 6,000 yards. For use at that distance the gun has an elevation of 19° 06′; the time of flight of the projectile is 23.7 seconds; its angle of descent 30° 42′; its remaining velocity 644 feet per second.

A comparison of the new and the old field pieces shows decreased proportional weight of gun to projectile, with greater velocity. Their relative accuracy may be gathered from the following figures which hold good at the distance of 4,000 yards:

	With the 16-pounder.	With the 13-pounder.
	Yards.	*Yards.*
Ten per cent. of rounds should fall within—		
A length of	48.4	38.4
A width of	5.22	2.28
A height of	13.54	10.40

These results are obtained by greater length of bore, 68.4 inches in the 16-pdr. and 84 inches in the 13-pdr., an increase of 9 calibers; by the use of a chamber, by the adoption of a gas check or expansion ring, and by the heavier rates of charge to projectile. In the new gun the charge is nearly one-quarter of the weight of the projectile.

It is worthy of remark that the use of wet sponges is forbidden with this gun on the ground of increased residuum in the chamber, after firing, which is difficult to remove on account of the "choke." Great care in sponging is, however, strongly urged. It would strike one accustomed to liberal amounts of water in this connection that the care recommended would be more in place in the subsequent loading. It is but fair to say that no ill effects were experienced through the adoption of this rule.

As was the case with everything else on wheels, the country proved too heavy for the guns, or the guns too heavy for the country, reducing all movements to a slow and painful drag. Six horses were originally assigned to each gun, but it was found necessary to increase the number to ten, fourteen, in fact, indefinitely, the war schedule of allowance being a mere estimate of probable needs.

The battery drivers carried revolvers only, a special issue for the campaign, the other men being armed for the most part with cavalry sabers or sword-bayonets, according to the nature of the battery, whether horse or field. Each battery has 24 Martini-Henry carbines. Two are slung on each limber (gun and wagon), on the ammunition boxes above the foot-board.

The ammunition column, F.I, was designed to convey 30 spare rounds per gun in addition to the assorted projectiles and charges in the limbers and wagons, besides 360,000 rounds of rifle ammunition, 40,000 rounds of carbine ammunition, &c. It was a reserve in all respects except that it brought out no guns. Four spare gun carriages were among its stores. It was expected that the column would serve as a distributor of ammunition of all kinds from the advance depot to the batteries and battalions at the front, the advance depot being in its turn supplied by the railway. The men and horses received the same special issues as those mentioned apropos of the cavalry.

As regards mess arrangements, each battery has one cook, who is rarely changed. Each subdivision (gun's crew) is served by an orderly detailed for the day. This man draws the rations and gives them to the battery cook, receives the cooked food when ready, and attends generally to all the mess interests.

The various detachments of the Royal Artillery embarked between August 3 and 9 at Portsmouth, Southampton, and London. The first to arrive at Alexandria was the field battery A.1, by the Palmyra, on the 14th, and the last, the ammunition column, by the Texas, on the 25th of the same month.

The artillery of the expedition was under the general command of Colonel W. H. Goodenough, R. A., who was given the local rank of Brigadier-General. The artillery of the 1st division was commanded by Lieutenant-Colonel B. F. Schreiber, R. A., that of the 2d by Lieutenant-Colonel F. C. Elton, R. A., and the Horse Artillery by Lieutenant-Colonel C. E. Nairnes, R. A.

The artillery took no part in the preliminary operations about Alexandria.

The disembarkation was begun at Ismailia on August 22, and was pushed with all speed.

The first engagement with the Egyptians in which the artillery took part was that of August 24, near El Magfar. At 5 a. m. of that day two 13 pdrs. of N.A, Royal Horse Artillery, under Lieutenant S. C. Hickman, started from Ismailia to join General Graham's force, then ordered to advance from Nefiche. They pushed on at once past Nefiche to El Magfar, and came into action on the right of the infantry, behind some low mounds, keeping up an unequal artillery duel all day, the Egyptians having twelve guns to assist this attack. At 5.45 p. m. the remaining four guns of the battery arrived from Ismailia, which they had left at 3 p. m., and the united battery soon silenced the Egyptian artillery, the range being from 2,000 to 2,600 yards. It was then shifted to the other flank near the canal, and an interchange of shell begun with the pieces on the Egyptian right, which lasted until dark. By this time Lieutenant Hickman's division had expended about one hundred rounds each, mostly shrapnel.

It is difficult to obtain minute details of the effect of the British shell either during this or the subsequent engagements of the campaign. Under the circumstances, it is necessary to accept the main fact, that the enemy's guns were silenced in twenty minutes. On the other hand begins the testimony, which is repeated on every occasion, that the Egyptians served their own guns with unexpected skill. "The enemy had the range, and burst his shells, as a rule, fairly well." It must be borne in mind that the *atmospheric phenomena peculiar to that region are known and understood by the native, while distressing and misleading to the foreigner, who, on this occasion, had the sun fairly in his eyes after midday.*

One result of the operations of August 24 was the demonstration that the wheeled vehicles supplied were almost useless in the desert across which the army was now to advance. Except in Lieutenant Hickman's division, all the ammunition wagons had been left behind, "having stuck on the road, where they remained over the following day." To get the guns and limbers along was about all the battery horses could accomplish even when exerting their greatest efforts.

The advance was strengthened during the night of August 24 and 25 by the arrival, among other corps, of battery, A.1 and, somewhat later, by two guns each of battery N.2, and battery G.B. In the march to the westward a ridge overlooking Tel-el-Mahuta was reached from whence the Egyptians could be seen at work on their intrenchments. At this point the artillery on both sides began firing, but the duel was of short duration, as the cavalry and horse artillery and two guns of A.1 turned the left flank of the Egyptians, who retreated to Mahsameh, throwing away arms, accouterments, and everything in their flight. The good work done by the cavalry and artillery did not cease here, but was repeated on beyond at Mahsameh. When within range of the camp there the guns which had accompanied the cavalry opened on the camp and railway station, which were speedily evacuated, the mounted troops then dashing in and capturing the place.

The artillery work on the August 28 is described from notes of that engagement by Captain G. B. Martin, R. A. (aid-de-camp to General Goodenough), to whom nearly everything that is of interest in this section is due.

Two guns of N.A arrived from Mahsameh at Kassassin about 11 a. m. (An 8ᶜᵐ Krupp gun had been mounted on a truck and protected by sand-bags and dragged up from Mahsameh. This gun continued in action throughout the day, and as soon as the men, the Royal Marine Artillery, became acquainted with the division on the tangent scale it rendered effective service.) The two guns N.A were in action on the right of the railway for an hour and then had to retire for want of ammunition. An ammunition-wagon, which had been sent after the two guns stuck in the sand, did not arrive until late in the day.

The remaining four guns of N.A advanced from Mahsameh with the cavalry in the afternoon, and reached the plateau north of Kassassin about 5 p. m.

These guns began the firing, which was succeeded by the moonlight charge of the Household Cavalry.

The artillery engaged in the affair of September 9, at Kassassin, was as follows:

N.A, Royal Horse Artillery.
G.B, Royal Horse Artillery.
A.1, Royal Artillery.
D.1, Royal Artillery.
7.1, Northern division, mule battery.
5.1, Scottish division, 3 25-pdr. M. L. R.
Royal Marine Artillery, 1 8ᶜᵐ Krupp B. L. R.
Royal Navy, 1 40-pdr. B. L. R.
The last two were mounted on railway trucks.
Captain Martin goes on to say:

The 8ᶜᵐ Krupp was in front of the 40-pdr. There being no siding at Kassassin, this could not be remedied. The 8ᶜᵐ gun made good practice at trains bringing on the enemy's troops. The 40-pdr. being masked could only fire occasionally. Both these guns had no motive power. Had there been any they would have been extremely useful. The Krupp opened fire at 7.30 a. m. in reply to some desultory firing of the enemy.

Of A.1 and D.1 he says:

These batteries were north of the camp, and fired at the enemy's guns (2,000 yards off) and at infantry (about 1,200 yards off). The enemy's guns were placed on Ninth Hill, their left extending beyond the British front and their right resting on the canal, with a few troops south of the canal. The Egyptian fire on the gun-pits was very good. * * * A.1 and D.1 left the gun-pits and advanced about 100 yards. D.1 fired from here at an Egyptian battery, A.1 at two batteries and infantry in right center. About 8.30 a. m., A.1 and D.1 advanced again, this time 1,000 yards to the right front, and continued firing for an hour or so. The enemy's infantry fire continued, but at this time their gun-fire became slacker. * * * Our troops were ordered to advance and drive back the Egyptians. A.1 and D.1 therefore advanced independently for two miles and a half or so, firing at various ranges. They shot down the detachments of two Egyptian guns, which were taken possession of by our line as it advanced. About 3 miles from Tel-el-Kebir a halt was made, all our artillery keeping much the same relative distance as they formed with originally. The Egyptians retired into their entrenchments. A final advance of 1,000 yards or so was made by our side to see the entrenchments and get an idea of them. At that time we were 5,000 yards or so from them. The action ended at 12.30, and the troops returned to Kassassin.

N.A was with the cavalry division on plateau north of camp. * * * This flank was kept refused throughout the day.

G.B about 7.30 a. m. was formed up some 1,500 yards to the right of A.1 on the north side of the camp. Their fire was directed chiefly towards the enemy's center. They advanced about 9.30 a. m. when A.1 and D.1 did, their movements conforming generally to those of the troops in our center.

7.1 came into the space between A.1 and G.B about 8.30 a. m. * * * They were also directed by the movements from our center.

Additional technical notes on this action, the principal artillery affair of the campaign, are quoted as of extreme interest. They were made by Lieutenant Apsley Smith, R. A., aid-de-camp to Lieutenant-Colonel Nairnes, R A., who directed the artillery on this occasion.

The enemy stuck to their guns, and both their elevation and direction were good, but they used chiefly common shell, and with so small a charge (about one pound) the shells dropped at a very high angle, sinking deep, and, though exploding, doing hardly any damage. Except at first against the camp and gun-pits, their fire was not concentrated, but seemed to be directed against whatever battery of ours happened to be firing at or near them. They appeared to make good use of any cover afforded by the ground, and, in one case, the position of a battery, as shown by the wheel tracks, was remarkably good. I believe their ammunition-wagons were kept well in rear, more so than is usual in our own service. One or two of their shrapnel burst on graze, the bullets ricochetting harmlessly along the ground, but I do not remember seeing any time-shrapnel bursts in air.

On our side the batteries worked independently as far as the nature of ammunition, range, and object aimed at permitted, though no advance of any extent was made without orders.

At first our shells, especially the 7* and 13 pdrs., burst short and high, but for some time previous to the advance one could see the time-shrapnel, especially on our left front, causing considerable disturbance among the enemy.

Although the batteries fired independently, each battery of six guns fired at the same or about the same object.

When once our artillery was fairly in action, and our infantry in position, the enemy never advanced another yard, and soon showed signs of wavering. But just at first, his fire was so quick and accurate that I thought personally we had more guns opposing us than we really had. The light was good, the sun being behind us, but, probably from want of a well-defined object to lay on, I did not hear, except in one case, of any Watkins range-finders being of use.

The wagons of our field batteries remained near them and were a good deal exposed.

In the advance the batteries hardly worked together sufficiently, the ones in front taking up their position without much regard to a battery perhaps still in action behind and to their flank.

I heard it remarked, with reference to this and other actions, that in ground like the desert it was a mistake to come into action just behind the crests of ridges, on account of the labor and delay of running up after each round.

The two guns on the railway, and the three 25-pdrs., I saw nothing of, but they expended a lot of ammunition, and I heard made good practice. The 25-pdrs. fired over the heads of our infantry advancing along the railway and canal banks. The 40-pdr. was handicapped by the Krupp in front, and could only fire to its right front.

---

* Of the mule battery, 7.1, Northern division.

The performance of the artillery at Tel-el-Kebir, being but a phase of the battle and not the principal part of it, is given in the section treating of that action.

The experience in Egypt with even the light 13-pdr. shows the carriage (or indeed any carriage) too heavy for use in such a country. It would seem desirable, for service over light sandy soils, *to devise some sort of broad tire capable of ready application to the wheels of all vehicles.* There were no instances of breakdowns from slightness of construction; all the mishaps arose from sheer inability to get the weights across the desert with any speed approaching satisfaction. Such a tire would have proved of value, and its design appears to present no insuperable difficulty. An alternate solution of the question might be found in a wooden track in pieces which could be shifted from rear to front by hand, as the wheels left them. Under the actual circumstances the draught power had to be increased enormously to obtain even the snail-like speed achieved.

It is impossible to avoid instituting a comparison between the wheeled and the mountain batteries employed during the campaign, to the advantage of the latter. The former threw heavier shell, but in range the latter was at least equal to the 16-pdr., while its greater mobility, the facility with which it could go anywhere and everywhere, across the desert or even along the narrow banks of the irrigation canals which cover the cultivated portion of Egypt as with a net-work, rendered it most valuable, and in the event of operations in the interior of the delta would have made it invaluable. The gist of this criticism is merely that Egypt is best suited to the employment of mule batteries.

The testimony is unanimous as to the value of shrapnel when the fuze is properly cut. The Egyptians did not use this projectile, as a rule, and their shell-fire occasioned more contempt than wounds, the British becoming accustomed to it and ceasing to dread it. The British artillery, *employing shrapnel almost exclusively, was more effective both physically and morally.* The part the two 13-pdrs. took at El Magfar in repelling the attack was as much due to superiority projectile as to more able management.

No step was made in this campaign towards solving the question of the muzzle-loader *versus* the breech-loader for a field piece. The British had none of the latter type to pit in technical rivalry against their new and admirable 13-pdr., while the Krupp guns of the Egyptians were of the old pattern of 1868, burning too little powder to make them equal to their British competitors at any but short ranges.

The skill, intelligence, and vigor which official dispatches attribute to the artillery operations of the campaign testify to admirable organization, careful equipment, and thorough training, and reflect credit on those immediately charged in the field with the direction of this branch of the British military service.

XXIII.

THE ROYAL ENGINEERS.

The engineer detachment in the British expeditionary force in Egypt was composed of six companies, two troops and a field park, the whole under the command of Colonel C. B. P. N. H. Nugent, C. B., R. E., to whom was given the local rank of Brigadier-General.

The companies according to their corps numbers were the 8th, 17th, 18th, 21st, 24th, and 26th, and the troops were A and C.

The 8th company receives special mention in Section XXIV of this report, under the title of "the Railway Company," and C troop in Section XXV, which treats of "the Telegraph Troop."

The 17th company, under Captain Elliott Wood, R. E., appears to have been a sort of maid of all work. Its *personnel* was composed of 2 captains, 2 lieutenants, 85 non-commissioned officers and men, a total of 89.

The company was armed with Martini-Henry rifles and sword-bayonets. It came from Malta in H. M. S. Northumberland, arriving at Alexandria on July 17, and was the pioneer of its corps in Egypt. It marched at once to Gabarri, each man carrying a tool of some kind ready to repair the defenses of the place. The men and officers slept in a large cotton storehouse during their stay in Alexandria.

The following paragraphs are taken from notes kindly furnished by Captain Wood:

Large quantities of stores, including 50,000 sand-bags and 1,300 shovels, had been brought with the company and were far in excess of what would accompany it in the field.

The company had started at a few hours' notice from Malta, and its transport had to be entirely organized, as drivers, even, did not exist. This was at once taken in hand, while defensive works were pushed with all dispatch.

These consisted in repairing or retrenching old breaches in the enceinte, one being of great extent; putting the draw-bridges in working order, laying fougasses, erecting heavy stone barricades, &c., on which working parties of other corps and Arabs were also employed under the Royal Engineers.

The hours for the Sappers were as follows: After breakfast of coffee and biscuit, parade for work at 4.30 a. m.; 12 to 2 p. m. dinner, cooked at the works; return to quarters at from 5 to 6.30 p. m.

On July 22, Lieutenant Heath and a detachment of Royal Engineers removed part of the railway beyond Mellaha Junction. (See Plates 44 and 45.)

This operation was conducted under fire from the enemy.

On July 24, half the company under Captain Wood accompanied the South Staffordshire Regiment and the 3d battalion of the Rifles in the advance to Ramleh, and began at once putting the water-works and water-tower in a state of defense, as detailed on p. 158.

On August 7, the 21st company, Royal Engineers, landed, so that the half company of the 17th left at Alexandria marched to Ramleh, having been in the meanwhile occupied as before on the defenses, constructing stone block-houses, sinking wells, &c.

The special services rendered by this company may be briefly mentioned thus:

On July 20, Captain Hyslop and 20 sappers with a strong covering party left, by night, in a train from Gabarri, while Lieutenant Thomson started with a similar party from Ramleh. The two detachments met at Mellaha Junction, repaired the lines at that point, and brought some rolling-stock around from Gabarri to the Moharem Bey Line, where it was much needed.

On another occasion, reports of an intended flank attack by Arabi caused the half company at Ramleh to be suddenly ordered out at midnight to throw up a gun breastwork across the line towards Mellaha Junction.

A covering party was thrown forwards as far as the Junction, and a working party from a line battalion assisted on the breastwork, so that a parapet revetted solidly with railway iron and sand-bags was thrown up and the party quietly withdrawn.

Other technical operations were conducted at Ramleh, some of them in exposed situations almost inviting attack.

On the afternoon of August 17, an order was given to embark at Alexandria, and that evening half the company, with 24 carts and six pack animals carrying equipment, started, while the remainder made an early march next day, and the surplus stores came in by train. These consisted of large quantities of sand-bags, tools, and pumps (tripod and Abyssinian or "Nortons").

The transport Nerissa, carrying the 17th company and the Royal Marine Artillery, was the first in the Suez Canal, but eventually stuck hard and fast about three miles from the pier at Ismailia, so that it was not until 2 a. m. on the 21st that a landing was effected in support of the small force holding the place. The Royal Engineers bivouacked in a street, and were early at work landing stores, improving roads (for each man landed with a tool), and making arrangements for watering-places.

A Royal Engineer park was started; the railway towards Nefiche repaired; the extension of the line from the station to the pier commenced, and the telegraph staff assisted.

The water in the Fresh Water Canal was husbanded by stopping the leaks in the locks and raising the overflow of the lower lock. This had to be done afresh whenever boats were passed up into the canal for water transport.

August 24, Lieutenant Heath with six sappers, three carts, and a working party of 18 of the York and Lancaster Regiment, accompanied the advance of General Graham's force beyond Nefiche, repaired the railway under distant shell-fire, reached the dam on the canal at El Magfar, and commenced hasty defenses.

The carts carrying two of the pontoons brought from Ramleh, drew a heavy shell-fire, but the shells, as usual, being badly fuzed, did no damage. These pontoons were rafted on the canal above the dam and carried rations on to the cavalry when land transport could not keep up owing to deep sands.

On August 25, the removal of the dam was commenced, and about midnight on the 26th Captain Wood and 30 sappers arrived by boat and set to work, so that by 4.30 a. m., the 27th, a passage for steam cutters was just practicable.

This dam is met with in all accounts of the advance to Kassassin. It received the united attention of both arms of the service, for Lieutenant King-Harman, R. N., was left behind from the Naval Battery, in its march of the 25th, and was told to do his best to blow up the obstruction. He had with him a small party of skilled men, charges of gun-cotton, fuzes, &c. He tried the effect of this explosive on the dam, varying the conditions each time, in the hope of success. The heaviest explosion was of a series of charges planted in two parallel lines 8 feet 6 inches apart, 33 pounds of gun-cotton in all. The effect was to cut a trench through the dam and pile up the mud which had been displaced at each end of the trench. Lieutenant King-Harmer calls it " a vile job," and says that the means adopted proved inadequate. It was finally necessary to resort to the slower process of removal by hand, and strong parties of the Guards brigade kept at work on it until a sufficient channel was made through it. Captain Wood continues:

A disabled dredge was got into working order and pushed through next day for the dam at Tel-el-Mahuta with Lieutenant Heath's party.

This dam was constructed of sand only, about 50 feet thick and 12 feet high, above the water, which was here about 70 feet wide. The dam at El Magfar, however, was far more formidable; it was formed of long, strong reeds, tied and matted together and solidly compressed by the superincumbent weight, so that neither picks, shovels, specially made hoes, nor rakes could make any impression on the part below water. Telegraph posts, tied together with wire, were bedded in it and piles also driven. Gun-cotton in coffee and biscuit tins, holding from 3 to 10 pounds, was resorted to, but the work was continually interrupted in order to haul boats through, and the level of the water was continually falling, so that the work was heavy and continuous.

On the evening of August 31 the company started for Kassassin, marching nine miles across the desert in three hours, the small pack-mules carrying 160 pounds, the large mules drawing 400 pounds, and a couple of spare mules, with lead traces, being ready to hook on in case of a difficulty; the heaviest stores, such as smith's forge, coal, ten tents, &c., coming by water on the ponton rafts.

Bivouac was formed with carts around, as an attack by Bedouins had been reported probable; and the next morning Kassassin was reached. Here defensive and other works were at once commenced. Millet was formed into fascines, and strong revetments formed by driving the butts of stalks into each row and bending the tops over into the parapet by which the fascines were securely anchored. The falling of the water in the canal rendered it necessary to send both subalterns back, each with twenty sappers, to the two dams to widen and deepen the channels.

This repeated labor on the obstructions in the Sweet Water Canal earned for Captain Wood's command the equivocal title of "the dam company."

The company was exposed on September 9 to the shell-fire of the Egyptian attack, and lost some of its animals.

On the 13th of September the company struck camp at 2 a. m., had coffee, and started with the following equipment, having orders to conform to the movements of the army and to open a passage through the dam near Tel-el-Kebir:

Eight pack-mules, carrying tool-chests and shovels (30 in a load weigh 160 pounds), and 15 carts, carrying, as usual, two days' forage, rations, valises, tools, demolition stores, rope, wire, sand-bags, reserve ammunition, stretchers, &c. One raft was made of 48 wheeling planks, carrying on it the composite beams and wheelbarrows. Two rafts, formed each of two pontons, and one single ponton, carrying pumps and hose, forge, $2\frac{1}{4}$ cwt. anvil, smith's tools, scaling ladders, sand-bags, gun-cotton, crowbars, shovels, and other stores. Total number of shovels, 200, of sand-bags, 3,000. Abundance of bill-hooks, gabion knives, fine wire and spunyarn for cutting and making millet into fascines was carried. The rafts were attached one in rear of the other, and a couple of mules harnessed on either bank so as to keep the rafts more easily in the middle of the stream and to keep them going when reeds or anything else interfered with the fraction on one side.

The company came under shell-fire, pitched camp at the dam, which was in the lines of Tel-el-Kebir, and commenced to remove it forthwith. It was 50 feet thick at the water line, but of small height, and was only constructed with sand, so that in twenty-four hours it was practically removed, the 17th company being relieved by the 24th and 26th companies, Royal Engineers.

Next day the 17th company left its camp for Cairo, the transport, with light loads, marching along the railway, reached Benha (42 miles) in two days.

This company still remains in Egypt and is stationed at Cairo. The rather lengthy account of its work is warranted by the prominent part it took in all the operations of the campaign and by the light it throws on the difficulties encountered in Egypt and the measures chosen to overcome them.

The 18th company of Sappers, 100 strong, under Major W. Salmond, R. E., remained at Ismailia as a reserve at the base, establishing the engineer park, and handling and forwarding as necessary the stores coming under that department.

The 21st company, under Captain A. R. Puzy, came from Cyprus to Alexandria on August 8. It numbered a subaltern and 54 men. It continued and concluded the work begun by its predecessor as well as contributing to the defense of the place in other ways. It remains in Egypt as part of the garrison of Alexandria.

The 24th company, under Captain C. de B. Carey, R. E., was attached to the 1st division, forming a portion of the divisional troops. Its *personnel* was 2 captains, 3 lieutenants, 1 surgeon, and 185 non-commissioned officers and men, a total of 191. It had 37 horses and 10 carts. It joined the 1st division, under General Willis, at Tel-el-Mahuta, on August 26. At this point, aided by fatigue parties from various line battalions, it shared with the 17th company the labor of removing the dam in the Sweet Water Canal.

On September 4 this company made an attempt to obtain a supply of drinking water by sinking tube wells. The blocking of the water above, and its enforced retention between the locks at Kassassin and Ismailia, had made it stagnant, the constant traffic through the canal had kept the mud stirred up, while the dead bodies in the canal, whether there by accident or design, had vitiated the water to an alarming extent. The attempt to obtain potable water elsewhere was not crowned with success. Brackish water was found at five feet below the surface, and although the tubes were driven ten feet further, no improvement in the quality of the water was detected. The army therefore continued to make use of the canal water, and, happily, without experiencing ill results. In other respects the history of this company is the history of the 1st division.

The 26th company, under the command of Major B. Blood, R. E., was attached to the 2d division as a field company. In organization, number, and equipment it was similar to the 24th company. For the sake of clearness the following table is added as giving the established organization of a field company of Royal Engineers:

Rank.	Mounted.	Dismounted.	Horses. Riding.	Draught.	Pack.	Spare.
Major	1		2			
Captain	1		2			
Lieutenant	3		6			
Surgeon	1		1			
Total	6		11			
Sergeants	2	6				
Corporals	1	6				
Second corporals	1	6				
Shoeing-smith	1					
Sappers		134	4	24	3	4
Drivers	26					
Trumpeters	1					
Buglers		1				
Batmen		12				
Total	38	165	4	24	3	4

Total *personnel*, 203; animals, 46; wagons, 6.

It was even later in reaching the front than its colleagues in the 1st division, only arriving at Kassassin a few days before the battle of Tel-el-Kebir. It took part in this action, being exposed to heavy fire on the extreme left near the canal bank. After the works were carried, the company was sent to remove a barrier which had been built across the railway as part of the general lines of Tel-el-Kebir, and to dig away the dam in the Sweet Water Canal. These proved no very serious obstacles, and disappeared after two or three hours' work. The company then pushed on to Benha. It is now in Cairo as part of the army of occupation.

The Pontoon Troop A, commanded by Major R. J. Bond, was not up to the standard organization in either men or equipment. Its *personnel* was 1 major, 1 captain, 3 lieutenants, 1 surgeon, 1 veterinary surgeon, 7 officers, and 194 non-commissioned officers and men, instead of 1 major, 1 captain, 4 lieutenants, 1 surgeon, 1 veterinary surgeon, 1 quartermaster, 9 officers, and 320 non-commissioned officers and men.

Its equipment was 61 horses, 10 pontoon wagons, and 20 carts (instead of 243 horses, 20 pontoon wagons, 4 trestle wagons, 6 store wagons), and 1 forge-cart, besides Berthon's collapsible boats and Blanchard's pontoons for three bridges each.

The pontoon bridge is formed of pontoons kept at 15 feet central intervals by balks fitting on to saddles resting on central saddle-beams.

The number of balks used is five for the advanced bridge and nine for the heavy bridge for siege artillery; they support chesses, which are kept in position by a riband on each side, racked down by rack-lashings to the outer balk, and leaving a clear roadway of 9 feet.

It was calculated that the pontoons should not be immersed to within

1 foot from the tops of their coamings when carrying their ordinary loads of infantry in marching order in fours crowded at a check, or car-

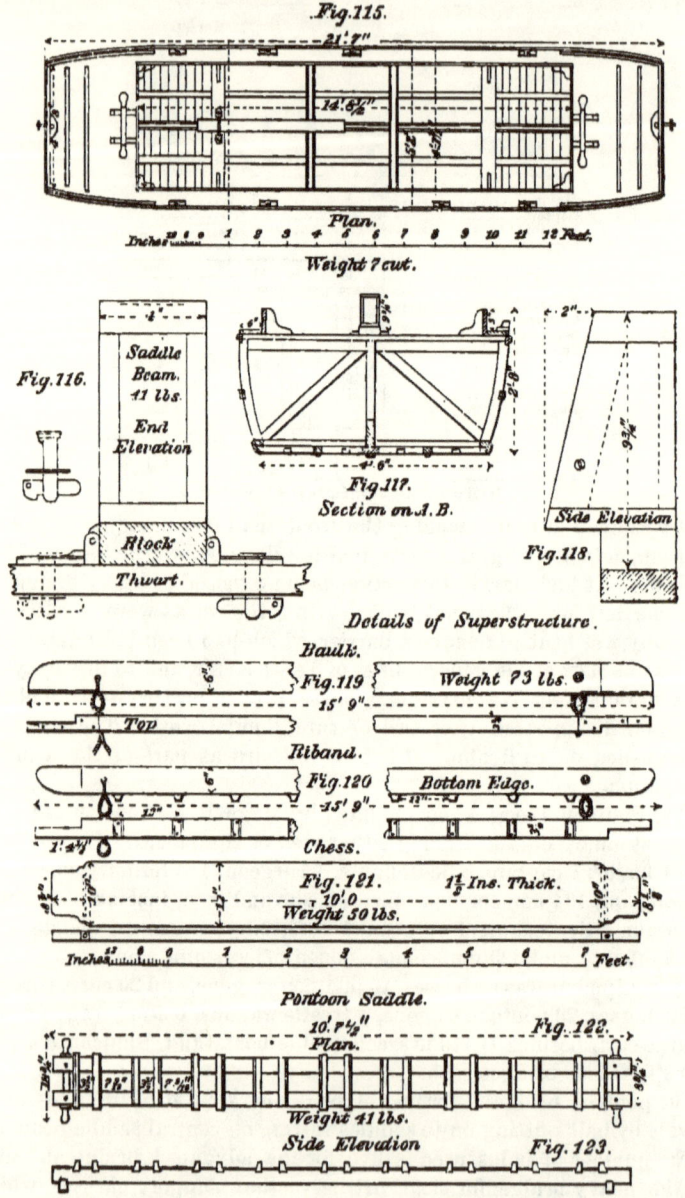

riages equal in weight to the 16-pdr. gun, weighing 43 cwt.; and that the pontoons should not be immersed to within 6 inches of the tops of their coamings when carrying extraordinary loads, such as disorganzed infantry, or weights such as the 64-pdr. gun, weighing 99¼ cwt.

The pontoon (Fig. 115 et sq.) is a boat with similar decked ends, and is partly decked at the sides, where eight rowlock blocks are fixed; there is also a rowlock at each end for a steering oar. The undecked portion of the pontoon is 14 feet 8½ inches by 4 feet 1½ inches, and is surrounded by coamings 5 inches high above the deck. The extreme length of the boat is 21 feet 7 inches; its extreme breadth is 5 feet 3 inches, and its depth amidships, including the coamings, is 2 feet 8 inches. The pontoon weighs (dry) from 750 to 800 pounds (say 7 cwt.), and draws when floating empty 2½ inches, and when in bridge 6 inches. Roughly speaking, every inch of immersion gives 500 pounds of buoyancy.

The pontoon consists of six sets of framed ribs connected by a deep kelson, two side-streaks, and three bottom-streaks. The sides and bottom are of thin yellow pine, with canvas secured to both surfaces by India-rubber solution; the canvas is coated outside with two coats of marine glue.

An iron ring is attached to the framework at each end, and connected with the kelson by an iron rod. There is a cleat for securing the cables on the deck at each end.

The bottom is provided with two plug-holes to let water out; it is protected outside by five longitudinal battens. On each side of the boat there is a side-rail, to which are secured eight handles by which the pontoon can be carried by hand. The second handle from each end is attached by wire rope, the remainder by hemp rope.

There are four thwarts which support a saddle-beam, which can be moved when the pontoon is to be used for ferrying troops; the saddle-beam is secured to the thwarts by iron pins going through the seat and keyed under it.

The saddle-beam is hollow, 10 feet 1 inch long at bottom and 9 feet 9 inches long at top, 8 inches deep, and 4 inches wide; it can be easily removed, being merely secured by the four iron pins before described. The top is beech, the rest of Baltic fir. The weight of the saddle-beam is 44 pounds. Shore transoms are also required for the far and near

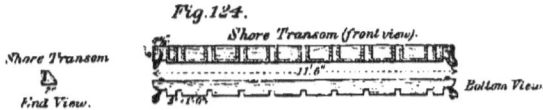

Fig. 124.

bridge-ends (Fig. 124), failing which they can be improvised from a plank 11 feet 5½ inches by 4¾ inches by 3 inches, laid flat, and with nine pairs of cleats 4 inches high and 1⅞ inches apart for the five ordinary and four extra balks.

A pontoon saddle is a framing of 10 feet 7 inches long, 8¾ inches broad, and 4¼ inches in depth, which fits over the saddle-beam. The saddle has five sets of curved cleats 10¾ inches by 2 inches, at equal distances, to receive the ends of the balks. There are four other sets of cleats

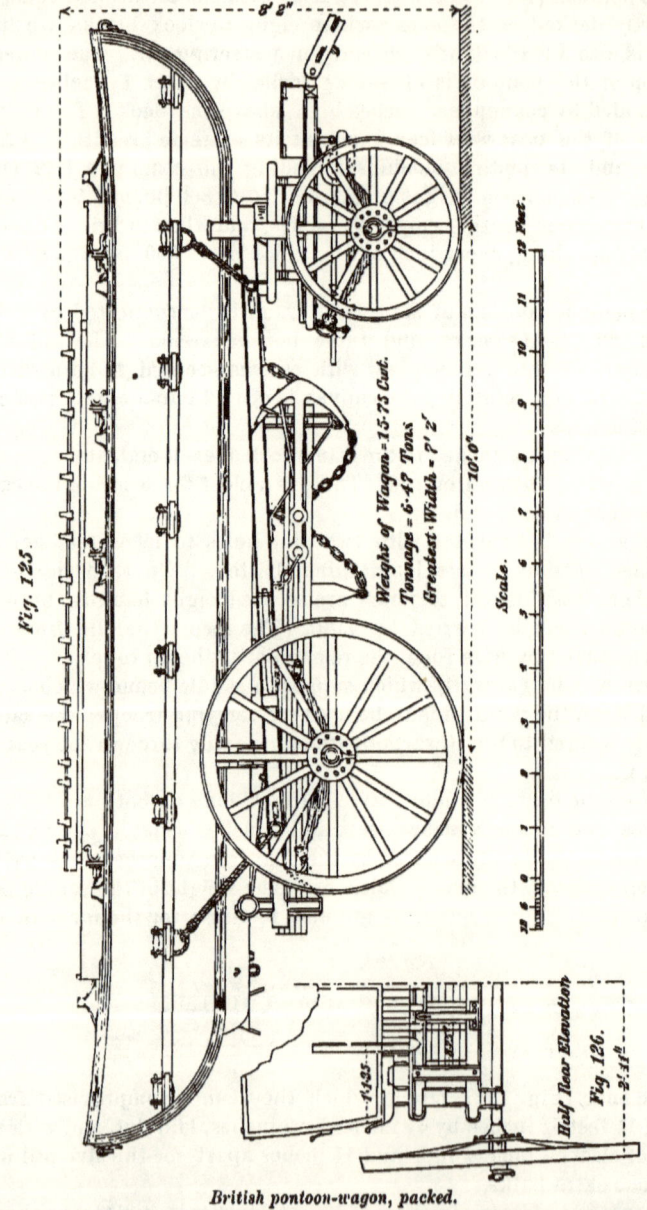

British pontoon-wagon, packed.

with square ends placed intermediately to receive the ends of the additional balks necessary for the passage of siege guns over the bridge.

There are handles at each end to enable the saddle to be lifted. The side-rails, 10 feet 7 inches by 2¼ inches by 2¼ inches, are of Baltic fir, and the remainder of American elm. The saddle weighs 41 pounds.

The balks are of Canada red or Kawrie pine, the length being 15 feet 9 inches, breadth 3¼ inches, and depth 6 inches. The ends of the balks are halved, but they are there strengthened by iron plates at top and bottom; the bottom plates are made with two claws to prevent the balk slipping off its saddle. A balk weighs, dry, 73 pounds; wet, 75 pounds.

The chesses are single planks of Kawrie pine, the length being 10 feet, the breadth 1 foot, and the depth 1½ inches; the breadth at each end is diminished to enable the rack-lashing to be passed between two adjoining chesses. A chess weighs, dry, 50¼ pounds; wet, 52⅓ pounds.

The ribands are of Canada red pine, 15 feet 9 inches by 3¼ inches by 6 inches, halved at each end, with 14 buttons, the first 1 foot 4½ inches from the end, and the remainder 12 inches from center to center. The distances from center to center of the buttons are painted alternately black and white.

The buoyancy of the pontoon bridge is sufficient to admit of the passage of siege artillery and steam sappers.

Berthon's collapsible boats are of waterproofed canvas over a folding frame of wood, the gunwales doubling down in the plane of the keel. The length is 9 feet and the width 4 feet; when opened the boat is retained in shape by the thwarts. When used in building bridges, a saddle or two-legged trestle is placed in cleats on the bottom boards of the boat and held in position by wire guys, extending from the gunwales of the boat to the saddle. On these saddles the superstructure is laid. It is made of four longitudinals, tapering from 3 inches in depth in the center to 1½ inches at each end, placed on edge, and connected by wooden pins. On top of this girder is laid a platform 18 inches wide and 8 feet long.

Two men can carry a boat, 109 pounds, slung on a pole, and two more the trestle, superstructure, anchor, and guys, 97 pounds, or a complete unit may be conveyed on one horse or mule.

The pontoon troop also had Blanchard pontoons, cylinders of tin with hemispherical ends, 22 feet 3 inches in length and 2 feet 8 inches in diameter, weighing 476 pounds, and having a displacement of 6,735 pounds. Two pontoons with their superstructure form one raft, which, with the roadway between it and the next raft, is carried on one wagon.

The troop was landed at Ismailia on August 29, and the pontoons at once utilized for transport on the Sweet Water Canal. The service pontoons, drawing but 18 inches of water when supporting two tons of load in pairs, were, as may be supposed, very useful in this connection.

On September 2 the troop was placed temporarily at the disposal of the general commanding the line of communications, for the purpose of working between Tel-el-Mahuta and Kassassin, receiving and forwarding at the former point the stores brought up by the canal boat-service under Commander Moore.

In addition to the pontoon equipment, a simple flat-bottomed boat devised by Captain Wood, R. E., was tried in the canal. (Figs. 127 and 128.

The gnu-wale and bilge pieces are identical in form, and are connected by stanchions, all being sawed out of inch stuff. The frame is then covered with two thicknesses of well-painted canvas.

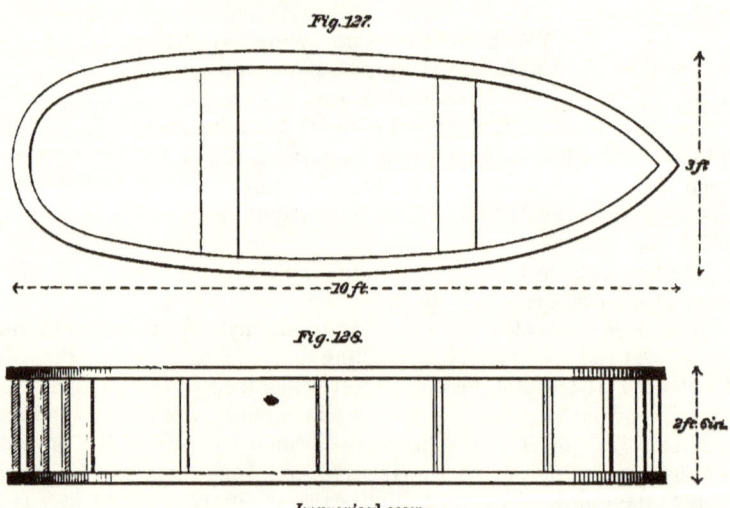

Improvised scow.

The only real pontoon work done by the troop was the construction of pontoon bridges at Tel-el-Mahuta and Kassassin to connect the camps established on opposite sides of the Sweet Water Canal.

The Field Park, under Captain C. A. Rochfort-Boyd, was composed of 33 non-commissioned officers and men, and had as its equipment 26 horses, 9 carts, and a printing wagon. It followed in rear of the army as far as Kassassin, carrying supplies of tools and material for all possible wants in the way of intrenching, &c. Its province was to act as a reserve to the other companies regularly attached to the fighting line.

XXIV.

THE RAILWAY COMPANY.

Of the six companies of the Royal Engineers, one, numbered the 8th, was organized and prepared for the work of building and operating railways. It is not, however, a permanent railway company. Indeed, there seems to be no such corps. The art of railway construction and management is taught at the School of Military Engineering, and a limited amount of practice is had with the railways about the Government workshops at Chatham and Woolwich.

The Government does not own the railways in Great Britain, and hence is debarred from utilizing them as a school of exercise for sappers. As might have been expected, the latter displayed occasionally in the field a lack of familiarity with the minor details of railway work, which showed them to be amateurs as was further proved by the improvement in the running of the railway out of Ismailia as time elapsed and experience increased.

When the sending of a force to Egypt became probable, No. 8 company was filled up by mechanics of the various kinds deemed desirable for railway work. Brought together early in July, they gained what acquaintance was feasible with the duties before them by volunteer labor on the lines of the Southwestern and the London, Chatham and Dover Railways, these corporations affording them every facility compatible with their regular train services. In this way they gained excellent practice in laying lines, putting down points and crossings, erecting signals, &c. The sappers especially selected as engine-drivers were permitted by the London, Chatham and Dover Railway to ride on the locomotives and occasionally to handle them, while the facilities of the Chatham station were secured for the experience of guards (conductors), station-masters, shunters, pointsmen, signal-men, &c. A very hurried and inadequate training, certainly, but better than none at all.

The organization of the company consisted of 3 lieutenants, 1 surgeon, 1 warrant officer, and 103 non-commissioned officers and men, under the command of Captain Sidney Smith, R. E. In addition, Major W. A. J. Wallace, R. E., went out as director of railways, with a staff of two officers and three men. Afterwards, Major J. C. Ardagh, C. B., R. E., was temporarily associated with Major Wallace.

The outfit comprised enough 72-pound steel rails for 5 miles of road, besides a small quantity of light 36-pound rails, with the requisite sleepers, ten points and crossings, four tank-engines, with complete sets of tools, two heavy cranes mounted on railway carriages, two breakdown vans containing all possible appliances for clearing away wrecked trains, such as jacks, bars, chains, shoes for getting cars back on the rails, three or four passenger carriages of each class (first, second, and third), cattle-cars and trucks, and brake-vans. All the rolling stock was of the usual English pattern.

It may be superfluous to mention that in England a locomotive is called an engine; passenger cars, carriages; covered freight cars are goods vans, and platform cars are trucks.

The light rail was designed for temporary repairs only. The experience had with it showed that it was totally unfitted for the purpose, and that time would have been saved by at once resorting to the heavier rail.

The sleepers, represented in the accompanying sketches not to scale, are simply iron plates about 8 feet long by 18 inches in width, dished in the center. The chairs, of the usual form, are bolted to the convex side of the sleeper.

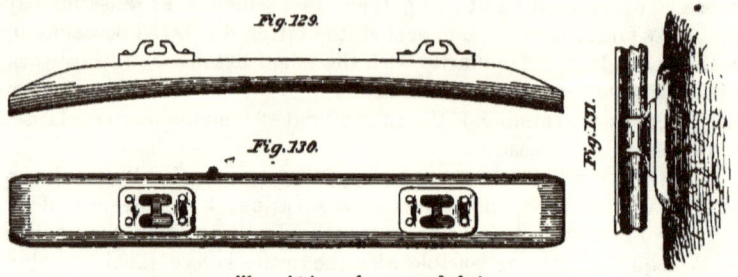

Wrought-iron sleepers and chairs.

In laying the rails the sleeper is worked down into the sand to the proper level, and the rail slipped in and keyed. Intended for use in light soils and in dry climates, the sleepers proved both convenient and efficient. Their natural tendency is to settle steadily and rapidly to a permanent bed. After this is reached the line is as solid as can be desired.

This sleeper is lighter than the wooden sleeper, and if separated from the chairs is much less bulky, stowing spoon-fashion. With the chairs attached it makes rather awkward stowage.

The key employed has long been in use in India, where the ravages of the white ant are the occasion of the substitution of metal for wood wherever economically possible. This key, therefore, while no novelty abroad, may be of interest at home. It is made of steel ribbon about a quarter of an inch square, wound on a tapered former, all of whose sections are rectangular, with the corners rounded off. The key is 8 inches long, 3 inches by 2 inches at the base, and 2 inches by 1 inch at the point. It is supposed to be driven between the rail and the chair over a wooden mandrel which is afterwards backed out. The turns of the spring towards the smaller end pass beyond the chair and serve to clinch the key, so to speak, in place. When properly driven it is said never to work out, although this tendency was complained of at Ismailia. The mishap appears to have arisen from the inexperience of those using it.

Railway key.

The locomotives were of a well-known type, light, four-coupled tank engines without tenders, having a coal-box in the cab and a water-tank over the boiler. Weighing less than 20 tons, they were not heavy enough for the traffic which the needs of the army subsequently developed.

Their water capacity, originally small, was increased by the improvising of a tender, a platform car or truck with four small tanks capable of holding 400 to 500 gallons each. A hand pump was rigged in the tender to deliver the extra water through a hose into the engine tank for feeding the boiler. The fireman assistant had, as a rule and without exaggeration, to work his passage every trip, so constant was the manipulation of this pump.

The selection of this light type was governed by the probable difficulty of getting the engines ashore in Ismailia; but, judged by the event, it was regrettable. All the engines used between the base and the front prior to the battle of Tel-el-Kebir, that is, during the whole of the actual campaign, were landed at Suez, where the facilities were so great as to permit the landing of large as well as small engines. There was, moreover, never any railway demand for the latter in preference to the former, as the traffic was always heavy, and the light engines with their meager trains blocked the single track to the front as completely as the larger ones. The hauling capacity of these small engines was in the neighborhood of ten trucks, carrying each from 5 to 6 tons net, while that of the larger engines usually working on the Egyptian railways is at least 50 per cent. greater.

The railway company embarked at Woolwich on board of the transport Canadian on August 8. On the way out from England the men were told off for, and instructed theoretically in, the various duties they would have to perform, as station-masters, assistant station-masters, storekeepers, engine drivers, guards, plate-layers, gaugers, &c., so that each knew what his own work was to be before arriving in the field.

The steamer arrived at Ismailia on August 23, and the company began landing at once.

There were two breaks in the line held at this moment by the British troops, an insignificant gap of two pairs of rails, which had been blown out by Lieutenant King-Harman, R. N., on the 21st, between Ismailia and Nefiche, the other a more serious interruption, 220 yards in length, near El Magfar, made by the Egyptians in their retreat. Near by the latter a second and very annoying obstacle was discovered, where a railway cutting from ten to fifteen feet deep had been filled in with sand for the distance of twenty-five yards. The removal of this obstruction consumed the greater part of four days, owing to the lightness of the soil and the impossibility of increasing the force at work beyond a certain limited number of men.

The small break near Nefiche was immediately repaired and traffic begun by means of half a dozen of some thirty trucks that had been secured at Nefiche by General Graham on August 21. Horses were employed to haul the cars as far as the gap at El Magfar, Arabi having run off all the locomotives on this part of the Egyptian railway system. In the mean time parties of the Railway Company went down to Suez to land some Egyptian locomotives from lighters towed around from Alexandria, as well as the English locomotives already mentioned.

At Suez, there being deep water close to the docks, the operation of getting the engines ashore was comparatively simple, while at Ismailia it would have been extremely difficult and attended with great risk. Work was also being pushed ahead at Ismailia, and a branch line laid with light rails from the station to the Central Wharf (see Plate 48). The Arab labor for this most valuable adjunct was secured by contract at heavy rates. This line was completed by August 26. By the same day the gap at El Magfar had been repaired.

The railway was now in good condition as far as the advance at Mahsameh and Kassassin, only lacking locomotives to begin a steam service at once, the amount of rolling stock having been increased by the capture of forty-five trucks, in the engagement of the previous day, at Mahsameh. The engines with them had uncoupled and escaped up the line, to the great chagrin of the British.

The wheeled and other land transports had not been able to keep up with the rapid advance of the fighting line, and the latter had already begun to suffer through want of supplies.

The first locomotive arrived from Suez in charge of Major Wallace at 3.30 p. m. August 27, and was received with a greeting which bordered on joy. A train service was begun on the following day. This engine belonged to the Egyptian State Railways, and had come around from Alexandria.

The speed attained between Ismailia and Kassassin, the point now occupied by the advance, was always, and of necessity, slow. The heavy engines brought up from Suez were in indifferent order, as might have been expected of complex mechanism which had been in the hands of semi-civilized people. In addition, the permanent way had been injured by the constant passage over it of animals and wheeled vehicles, for it must be remembered that such a thing as a road is unknown in this part of the world. The Egyptian lines are laid on large cast-iron chairs, better known as "pot-sleepers," connected by wrought-iron tie-rods, Figs. 134, 135. The effect of this heavy extraneous traffic was to bend the tie-rods and drag the rails together, and thus to produce the phenomenon known among engine-drivers as "grinding."

The schedule at this time was limited to one train a day each way. The train went to Kassassin in the morning and returned in the afternoon to Ismailia.

A second branch line about a mile long was laid by the Indian sappers from the station at Ismailia (see Plate 48) to the base hospital and thence to the commissariat landing place at the mouth of the Sweet Water Canal. This branch proved of great value in bringing the wounded and sick from the front direct to the hospital, while it was also used for all commissariat stores which were loaded on the trucks and hauled by draught animals to the station ready for forwarding. This

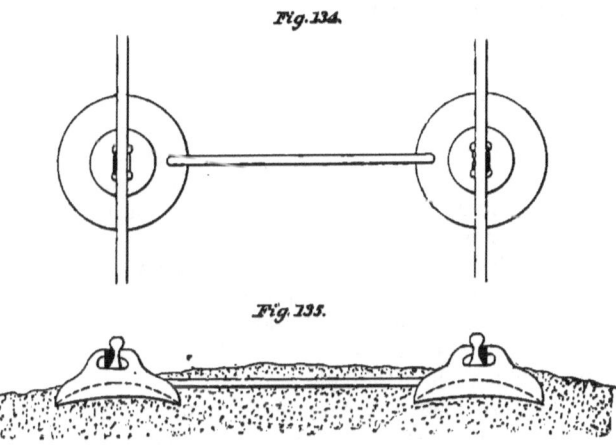

Pot-sleepers, Egyptian permanent way.

particular service was in the hands of the Commissariat and Transport Corps.

On August 31 two more Egyptian locomotives arrived from Suez, making three in all. Of these, one was large, capable of hauling from fifteen to twenty trucks loaded to five tons each, and two were smaller ones, only able to haul from ten to twelve trucks each. The number of trains was at once doubled. The time table was by no means fixed, but was subject to daily modifications according to necessity, and was established by the general in command of the Line of Communications. As a rule at eight o'clock in the morning a train left Ismailia for Kassassin direct with supplies for this advanced post, followed at eleven o'clock by a mixed train which stopped wherever needed. Both returned in the evening. The round trips usually occupied about eleven hours.

With this increased traffic, the want of additional sidings became more apparent, there being but one turn-out, that at Mahsameh, between Nefiche and Kassassin, and originally none at all at the latter place. As soon as the concentration of the army at this position was determined upon, a siding was constructed 230 yards in length, with points having a lead of one in ten. Watering stations were improvised at Tel-el-Mahuta and Kassassin, using tanks similar to those fitted in the jury tenders. To keep up the supply of water for the locomotives the regimental water-carts were employed, being filled at the Sweet Water Canal and emptied into the tanks. It required the constant services of at least two of these carts at each station, with large fatigue parties from the camps, to meet the demand for steaming water. From the tanks it was pumped by hand into the tender. The railway further needed the daily labors of other detachments of men to clear the sand away from the rails as it gradually accumulated, driven by the prevailing northerly wind and kicked up by the men and animals that used the railroad habitually as a highway.

Each train had an engine-driver and fireman on the engine and a guard or conductor in charge of the train, besides a brakesman and an armed escort. The trucks and vans carrying stores bore written lists of their contents and destinations, the guard being furnished with a way-bill. No one, officer or man, was allowed to ride on the train without a pass from the Railway Staff Officer at the station of departure, and no animals were ever transported by rail.

The history of the railway during the early days of September is made up of a series of small mishaps: sand piled up on the rails by foot travel high enough to throw trains off the track; petty accidents to locomotives; blocks on the line; insufficient water, and that very dirty; trucks left at the wrong place or carried past their destination; trains not properly made up, &c.; none serious, but some of sufficient importance to interfere with and retard the traffic. On September 3, for instance, the number of trains each way was reduced to one.

So insufficient was the motive power, that barely enough stores for daily consumption could be hauled to the front. The inability to accumulate supplies involved the consequent inability to make an advance It was at this time and for this reason that the prospects of the expedition seemed least bright.

The accession of two more English engines from Suez, on September 9, relieved the pressure, particularly in permitting the extensive use of steam power in shunting. The next day two more engines came up and the railway was now fairly well equipped. In all there were seven locomotives in use, the eighth, a large one, not arriving until September 9. The larger engines were in very indifferent condition, however, and the smaller ones were too weak, so that a full development was not obtained; still it became possible to run three trains to the front every day and to begin the accumulation of provisions and forage at Kassassin, in addition to keeping pace with the current demands.

Every effort was made by Major Wallace and his colleagues to expedite the work. The actual dispatching of trains was simple enough, but the railway company was deficient in one essential point. It had no man familiar with "yard work"; that is, the making up of trains and the distributing of cars, that ceaseless backing and filling of the switching engine at every important station which seems to the looker-on such a misdirection of energy. The ability to carry on this operation, if on a large scale, without undue loss of time, involves an extremely quick intelligence, sharpened by long experience. The result is the proper composition of the train, so that the cars destined to go to the most distant point are nearest the locomotive, those for the nearest bringing up the rear, where they can be readily dropped. With English cars, that have, as a rule, no brakes, each train concludes with a covered car fitted with brakes, and called a brake van. In a mixed train, the proper placing of these brake vans, whether one, or more than one, in number, introduces further complication into yard work.

Good results were, of course, reached at Ismailia, but at the expenditure of more time and trouble than could well be afforded at the moment. The engine-drivers, too, were unskillful at first, although zealous and untiring. In the words of an officer dependent upon the railway for the efficient discharge of his own duty, "The sappers did extremely well, but were not professional drivers." In fact all the railway duties were performed with great zeal and in a manner generally satisfactory, regard being had to the circumstances of the case. The work was not always free from risk, although the Egyptians never molested the trains. No complaint was heard against their faithfulness and energy in all branches of their never-ending duty.

With the seizure of the Egyptian systems between Tel-el-Kebir and Zagazig, Zagazig and Benha, Benha and Cairo, Benha and Alexandria, after the battle of Tel-el-Kebir, the responsibilities of the railway company were suddenly enormously increased for a brief time. The Egyptian railway officials were, however, at once restored to their old positions and the service and material turned over to them with all possible speed. For the first few days the British Railway Staff Officers exercised a general control over the arrival and departure of trains, but even this management was soon abandoned, the Egyptians resuming full sway, subject only to occasional requisitions for special or extra service from the British military authorities.

In considering the labors of the 8th company, Royal Engineers, it is imposble to avoid being struck by the very slight nature of the damage done to the railway by the retreating Egyptians. The explanation may possibly be found in the fact that the war was seen to assume from point to point a character very different from that which their inflated ideas had caused them to expect. Their leaders must have known, supposing them to have possessed a modicum of intelligence, and some of them were really clever men, that resistance to the British force would necessarily involve hard work and hotly contested engagements, with a chance, remote if they would, yet still a chance worth considering, of having to retreat. It was this chance which crystallized into the event, but, even then, to have inflicted serious injury to the railway would have given tangible proof to the rank and file that the issue of the war was inclining strongly against them, and have tended to weaken that belief in their own invincibility which alone held them together.

This blind belief acted in the matter of the railway, as it did in others, as a positive help to the British. A civilized enemy in the position of the Egyptians would have torn up the railway as he retreated, and during his halts have bent his energies to cutting the communication with the base by raiding in rear of the attacking force. The severing of this main artery of supplies might have been effected with comparative ease, and mere attempts at it would have proved fruitful in embarrassment.

The stupidity of the defense is nowhere more clearly shown than in this neglect. As elsewhere, this stupidity was recognized in advance, and was relied upon with perfect reason as a factor in the general product. The tactics of the campaign would have been very different if both sides had possessed fairly equal intelligence.

XXV.

THE TELEGRAPH TROOP.

The importance of rapid and trustworthy communication between the headquarters of the Commander-in-chief and the various subsidiary centers of an army in the field is so great that, in every military service, the development of means to this end has received careful thought and elaborate experiment. The oldest mode of conveying intelligence is by messages, verbal or written, carried by men either mounted or on foot. A second method is by visual signals, considered elsewhere; and a third is by the use of the electric telegraph. The advantages of the latter are rapid, unobserved, and accurate working, yielding, if desired, a permanent record. Although requiring, when once laid, a comparatively small working staff, it still involves a costly and rather cumbersome plant, and hence its use is generally restricted to maintaining communication with the base of operations, and between the wings and headquarters. Being wholly within the lines, all its delicate parts receive the benefits of the general defense.

During the campaign in Egypt the field telegraph was comparatively little used, owing to the fact that the advance of the army was along a route supplied with three permanent telegraph lines, which had been merely damaged but not destroyed by the retreating enemy, and which were utilized for keeping up communication between Ismailia and the advanced depot. An account of the history and organization of the telegraph companies and of what is known as C troop, Royal Engineers, will not be without interest.

It should be borne in mind that in England, the entire telegraph system, being part of the Post-Office Department, offers facilities, in the way of instruction and practice to other branches of the Government requiring them, which are not attainable in a country like our own, where the telegraphs are in the hands of private individuals or corporations. Even in England much opposition was experienced by the Royal Engineers in obtaining access to the telegraph offices of the kingdom. It is due to the long-continued exertions of Lieutenant-Colonel C. E. Webber, R. E., an electrician of high standing, now president of the Society of Telegraph Engineers, that the post-office authorities were induced to agree to the plan in operation at present. By this plan the members of the two Telegraph Companies, the 22d and 34th Royal Engineers, are admitted into the postal telegraph department, where they are permanently employed during peace in the construction and maintenance of all the lines in the southern counties of England.

The recruits for these companies are enlisted not under eighteen years of age. In addition to the usual qualifications they must be approved by the Postmaster-General, through his inspectors, as thorough telegraph operators. They are at once sent to the School of Military Engineering at Chatham, where they pass eighteen months under instruction as soldiers and sappers. From the school the recruit is sent to one or other of the two Telegraph Companies, rated as "Indoor Telegraphist" or "Outdoor Telegraphist" according to his proficiency. It will be noted that the latter position calls for wider knowledge of the art, including, as it does, an acquaintance with all that relates to batteries and office instruments in addition to experience in line work, with its peculiar functions in the matter of faults of all kinds, and the practical erection of wires.

The soldier telegraphist, then, usually settles into the place of "lineman," senior telegraph clerk (operator), or other position of responsibility in the Post-Office. For six years he is credited with active service, and indeed is in the first line of the army. After that time he passes into the reserve, remaining, in most cases, in the Post-Office as a civil employé.

There are now about 400 of these Military Telegraphists in the Active Line and Reserves, liable to be called upon to join the Royal Engineer Telegraph Companies when war breaks out, and the number, through the operation of this admirable system, is constantly increasing.

Another result is attained in the steady supply of telegraphists for Indian and colonial service, for the Persian Government telegraphs, military telegraphs at various home and foreign military stations, and for the torpedo service (submarine mining).

As a body of men, subject to military discipline, and accustomed to unquestioning obedience, these engineer telegraphists are most valuable on occasions of sudden emergency. In 1872, when a strike arose among the civil employés of the Postal Telegraph, forty-five of these engineers went to Ireland at a few hours' notice and took entire charge of the lines at Dublin and Cork. The rapid restoration of the telegraph service at this juncture had a salutary influence upon the strikers.

The Post-Office organization was first tested during the Ashantee war in 1873. At forty-eight hours' warning, a complete force of officers and men trained in the postal telegraph service was sent out, with stores, instruments, batteries, &c., all drawn from the Post-Office. The success which this body of experts achieved was signal, and it received well-merited approbation.

Besides these two Telegraph Companies, there is a third corps of Royal Engineers, known as C troop, charged with the special work of telegraphy. The headquarters of this troop are ordinarily at Aldershott, where it is exercised in practical field work, laying ground cables, putting up overhead lines, &c.

For many years the equipment of C troop was in imitation of the German outfit, consisting mainly of a ground cable worked with polarized Morse recorders on a closed circuit. It seems to have been taken for granted that no better method of running a line could be found than by paying out an insulated cable on the ground. The fact that such a cable would be greatly exposed to accidental damage was recognized, and it was to reduce the ill-effects of this damage to a minimum that this type of receiving instrument was adopted. The polarized armature being worked by feeble currents permits considerable leakage without interruption of the service, but the instrument is delicate and complex. As might have been foreseen, much difficulty was experienced in the practical working of this equipment. The condition of the troop as a whole was not as satisfactory as its friends could have wished during a period of several years.

In 1874 the dissatisfaction with the outfit bore fruit in the adoption of a new equipment, notably of an overhead air line in addition to the cable, and simpler forms of instruments. Since then the equipment has undergone constant improvement.

The members of C troop, while intelligent and well instructed, are not necessarily professional telegraphists. The backward condition of the troop for so many years was doubtless due to the fact that during this time no practical telegraphist, officer or man, was appointed to it. It is now, however, in more efficient condition, having abandoned with profit its rigid conservatism.

The old organization was subjected to a severe trial during the Zulu war, when, strengthened by about twenty Post-Office clerks, C troop went to the front. On arriving at Natal the equipment proved defective and the best work was by the Post-Office clerks, who took over the colonial telegraphs and worked them for military purposes. The field lines were at fault because too lightly put up. Altogether this expedition was not very successful.

After the Natal experience a mixed *personnel* went out under a thoroughly experienced officer, trained in the post-office. The equipment included a light overhead wire. The work was well done in every way. The combination of generally trained intelligence with special expertness could not fail to produce good results.

The occurrences just referred to were among the causes which led to the forming in 1881 of a board of officers at Aldershott, presided over by Lieutenant-Colonel Richard Harrison, C. B., R. E., for the consideration of the subject of field-telegraph organization and equipment. This board recommended a complete amalgamation, in time of war, of C troop and the two telegraph companies, 22d and 34th. In the mean time it secured marked improvements in poles, wire, insulators, and instruments.

The outfit at present is chiefly as follows:

The ground cable is manufactured by Messrs. Siemens Brothers, of

London. It consists of a core composed of seven wires No. 22 B. W. G.
The central wire is of steel, the others of copper, tinned. The dielectric
is of rubber, the first layer being soft, the outer layers semi-vulcanized
and vulcanized. Over this is a wrapping of India-rubber tape, and the
whole is inclosed in tarred jute braiding. The total diameter is .24 inch.
The resistance of the conductor is 28.7 ohms at 75° Fahrenheit. The
resistance of the dielectric is not uniform (the dielectric being so slight),

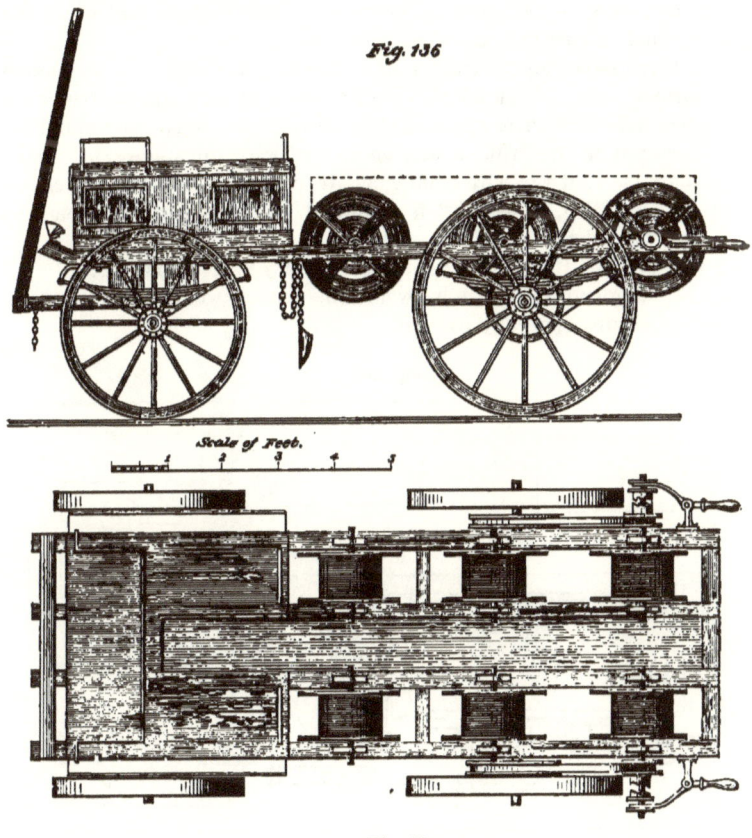

Fig. 136

Fig. 137

Telegraph wagon.

and is not guaranteed by the maker. The cable weighs 170 pounds per
statute mile, and has a breaking strain of 270 pounds. It is carried on
drums, each capable of holding five-sixths of a mile, which rest on a specially designed wagon. (See Figs. 136 and 137.) Here they are secured by
cap-squares and latches. An arrangement is fitted on either side of the

wagon for winding up the wire on the rear reel. It consists of a wooden drum fixed upon the back of the hind wheel of the wagon and concentric with it. From this an India-rubber band passes over a small bandwheel held in an iron bracket on the side of the wagon. The ends of this band are fitted with clips, and may be disconnected at will. The axis of the band-wheel lies in the prolongation of the spindle of the wire-drum, and has upon its inner side a clutch. Corresponding to this is another clutch on the spindle of the drum. These clutches can be thrown in or out of gear as desired. When in gear, and when the carriage moves forward, the wire is wound up.

The three boxes on the front part of the wagon frame may be opened and formed into a field office. Inside the near box are instruments and terminals with wires running to the bearings of the drum's spindles. The terminal on the drum is also connected with the spindle by means of a plate, so that the wire from each drum may be coupled as desired in the field office. "Earth" is obtained by wires running from the naves of the wheels along the spokes to the iron tires.

The weight of the cable wagon when empty is 1,758 pounds.

In the longitudinal space between the drums twenty light iron telescopic poles are generally carried.

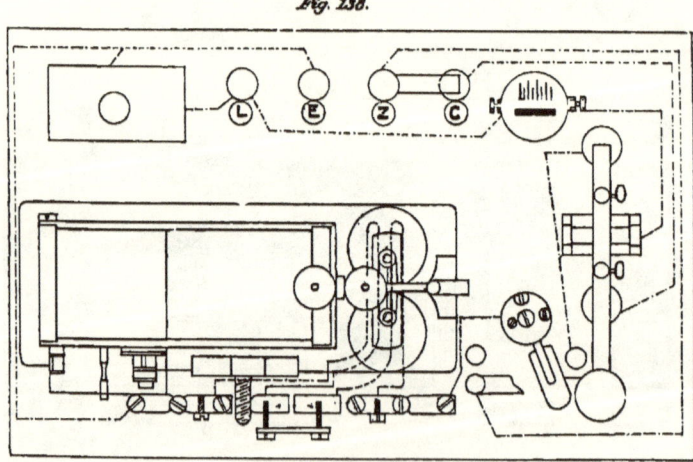

Fig. 138.

Military Morse recorder.

The overhead line is a strand of three galvanized-iron wires, each No. 18 B. W. G., having a resistance of 240 tons and weighing 120 pounds to the mile, very pliable and strong, carried on light poles (bamboo is the material selected), 14 feet long, capped with simple ebonite insulators.

The instruments employed were military Morse recorders, of which a top view, with the connections, is given in Fig. 138. This instrument can be used as a direct inker on a closed circuit, or as a local inker with either single or double current. This instrument is small, compact, simple, and efficient. It is made by Siemens Brothers.

It has been proposed to use the telephone for hasty field work, and sets of receiving and transmitting instruments, based on this principle, were issued to C troop for experiment and trial. The transmitter is represented in Fig. 139. When the key is down the current passes through the coils of the electro-magnet and through the armature as well. The latter being attracted leaves a stop-screw on the standard and the current is broken. As the armature is carried by a spring, the making and breaking of the current, which now takes place, is very rapid, occasioning a buzzing sound that is transmitted through the line wire to

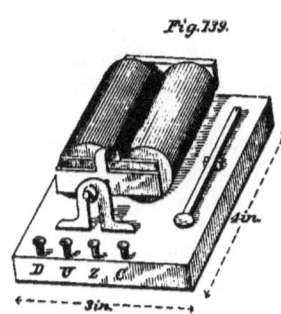

Fig. 139.

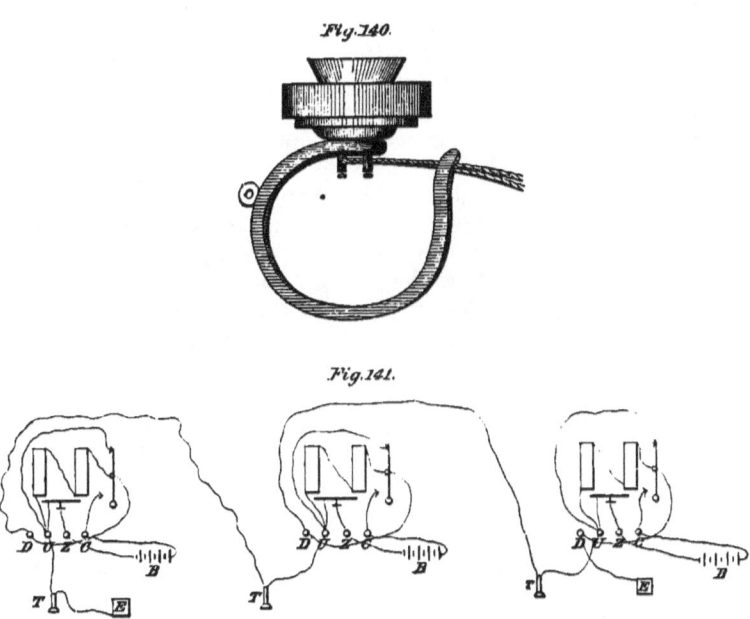

Fig. 140.

Fig. 141.

the telephones of all the stations. The special form of telephone employed is shown in Fig. 140, while Fig. 141 is a conventional diagram of the electrical connections of the stations in circuit.

Concerning the value of the apparatus, different opinions were encountered. Lieutenant-Colonel Webber thinks the Tyler sounder a toy, and states that the contacts are very apt to foul, while Major Sir Arthur Mackworth experienced no fault in its working in the field, and found its behavior satisfactory even when sending messages over a leaky cable.

The batteries that entered into the outfit of C troop were small Leclanché elements in square vulcanite jars, ten in a box, and coupled in series. They were all ready for use, except that water had to be added through a plugged hole when needed. The tops of the cells were sealed with a bituminous composition, which in the hot climate of Egypt melted and flooded the batteries, rendering many of them useless. The Leclanché element is not adapted to continuous work on a closed circuit, and hence the advisability of its employment with the Morse recorders is open to question.

For field work, the ordinary post-office detector galvanometer was issued. This has a vertical needle and two resistance coils, and is a good instrument for rough purposes.

Each unit or section was provided with an "office box" containing a complete equipment of stationery, spare parts of instruments and batteries, tools, &c. These boxes were found to be too heavy for transportation from Ismailia. They were therefore opened and the necessary articles taken out for use and forwarded to the front.

A portion of the equipment was arranged for conveyance on pack saddles, suitable boxes being made to contain spare parts, tools, spun-yarn, gutta-percha, covered wire, &c.

As an outcome of the report by Lieutenant-Colonel Harrison's board, when the expedition to Egypt was resolved upon, the mounted portion of C troop and sixty men from the Postal Telegraph Companies were formed into a Telegraph Corps under the old designation of C troop, the command being given to Major Sir Arthur Mackworth, R. E., a capable and energetic officer, not a post-office trained telegraphist. Associated with him were one captain and five lieutenants. The rank and file numbered 184 men. The transport consisted of 66 horses, 12 telegraph wagons, 14 Maltese carts, 4 water-carts, and a forge wagon, and was only meant to carry the stores needed at the front, other modes of conveyance being looked for after landing, for the outfit comprised enough wire to reach from Ismailia to Cairo, and weighed between 300 and 400 tons. It was found that the heaviness of the country prevented the use of all the vehicles brought out. The horses could never move more than 10 wagons and a few two-wheeled carts. The drivers and mounted men were armed with revolvers, and the others with carbines.

The troop assembled at Aldershott and marched with horses and wagons to London, where it embarked on August 9 on board the hired transport Oxenholme lying in the south West India docks. In the mean time the entire equipment, providing against every possible want, had been sent from the Woolwich Arsenal and put on board the ship. Unfortunately, those most interested had not superintended the stowage of the cargo, and, as a natural consequence, what ought to have been on top was at the bottom, an arrangement very fertile in subsequent embarrassment.

The importance of the prompt arrival of so valuable a corps as the Telegraph Troop would seem to have been obvious, and yet the Oxenholme, selected to bring it out, together with the Pontoon Troop and the Field Park, was one of the slowest of the transport fleet. Sailing from London on August 9, she only reached Alexandria on the 26th, and Ismailia on the 28th of the month, when the advance of the army had already arrived at Kassassin. The inconvenience of stowage, already referred to, was experienced at once; the whole equipment had to be broken out and reassorted in order to select the two or three tons required for immediate use. The outfit of stores, material, tools, &c., was to have been divided into five portions, each article or set of articles being in quintuplicate. One portion was designed for a reserve at the base, and the others for use with the four independent sections which composed the troop. Owing to the Oxenholme's late arrival at Ismailia, and to the time taken in reassorting the ill-stowed cargo, the scheme could not be carried out.

Men and wagons were landed and pushed on at once without proper material, tools &c. * * * It was found too late that the work on hand differed from the drill at Aldershott, and that, as practical telegraphists, the first thing to be done was to restore as quickly as possible the Egyptian system, which had been broken down.

It has been mentioned that there were three wires along the railway from Ismailia to Zagazig. In addition to these were two through wires belonging to the Eastern Telegraph Company, and having no connection with the Egyptian office *en route*. The first three were Egyptian Government lines, with stations originally at Ismailia, Nefiche, and Mahsameh. All of these wires were more or less damaged, the Eastern Company's having especially suffered. Many of the latter's poles, which are of iron, were thrown down. This group of wires was not repaired or used by the Telegraph Troop.

As General Graham, who commanded the advance post, had been beyond the reach of the telegraphs for four days prior to the arrival of the Oxenholme, Major Mackworth had at once to establish the desired communication as well as to get his men and material ashore.

The disembarkation was completed, as far as necessary, by 11.30 p. m. of August 30, the troop marching at once to Tel-el-Mahuta, ten miles distant from Ismailia, where it arrived at 4.30 a. m. of the 31st and rested for a short time. August 31 was spent in labor on the broken Egyptian system. By 4.30 p. m. the line was "through" from Kassassin to Tel-el-Mahuta, and by 9 a. m. of the following day was "through" to Ismailia.

This was effected by passing across the breaks from one to another, an expedient yielding temporary success, but much subsequent inconvenience, the "leads" being badly intermingled.

The next few days were occupied in repairing and re-establishing the old lines and in forming an advanced field-telegraph post at Kassassin. By the morning of September 7 Major Mackworth describes himself as "pretty well off."

Of the three lines that had been restored, one was a through wire used mainly by General Wolseley for his dispatches to the base and to England; the second passed through all stations; and the third was reserved exclusively for the railway management. On September 12 there were two telegraph offices at Ismailia, one at the railway station and the other under a tent in the yard adjoining the headquarters of the base commandant. One station was at Nefiche, one at Mahsameh, besides the railway and staff offices at Kassassin. Before or at about this time Major Mackworth appears to have given up charge of the permanent lines from the front at Kassassin to the base at Ismailia to Lieutenant-Colonel Webber, and to have confined his attention to the operations of the field telegraph.

During a reconnaissance on September 8 a small detachment followed up General Graham, and maintained communication with General Willis' headquarters at Kassassin by means of a ground cable.

The Egyptians appearing in superior force, Graham was obliged to retire more rapidly than was compatible with reeling up the wire. Major Mackworth used every exertion, holding on until the enemy was within 600 yards of him before cutting the cable, about half a drum of which was lost. This was the "torpedo wire" which Arabi speaks of as having captured. (See p. 144.)

September 12 the plans for the general advance of the next day upon Arabi's position at Tel-el-Kebir were elaborated. It was decided that a portion of C troop should run a ground cable from Kassassin to the Commander in-Chief's headquarters in the field, on the northern side of the canal, while General Macpherson, commanding the Indian Contingent, was to be kept in communication with the same point, and thence with General Wolseley, by means of an overhead line to be run by the Indian Sapper Telegraph Train. In addition, Major Mackworth planted a row of telegraph poles, $2\frac{1}{2}$ miles long, at intervals of 150 yards, to mark the direction of the night march. Lieutenant-Colonel Webber and Lieutenant R. W. Anstruther, R. E., with another detachment of C troop, were to follow up and repair the Egyptian permanent wires along the railway.

The army marched from Kassassin during the night of the September 12-13, the two wings being in constant telegraphic communication until 2.30 a. m. of the 13th, when the Indian Contingent's line south of the canal was interrupted. It was afterwards ascertained that the break was caused by a pontoon wagon, which accidentally struck and tore down the overhead wire. General Wolseley, however, was always in connection with Kassassin, although the actual telegraph work involved stopping from time to time to make "earth." The dry, sandy nature of the soil necessitated a special apparatus for this operation, a pointed and perforated galvanized-iron pipe, 3 feet long, which was driven into the ground. Water was then poured in, the end of the cable connected with the pipe, and "earth" obtained at once.

Fig. 142

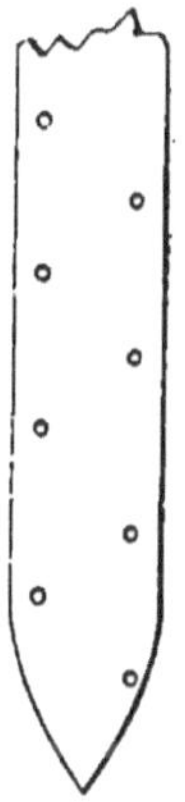

During the battle of Tel-el-Kebir, General Wolseley sent three messages over the field cable, and received several in return. When the fight was ended Major Mackworth pushed on as rapidly as possible to Tel-el-Kebir railway station, paying out his cable as he went. The last three miles were laid in thirty minutes, ten in all being run. At 8.30 a. m. he received messages to the Queen and to the Secretary of State for War. He got them off at 8.41, and at 9.15 Her Majesty's reply was received.

The end of Major Mackworth's field cable was connected with one of the Egyptian wires two miles west of Kassassin. As tending to introduce confusion into the subsequent regular telegraph service this would appear to have been a mistaken economy of time and material. Notwithstanding the fact that men were immediately dispatched back along the railway to meet Lieutenant-Colonel Webber, it was not until 6 p. m. that the latter was able to send word to Major Mackworth to shift on to the permanent lines and to pick up his cable.

Lieutenant-Colonel Webber, who, as has been stated, was to follow up the Egyptian wires along the railway, found Nos. 1 and 3 gone in several places, but No. 2 was still on the poles throughout, although damaged here and there. He passed the intrenchments with General Macpherson and reached Tel-el-Kebir railway and telegraph station at 7 a. m., finding one wire "through" to Cairo. He was trying in vain to communicate in English, when in came the superintendent of Egyptian telegraphs, an Englishman named Clark, who immediately began conversing in Arabic, as if he were a friend in Arabi's camp, but not revealing the exact state of affairs. The consequent lack in Cairo of trustworthy information had doubtless something to do with the irresolution of Arabi's party there, and may have helped to save the city. On the other hand, Mr. Clark sent the news of the battle to the operator at Zagazig, assuring him that, if his behavior was satisfactory, the English would spare his life. In this way the integrity of the lines was secured from Tel-el-Kebir to Cairo, leaving the sole gap between the army and its base in the Tel-el-Kebir–Kassassin section. To restore this link to proper working order, two valuable days were consumed at a critical moment, the officer specially charged with the work being suddenly ordered away and on to the front.

Details of linemen and operators were sent on with the advance in both directions. The office at Zagazig was seized that afternoon, and by 9.30 a. m., September 15, the other stations on the railway at Benha, Belbeis, Calioub, and Cairo were occupied. They were held until the Egyptian Government official service was established—an operation rapidly effected.

The peculiar nature of the soil is a sufficient explanation of the immunity from accident enjoyed by Major Mackworth's ground cable, over which numberless wagons of all kinds passed freely from midnight until sundown September 13.

It is not out of place to record the general good conduct and performance of C troop. The office work was particularly severe and almost unremittent, giving little rest to the operators, who were nearly worn out by the constant strain. Their efforts to keep at their desks when overcome by fatigue and loss of sleep were most creditable.

A regular order of precedence in the forwarding of dispatches was maintained. The general features were as follows, viz:

1st. Dispatches to or from the Commander-in-Chief.
2d. Railway dispatches.
3d. Official dispatches relating to the sick or wounded.
4th. Other official dispatches in order of receipt, unless made "urgent" by proper authority.
5th. Private dispatches relating to the sick or wounded.
6th. Other private and press dispatches in the order of their receipt.

For classes 5 and 6, payment was exacted according to a regular tariff.

As might be presupposed, the loudest expressions of discontent with the telegraph service came from newspaper correspondents, who were not always reasonable in their demands, and who failed at times to understand how official dispatches could be of greater importance than their own. It must be remembered, however, that even so conservative a body of men as army officers cannot be entirely exempt from the influence of the tendency of to-day to substitute the telegram for the written letter, that a large proportion of the dispatches marked "official" need not necessarily have been urgent, and therefore the business they were designed to transact would have lost nothing by a slower process of transmission. From various causes, there arose at times heavy blocks in the telegraph lines in spite of the unusual advantage of three wires. It was during one of these blocks that a distinguished officer was able to say, humorously but truthfully, that he had sent three simultaneous dispatches from Ismailia to Kassassin: one by boat on the Sweet Water Canal, the second by railway, and the third by telegraph, and that they arrived at their destination in the exact order given.

It is only fair to remark that the lateness of the arrival of the troop at the base and the extreme brevity of the campaign prevented a settling down to an organized routine and gave an appearance of confusion which was to some extent unavoidable. The work would, it is believed, have been better done had the absolutely distinct parts of the troop been occasionally associated for joint practice prior to amalgamation.

Military telegraphy cannot be an amateur's toy. It is valueless unless trustworthy in its material and managed by capable persons. The simplest and best instruments are required in conjunction with a well-insulated line, either ground or overhead. If the latter, it is not enough to bring the ends of the wire into the terminal stations. The intermediate points must be out of the reach of accidental mechanical injury and reasonably free from electrical faults. A little more time and trouble spent in setting the poles, in making electrically sound joints, and in securing good insulation will, in the end, be found to be time saved.

The result of the practical comparative experiment on September 13, with a ground cable on one hand and an overhead line on the other, only emphasizes the necessity of thorough work, without deciding the relative merits of the two methods. Each has its own province, the former in supplying, in a rapid advance, a communication which is only meant to be temporary, while the latter is more or less permanent according to the circumstances of the case. It follows that both kinds of conductor should enter into the outfit. But above and beyond mere mechanical appliances is the importance of a thoroughly-trained *personnel*, one part familiar with the press of office work conducted amid noise and confusion, the other with the conditions and phenomena of engineering and line work, and both parts accustomed to action in concert. The combination of these elements, directed by clever and energetic officers, will alone produce such results as will justify the heavy expenditure of men and money in making the army telegraph a valuable adjunct, not a delusion and a snare.

XXVI.

THE CORPS OF SIGNALERS.

The earliest mode of transmitting intelligence, the written or verbal message, possesses certain great advantages. Written dispatches destroy all chance of error, and hence are resorted to when time permits and the importance of their contents demands this additional precaution. Besides being slow, the system presents the drawback of being excessively cumbersome, requiring a man and a horse, or a man alone, for each message, and, over great distances, for each stage of the journey accomplished.

Visual signaling, the second method, historically speaking, possesses the merits of cheap and simple equipment, a *personnel* not very highly trained except in one direction, the ability to begin work the instant the stations are reached, while its great mobility enables it to be used at and among the extreme outposts. On the other hand, these stations must always be selected with reference to the facility of signaling from one to the other, and not to the convenience of the Commander-in-Chief, while each obstacle intervening in the line of sight introduces a repeating station with its consequent chance of error. Again, this method, depending for its successful employment upon an unobstructed view, is at the mercy of the weather. Five minutes of fog may imperil the success of an important military movement. It finds its most complete scope in hilly countries, where the sun is rarely obscured. Under these conditions, its range, so to speak, has almost no bounds. Thus, as an extreme case, it is known that in the triangulation carried across the Rocky Mountains observations have been taken between peaks one hundred and fifty miles apart, mirrors being used to reflect the sunlight from one to the other. Messages might have been and possibly were exchanged between these points by flashing the reflected light.

Visual signaling in the British army is based on "flashes," long and short. The code, composed of dots and dashes, and being what is known among telegraphers as the "Morse Continental," is given below.

A · —   H · · · ·   N — ·   T —
B — · · ·   I · ·   O — — —   U · · —
C — · — ·   J · — — —   P · — — ·   V · · · —
D — · ·   K — · —   Q — — · —   W · — —
E ·   L · — · ·   R · — ·   X — · · —
F · · — ·   M — —   S · · ·   Y — · — —
G — — ·   Z — — · ·

Comma · — · — · —
Period · · · · · ·
Preparative and erasure · · · · · · · · · · · · · · · · · ·, &c.
Stop — — — — — — — — —, &c.
General answer — (T)
Station sign · — · · (P)
Repeat · · — — · ·
Right · — · — (R T)
Cipher — · — · — · — · (C C)
Numerical, — — · · (Z)
Signaler's indicator · — · —
Obliterator · — — · — ·

This phase of the Morse code is universally employed in the telegraphs of Great Britain and the continent of Europe. By its adoption for the army and navy a long step is made towards rendering signalers tolerably efficient substitutes for telegraphists in case of emergency. It differs from the Morse code in use in America by the suppression of the space as a code unit, which, it may be remembered, enters into several of the most important letters of the alphabet, viz, c, o, r, and y, and in containing no combination of more than four elements. The continental is, therefore, an improvement upon the earlier code. Its application to visual signals is very simple, any motions or exposures, which may be made long and short, affording a means of transmitting intelligence. It involves but the one notion of time; that is, of one thing lasting longer than another. As practiced, it is entirely devoid of direction of motion, the fundamental principle of the Myer code, as it is of the relative position of objects, the key to the semaphore, that rapid method of signaling employed in the British navy.

During the day army signals are made either by the heliograph or by flags. The latter are white or blue, according to the nature of the background, and are of two sizes, 3 feet square, mounted on a staff 5 feet 6 inches long, 1 inch in diameter at the butt, tapering to $\frac{1}{2}$ inch at the top, and 2 feet square, mounted on a stick 3 feet 6 inches long. The signalman stands so that the motions of the flag are in a plane at right angles to the line of sight. The normal position of the staff is 25° from the vertical. If the wind serves the motions are made to windward.

The dot, or short flash, is made by waving the flag from the normal position to a corresponding position on the opposite side of the vertical, and immediately back again to the normal position. The dash or long flash, equivalent in length to three dots, is made by waving the flag from the normal position until the pole almost touches the ground on the opposite side of the vertical, then, after a short pause, back again to the normal position. The various letters and signs are made by combining the dots and dashes according to the code, a pause equal in length to a dash intervening after each letter of a word. At the end of the word the flag is lowered or gathered in, when the receiving station makes a dash to indicate that the word is understood. "Right" (R T) is the final answer at the end of a message.

The station sign (P) followed by a letter calls the station to which that letter has been given, the called station responding by "right" and the letter of the calling station, as for instance P B and R T A when station A calls station B, and the latter signifies its readiness to proceed with the reception of the message. The station sign is also used to indicate the completion of the message.

The digits are indicated by the first ten letters of the alphabet in order, J being omitted, and K substituted in its place. When the numeral sign (Z) is followed by a letter or series of letters the combination is to be read as a number; thus Z C H would be 38.

The "signalers' indicator" precedes directions intended solely for the signalers and not forming part of the message, abbreviated thus:

Fresh reading	G Q
Go on	G
Move to your right	R
Move to your left	L
Move higher up	H
Move lower down	O
Stay where you are	S R
Separate your flags	S F
Special message	S M S

Use blue flag	B
Use white flag	W
Use large flag	L F
Use small flag	S
Your light is bad	L B
Turn off extra light	T E L
Wait	M Q

L B and T E L have reference to the heliograph. The "obliterator" annuls what precedes and is answered by the obliterator.

Time is signaled in code and is followed by a. m. or p. m. as the case may be. Fig. 143 is a clock-dial lettered according to the code. The

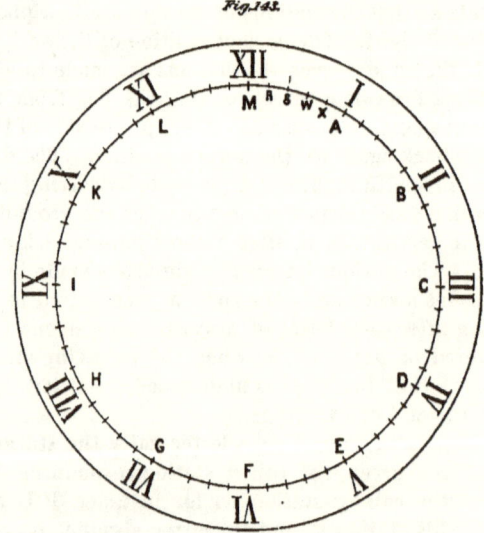

twelve hours each bear a letter and the four individual minutes intervening between each hour-mark and its successor are known by the letters R S W X, respectively repeated around the dial. Thus 8.29 p. m. is <H E X p. m.

The second means of making signals during the day is the heliograph, an instrument for directing the reflected rays of the sun in any desired direction alternately on and off a distant station.

A fairly correct idea of the principle and mode of use of the heliograph is given in Fig. 144. A small circular mirror is mounted on a U-shaped frame. The frame, which can be turned in any direction, is supported by a tripod. The mirror is movable about a horizontal axis, and can be set at the necessary angle of inclination by a screw-rod at the back working inside a nut, a. The nut, which can be turned at will, is carried at the top of a small cylinder, into which the rod passes as the mirror is more and more inclined. The cylinder is fixed to the top of what, for clearness, may be called a telegraph key, by means of lugs and a pin. Depressing the key turns the mirror through a small angle, and, if the instrument is adjusted, throws the flash of light on the receiving station. This flash is a dot or dash of the Morse code, according to its duration. When the key is released, a spring returns the mirror to the original position, and the light is no longer seen by the other station. A hole through the center of the mirror is for directing the heliograph. The arm b carries a fore-sight in the shape of a very small white metal disk. When the distant station and this index are in one line, as seen by the eye placed at the back of the mirror, the instrument is properly pointed. The mirror is now moved until the sun's reflected ray falls full upon the disk when the key is down. In the very center of the mirror a small circle is left unglazed. The reflection from the mirror shows this as a black spot on a bright ground. This spot must be brought into the center of the fore-sight disk. The disk is then turned in its socket so as to present its edge to the beam of light, and the signaling may be proceeded with. As the sun shifts its position the heliograph must be constantly readjusted, but the operation is merely a slight correction of the original adjustment.

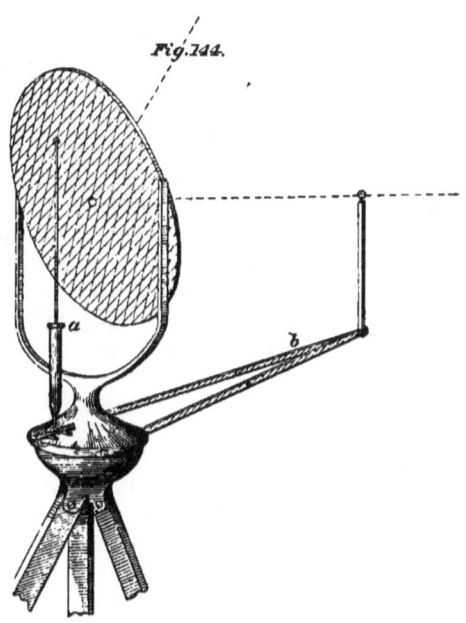

Fig. 144.

If the sun is behind the sending station as seen from the receiving station, a second circular mirror is substituted for the fore-sight. The course of the beam of light is then as seen in Fig. 145.

The heliograph was invented by Mr. G. B. Mance of the Indian telegraph service, who received £1,000 sterling from the Indian Government as a reward. (Mr. Mance's name is identified with a well-known and very clever method of measuring the internal resistance of an electrical battery.) It was first employed in the Kaffir campaign, in 1877. During the last Afghan war it was constantly used to great advantage, the conditions mentioned in the opening paragraphs of this section finding a complete fulfillment. It may be remembered that the first intimation of the approach of the army under Major-General Sir F. S. Roberts, which marched to the relief of Kandahar in 1880, was by means of this instrument, when at the distance of *forty-eight miles* from the town. As no previously concerted plan had been agreed upon, this fact sufficiently indicates the ease with which one station may attract the attention of another, the brilliant spot of steady reflected light being unmistakable.

The range of 58 miles between Kandahar and the station at the summit of the Maiwan Pass was habitually covered, while, in the same country, it was occasionally employed between parties 70 miles apart. In the Transvaal, in 1881, Lieutenant Davidson, of the King's Royal Rifle Corps, maintained communication over a line 200 miles in length, using but four intermediate stations. These facts give an idea of the great value of the heliograph under favorable circumstances.

The heliograph may, of course, be used with any source of illumination, its range depending upon the strength of the light, and indeed it is so convenient an instrument that its employment at night for flashing signals has grown into great favor with signalers. During this campaign it was used between Kassassin and Mahsameh for signaling with the light of the moon at its full.

The "call" with the heliograph is most simple. Turn the spot of light upon the other station, and wait until it answers by showing its light in return.

The request for the adjustment of the heliograph at another station during the transmission of a message is effected by merely keeping the light turned on. When the latters light is adjusted to shine full and clear, the asking station's light is dropped.

The apparatus for night work consists of a lime light and a hand lantern, both fitted with shutters moved by keys so as to vary the exposure at will. The former is accompanied by all the paraphernalia necessary for making and holding oxygen. A powerful lens secures parallelism of the rays of light. An outside view of this lamp is given in Fig. 146. The combustible is spirits of wine contained in a large reservoir forming the base of the lamp. The lime pencil is carried by a holder capable of adjustment by means of a rack and pinion not seen in the sketch. The gas is brought to the lamp from a gas-tight bag through a rubber pipe, and its flow is regulated by the tap *a*. At *b* is a small hole provided with a darkened eye-piece, so that the signal-man may inspect and adjust the light without injury to his eyes. On a clear dark night this light can be seen over 20 miles. The hand lantern is used for distances not exceeding from 4 to 6 miles. It burns colza oil.

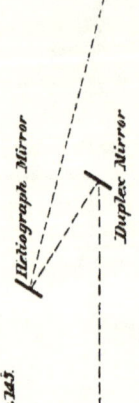

Use of the duplex mirror in heliographing.

A view of the exterior with dimensions is given in Fig. 147. The key for operating the shutter is conveniently placed at the top of the handle. Both forms of lantern are supplied by J. De Fries & Sons, London.

Each cavalry regiment in the British army has four non-commissioned officers and eight men in their signal corps, or four complete "stations" of three men each. Each infantry battalion has two non-commissioned officers and four men, or two "stations." In addition, each cavalry troop and infantry company has a supernumerary trained signal-man.

The instruction and practice necessary to keep the signal-men and

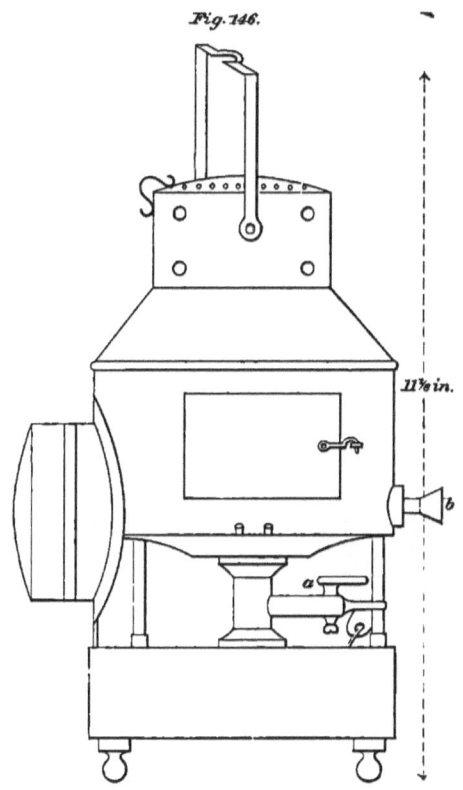

Fig. 146.

supernumeraries up to their work is conducted by a specially selected officer of the regiment or battalion, and amounts to three days per week for the former and one day for the latter. A quarterly return is made to the lieutenant-colonel commanding by this officer, giving the names and proficiency of the men under his instruction. One column of the return calls for the "rate of sending," as a comparative test. It has been found that if the letters of the alphabet be repeated three times, mixed together, and then separated into twenty groups of unequal length, the time occupied in their transmission is the same as that required for a message of twenty words of different lengths averaging five letters to the word. The time spent in sending this message is then reduced to "words per minute." Ten is considered fair signaling with large flags, but higher rates are reached with the small flag, lamp, and heliograph.

The signal officers and men of the regiments and battalions are sent to the Camp of Maneuver at Aldershott, where they receive instruction

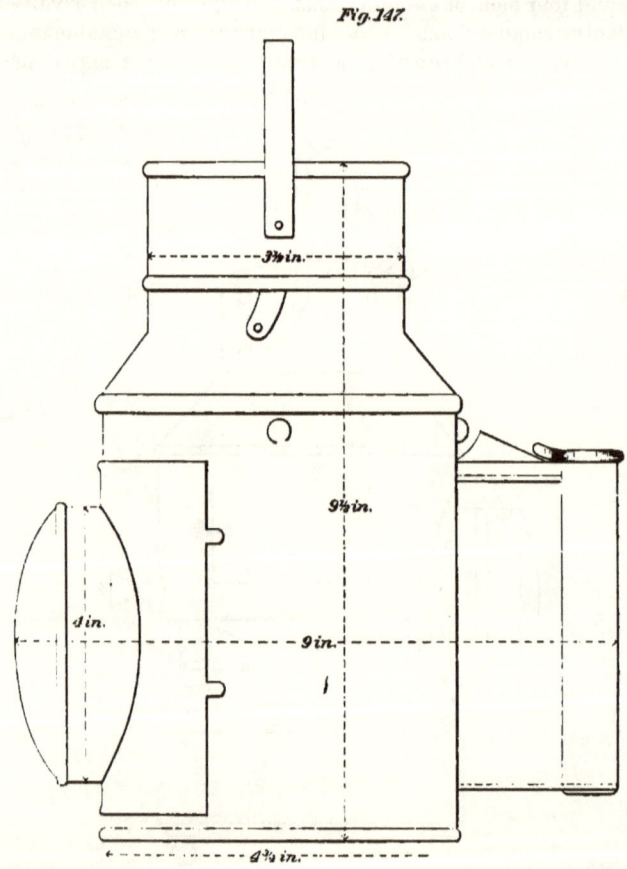

Fig. 147.

in field and brigade signals under the immediate supervision of Major M. F. Thrupp, the Inspector of Army Signaling, who also examines and passes the regimental instructors.

Signal-men in the field are armed with the sword-bayonet and short Martini-Henry carbine slung over their back. The heliographs are carried in neat leather cases over the shoulders. Three men form a complete party, and, as a rule, are provided with an outfit consisting of two flags (one large and one small), with the requisite poles, one heliograph and stand, one hand lantern, one lime light and stand, with the accompanying gas and pressure bags, retort and chemicals for generating oxygen (chlorate of potash and binoxide of manganese), together with printed blank forms in blocks; one set as a record of dispatches sent, the other of dispatches received.

Generally speaking, in the late campaign the transport of one party comprised three mules, one for provisions and signal apparatus, packed in convenient boxes; the second for the men's kits and camp kettles, the third for the tents, &c. A fourth man is usually added to the group of three, for cooking, &c., and a relief in case of need. Cavalry signalers, not being designed to form permanent stations, carry only flags and heliographs, in leather buckets strapped to the saddle.

The Corps of Signalers in this campaign was composed of 1 captain, 2 lieutenants, and 90 men, volunteers from various regiments, under the command of Lieutenant-Colonel F. C Keyser, of the Royal Fusiliers, an officer of experience in the late Afghan war. This corps was for duty under the Chief of Staff, and had no connection with the regimental signalers.

The men appear to have been selected solely with reference to their proficiency as signalers, without regard to other desirable qualities. Their behavior was not what should have been expected from persons charged with such responsible duties.

The work they did in Egypt was not of very much importance. The flatness of the country and the frequent mirage greatly restricted the use of the heliograph, their most powerful instrument.

A line of four stations was maintained between Ismailia and Kassassin, a distance of twenty miles, and was worked by heliographs, flags or lime light, as occasion demanded. These stations would have sufficed, but an extra one was kept up at Tel-el-Mahuta to control the canal traffic.

The first warning of the approach of the Egyptians in the action of August 28 was conveyed by heliograph from Major-General Graham, at Kassassin, to Major-General Drury-Lowe, commanding the cavalry encamped at Mahsameh. The sending instrument was advantageously placed on a small house at the former place, and was doing excellent work when one of the Egyptian shells struck the building, and the signalers, to use Colonel Keyser's expression, "incontinently bolted," deserting their post at a most critical moment and leaving General Drury-Lowe without information of the occurrences at the front. The absence of an officer at so important a station seems odd, to say the least.

The Corps of Signalers started out with a full supply of wheeled transport, which as usual broke down on the first march out from Ismailia. All spare carriages and store-wagons had to be left behind and recourse had to mules. One animal then carried two complete sets of day and night apparatus in panniers, the heavy boxes of spare articles, &c., being forwarded by train.

The final labors of the signalers were in Cairo, after the occupation, where they maintained heliographic and lime-light communication from the roof of the Abdin palace, the headquarters of the Commander-in-Chief, to the citadel, which, from its commanding position, was used as the repeating station to the cavalry camp at Abbasieh, the infantry camp across the Nile, at Ghezireh, and the barracks at Kasr-el-Nel. This service was soon replaced by telephones, and Colonel Keyser's men returned to England.

XXVII.

THE MILITARY POLICE.

The provision made for the maintenance of order in the various camps and outside the camps, in the towns and villages where portions of the army were quartered, included a Provost-Marshal, Colonel H. G. Moore, V. C., Arygle and Sutherland Highlanders, as administrator, assisted by a corps of Military Police, some mounted and some on foot; in all, 4 officers and 138 men.

Of the mounted police, 39 were drawn from the regular establishment of the permanent camp of instruction at Aldershott, and 34 were volunteers from various cavalry regiments, especially recommended by their commanding officers for sobriety, good behavior, intelligence, and force of character. They were assembled at Aldershott for organization and equipment. They were armed with swords and revolvers, and were given a light outfit of transport, a Maltese cart and a water-cart, for use when marching as an independent military unit, as at Tel-el-Kebir.

Of the foot police, 55 were volunteers from the London Metropolitan Police, selected on account of their zeal and capacity and of their familiarity with the habits of criminals, while the remainder, 10 in number, were volunteers from regiments at home who had been named for vigor and good conduct by their superior officers. This detachment had a similar amount of equipment to that given their mounted colleagues. The men carried revolvers and sword-bayonets.

All the members of the Military Police Corps were made permanent or acting non-commissioned officers, in order to give them that authority over delinquents which is derived from higher rank. To distinguish them, each man wore on his left arm a broad white canvas band, with M. P. in large black letters stamped upon it.

In former times the provost-marshal had the power of summary punishment, and could inflict on any offender lashes not to exceed 50 in number. Since the abolition of flogging, in 1881, this rapid canceling of a score is no longer possible, and the provost-marshal's duties are confined to the arresting of delinquents and the reporting of the facts of the case to the commanding officer of the regiment or corps to which the delinquent is attached.

The Military Police are charged with the general good order of the camp or town as distinguished from that of the special encampment of a particular troop or battalion, patrolling the whole neighborhood day and night. Under the military commandant, a guard-house is established, where all straggling and drunken soldiers are confined, as well as all caught breaking the peace in any way. The prisoners are sent back to their own quarters every morning, and the charges against each are heard and the punishment awarded according to the Army Act in force.

The instructions governing the Military Police are very clear:

They are to prevent soldiers from committing outrages on civilians; to protect their property from trespass and depredation; to apprehend soldiers who are beyond bounds without passes, or who, having passes, may behave improperly, or who are not dressed according to regulations. They are to examine the passes of all ranks below that of sergeant. In carrying out their orders they must be particular not to give cause for complaint, to be prompt and decided, but civil and temperate on all occasions in the performance of their duty. They must be clean and smart in their appearance and a pattern to other soldiers.

In an advance, and particularly after an engagement, the mounted portion of the Military Police are ordered to keep well to the front, in order to prevent pillage, ravishing, and other crimes likely to be committed in the heat of excitement.

The provost-marshal issues licenses to shop-keepers to open refreshment saloons, where beer or light wine is allowed to be sold to the troops. In Egypt, all persons detected in the act of selling strong spirits to the soldiers were flogged by the native authorities (the lashes not exceeding 300 in number), and their liquor was confiscated and destroyed.

The Military Police were late in joining the army, only arriving at Ismailia September 2. Their presence, which was much needed on account of certain irregularities that had manifested themselves, soon brought about an improvement in discipline. It may be remarked that they had, as a whole, absolutely no affiliations with the troops, were a body of men with entirely different traditions and associations, and had nothing in common with the soldiers whose infractions of discipline they were espeially designed to check.

The police work in the desert was very light, as might have been expected, but it increased greatly after reaching Cairo. The good behavior of the troops on the whole was a matter of constant remark. The writer of this report takes pleasure in recording, as the result of his own observation, extending over many weeks, the rarity of cases of intoxication or other misdemeanor, the soldierly bearing, neat appearance, and generally good behavior of the British troops in Egypt.

Exceptions to this rule did occur, as a matter of course, one being of a serious and disgraceful nature. Two men of the Royal Irish Regiment committed a grave crime in the village of Tel-el-Kebir, just after the battle, and received in punishment seven years' penal servitude.

Great dissatisfaction was felt on the part of the British officers with the lack of a means of summary punishment to take the place of flogging. Confinement remains now, practically, the sole mode of punishment. *The guarding of one prisoner involves the labor of at least four other men, whose services are lost in more useful ways, while the prisoner himself is relieved of disagreeable, painful, and at times perilous duty, is well sheltered, well fed, and otherwise scrupulously cared for.*

During the campaign men sentenced to imprisonment of less than six weeks were retained with their regiments or corps; if more than six weeks and less than six months, they were sent to a base prison at Alexandria, and if of more than six months, they went back to England.

The hands of the Provost-Marshal were greatly strengthened by the co-operation of the native magistrates, who might be trusted to mete out a full measure of justice to inhabitants apprehended in acts prejudicial to the good order of the troops or to the peace of the neighborhood. Under other and ordinary circumstances the Military Police itself must have had cognizance of and jurisdiction in all such cases.

The plan of having a separate corps clothed with special powers, to look after instances of disorder among the troops, derives further warrant to careful consideration from the success which attended its practice during this campaign.

XXVIII.

THE MEDICAL DEPARTMENT.

This section is rather a collection of notes, which may serve to make the arrangements and methods adopted in Egypt reasonably clear, than a treatise on the subject of army hospitals and hospital practice in general.

The Medical Department of the British army has undergone within the last fifteen years important and wide-reaching changes. Formerly the Surgeon was an officer regularly attached to a regiment or corps, and he served with it until promoted to wider fields of usefulness. Identified with the fortunes of the regiment and intimately acquainted with the physical history of the men, his value was great if his sphere was somewhat restricted.

The withdrawal of the Surgeons from the direct authority of the Principal Medical Officer of the station or district, which was involved in their being made subject to their immediate military superiors in the corps to which they were gazetted, was regarded with disfavor, and the system known as "unification" was introduced. According to this, a Surgeon is assigned to temporary duty with a particular body of men after they reach their destination. Thus a battalion proceeding to the West Indies would leave England either with its former Medical Officer retained for the voyage out or with one detailed for the time being. On arrival at its post, the local Principal Medical Officer would order one of his subordinates to care for the wants of its members.

This unification is a hotly-debated point, much being advanced in way of argument on each side. In its favor are urged a more direct professional accountability for proper methods and treatment, as well as record, an escape from non-professional military control, simplification of the hospital service, and increased economy. Against it may be put the testimony of individual representatives of the medical corps, to the effect that the younger officers are not so desirable socially now as formerly; that the surgeon no longer knows his patients, thus rendering malingering much more easy than previously; that the medical officers are too anxious for military distinction, pressing to the front to the neglect of their own duty, &c. When doctors disagree, who shall decide?

One result is the concentration of power and responsibility in the hands of the Principal Medical Officer of the Force or District. He exercises command over all officers and men of the Medical Department proper or the Army Hospital Corps, and medical supervision and superintendence over all hospitals.

These responsible duties were performed in Egypt by Deputy Surgeon-General J. A. Hanbury, M. B., C. B., with the local rank of Surgeon-General.

As his chief assistant, under the title of "Sanitary Officer," was Brigade-Surgeon J. A. Marston, M. D., with the temporary rank of Deputy Surgeon-General.

It may be well to remark that in England a special corps, the Army Hospital Corps, is organized to carry on the hospital service and to direct the "bearer columns" charged with the collection of the wounded after a battle, and their transport to the stations where the wounds are temporarily dressed, prior to removal to the established hospitals. This corps may be described as a sort of lay handmaid to the Medical Department. Its officers are "Captains of Orderlies" and "Lieutenants of Orderlies," and it is mostly recruited from the ranks of the army.

For the second service mentioned in the foregoing paragraph, the handling of the wounded, what are known as "bearer companies" are formed, the professional *personnel* and equipment being drawn from the Army Medical Department and the Army Hospital Corps, while the necessary animals and drivers are furnished by the Commissariat and Transport Corps.

In Egypt, each bearer company was organized as shown in the annexed table.

Corps.	Surgeons-major.	Surgeons.	Captains of orderlies.	Lieutenants.	Warrant officers.	N. C. O. and men.	Drivers.	Batmen.	Horses. Officers. Private.	Horses. Officers. Public.	Horses. N. C. O.'s.	Horses. Draught.	Mules.
Army Medical Department	4	4	....	....	....	....	....	6	2	6	....	1	....
Army Hospital Corps	....	....	1	....	1	145	....	....	....	....	5	19	61
Commissariat and Transport Corps	....	....	....	1	1	10	55	1	....	....	5	6	17
Total	4	4	1	1	2	155	55	7	2	6	10	26	78

The mules were mainly to carry 26 litters and 60 cacolets in pairs. A cacolet is a frame for transporting a man in a sitting posture—a sort of arm-chair at the side of a mule.

Each bearer company has two operating tents and a full equipment of materials for establishing dressing stations.

Sick-carriage is provided at the rate of 10 per cent. of the force.

Dressing stations are pitched as near the battle-field as practicable, and are indicated by the Geneva Cross.

The two bearer companies were divided into half companies. The latter were distributed as follows:

Right half of No. 1 Company, 1st division.
Left half of No. 1 Company, 2d division.
Right half of No. 2 Company, cavalry division.
Left half of No. 2 Company was left at Alexandria for use there and at Ramleh.

The field hospital is planned to accommodate 200 patients, and is arranged in four sections. The establishment is as follows: Surgeons-major, 3; Surgeons, 4; Captain of Orderlies, 1. Total officers, 8; non-commissioned officers and men, 37.

The field-hospital tent is of the Bell pattern, double fly, and can contain four patients. Of these there are fifty, besides ten operating tents and tents for the *personnel*.

The field hospitals were eight in number, distributed as follows:

No. 1 at Alexandria.

No. 2 was stationed at Tel-el-Mahuta, afterwards at Kassassin, and was attached to the 1st division. It was closed at Ismailia on September 21.

No. 3 acted as a base hospital at Ismailia for a few days. It afterward proceeded by rail to Kassassin, and finally to Cairo.

No. 4 remained at Ismailia as part of the base hospital until moved to Cairo, after the occupation.

No. 5 at Ramleh.

No. 6. Of this, one half remained at Ismailia with the base hospital, the other at Mahsameh, at the cavalry camp. The two were amalgamated after Tel-el-Kebir and brought to Cairo.

No. 7 acted as part of the base hospital at Ismailia, and afterwards was transferred to Cairo.

No. 8 at Ismailia.

Each field hospital had a *clever carpenter* capable of making any desired form of splint.

The mattresses supplied *are in four parts* (divided transversely), so that any portion may be removed from under a patient for purposes of inspection or operation.

Two base hospitals were formed.

One at Alexandria, administered by No. 1 field hospital, was supplied with cots from home. Its capacity was 500 beds. A cotton warehouse was appropriated for this purpose; a large, airy building, well adapted to such use.

At Ismailia, as already mentioned elsewhere, the Khedive's palace was utilized as the principal base hospital. This is a large two-storied edifice, in the Italian style, with ample wings and high ceilings. It was most valuable in this connection, the walls being thick enough to resist the rays of the sun, while the window-shutters permitted the keeping out of the brilliant light, and, what was of even more importance, the persistent Egyptian fly.

The principal want in this hospital was a sufficient distribution of water. The latrines were even here in shocking condition and of a type not known in Christian countries. Earth-closets were soon provided and the latrines closed.

The accommodation afforded by the palace was supplemented as needed by tents. The *personnel* was drawn from No. 4, a portion of No. 6, and the medical staff of No. 7 and of No. 8 field hospitals.

Reserve hospitals were established at Cyprus and Gozo. The former had 400 beds, with a staff of 8 medical officers, one officer of orderlies, and 20 non-commissioned officers and men; the latter, 200 beds, with 4 medical officers, one officer of orderlies, and 12 non-commissioned officers and men.

Two hospital ships were stationed at Ismailia—the Carthage, a fine, large, new mail steamer of the Peninsular and Oriental Line, and the Courland, designed primarily for wounded and bad cases. Their capacity was 270 beds, and their *personnel* was 8 medical officers, 1 officer of orderlies, and 26 non-commissioned officers and men.

The messing for sick or wounded was at the rate of 3s. 6d. per diem, and was undertaken by the owners.

These vessels were supplemented by five auxiliary hospital ships, the Orontes, Tamar, Iberia, Lusitania, and Nepaul, whose services could be utilized as desired. Each was capable of making up, on the average, 300 beds, with a due proportion of medical officers and hospital orderlies.

To supply ice, that essential in medical or surgical practice in hot countries, *four large ice-machines were sent out.* One was mounted at Ismailia, at the mouth of the Sweet Water Canal, and one at Alexandria. Two others were brought out in the Carthage, but never set up. Five cwt. of the article was sent daily to the front.

As volunteer aids, 23 female nurses and 2 superintendents came from England, members of the Netley National Aid Society. These good women and invaluable assistants were distributed as follows:

Four nurses on board the hospital ship Carthage.
Four nurses at base hospital, Alexandria.
Seven nurses at base hospital, Ismailia.
One superintendent and four nurses at Gozo.
One superintendent and four nurses at Cyprus.

The medical comforts were provided on a liberal scale. They consisted of brandy, champagne, other wines of various kinds, soups, beer, milk, arrowroot, jelly, ice, &c. They were distributed among the base and field hospitals for use, besides a large supply at the advanced depot at Kassassin.

The hospital diet was the army ration supplemented by such medical comforts as were deemed necessary.

The men who became ineffective were shipped as fast as possible to England, Malta, &c. It was thought best to keep the hospitals in Egypt free, as well as to give the sufferers the increased chance afforded by cooler climate and more favorable surroundings. The question of temporary or permanent invaliding was decided later, according to the merits of each case.

The diseases mostly encountered were dysentery, diarrhea, heat apoplexy, fever, and a small amount of ophthalmia towards the end of the campaign. The number of cases, percentage, &c., could not be determined.

The Sweet Water Canal, whose condition has been frequently referred to in this report, did not, as was feared, give rise to disease, or if it was instrumental in producing, for instance, diarrhea, it could only have been to a very slight extent, for this class of malady was found even among men who drank distilled water exclusively. The muddiness of this particular water was of small moment, as pocket filters were issued to the troops at the rate of one to about every fifteen men; and lacking these, filters could be readily improvised from tin cans, &c., or the sediment could be precipitated by the addition of a small quantity of alum. It must rather be accepted as a fact that the dysenteric troubles found their cause in the heat and exposure to which the soldiers were subjected.

Antiseptic surgery was employed from the first. The wounds, when ready for dressing, were washed with very dilute carbolic acid and then dusted with iodoform. The bandages were either of carbolic-acid gauze or boracic-acid lint, a protector inclosing all. Before the operation the surgeon's hands and the surgical instruments were dipped in weak carbolic acid. The results of this treatment were considered to be good, but they had not been worked out in detail or tabulated.

Heat apoplexy was probably the only true climatic disease.

The arrangements at Tel-el-Kebir comprised a dressing station of twenty-five tents near the dam in the Sweet Water Canal, under Deputy Surgeon-General Marston, aided by 2 surgeons-major, 3 surgeons, 3 temporary assistants, and 1 volunteer, 10 in all, with 17 men of the Army Hospital Corps.

The plan pursued in each case was:

1st. To give the wounded man a little opium. This had the effect of quieting him until his turn came for operation.

2d. A drink of water was administered and then such food given as seemed advisable, beef, beef tea, milk, &c. By this time the patient was as nearly comfortable as possible, and could await without uneasiness the leisure of the surgeon.

3d. Examination of the wound.

4th. Such operation as was absolutely necessary.

5th. Transport down the canal to Kassassin, the sufferer being thoroughly nursed and nourished. A medical officer accompanied each tow.

Three Egyptian tents were utilized at Tel-el-Kebir. Two amputations were made and numberless other operations. In all, 180 Europeans were treated and nourished at this station.

The following paragraphs are from notes of a conversation with Deputy Surgeon-General Marston, and contain some of the suggestions of his experience. The language is not his.

Do not hesitate to move a wounded man, if necessary. Do not move him from the stretcher he is on, unless necessary. It is far better to move the wounded than have the wards crowded.

There are usually too many paraphernalia about a hospital and too much medicine. All medicine should be put up in its most compact and concentrated form. The necessary solution can be made on the spot.

The first dressing of a wound on the battle-field should be as simple as possible, for usually there is not time to do the work well. It should be a small bandage lightly put on, otherwise the limb swells above and below and gives pain to the patient and trouble to the operator.

Every officer and man should be labeled in some simple and effective way for identification if killed, or wounded beyond the power of speech.

Iron tubing ⅜ inch in diameter can be fashioned by an ordinarily good smith into a great variety of useful appliances.

A very simple yet efficient mode of relieving a wound from pressure is by means of a rough cage made of three wooden battens bent into shape, pushed under the bed-clothes. A large one covered with mosquito netting may be used to keep out insects. On the inside at the top a hook is placed, to which is hung a bottle containing antiseptic lotion, with a camel's-hair brush in the mouth of the bottle. The patient, if strong enough, is ordered to use this on his wound or bandage frequently (thus giving him an occupation), and to throw it into the fire when the wound is healed.

The disposition of offal is an important point. If a harbor is at hand, an easy method is by filling the windpipes of slaughtered animals with sand and sinking them in the sea. On shore, dead animals should be buried to leeward of mounds or sand hills with reference to the prevailing wind. It was found in Egypt that if buried to windward they were soon uncovered. If it is not possible to bury animals, they should be ripped up and the viscera interred and fire applied to the inside of the body. Lastly, if even this be impracticable, stab the body all over; it will soon dry up and give little or no offense.

The dry-earth system of latrines, if well looked to, leaves nothing to be desired. An ounce of MacDougall's powder should be added to every few pounds of earth. If doors and windows are left open amputations may be made without fear. The stools should be removed twice daily without fail.

In dry climates a little carelessness about nuisances buried will produce no harm, but if the weather be rainy it is impossible to take too great precautions in this matter.

The necessities of a hospital may be arranged in the following order of importance:

1st. Feeding.
2d. Latrines.
3d. Washing accommodation.
4th. Nursing and clothing.
5th, and last. Physics.

In selecting a building for temporary use as a hospital, the first thing to attend to is ample movement of air. Knock out window-sashes, make holes in ceilings and in gable ends, but be sure to get fresh air in abundance.

Tools, materials, and other accessories are of secondary importance. A very few appliances will suffice, but the men must be well trained.

The practical good sense of the foregoing remarks is obvious, and should be of value to the layman as well as to the professional man.

The temperature in Egypt was the only meteorological phenomenon subject to much change. The wind was constant from the northward and the sky rarely clouded. Of rain there was none.

The thermometer ranged in the daytime from 90° to nearly 100° Fahrenheit. A few observations on this score may be quoted.

August 27, 1 p. m., 94°; August 31, 96°; September 1, evening, 80°; September 11, 11 a. m., 93°, with fresh breeze blowing at the time.

Each man carried on his person a supply of lint and bandages for preliminary dressings.

The medical comforts issued at Kassassin on September 9 included such unwonted delicacies as iced champagne.

Although no pains had been spared by the authorities to provide for the proper treatment of the sick and wounded, it would appear that the details were not always carried out with the same scrupulousness, and much discontent was felt and expressed. One officer who was sent wounded to the Carthage found the food provided scant in quantity and indifferent in quality, while the medical officers on board lived in comparative luxury. His indignant complaint was attended by an improvement in fare. He exonerated the medical authorities from blame, attributing the faults to the steamer people, " who had to make three shillings and sixpence worth of food do for one person." But should a wounded officer be obliged to protest against such treatment in a hospital ship?

Another officer presented himself wounded at the field hospital at Kassassin after the night charge of August 28. He found no food or water, and there was no latrine for his use. When he complained of hunger he was merely asked why he had not brought his rations with him.

The whole subject has been investigated by a parliamentary commission, whose report* is not yet made public, but it is believed that the deficiencies were in minor matters, and were mainly experienced in the early stages of the campaign, when all corps were alike hampered by lack of transport.

A ready means of recognizing the surgeon at a distance is absolutely indispensable. His uniform should be so distinct from all others that no doubt can exist on this point.

---

*This report, contained in a Parliamentary blue-book of over 700 pages, gives much valuable information: Army Hospital Service Inquiry Committee, printed by George E. B. Eyre and William Spottiswoode, East Harding street, Fleet street, London. Price, 10 shillings.—O. N. I.

XXIX.

THE ARMY POST-OFFICE.

Mail facilities were provided for the army in the field by the only organization in Egypt which contained no regular troops, but was composed of volunteers exclusively. Its members were taken from the 24th Middlesex Regiment, of the Rifle Volunteer force, a regiment formed of employés and officials in the General Post-Office, in London.

Fig. 148.

Fig. 149.

The corps consisted of Major George H. Sturgeon, 1 captain, 1 staff sergeant, 4 sergeants, 4 corporals, and 33 men, all of whom had applied for this service. The sergeants had all been postmasters at various branch offices. During their absence they were granted a continuance of their salaries from the Post-Office, and, in addition, received army pay; that is, sergeants 2s. 4d., corporals 1s. 8d., and privates 1s. per diem. The non-commissioned officers wore swords and revolvers, the privates swords only.

A complete and light field equipment was provided, some points of which are worthy of mention as being serviceable and convenient.

The tent is shown in Fig. 148. The frame is of round wooden poles, socket-jointed at the middle, about 2½ inches in diameter. The uprights set into square sill pieces, also in two parts, pinned together. The corner junctions are sketched roughly in Fig. 149. The gable-ends are made by longer poles which project beyond the roof and carry a second ridge pole, over which a second roof or fly may be drawn backwards or forwards as desired. The rear may be raised to make a sort of booth and give increased space under cover. The ground dimensions are 10 feet square. The uprights are secured by rope guys, which run from the upper extremities and are made fast to the sill pieces. The total weight is 156 pounds.

The newspaper sorting box is shown in Fig. 150. The back is of canvas. By withdrawing the retaining keys $a\ a$ the sides can be folded around upon the top and bottom, to which they are respectively hinged.

The hinges at the corners of the pigeon-holes permit the shelves to fold together, and the whole affair makes a compact package, 4 feet 9 inches by 1 foot by 10 inches.

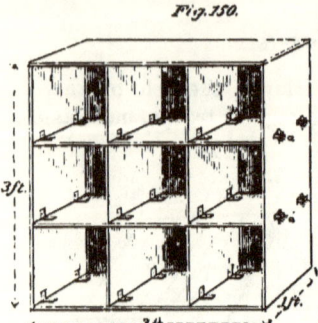

Fig. 150.

The sorting box for letters is similar in design, but smaller, being 3 feet long by 2 feet wide and 8 inches deep. It has forty pigeon-holes.

A very handy sorting pouch, made of canvas and used at temporary stations, is shown in Fig. 151. It can be strapped to the ridge pole or eaves pieces of the tent.

The portable table has a deal top, to which a stamping pad is fixed. The legs fold up underneath, or are spread out and hooked in place, as desired.

The sorting boxes are transported in a large canvas bag, together with the table.

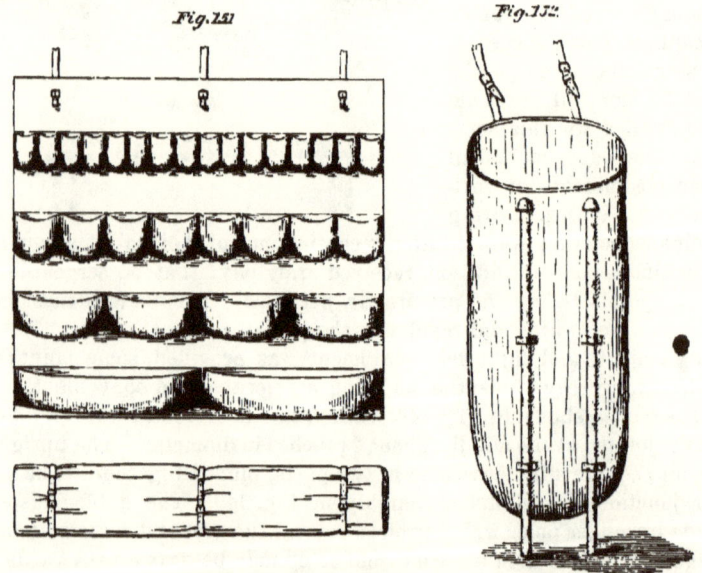

Fig. 151.   Fig. 152.

Fig. 152 represents a standing canvas pouch supported by sticks passing through canvas lugs on the outside, and entering canvas caps, as shown. This was convenient when placed at the end of the stamping table.

The office lanterns were simple tin frames with three glass sides.

A field office was established at Ramleh, and one sergeant and four men were left to operate a main distributing office at Port Said. Here the mail for each battalion or corps was put into a bag by itself and sent to the front. Field offices were maintained at Mahuta, Mahsameh, and Kassassin, and a daily service kept up after August 27. The home mails were three in number weekly, each way. These post-offices afforded the same facilities for transmitting small amounts of money as are offered by those of the United Kingdom.

The service was carried on to the satisfaction of those in the field, and no complaints were heard.

XXX.

THE INDIAN CONTINGENT.

The soldiers from the United Kingdom, spoken of collectively as "Imperial Troops," were in large majority in the British expeditionary force in Egypt. They were the earliest to arrive, and some of them still remain supporting the Khedive's authority. They were the first in individual importance to the people at home; they received constant and kindly notice at the hands of the newspaper press; they were massed together at Tel-el-Kebir, and they won the principal part of the honors of that day. But they were not alone in their work. Soon after reaching Kassassin they were joined by a strong detachment of Her Majesty's Indian subjects, known as the "Indian Contingent," a body so peculiar in all respects as to require notice apart, the differences in organization and equipment between it and the Imperial Troops being too great to permit of joint treatment.

The approximate strength of the Contingent was to be as follows:

European troops	2,000
Native troops	3,900
Total effective	5,900
To which should be added—	
Native followers	6,400
Total	12,300
Horses	1,600
Mules	4,000
Ponies	700

The force was to be composed of—
One battery of field artillery.
One battery of mountain artillery.
Two companies of sappers and miners.
Three regiments of cavalry.
Two battalions of British infantry.
Three regiments of native infantry.

It was organized as follows:

ARTILLERY.

Lieutenant-Colonel T. VAN STRAUBENZEE, R. A., commanding.
H Battery, 1st brigade, field battery.
7th Battery, 1st brigade, Northern division, mountain battery.

SAPPERS AND MINERS.

Colonel J. BROWNE, C. S. I., R. E., commanding engineer.
A Company, Madras Sappers and Miners.
I Company, Madras Sappers and Miners.

CAVALRY BRIGADE.

Brigadier-General H. C. WILKINSON commanding.
2d Regiment Bengal Cavalry.
6th Regiment Bengal Cavalry.
13th Regiment Bengal Lancers.

INFANTRY BRIGADE.

Brigadier-General O. V. TANNER, C. B., commanding.
1st Battalion Seaforth Highlanders.
7th Regiment Bengal Native Infantry.
20th Regiment Bengal Native Infantry (Punjaub).
29th Regiment Bombay Native Infantry (Beloochees).

ADDITIONAL.

1st Battalion Manchester Regiment.

A reserve to this force was established at Aden, which is officially, if not geographically, a portion of India, composed of two native regiments, the 4th and 31st Madras Native Infantry.

Approximate contemplated strength, &c., of the Indian Contingent.

Corps or department.	British officers.	Warrant officers.	Hospital assistants.	British N. C. O. and men.	Native officers, N.C.O., and men.	Followers.	Horses.	Ponies.	Mules.		
									Transport.	Water.	Others.
ARTILLERY.											
H Battery, 1st brigade	5			140		130	114	57	4		
7th Battery, 1st brigade, Northern division.	5		2	106	156	81	5		156	2	221
SAPPERS AND MINERS.											
A Company, Madras	4		1	3	121	33	3		104	2	
I Company, Madras	4		2	2	121	39	3		68	2	36
CAVALRY.											
2d Regiment, Bengal	8		2		376	214	391	188	150	6	1
6th Regiment, Bengal	9		2		422	340	465	231	150	6	1
13th Lancers, Bengal	9		2		499	383	538	267	150	6	1
INFANTRY.											
1st Battalion Seaforth Highlanders.	29			804		164	8		630	16	

Approximate contemplated strength, &c., of the Indian Contingent—Continued.

Corps or department.	British officers.	Warrant officers.	Hospital assistants.	British N. C. O. and men.	Native officers, N.C.O., and men.	Followers.	Horses.	Ponies.	Mules. Transport.	Mules. Water.	Mules. Others.
ARTILLERY—Continued.											
7th Bengal Native Infantry	8	......	2	......	788	99	8	......	356	16	1
20th Bengal Native Infantry	10	......	2	......	614	114	10	......	356	16	1
29th Bombay Native Infantry	9	......	2	......	639	78	9	......	356	16	1
1st Battalion Manchester Regiment.	25	2	......	694	......	216	9	......	620	16	......
MISCELLANEOUS.											
Medical Department	29	......	56	......	23	500	......	......	......	......	250
Ambulance	......	......	......	5	......	1,497	......	......	......	......	......
Transport	5	......	......	12	......	2,076	4	10	......	......	......
Commissariat	2	......	1	3	......	100	......	......	390	......	......
Engineer field park	3	......	......	2	14	18	3	......	100	......	......
Ordnance Department	......	......	......	......	......	......	......	......	423	......	......
Sapper telegraph train	1	......	......	4	44	......	1	......	......	......	20
Total	165	2	76	1,775	3,817	6,184	1,571	753	3,803	104	533
ADEN RESERVES.											
4th Madras Native Infantry	10	......	3	......	784	115	10	......	......	......	......
31st Madras Native Infantry	10	......	1	......	743	97	11	......	......	......	......

A portion of this reserve, the 31st Regiment of Madras Native Infantry, and a small detachment of others, numbering less than 100, were dispatched from Aden a day or two before the battle of Tel-el-Kebir, but were turned back when the news of the fight could be given them.

The total of the force actually embarked for Egypt is as follows:

British officers	192
Warrant officers	133
British non-commissioned officers and men	1,727
Native non-commissioned officers and men	4,677
Total effective	6,729
Add followers	6,740
Grand total	13,469

Of animals embarked the account stands thus:

Horses	1,775
Ponies	775
Mules	4,742
Slaughter cattle	228
Slaughter sheep	1,000
Total	8,520

The table subjoined gives the details of each corps as it went on board the transports, and shows incidentally the plan of sea transport adopted.

Corps.	Name of transport.	Date of arrival at Suez.	British.			Native.		Animals.		
			Officers.	Warrant officers.	N. C. O. and men.	Officers, N. C. O., and men.	Followers.	Horses.	Ponies.	Mules.
Sir Herbert Macpherson and staff.	Hydaspes	Aug. 21	13	....	....	....	66	19	....	....
Brigadier-General Wilkinson and staff.	...do	Aug. 21	3	....	....	....	14	7	....	....
Others	Deccan	Sept. 4	6	....	....	....	10	4	....	....
Others	Sirdhana							3		
H Battery, 1st brigade	Deccan	Sept. 4	7	1	160	....	113	162	....	....
7th Battery, 1st brigade, Northern division.	Galatia	Aug. 22	4	2	54	100	55	7	....	146
	Armenia	Aug. 22	2	2	48	58	72	3	....	154
	Chindwara				2					
Total			6	4	104	158	127	10	....	300
2d Bengal Cavalry	Tenasserim	Aug. 24	4	....	....	78	74	92	47	14
	Dryburgh Abbey	Aug. 23	1	....	....	56	50	62	30	14
	Ethiopia	Aug. 26	1	....	....	51	50	57	30	12
	Iris	Aug. 28	1	....	....	66	60	72	40	9
	Hampshire	Aug. 28	1	....	....	94	70	102	48	14
	Norfolk	Sept. 3	1	1	....	76	65	78	40	38
Total			9	1	....	421	369	463	235	101
6th Bengal Cavalry	Hydaspes	Aug. 21	2	....	....	55	75	58	34	16
	Khiva	Aug. 25	1	....	....	50	45	57	26	14
	Culna	Sept. 4	1	1	....	66	50	70	35	18
	Hazara	Sept. 9	3	....	....	87	65	85	42	15
	St. Columba	Sept. 7	1	....	....	94	86	99	50	15
	Corinth	Sept. 13	2	....	....	88	80	118	50	6
	Sirdhana*					32	28	25	19	....
Total			10	1	....	472	429	512	266	84
13th Bengal Lancers	Kangra	Aug. 25	1	....	....	80	60	87	43	13
	Booldana	Aug. 22	2	....	....	88	59	82	50	12
	Northern	Aug. 23	1	....	....	73	62	87	43	14
	Bhandara	Aug. 23	3	....	....	84	59	88	46	9
	Chindwara*		2	....	....	73	66	79	36	15
	Wistow Hall	Aug. 27	1	1	....	83	61	88	59	18
Total			10	1	....	481	367	511	277	81
1st Battalion Seaforth Highlanders.†	Bancoora	Aug. 8	24	....	579	....	92	7	....	....
7th Bengal Native Infantry	Merton Hall	Aug. 20	3	....	....	470	70	6	....	147
	Sicily	Aug. 22	8	....	....	327	57	4	....	48
Total			8	....	....	797	127	10	....	195
20th Bengal Native Infantry (Punjaub).	Allegheny	Aug. 28	5	2	....	313	60	6	....	80
	Naples	Aug. 28	4	2	....	260	105	3	....	114
Total			9	4	....	573	165	9	....	194
29th Bombay Native Infantry (Beloochees).	Clan Macdonald	Aug. 25	6	2	....	377	104	7	....	110
	Inchrona	Aug. 27	3	2	....	373	28	3	....	84
Total			9	4	....	750	132	10	....	194
1st Battalion, Manchester Regiment.	India	Sept. 3	24	7	644	....	231	4	....	....
Ordnance Department	Kangra	Aug. 25	1	8	....	....	5	....	....	....
	Chanda	Aug. 27					39			
	Wistow Hall	Aug. 27					5			
Total			1	8	....	....	49	....	....	....

*Arrived after September 13. † From Aden.

Corps.	Name of transport.	Date of arrival at Suez.	British.			Native.		Animals.		
			Officers.	Warrant officers.	N. C. O. and men.	Officers, N. C. O., and men.	Followers.	Horses.	Ponies.	Mules.
Engineers:										
A Company, Madras Sappers.	Bhandara	Aug. 23	3	8	....	121	49	3	....	96
I Company, Madras Sappers.	Malda	Aug. 8	5	....	4	121	74	4	....	72
Field-telegraph train	Kerbela	Sept. 1	....	....	2	22	25	....	....	20
Field park	Hydaspes	Aug. 21	....	....	....	....	10	....	....	....
	Wistow Hall	Aug. 27	....	1	....	....	....	....	....	....
	Lucinda	Sept. 1	....	....	....	....	6	....	....	....
Total			....	1	....	....	16	....	....	....
Veterinary Department	Wistow Hall	Aug. 27	1	....	....	....	2	1	....	....
	Kerbela	Sept. 1	1	....	....	....	2	1	....	....
	Cambodia	Sept. 1	1	....	....	....	....	....	....	....
	Darien	Sept. 7	1	....	....	....	2	1	....	....
Total			4	....	....	....	6	3	....	....
Commissariat Department	Peshwa*	Aug. 9	....	....	....	1	211	....	....	....
	Hydaspes	Aug. 21	....	30	....	....	20	3	....	....
	Zambesi	Aug. 23	2	35	....	....	380	3	....	88
	Khiva	Aug. 25	....	....	....	....	53	....	....	....
	Chanda	Aug. 27	....	1	....	....	....	....	....	....
	Kerbela	Sept. 1	....	4	....	....	8	1	....	....
	Boskenna Bay	Sept. 7	....	....	....	2	1	....	....	....
	Khandala	Sept. 9	....	2	....	....	6	....	....	....
Total			2	72	....	3	679	7	....	88
Transport Department	Chanda	Aug. 27	....	1	....	....	66	....	....	155
	Principia	Aug. 30	....	1	....	....	80	....	1	185
	Inchmornish	Aug. 31	....	1	....	....	203	....	1	190
	Kerbela	Sept. 1	1	....	....	....	114	1	1	230
	Cambodia	Sept. 1	1	1	....	....	147	1	....	344
	Culna	Sept. 4	....	....	....	....	15	....	....	36
	Boskenna Bay	Sept. 7	....	....	1	....	30	....	....	80
	Darien	Sept. 7	....	....	1	....	128	....	....	306
	St. Columba	Sept. 7	....	....	....	....	14	....	....	14
	Khandala	Sept. 9	....	....	1	....	88	....	....	190
	Hazara	Sept. 9	....	....	....	....	13	....	....	38
	Corinth	Sept. 13	....	....	....	....	13	....	....	24
	Ischia	Sept. 13	....	....	....	3	200	....	1	440
	Sirdhana‡		1	2	1	....	90	1	....	195
	Maharajah‡		1	1	1	....	118	....	1	238
	Africa‡		2	1	....	....	98	....	....	224
	Egbert‡		1	....	1	....	104	1	....	200
	Chilka†		....	....	2	....	136	....	1	173
Total			7	8	11	....	1,657	4	7	3,262
Bazar establishment	Galatia	Aug. 22	....	6	....	....	....	....	....	....
Conservancy	Wistow Hall	Aug. 27	....	1	....	....	....	....	....	....
Field pay establishment	Bhandara	Aug. 23	....	....	....	....	4	....	....	....
	Wistow Hall	Aug. 27	1	2	....	....	2	1	....	....
Total			1	2	....	....	6	1	....	....
Medical Department	Khiva	Aug. 25	1	....	....	....	3	1	....	....
	Chindwara‡		....	....	....	....	1	....	....	....
	Iris	Aug. 28	1	....	....	....	2	1	....	....
	Avoca	Aug. 31	1	1	....	....	1	....	....	....
	Cambodia	Sept. 1	....	....	....	1	2	1	....	....
	Culna	Sept. 4	1	....	....	....	2	1	....	....
	Deccan	Sept. 4	2	....	....	....	4	2	....	....
	Boskenna Bay	Sept. 7	1	3	....	....	1	1	....	....
	Darien	Sept. 7	1	....	....	....	....	....	....	....
	St. Columba	Sept. 7	1	....	....	2	....	....	....	....
	Kandala	Sept. 9	....	2	....	1	2	....	....	....

* 228 beeves and 1,000 sheep.
† This transport broke down between Bombay and Aden and was towed back to India.
‡ After September 13.

			British.			Native.		Animals.		
Corps.	Name of transport.	Date of arrival at Suez.	Officers.	Warrant officers.	N. C. O. and men.	Officers, N. C. O. and men.	Followers.	Horses.	Ponies.	Mules.
Medical Department	Hazara	Sept. 9	1				2	1		
	Corinth	Sept. 13	1			1				
	Ischia	Sept. 13				1				
	Sirdhana*			1		4	176			
	Maharajah*					1				
	Egbert*					2	56			
	Chilkat					1				
Total			11	12		12	252	8		
Ambulance column transport	P. and O. steamer Sutlej.	Aug. 30	1				397	1		
	Avoca	Aug. 31	1	1			525	1		
	Boskenna Bay	Sept. 7	1	1			498			
Total			3	2			1,420	2		
General Hospital	Khandala	Sept. 9				3	122			
Postal Department	do	Sept. 9					10			
Others, various			1		2		1			

*After September 13.

The force, it will be observed, was composed of about one-third British troops serving in India and two-thirds "natives." The former ceased to receive the extra pay allowed by the Indian Government after passing Aden, which is under the Bombay presidency, and technically the western limit of India.

The peculiarities of organization are so many and so great that it will only be possible, in the limits of this report, to mention the most striking.

Taking the British soldier first in order, it may be broadly stated that when employed under the Indian Government every effort is made to render him a mere fighting machine by relieving him as far as possible of the cares and routine duties generally incident to camp life. He has a native cook to prepare his food for him; a "dhobie" or washerman to keep his linen clean; water-carriers, scavengers, sweepers, and diggers. His shoes are brushed for him, and, at night, in barracks, he is insured cool and refreshing sleep by the fanning of "punkahs" moved by natives. If a mounted man, his horse is groomed and fed for him. This extraordinary consideration is a legacy from earlier days, and seeks its justification in the necessity of maintaining, in India, the prestige of the European as a superior being.

The number of non-combatant natives associated with the Indian troops in these and other capacities, under the term "followers," is made the larger through the operation of that singular and apparently ineradicable institution, "caste," which limits every man's occupation to one thing and no more. In garrison, for instance, where the exigencies of actual campaigning do not occur, the number of servants that the least exacting of European subalterns must retain is simply incredible. One brings the water, another cleans the boots, a third sweeps the house, a fourth waits at the table on the master of the house alone, a fifth serves the guests, a sixth is the body-servant, &c.

The British soldier enjoys in a less degree the benefits of the same system. Such a service, sweetened by increased pay, is certainly the ideal of military life, but the reverse of the picture is less attractive. The acclimation in India of a newly-arrived regiment is accompanied by a terrible loss of life; only those who survive the process can reap the rewards, which are great in proportion to the risks incurred.

The native troops, through employment in the Empress-Queen's service, acquire, *ipso facto*, a special distinction among Hindoos. They also have followers, although in smaller numbers than their European colleagues. It must be remembered, however, that they are recruited from a class of the population accustomed to having servants, and that to serve the Queen is honorable in the highest degree.

A minor but sometimes important advantage flowing from military service is derived from the right of all soldiers to priority of hearing in the native courts, if embroiled in litigation, and from the feeling that they never receive less than a full measure of equity.

It is readily conceivable that such a system would naturally tend to gradual expansion, and would require, on the part of those in authority, a careful watchfulness against abuse. The experience of the late Afghan war showed the necessity of reducing the number of non-combatants in camp to a minimum, and in 1879 a circular was issued by the Military Department of the Government of India, covering the point with great minuteness, establishing for all troops in the field a uniform schedule of baggage, camp-equipage and followers, known as the Kabul scale. This scale, the standard used in fitting out the Indian Contingent is given in the following table in so far as it was applicable:

Kabul scale of camp equipage.

For whom, &c.	Battery, field artillery.	Battery, mountain artillery.	Battalion, British infantry.	Company, sappers and miners.	Regiment, native cavalry.	Regiment, native infantry.
Commanding officer............each.	150 pounds.	150 pounds.	150 pounds.	150 pounds.	150 pounds.	150 pounds.
Other officers.................each.	80 pounds.	80 pounds.	80 pounds.	80 pounds.	80 pounds.	80 pounds.
For every 8 officers or under.	1 mess tent (Lascar pal), or 36 pounds each.	1 mess tent (Lascar pal), or 36 pounds each.	1 mess tent (Lascar pal), or 36 pounds each.	1 mess tent (Lascar pal), or 36 pounds each.	1 mess tent (Lascar pal), or 36 pounds each.	1 mess tent (Lascar pal), or 36 pounds each.
For every 50 followers.	1 Sepoy tent of 2 pals.	1 Sepoy tent of 2 pals.	1 Sepoy tent of 2 pals.	1 Sepoy tent of 2 pals.	1 Sepoy tent of 2 pals.	1 Sepoy tent of 2 pals.
Except the cavalry, who have.					10 pounds.	
Medical subordinates, including surgery, &c....each.	1 Lascar pal.	1 Lascar pal.	1 Lascar pal.	1 Lascar pal.		
Hospital assistants..........do.	40 pounds.	40 pounds.				
Native officers and hospital assistant......every 22..do.	1 Sepoy tent of 2 pals.	Authorized equipment.	1 Sepoy tent of 2 pals.	40 pounds.	40 pounds.	40 pounds.
Non-commissioned officers and men, every 44..do.		Authorized equipment.				
British non-commissioned officers.				1 Lascar pal.		
Native non-commissioned officers and men, every 44.				1 Sepoy tent of 2 pals.	Each 12 pounds.	1 Sepoy tent of 2 pals.
Hospital establishment.	1 Lascar pal for 8 sick at 10 per cent. of troops and followers.	Authorized equipment.	1 Lascar pal for 8 sick at 10 per cent. of troops and followers.	1 Lascar pal for 12 sick at 8 per cent. of troops and followers.	1 Lascar pal for 12 sick at 8 per cent. of troops and followers.	1 Lascar pal for 12 sick at 8 per cent. of troops and followers.
Quarter guard.	1 Lascar pal.	Authorized equipment.	1 Sepoy tent of 2 pals.	1 Lascar pal.	2 Lascar pals.	2 Lascar pals.
Rear guard.			1 Lascar pal.			
Office.			150 pounds.		150 pounds.	150 pounds.

305

Kabul scale of baggage.

For whom, &c.	Battery, field artillery.	Battery, mountain artillery.	Battalion, British infantry.	Company, sappers and miners.	Regiment, native cavalry.	Regiment, native infantry.
Commanding officer........................each..	120 pounds..	120 pounds..	120 pounds..	120 pounds..	120 pounds..	120 pounds.
Other officers................................do..	80 pounds..	80 pounds..	80 pounds..	80 pounds..	80 pounds..	80 pounds.
Officers stable gear.................per horse..	15 pounds..	15 pounds..	15 pounds..	15 pounds..	15 pounds..	15 pounds.
Officers mess stores........................each..	40 pounds..	40 pounds..	40 pounds..	40 pounds..	40 pounds..	40 pounds.
Officers' cooking utensils....................do..	10 pounds..	10 pounds..	10 pounds..	10 pounds..	10 pounds..	10 pounds.
Followers......................................do..	15 pounds..	15 pounds..	15 pounds..	15 pounds..	15 pounds..	15 pounds.
Medical subordinates.........................do..	60 pounds..	60 pounds..	60 pounds..			
Hospital assistants............................do..	40 pounds..	40 pounds..				
Non-commissioned officers and men.........do..	45 pounds..	45 pounds..	45 pounds..	40 pounds..	30 pounds..	30 pounds.
Native officers and hospital assistants.......do..				45 pounds..	40 pounds..	40 pounds.
British non-commissioned officers...........do..						
Native non-commissioned officers, men and artificers.						
Artificers....................................each..	30 pounds..	30 pounds..		30 pounds..	30 pounds..	
Native artificers and drivers..................do..	30 pounds..	30 pounds..				
Cooking utensils:						
Non-commissioned officers and men.....	360 pounds..	240 pounds..	240 pounds.(a)		160 pounds.(b)	160 pounds.(e)
Native drivers and farriers...............		240 pounds..		20 pounds..		
British non-commissioned officers.......				190 pounds..		
Native non-commissioned officers and men						
Medical stores:						
Camels (c)...............................	2..	3..				4
Mules...................................	1..	1..	6..	2..	3..	
Camp hospital furniture..................			1..		3..	4
Camels (c)...................................					3..	
Mules....................................mules..	1..	1..			3..	
Veterinary stores............................mules..	6..	6..			3..	
Stable gear per horse..........................			80..		15 pounds..	80 pounds.
Office...			8..		80 pounds..	12
Intrenching tools..........mules.					1..	
Armorers' tools and stores, forge and saddler's shop........mules.			1..	1..	10..	1..
Arms of sick per company or troop...camel (c)..			1..	1..	1..	1..
Paymaster's office............................do..						
Signaling implements.........................			60..			

a Per company.   *b* Per troop.   *c* Or mule equivalent.

948 EG——20

Kabul scale of followers.

Followers, &c.	Battery field artillery.	Battery mountain artillery.	Battalion British infantry.	Company sappers and miners.	Regiment native cavalry.	Regiment native infantry.
Officers	1 personal servant each; 2 servants for each authorized charger; 1 mess servant for every three officers.					
Native officers	1 servant to every two officers; 1 groom and 1 pony for each.					
Muleteers	1 for every 3 mules.					
Camelmen	1 for every 4 camels.					
Litter bearers	6 for each large litter (or dooly) carried by 4 men.					
Litter bearers	4 for each small litter (dandy) carried by 2 men.					
Mates (in charge of litter parties)	1 for every 4 doolies and 1 for every 6 dandies.					
Pony boy and pony	1 for every 2 troop horses.					
Drivers	As needed.					
Artificers and workmen	All necessary for executing repairs.					
Hospital establishment	As per regulation.					
Bazaar	2 per cent. on strength, to be selected by the commanding officer.					
Sick-carriage	(a)	(a)	(a)	(b)	(b)	(b)
Cooks and washermen	6	4	c4	3		
Cooks			3		d2	c2
Spare horses					d2	
Grooms			4			
Grooms for each 10 per cent. of troop horses and for each spare horse.					1	
Puckalees (e)	3	2	c2	2	d1	c1
Bhisties (f)	3	2	c2	2	d1	c1
Sweepers	3	2	12	2	d1	c1
Diggers	2		4	1	2	2

a For 7 per cent. of troops and 3 per cent. of followers.
b For 5 per cent. of troops and 3 per cent. of followers.
c Per company.
d Per troop.
e Drivers of pack animals carrying each two large leather water-skins (puckals). The animal in India is usually a camel or a bullock. Mules were, however, specially substituted in this campaign.
f Men whose duty it is to do the dirty work about the camp.

It is in the organization of the cavalry that the greatest differences are to be found between the European and Indian regiments. For this reason the cavalry is more minutely described here than the other corps.

It must be remembered that, in the first place, every native regiment, mounted or unmounted, is commanded by a British officer, known simply as the Commandant, with a second in command. Every squadron of cavalry and each wing of an infantry battalion has a British Commander and a British subaltern on probation. Each regiment of either branch has a British adjutant, a surgeon and two probationers. These officers belong to the staff corps of one or other of the three Indian presidencies, Bengal, Madras, and Bombay, each of which maintains its own army, subject to the control of the central Government of India. The army-list titles and the rank and precedence of these officers are similar to those of the Imperial Officers, but the pay is much greater, being in fact enough to live on. They take precedence over all native officers, who are never allowed to rise beyond the command of a cavalry troop or an infantry company.

The Indian cavalry regiments consist of six troops. The standard strength is 550 of all ranks. They are armed with the Snider carbine.

The scabbard of the cavalry sword is of uniform pattern, but the blade is selected by the trooper to suit his own taste.

The pay of native officers and men is according to a very complicated scale, reaching for the former as high as 300 rupees per month. Certain medals are accompanied by pensions, so that their possessor may receive as much as 60 rupees per month in addition. (A rupee is worth about 44.5 cents.) These pensions continue not only during the enlistment but until death.

In the cavalry regiments, the pay begins with 28 rupees (about $12.50) a month. Enlistments are for a term of three years, but the service is so popular that the soldier usually re-enlists over and over again until he becomes entitled to the pension of 4 rupees a month and upwards, awarded after fifteen years of service, or to the 40 rupees given after thirty years of service. The average period of service is between fifteen and twenty years. The measure of the popularity referred to above may be obtained from consideration of the fact that a roster is kept in each regiment of the applicants for future vacancies, a roster amounting in some cases to many times the possible wants, and that, on enlistment, the recruit must make a cash deposit of from £30 to £35 sterling (roughly from $150 to $175). This deposit is to cover the expense of his outfit, including his mount, his uniform, his share of tent and mess equipment, everything, in fact, except his arms and ammunition. It is returned to him when discharged.

Every two troopers have one follower, as groom and servant, and one pony to carry their kits, tent, &c. This tent is a light canvas shelter weighing but 30 pounds. The pony can always carry these articles and two days' rations. If a larger quantity of provisions be ordered to be carried, the transport department supplies the necessary mules.

The entire expense of maintaining the follower and pony is borne by the two troopers jointly. Moreover, in India, the trooper has to feed and clothe himself and feed his horse. It is evident that but little can remain of his pay at the end of the month; still, something is saved, and the accumulation continues slowly but surely, for a native's wants are slight, and his groom (or syce) usually finds and cuts forage for horses and pony in the open fields.

The six troops are again divided into three squadrons. In order to prevent too great concert of thought and action, the plan was adopted after the Indian mutiny of introducing heterogeneous and opposing elements into each military unit. As a general rule, therefore, one squadron in every regiment is composed of Sikhs, one of Mohammedans, and one of Hindoos. Other races are also drawn upon for squadrons occasionally, but these three make the most frequent combination. The natural jealousy existing between these people serves to suppress coalition on the one hand, and, on the other, to stimulate a wholesome spirit of **emulation.**

This arrangement is not without its disadvantages, however, caste and prejudice bringing great complexity into the internal economy of the camp, as to cooking, &c., and particularly as to latrines.

The powers of punishment lodged in the hands of the Commandant are very extensive, including imprisonment up to two years, dismissal, and the minor methods universal in military services. Flogging is still permitted, its abolition in the British army not having affected the Indian troops. The offenses are usually of a mild character, for the men are very docile. They require, however, a special treatment on the part of their officers, many small points of discipline essential with Europeans being entirely and purposely overlooked with them, while in other respects they are subjected to a very taut rein.

The Commandant holds a species of police court twice a week, when all the officers, British, native, and non-commissioned, that can be spared from duty are present. Here breaches of discipline are adjudged, complaints, requests, &c., heard and attended to. Much of the good feeling in these composite bodies depends upon the publicity of these "durbahs," every effort being made to cultivate respect for and confidence in the justice and probity of the superior officers. As the uniform and kits are generally maintained by the natives themselves, all regimental expenditures involving them directly or indirectly are discussed on these occasions, materials and manufactured articles being purchased by contract in open board where every one has the right of speech.

Each man pays 2 rupees a month into a regimental remount fund which is used to replace horses worn out in ordinary service. The Government furnishes substitutes for animals that are killed or disabled either in action or through fatigue incurred in long marches or through excessive exposure.

Great attention is paid by the commandant to physical education and technical sports, such as tent-pegging, mounted sword exercise, swimming parades across rivers on horseback, steeple-chases, with prizes, &c.

The drill is according to the British tactics, even the English words of command being retained, but very rigid adherence to the details is neither exacted nor expected.

The principles above mentioned for the cavalry hold as well for the infantry, being modified in application to suit the altered circumstances of the case.

The foot soldier receives less pay, about £1 sterling per month, but his expenses are proportionately less. He has no horse or pony to keep, and his tentage and other camp equipage are supplied and transported for him. On enlistment he receives a bounty of 30 rupees, and after eighteen months' service he is allowed 4 rupees annually for clothing.

The composition of an infantry regiment in India is similar to that of a British battalion, viz, eight companies. The war strength is, however, much less. For the Egyptian campaign the total effective was ordered to be 832 of all ranks. The service arm is the Snider rifle.

When the difficulty of living fairly well and putting aside for a rainy day in a country so poor as India is considered, together with the prestige enjoyed by the soldier as belonging to the Queen's service, the certainty of being above want, the probability of retiring with a good pension, and the comparatively high social class from which the recruits are drawn, it is not to be wondered at that Her Majesty's native Indian troops should be a fine set of men. In fact, they exhibit their pride and self-respect in a singularly dignified bearing and in a military record of much merit. Nothing could surpass the grace with which these men walked their posts as sentries or executed their maneuvers, while their small-arm drill is precise and formal to the verge of solemnity.

On outposts the cavalrymen are peculiarly valuable. They are very keen-sighted, alert, and alive to their responsibility.

The main fault these troops exhibit is an absolute incapacity to understand that anything wanted by the Queen's soldiers should not be seized at once and as a matter of course. The formality of requisition and payment produces in their minds a feeling of good-humored contempt. Having the might, they marvel at not being permitted to exert it.

The engineer equipment was particularly strong in sand-bags and water-troughs (both iron and wood), and about five miles of steel rails were sent out with all of their fittings. In the railway work done by the Indian sappers at Ismailia the plant from England was used.

The telegraph outfit was of a light overhead wire.

The artillery was fitted out with 500 rounds per gun, and 300 rounds per carbine; the infantry with 500 rounds per rifle; the cavalry with 300 rounds per carbine.

Of the two batteries in the Indian Contingent, one of 9-pdrs. was known as H battery, 1st brigade. Its officers were a major, a captain, and three lieutenants, besides a surgeon and a veterinary surgeon.

The 9-pdr. gun is being replaced by newer and more powerful pieces. It may, therefore, be dismissed with but few words of description. In form it resembles the 13-pdr. Its caliber is 3 inches, its length of bore is 66 inches. It has but three grooves, and it throws studded projectiles (similar to the 16-pdr). of the usual type.

H.1 was only engaged at Tel-el-Kebir.

The other battery, technically 7.1, Northern division, consisted of six 7-pdr. screw-jointed steel guns, Fig. 153, designed and made by Sir William G. Armstrong & Co. These guns are in two parts, each weighing two hundred pounds, a practicable load for a pack animal. The gun is specially intended as a mountain howitzer of high power. It is thought that the results of practical experience had with these guns warrant a detailed account of their construction, equipment, and performances.

The gun is separated into two portions underneath the trunnion band

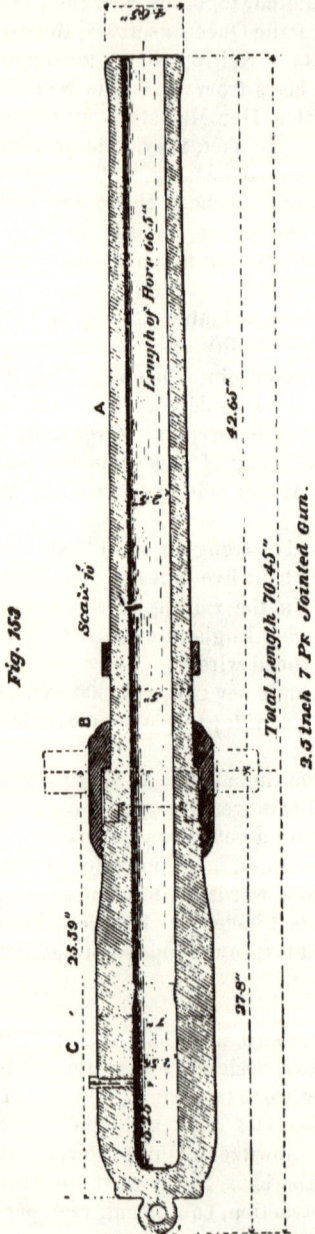

Fig. 153

B, Fig. 153, which slips loosely over the chase A. At the end towards the breech B is threaded internally. This female thread corresponds with a male thread cut on the front end of the breech portion C. An ordinary pipe coupling will give an idea of the principle. To make the joint tight, a steel ring or gas-check is inserted between the nose on the breech portion and the seat in the muzzle portion, after the manner of a gasket.

The parts of the gun are easily handled by three men. A leather cap over the thread on the breech part (see Fig. 154) protects it from injury, while a soft wooden plug, with a leather apron, performs the same office for the female thread on the muzzle portion. The general description of the gun is as follows:

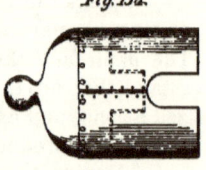

Fig. 154.

Length:
```
   Nominal.....................inches..  68.25
   Total..........................do....  70.45
   Of breech portion..............do....  25.7
   Of muzzle portion..............do....  45.5
   Of bore........................do....  66.5
   Of rifling.....................do....  55.5
```
Preponderance, average, 17 pounds at 24 inches from center of trunnions.
```
Caliber.........................inches..   2.5
```
Weight, average:
```
   Of breech portion..........pounds..  200
   Of muzzle portion..............do....  200
   Total..........................do....  400
```
Rifling:
  Grooves—
```
      Number .............................  8
      Width ......................inch..  0.5
      Depth.........................do...  0.05
```
Spiral increasing from 1 in 80 at breech to 1 in 30 at muzzle.

Commencing at 11.17 inches from bottom of bore.

Vent of hardened copper, 5.25 inches from bottom of bore.

Powder chamber enlarged to 2.56 in diam.

The gun is sighted on right side only, and the tangent scale set at an angle of 1°, to correct drift.

The following sights are supplied with the gun: One tangent scale of steel, graduated in degrees, from 0° to 15°. The head of the scale has a slow-motion arrangement for reading to minutes, and a deflection

Fig. 155.

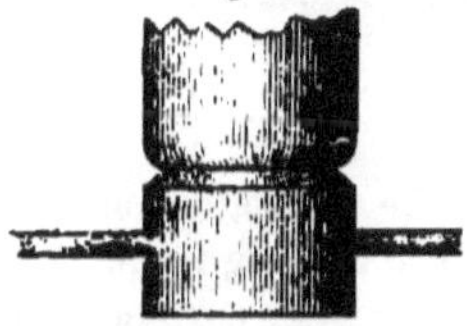

Fig. 156.

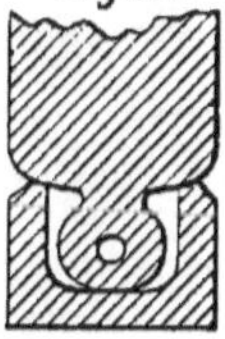

Fig. 157.

Method of uncoupling gun.

leaf. Immediately beneath the sighting-notch is a small circular hole, which is used for fine laying in combination with the cross-wire fore-sight. One fore-sight, screwed into a sight-ring shrunk on to the chase in front of the trunnions. It consists of an ordinary hog-backed sight, standing on a small open frame containing cross-wires.

The gun consists of three parts—the chase A, the trunnion B, and the breech-piece C.

Fig. 158.

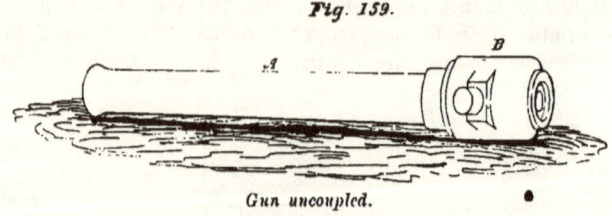

Fig. 159.

Gun uncoupled.

On service, the trunnion is always attached to the chase, but slides loosely on it, being prevented from coming off by the fore-sight ring.

To insure the breech-piece and chase coming together correctly, a key is fixed on the end of the chase, and this key enters a recess cut in the corresponding end of the breech-piece.

A steel gas-check is fitted into the joint, but this gas-check remains permanently in the breech-piece, and it is not necessary to remove it.

When the breech and chase ends of the guns are placed together they are firmly connected, simply by screwing the trunnion, which may be regarded as a connecting nut, until the lines on the trunnion and breech-piece correspond, or nearly so. The band is run up by hand as far as possible, then a protecting-ring of iron is put over one trunnion and struck sharply with a sledge, which is ordinarily carried alongside of the trail of the gun. In the joining of the two parts the gun is always placed vertically, the breech sitting in an iron block placed in the toe-plate of the trail, and shaped to receive the cascabel, through the ring of which an iron bar is passed. (Figs. 155, 156, 157). By this means the breech is prevented from turning through the effect of the blow.

The trunnions are stamped T and S, respectively, to indicate which is to be struck to tighten and which to slacken.

The projectiles are shown in the figures 160, 161, 162, and 163.

The case shot has 78 bullets of 16½ to the pound, filled in with clay and sand. Fig. 160.

The shell, Fig. 161, weighs, empty, 6 pounds 12 ounces; when filled and fuzed its weight is 7 pounds 6 ounces. The bursting charge is 4 ounces of powder.

The shrapnel are of two patterns, as shown in Figs. 162 and 163, both weighing 7 pounds 6 ounces.

The old pattern contains 40 bullets, at 55 to the pound, and 48 at 40 per pound; the new has 56 bullets at 26 to the pound and 18 bullets at 32 to the pound, and 10 segments. In both, the bursting charge is one-half ounce powder.

The time fuze employed has already been described (see page 19). The percussion fuze is given in section in figure 164.

The charge is 1 pound 8 ounces of R. L. G. powder, in a serge bag.

All the ammunition is of Armstrong's make, that house supplying the battery complete in every detail except men and mules.

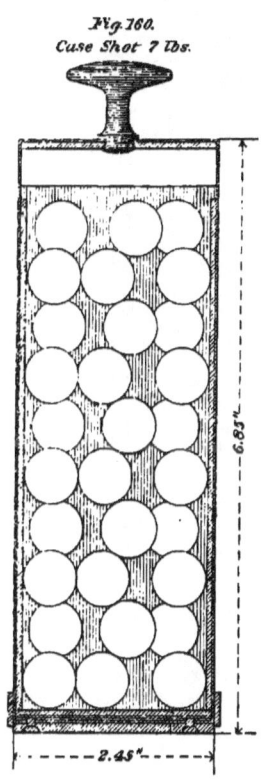
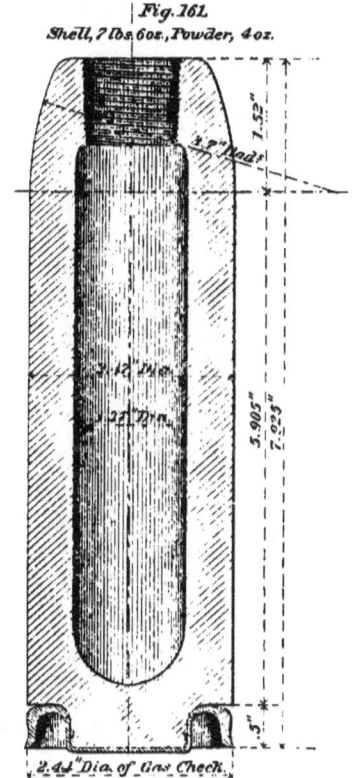

The carriage is formed of two bracket sides of plate steel, the edges of which are flanged outward to give the] rigidity of angle irons, with less weight. These bracket sides are connected by three steel transoms and a steel toe-plate, and are formed to receive] the gun trunnions and steel axletrees. A brass mounting]following the form of bracket side and of trunnion and axletree is fitted to each bracket, to give stiffness and bearing surface. The axletrees are removable for purposes of transport.

The wheels are 3 feet in diameter, the spokes and felloes of wood, the tire of iron, and the nave of gun-metal.

The carriage is fitted with a stool-bed of T-iron, the front of which hooks loosely upon a cross-bar carried by the bracket sides, and at the rear has a cross-bar, the ends of which rest in notched racks riveted to the brackets. A sliding brass quoin is attached to the stool-bed by clips. The quoin is worked, as required, by a hand-wheel which turns a screw resting in the end of the stool-bed and working through a screwed part of the quoin. A cap of wood is laid on the face of the quoin to cushion the shock and prevent indentation of the surface.

A toggled check-rope is passed through the wheels and over the toe,

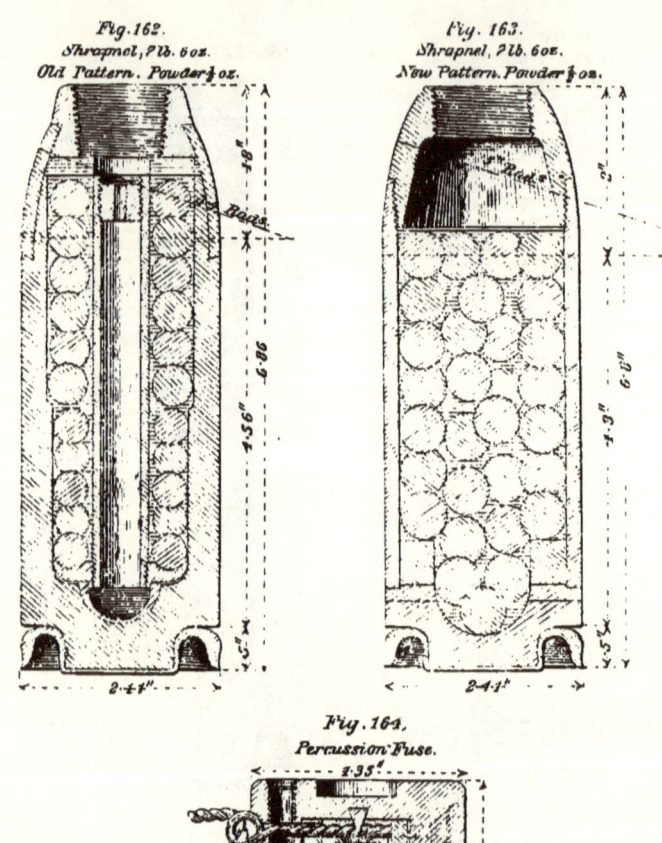

Fig. 162.
Shrapnel, 7 lb. 6 oz.
Old Pattern. Powder ½ oz.

Fig. 163.
Shrapnel, 7 lb. 6 oz.
New Pattern. Powder ⅜ oz.

Fig. 164.
Percussion Fuse.

under the trail handspike, to lash the wheels and check the recoil on firing.

Upon each bracket there is a staple and strap to secure it when packed on a saddle.

A grease-tin is carried on the bracket side.

DIMENSIONS AND WEIGHTS.

	Feet.	Inches.
Height, center of gun	2	2
Length of carriage with wheels	5	1
Length of carriage without wheels	4	2¼
Length of axletree	3	7
Angle of trail	33°	

315

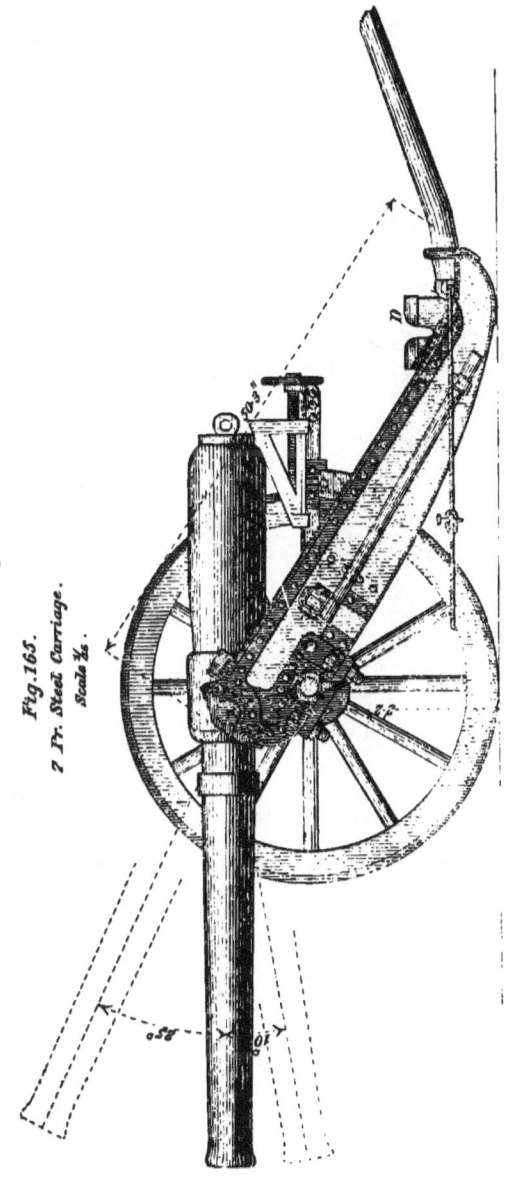

Fig. 165.
7 Pr. Steel Carriage.
Scale ⅛.

Elevation, maximum:
    Bottom step .... 25°
    Second step .... 17°
    Third step .... 7°
    Top step .... 2°
Depression, maximum, top .... 10°

Wheels:

	Feet.	Inches
Track	3	0
Diameter	3	0

	Cwts.	Qrs.	Lbs.
Carriage complete, but without gun	4	2	20
Trail	1	0	27
Wheels	1	2	25
Elevating arrangement	0	1	11
Dismounting block and trunnion collar	0	1	1¾
Axletree	0	2	23

The parts of the gun and carriage, the equipment and ammunition are all carried on the backs of mules in specially-designed pack-saddles. The projectiles and charges stow in strong leather cases shown in the accompanying drawings, Figs. 166 and 167. Each gun requires six

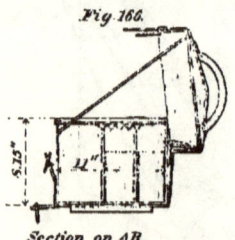 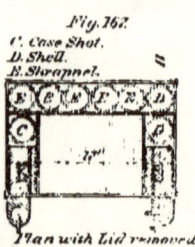

Fig. 166. *Fig. 167.*
C. Case Shot.
D. Shell.
E. Shrapnel.

Section on AB. *Plan with Lid removed.*

Ammunition boxes—leather.

mules for the first line, the loads being distributed among them as follows:

Muzzle portion	first mule.
Breech portion	second mule.
Carriage	third mule.
Axle, coupling block, trunnion guard, elevating gear, and two store-boxes	fourth mule.
Wheels	fifth mule.
6 ammunition boxes	sixth mule.

In each box were five shrapnel, two shell, and one canister, and eight charges, making, with those carried on fourth mule, fifty-two rounds with the piece.

In action each gun is attended by a second line of five saddled mules as reliefs to the first five enumerated above, of three more mules carrying a reserve of forty-eight rounds of ammunition, and four spare mules, one of which is saddled as a spare-ammunition mule. Altogether, each gun requires eighteen mules in the fighting lines.

A pioneer mule accompanies each subdivision (pair) of guns, and three others are loaded with tools of various kinds.

The following is the detail of the weights carried by the battery mules:

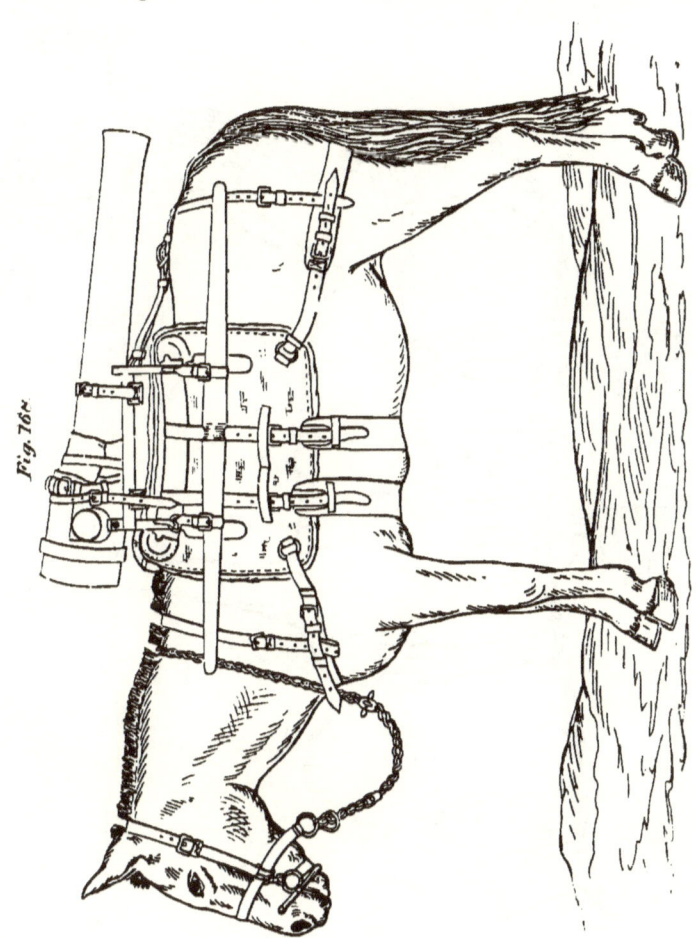

First gun mule.

	Lbs.	Oz.
Chase and trunnions of the gun	200	0
Canvas apron		
Leather cap (on gun)	4	8
Gun cradle, with straps	20	8
2 wooden gun bearers	7	4
Saddle and bridle	19	0
Picketing chain	2	8
Nose-bag	2	8
Spare shoes and nails	1	10
Tarpaulin, 6 by 4 feet	6	0
Surcingle	1	0
Total	264	14

318

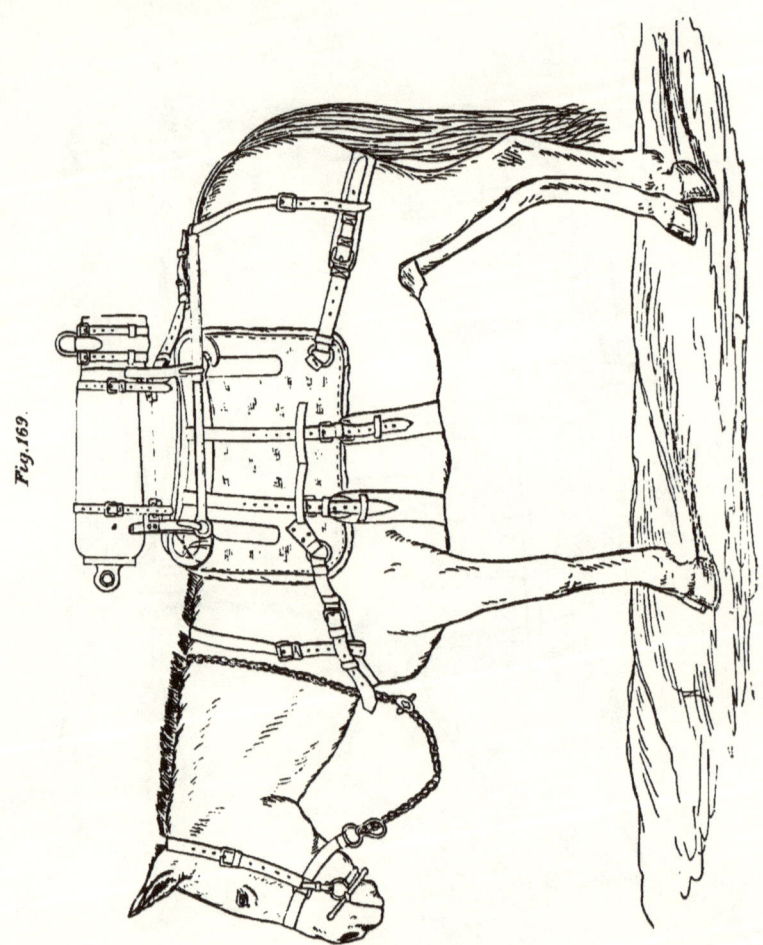

Fig. 169.

Second gun mule.

	Lbs.	Oz.
Breech of gun	200	0
Leather vent apron		1
Leather cap on gun	7	0
Gun cradle, with straps	19	8
2 iron gun bearers	13	
Saddlery as on first gun mule	32	10
Total	272	3

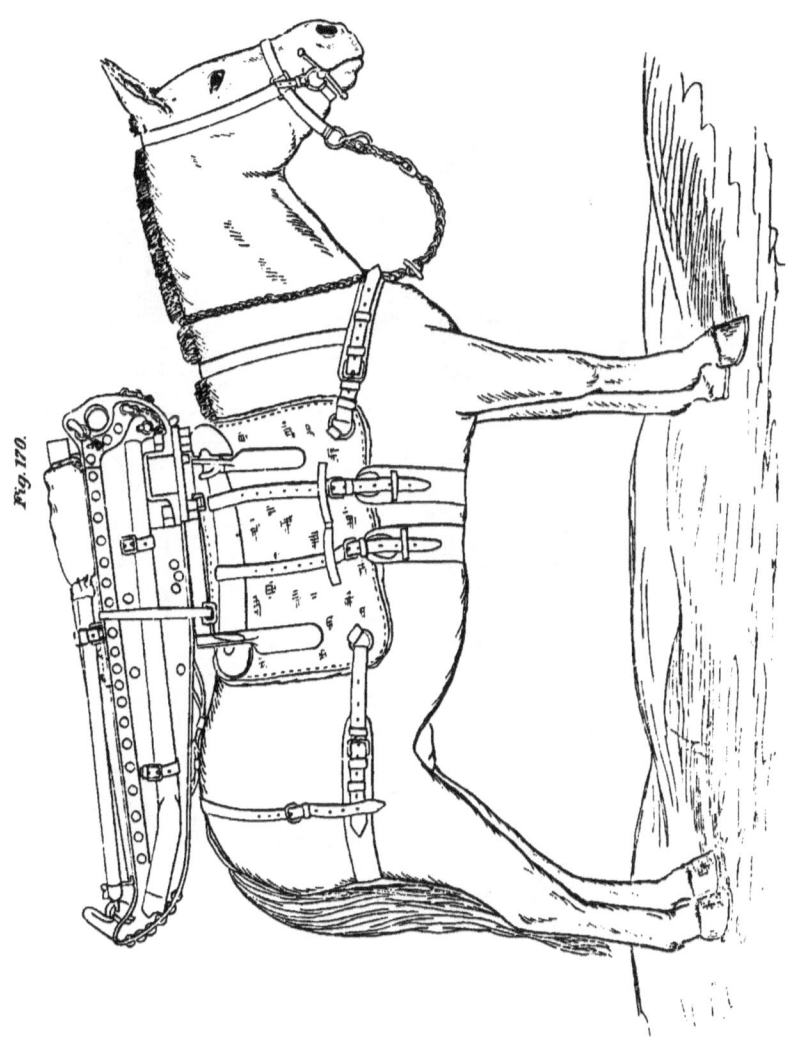

Third gun mule.

	Lbs.	Oz
Carriage, without wheels, axletrees, or elevating gear	167	0
Carriage cradle, with straps	21	0
Trail handspike on carriage	5	8
Rammer and sponge, with cap and jointed handle, on carriage	8	12
Set of priming wires on carriage		4
Sledge, on carriage	7	4
Tin grease-box, filled	1	5
Saddlery as on first gun mule	32	10
Total	243	11

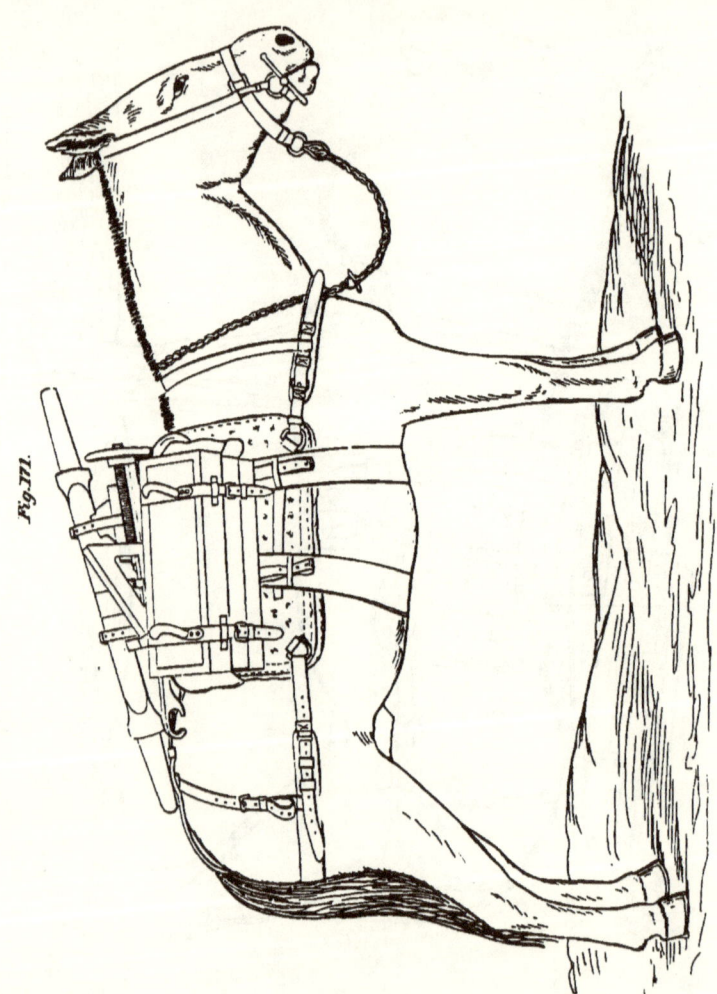

Fourth gun mule.

	Lbs.	Oz.
Cradle	21	0
Steel axletree	79	0
Elevating gear	39	0
Dismounting block and trunnion guard	47	0
2 leather boxes for stores, tools, &c., and four canisters and cartridges	71	13
Saddlery as on first mule	32	10
Total	290	7

Fifth gun mule.

	Lbs.	Oz.
Wheels	193	0
Axle arms, with girth and strap	14	4
Saddlery, picketing chains, nose-bag, shoes, tarpaulin, &c	45	10
Total	252	14

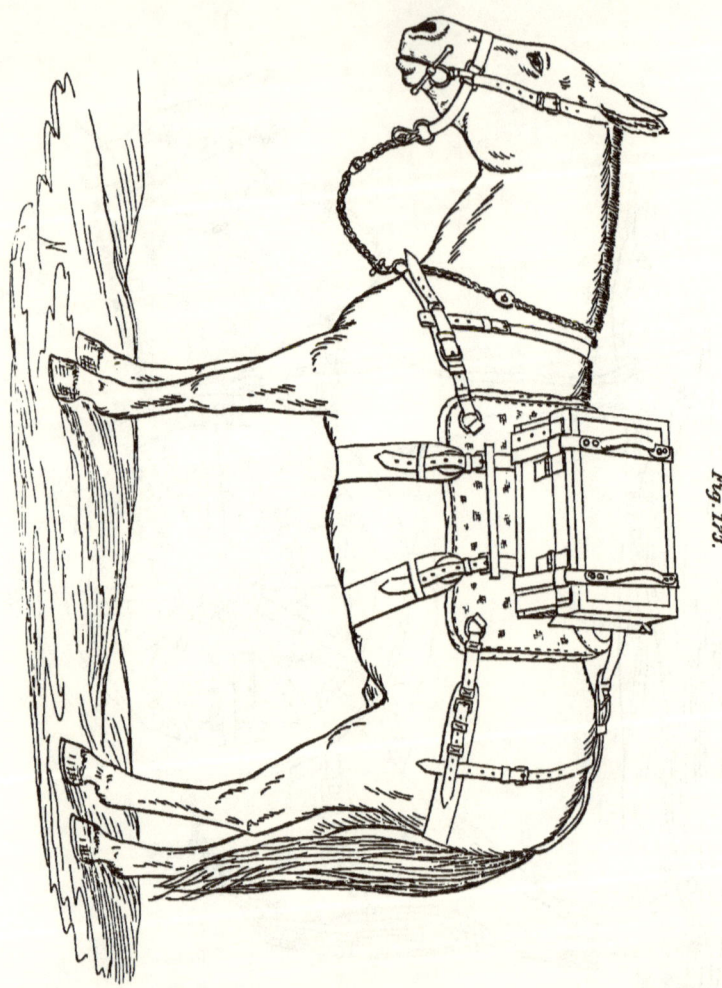

Ammunition mule.

	Lbs.	Oz.
2 leather ammunition boxes	41	8
2 canvas cartridge-bags	2	12
16 cartridges	25	0
12 combination fuzes	7	3
6 percussion fuzes	2	6
4 shell filled	29	0
10 shrapnel	70	0
2 case-shot	14	4
Sundries	1	0
Saddlery as on first gun mule	32	10
Reaping hook, stable gear, &c.	29	8
Total	255	3

Each gun's crew consists of 9 men. The total *personnel* of the battery was 106 British non-commissioned officers and men and 147 fighting natives, drivers, &c., all enlisted men. There was the usual allowance of artificers, viz, a farrier, four shoeing smiths, two collar-makers, and two wheelers. The number of followers is given in preceding tables.

Besides the battery-mules were 82 others for transporting the camp equipage, kits, cooking utensils, &c. These make up a total of 230. As additional transport, 78 mules were allotted to the battery, sufficient to carry 6 days' rations.

The men are unmounted, except the sergeant-major, the quartermaster sergeant, two trumpeters, a farrier sergeant, and the collar-maker. The muleteers who drive the baggage mules (one to three mules) are hired followers and not enlisted men. The same may be said of the water-carriers, nine in number, who distribute water on the march.

When it is remembered that this was the first battery equipped with these jointed guns, the comparatively small number of defects in design and construction developed by actual service is quite noteworthy.

The saddles are being constantly modified into the object of lessening the height of the load. The gun portions will, of course, always be transported, as now, on the back of the animal, and fore and aft, so to speak, but the load is a difficult one to carry, being both heavy and top-heavy. The girths must be kept extremely tight, or else sore backs and accidents ensue. The mules carrying these loads are more frequently relieved than the others. Of all the gun loads, the wheels are the easiest to carry, as they balance perfectly and have a low center of gravity.

The brass facing on the bracket, Fig. 165, which receives the axle, is too light and yields under the shock of the heavy recoil. In nearly all the carriages, this part had been strengthened by iron plates riveted on by the battery smiths. Fig. 174.

The rear-sight socket, a piece of copper screwed into the gun, is liable to work loose and affect the pointing, while it is exposed to injury in mounting and dismounting.

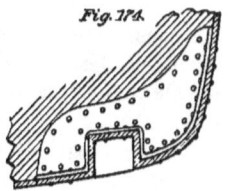

Strengthening plate on carriage-bracket.

Similarly, the front sight screws into a copper bouching which frequently moves in its seat.

The trunnions being fixed and the breech free to turn about its axis, if sufficiently urged, it is noticed that firing the gun is apt to slacken the joint, the passage of the shell along the bore tending to unscrew the breech from the trunnion band. No accident has as yet arisen on this score, because the guns are carefully watched and the coupling set up afresh whenever necessary. The existence of a leak of gas at the joint would be shown by its exit through an escape channel drilled in the center of each trunnion.

The feather marks on the outside of the gun to indicate that the joint is properly made are exact only when the gun leaves the maker's hands. In practice it is found that each gun requires separate adjustment, so that it becomes highly necessary for every crew to know its own gun, not only in order to have no leakage of gas, but also to make the allowance in sighting occasioned by the rotation of the breech portion away from the normal position in one direction or the other.

The vent projects beyond the surface of the gun, as seen in Fig. 153, in order to give the necessary length of socket for the friction tube.

Great care has been taken that no accident to the vent should arise from this peculiarity of construction. It would appear, however, desirable to devise some other equivalent scheme.

The recoil is very heavy, owing to the lightness of the gun and carriage, but this disadvantage is unavoidable.

The cascabel hole and bearer are inconvenient in practice. Lieutenant H. H. Rogers, R. A., one of the officers of the battery, suggests that the knob be shaped as shown in Fig. 175, the straight bar to fill into the dismounting block (made square in section), and thus holding the breech against turning. In place of the iron bearer he would substitute a stout wooden bar with an iron devil's claw.

Fig. 175.

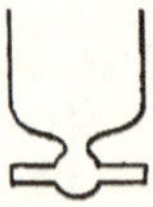

Proposed form of cascabel knob.

A wooden bearer through the trunnion holes is used for handling the carriage. If this is not placed and maintained fairly, an awkward lift results during the operation of packing on the mule. It would be well, as suggested, to do away with this bearer, and replace it by a pair of short iron levers, 14 inches long, permanently hinged to each bracket. When not in use, they would be close to the carriage; when in use, they would stand at right angles to it.

The proof of the practicability of jointed guns is found in the fact that the construction of others in three pieces is seriously contemplated in official circles. It is probable that the interrupted screw will be tried in this connection as an experimental substitute for Armstrong's coupling.

Against the disadvantages of the 7-pdr., some of which are enumerated above, a portion remediable, the others inherent in the system, must be weighed the comparatively high powers in this its earliest expression, burning more than one-fifth of the weight of its projectile in powder, giving a good muzzle velocity (1,440 feet per second), and working range of 4,000 yards; its lightness and transportability; the ease and rapidity of coming into action, the evolution requiring only 35 seconds; its ability to go wherever a mule can find footing; the accuracy of its fire, and the size of the shell it throws. The piece and equipment were spoken of in high terms by the officers of the battery, after several years' acquaintance and experience with it, these terms amounting to positive enthusiasm.

The battery left Bombay on August 9 and reached Suez on the 22d, where it remained several days inactive. It arrived at Ismaili on September 2. On the morning of the 4th it started for the front, reaching Kassassin the next morning, having bivouacked at Tel-el-Mahuta. At 9 a. m. it was ready for work, having with it all the camp equipage and 6 days' provisions for man and beast.

(The usual rate of progress of a mule battery is somewhat over 4 miles an hour on a good road.)

The 7-pdrs. took part in the fight of September 9, being at gun-drill when the Egyptians made their appearance. They fired between 50 and 60 rounds before the enemy withdrew. The guns were limbered up, pushed ahead, and brought into action again at 2,800 yards, the Egyptians now "running like hares." A second advance was made and the battery engaged for a third and last time, the total expenditure of ammunition being 90 rounds per gun. The practice was excellent. One shrapnel alone is credibly reported to have killed ten Egyptians; good work for so light a piece at such long range.

At Tel-el-Kebir the battery accompanied the Indian Contingent along the south bank of the Sweet Water Canal, coming into action in *échelon* divisions right and left, engaging a battery of seven Lahitte howitzers, in gun-pits on the canal bank, in advance of the main line of defenses, as well as the guns in the redoubts on either side of the canal. For a few minutes the fire was very hot. After the lines were carried by the Seaforth Highlanders, the 7-pdrs. shelled the native village lying south of the intrenchments. A heavy redoubt on the other side of the canal, about 1,800 yards distant, was still giving much trouble with its cross-fire on the advancing troops, when the screw-guns concentrated their fire on it and blew up its magazine.* After this the battery shelled the Egyptians, who were running away from all points, and advanced past the intrenchments, firing at the main camp and the railway station. The battery then ceased its fire, having expended about 60 rounds of ammunition, mostly shrapnel, during the action.

With the balance of the Indian Contingent it went to Zagazig, making at the start an awkward mistake in marching two miles up the wrong side of the canal and having to retrace its steps to the bridge at Tel-el-Kebir. From Zagazig it proceeded with the Contingent to Belbeis, Khankah, and Cairo, the only corps of British troops that marched the entire distance from Ismailia.

From the time of leaving its post on the northwest frontier of India, near Abbottabal, until it reached Cairo, not a single animal was lost, and the men enjoyed unusually good health.

Before the Indian Contingent left Bombay three months' advance pay was given to every man and officer desiring it, and arrangements for re-

---

* This statement is made on the authority of Lieutenant Rogers.

mittances were perfected in all details. This shows the care which marked the organization and preparation of this force.

Long experience and constant practice in the field, marching and campaigning for years together, have brought these troops to a high pitch of facility in movement and transport. Before starting on this expedition every person knew his own duty, and if it was necessary, he could readily know his neighbor's duty as well, each point being worked out and clearly put in a pamphlet issued for the occasion by the military department of the Indian government.

A three months' supply of provisions was shipped with the Contingent. The ration for native troops was as follows:

Atta* or Rice	pounds.. 2 / do.... 1½
Dhal†	ounces.. 4
Ghee	do.... 2
Salt	do.... 0½
Onions	do.... 1
Peppers	do.... 0½
Chillies	do.... 0½
Turmeric	do.... 0½

Once a week one pound of fresh meat was issued, the rice or atta allowance being reduced one-half on that day. Tea and sugar are given to the sick and wounded only, but may be issued on special occasions after great fatigue or exposure or in a bad climate. Tobacco is issued on payment at the rate of one ounce per diem. The price charged is the first cost to the Government.

For followers the ration was simpler, viz:

Wheat flour or rice	pounds.. 1½
Dhal	ounces.. 4
Ghee	do.... 1
Salt	do.... 0½

The forage ration for horses was 8 pounds of grain daily, with 14 pounds of hay in lieu of grass. For ponies the ration was half that for a horse.

The commissariat and other stores used in India are put up, as far as possible, in packages of the uniform weight of 100 pounds. The advantage of this plan lies in the facility with which animals may be loaded, these packages necessarily balancing, no matter what their nature, on opposite sides of the saddle. The economy of time and trouble is obvious.

---

*Atta is the native flour.   † Dhal is a species of grain.

An extra issue of clothing, &c., was made for the occasion, as shown in the following table:

Articles.	British troops.	Native troops.	Followers.
Waterproof sheets	1	1	1
Jerseys	2	2	2
Boots, pairs	1		
Puttees, on payment	1	1	
Extra blanket	1		
Canvas frock for shipboard	1	1	
Flannel belt	1	2	1
Quart tin mug for shipboard	1		
Hammock, pillow, &c	1		
Shoes (native), pairs		1	1
Blanket, country		1	1
Lascar or follower's coat			1
Great-coat			1
Pyjamas			1
Tin canteen			1
Haversack			1

When campaigning, a small grant of money, called *batta*, is made to men of all grades. It varies according to the rank of the recipient, and is supposed to compensate to some extent for the expense of getting ready, for fitting out generally, and for wear and tear of clothing on active service. In Egypt the *batta* was increased by one-half to followers and by other proportions to the native troops.

The Transport Department, under Lieutenant-Colonel Charles Hayter, was particularly strong and well up to its work.

As before stated, the troops in India are constantly in the field. Marching is a habit with them, and the preparations for a move a matter of small moment. The mode of packing the equipment is a subject of careful drill, according to a regularly established system. In the words of a distinguished British officer, speaking of this system, "even the colonel's mustard-pot has its own place."

Wheeled vehicles were definitely discarded and pack-animals exclusively employed. A large number of camels were to have been secured at Suez, but this expectation was not realized.

The animals allotted for regimental transport, together with rations for two weeks, were, as far as possible, shipped on board the same steamer with the troops. This wise provision enabled the latter to march to the front as soon as landed at Ismailia, without waiting. The result was in marked contrast with the delay occasioned by the dilatoriness of the British Transport Service.

The liberality of the scale upon which the Indian Transport was organized is seen in the fact that the sick-bearers or litter-men numbered over 1,400, and the muleteers, &c., belonging to the Transport Corps proper, including non-commissioned officers, drivers, veterinary and farriers' establishment, saddlers, and other artificers, no less than 1,900 more. The nature of the country in which the operations were to take place was thus appreciated in advance and every precaution taken to insure adequate and practicable modes of conveyance.

The impression prevailed in the early stages of events that the Indian Contingent would march from Suez across the desert to Cairo, a line offering vastly more difficulties and obstacles than that actually selected. The fact that the preparations made would have sufficed for the greater undertaking made the lesser the more easy of accomplishment.

The Transport Corps supplied animals and drivers to each regiment, &c., to carry out the provisions of the Kabul scale, and to convey two days' rations and stores in addition. To every eight drivers there was a native sergeant, and to every two sergeants a native officer (entitled jemadar) of standing equivalent to that of our warrant officers. The Transport Corps was thus arranged in units of 25 animals, 24 pack and 1 spare, the sections being capable of indefinite combination or division. The drivers were public followers, unarmed non-combatants. They wore a simple blouse of drab drilling under a broad leather belt, with A. T. on the buckle.

With the exception of the 20th Bengal and 29th Bombay Regiments, which sailed from Karachee, and the Aden reserves, which sailed from Madras, the troops were all embarked at Bombay.

The recently constructed Prince's Dock at that port rendered the embarkation simple in the extreme. Each transport was first taken alongside a coal-shed, the bunkers filled with coal, and the internal fittings put up in accordance with the Transport Regulations. She was then hauled a short distance ahead, abreast of large warehouses, whence she received her stores of all kinds, provisions, forage, &c., and finally moved close to the railway terminus. The troops were kept back in the hills, twelve hours distant from Bombay, and were only brought to the seaboard when the transport was ready to receive them. Each detachment was railed alongside its own transport in the morning, and embarked without delay or confusion, a few hours only being required to get 400 men on board from the time of reaching Bombay until steaming out of the dock.

In spite of every exertion on the part of the central authorities, and of their well-digested code of rules, a number of animals were badly damaged on the voyage to Aden through careless stabling, as the ships had to cross the Arabian Sea in the trough of the swell raised by the southwest monsoon. The 13th Bengal Lancers is stated to have lost over 40 horses through injuries and overcrowding.

The same orderly method which marked the embarkation prevailed at Ismailia. The readiness of each corps as landed to proceed at once in obedience to orders elicited the commendation of those in a position to observe. Nor was this commendation qualified by any subsequently developed deficiency. It is stated by an officer of high standing that "the commissariat and transport of this contingent were simply perfect."

The medical arrangements were based on a hospital provision for 15 per cent. of sick of the estimated effective strength of the force, and for 3 per cent. of the estimated number of followers; that is, for 815 sick, one-third being accommodated in field hospitals and two-thirds in general hospitals. A base hospital was established at Suez.

The old system of regimental hospitals has been abandoned. Under the present *régime* the surgeon attached to any corps is supposed to render only such temporary assistance as may be required in camp, on the march, or during an action, sending all cases needing treatment for more than twenty-four hours to the field hospital, if there be one at hand. In action they apply but the first dressings to wounds, and are not to undertake any serious surgical operation. Field dressings were supplied in packages of uniform pattern. They were composed of pieces of dressing (simple ointment with 2 per cent. carbolic acid, spread on the lint), a piece of gutta-percha tissue, and some pins.

The field hospitals were equipped for 100 beds each, and were in four sections, each a working unit by itself. The *personnel* consisted of 1 senior surgeon, or surgeon-major, in charge, 4 assistants, 7 apothecaries, or other medical subordinates, and 20 ward servants (nurses). In the wards for the native troops it was necessary to have the nurses of proper caste, out of respect to religious prejudice. Besides, there was a long list of cooks, water-carriers, sweepers, scavengers, writers, storekeepers, carpenters, a cutler, tailors, washermen, &c., in all 80 men.

The outfit of stores was an estimated supply for three months. The instruments, surgical apparatus, and library of professional books were selected. Under the head of "medical comforts" were such articles as brandy (3 dozen), Tarragona wine (6 dozen), lime juice, sago, arrowroot and barley, extract of beef, condensed milk, concentrated soups, preserved potatoes, compressed vegetables, &c.

For the European sick the usual field ration was supplemented by such medical comforts as were necessary.

The diet for the native sick consisted of such parts of the ration as they could consume, with one-half ounce tea and three-fourths ounce sugar (for tea), 2 ounces rice and 1 ounce sugar (for rice), with medical comforts.

In addition to the foregoing articles were full sets of toilet and kitchen utensils, special clothing, bedding, lamps, &c. Each field hospital flew the Geneva Cross.

The tentage was on a liberal scale—29 double-fly and 34 single-fly tents (the former 12 by 8 feet and the latter $12\frac{1}{2}$ by 10 feet) to each field hospital.

In providing for the carriage of the sick all ambulances were discarded and only litters employed. Of these there were 290 in all, 68 doolies (large litters) and 222 dandies, with the requisite bearers, mates, &c.,

divided into three bearer columns, each in charge of a warranted medical officer, as shown in the following table:

Corps.	Litters.		Bearers.		
	Doolies.	Dandies.	Sirdars.	Mates.	Bearers.
No. 1 Bearer column	23	74	5	19	476
No. 2 Bearer column	23	74	5	19	475
No. 3 Bearer column	22	74	4	19	475
	68	222	14	57	1,426

It will be seen that nearly 300 wounded could be transported at once. With each litter were two leather water-bottles.

The columns again were divided into five companies of 100 men each, under the supervision of one "sirdar" or superintendent, and the companies into sections of 25 each, under a "mate."

It may be well to explain that these litters are simply cots slung from poles, which rest on the shoulders of the bearers. The duties of the latter included general work in and about the hospitals, pitching and striking tents, &c.

The veterinary department appears to have been the weak point of the expedition, four officers to over 6,000 animals. In this respect the Indian Contingent contrasts unfavorably with the Imperial Force, in which the veterinary arrangements were especially well ordered.

The "bazar," an authorized sutler's establishment, found its place in the Contingent, as seen in the table, page 306.

Another expression met with in the same table may need a word of explanation. "Conservancy" is used to denote the general cleaning of camps, the care of latrines, &c. In this force the duty fell to certain of the followers attached to the various corps for the purpose.

The probability of warlike operations in Egypt began to assume definite shape after the massacre at Alexandria on June 11, and the possibility of dispatching a force from India was seriously considered in that country. The Indian Government, acting under instructions from home, began at once preparing an expeditionary body to be held subject to telegraphic orders. The selection of the regiments was made, the men and officers warned to be in readiness to start at a moment's notice, the stores and equipments were collected at Bombay, and a list of steamers available for transport duty was made out.

The first detachment to start was Company I, Madras Sappers, in the Malda, which left Bombay on July 21. It was intended to accumulate a number of troops at Aden, distant only about 1,200 miles from Suez, while awaiting definite sanction for their employment in Egypt.

The war may be said to have begun officially on July 28, when the British Parliament agreed to the vote of credit for the expenses of the expedition. The following day the Indian Government issued an order for the embarkation of its portion of the force, although, technically, the co-operation of Indian troops was only authorized on the 31st, when a resolution was offered in the lower house of Parliament, and passed by both branches, authorizing the diversion of enough of the Indian revenue to cover the necessary outlay. This sum was subsequently estimated to be about £1,800,000 sterling.

On August 8, the advance of the now well-known Indian Contingent, consisting of one company of Sappers and Miners and the 1st battalion of the Seaforth Highlanders (late 72d foot), arrived from Aden at Suez, which had been previously occupied by British blue-jackets and marines of the East India squadron, under Rear-Admiral Hewett. Here the troops just named remained until August 20, the day previously agreed upon for the seizure of the Suez Canal; when 400 of them marched 8 miles to the northward towards Chalouf, returning at 4 p. m. without having encountered the enemy. They suffered severely from the heat, having moved out in heavy order under the terrible sun over the sands of the desert. The balance of the battalion took part in the operations of the day, as detailed in Section XI of this report, which treats of the seizure of the canal.

The day following, August 21, the main body came up the canal in the Sphinx, a small hired steamer, which joined the gun-boats Mosquito and Seagull at Chalouf. (See Plate 47.) The latter, with two companies of the same battalion, remained at Chalouf to guard that portion of the canal, while the Mosquito, with the Sphinx following, pushed on slowly to the northward, landing from time to time to reconnoiter. The results were only negative. Near the southern end of the Little Bitter Lake is a lock in the Sweet Water Canal, where it was known that the Egyptians had been encamped. The gun-boat shelled this place on approaching, prior to the landing of a party of the Highlanders. The camp was found deserted and a sluice-gate in the canal open, through which the water was running freely into the desert. The gate was closed, the telegraph line destroyed (severing communication between Nefiche and the stations near Suez), and the detachment returned to the ships, having fired at a small party of Egyptians, who took to their heels at once.

The Mosquito and Sphinx now crossed the Bitter Lakes and passed into the short stretch of 7 miles intervening between them and Lake Timsah. At Serapeum, 2½ miles from the Bitter Lakes, the land is higher than at any other point in the southern half of the canal, with a rocky substratum, furnishing an admirable position for the defense or blocking of the canal. It was supposed that the Egyptians would make a stand here. For this reason the place was shelled from a distance. There being no response to the fire, the Seaforth Highlanders landed. Finding none of the enemy in sight, they marched a mile inland to close another opened lock in the Fresh Water Canal. This done they returned to Serapeum, where they encamped for several days. Serapeum was the only point on the canal even temporarily guarded by the army.

The troops from India proper began to arrive at Suez on August 20, the 7th Regiment of Bengal Native Infantry preceding. On the 21st Major-General Macpherson arrived in the Hydaspes and assumed general command.

The impression which had originally prevailed that the Indian Contingent would operate independently from Suez, as a base, towards Cairo, as an objective point, now gave place to the certainty of joint action with the British troops along the Ismailia–Zagazig line. Guards from the Contingent were established at the various railway stations between Suez and Nefiche, at Serapeum, Fazoid, Geneffe, and Chalouf, to protect the railway, which afforded the only means of getting locomotives to Ismailia.

The 13th Bengal Lancers were the first to reach the front, a detachment arriving at Ismailia on August 25 and pushing on immediately to Mahsameh. Two days later the Cavalry Division, under Major-General Drury-Lowe, had been strengthened by portions of the 2d Bengal Cavalry and 13th Bengal Lancers. On the 29th the Seaforth Highlanders left Serapeum for Ismailia, and with all convenient speed the Contingent was concentrated at Kassassin. Its military operations from this time on merge into those of the army as a whole.

Instead of acting as an independent unit at Tel-el-Kebir, its brigade of cavalry joined General Drury-Lowe, and one of its two batteries (H.1) was attached to the Artillery Brigade, under Brigadier-General Goodenough, R. A. There was thus left but a comparatively small force under General Macpherson's immediate command. This force was made up of the Seaforth Highlanders, such portions of the three native infantry regiments as were left after supplying entire guards from Suez to Ismailia, and parts of the guards from Ismailia to Kassassin, a squadron of the 6th Bengal Cavalry, and a company of Madras Sappers. Associated with it on the other side of the canal, and acting under General Macpherson's orders, were the Naval Light Battery, the Naval 40-pdr. railway gun, and the captured 8^{cm} Krupp, also on a railway truck.

Excellent work was done in this part of the battle-field, and twelve guns were captured. The dash displayed by the Indian Contingent rivaled that shown by the 2d and Highland brigades, on the right of the line. The details of the fight are given elsewhere, together with the high praise awarded the Contingent by the Commander-in-Chief.

One instance may be permitted to show the stamina of the Indian trooper and his horse. The last detachment of the Contingent to arrive in time for the fight was a troop of the 6th Bengal Cavalry. After a sea voyage of sixteen days, it landed at Ismailia at 8 p. m. on September 11. At 11 p. m. it started for Kassassin, which it reached the following afternoon. It joined the cavalry division, marched on Tel-el-Kebir, and thence to Cairo, not a man or horse having fallen out on the way during the three days of forced marching. Cavalry capable of such a performance is not cavalry to be thought lightly of.

As a hasty review of the work done by the Indian Contingent, it may be broadly stated that whatever duty it was called upon to execute was accomplished rapidly, quietly, and well. A long campaign might have developed defects in organization, administration, or *morale* not manifest during the scant fortnight of its share in the war in Egypt. On this point speculation is open to all; but taking the Contingent upon its record, one is forced to the conclusion that Lord Beaconsfield's so-called "*coup de théâtre*" in 1878, when Indian troops were brought to Malta as a reserve in the event of hostilities with Russia, was a real menace, whose complete meaning was only made clear four years later. These oriental soldiers of the British Empire can be brought on any field of action by the scores of thousands (there are about 17,000 cavalry and 100,000 infantry habitually under arms); indeed, the number has hardly any limit. That the practice, once begun, of drawing upon this reserve will ever be abandoned, should future complications require a sudden reinforcement of her military strength, cannot be hoped for by any possible enemy of England. It must, on the contrary, be taken into account in the problem as a factor capable of almost indefinite expansion.

The recovery of Great Britain's former military prestige was merely a question of time and opportunity, but it is impossible not to believe that for this recovery she is indebted, to a certain extent, to the real worth and unbounded possibilities of her Indian Contingent.

XXXI.

MISCELLANEOUS.

In this section are gathered such items and conclusions as are of interest, either technical or general, but which do not find a proper place in the preceding subdivisions of the report.

ARAB MARES.

1. It was remarked as a singular and suggestive fact that among the horses captured from the Egyptians or found in various parts of the country as occupied there were no Arab mares. These valuable and usually unpurchasable animals must have been very carefully hidden, in the fear that they might possibly fall into the hands of the British.

FOULNESS OF LAKE TIMSAH.

2. The speedy return of the base to Alexandria after the battle of Tel-el-Kebir was further advisable on account of the condition of Lake Timsah. There is no tide in this harbor, only a slight general set of

the water in the Suez Canal according to the season. The presence of so many ships packed closely together, in the small basin, had resulted in the accumulation underneath them of all sorts of filth, rubbish, offal, &c., thrown overboard. Through the lack of a strong cleansing current, the water had no chance of adequate renewal, and hence was very foul, while the bottom, as found on heaving up an anchor, was reeking and noisome.

BERTHING CAPACITY OF LAKE TIMSAH.

3. The normal capacity of Lake Timsah as a harbor was greatly enhanced by the fact that the wind was constant in direction. In consequence the transports could be anchored in lines abreast, close to each other, without regard to the ordinary necessity of "swinging room."

The berthing of the arriving ships was in charge of Staff Commander Patch, R. N., of the Orion, who was appointed Harbor-Master. So well was this duty performed that the port, which had been pronounced by the president of the Suez Canal Company barely sufficient for two vessels, was made to contain no less than 103 at one time.

THE BELL TENT.

4. The regulation army tent is of the Bell pattern, 10 feet high and 12 feet 6 inches in diameter at the base. There are two flies inside and out, with ventilating holes at the top. It is intended to accommodate 15 men. At the bottom is a deep flap, which can be buttoned up to admit air. The pole is 2 inches in diameter, in two parts (for convenience of transport and storage), connected by a socket joint.

COINCIDENCE OF THE TERMINATION OF THE CAMPAIGN WITH THE NILE HIGH WATER.

5. The annual high water in the Nile occurs towards the end of September, and the water falls but very slowly for several weeks. The coincidence of the termination of the campaign with the Nile rise was more than a mere matter of chance. Had Arabi not been crushed at Tel-el-Kebir, the result to the British force would have been very damaging. With full control of the water-flow in the numerous canals and ditches spread out over Egypt, the Egyptians could have carried on a strong defensive fight, with all the advantages on their side.

TACTICAL PROBLEMS OF THE CAMPAIGN.

6. It can hardly be said that any tactical problems were solved in the campaign. It was demonstrated that a night march in attacking order could be made to end in a successful engagement, but it may be considered as legitimately permissible to question the possibility of repeating the advance on Tel-el-Kebir under other and less favorable conditions of soil, atmosphere, and enemy.

INCREASED PROBABILITY OF ATTACK AT DAWN IN THE FUTURE.

7. On the other hand, General Wolseley has proved by the logic of events the efficacy of the strategy involved in an attack at early dawn, a point always urged by him as the outcome of the improvement in modern weapons. In future wars it may be safely predicted that the defense will be frequently subjected to assaults at this moment, and will be forced to increased vigilance and stronger outposts towards the end of the night to repel the enemy or keep him at a distance until the day has completely broken.

The campaign was fruitful in at least one strategical lesson of great importance.

CONCERNING UNIFORM.

8. Contrary to generally received ideas, the red coats of the British were less conspicuous than the white or blue uniforms worn by the Egyptians. Visibility is merely a matter of background, after all, and the sand and glaring light of the desert were relatively worse for the latter than the former.

Towards the end of September, a gray serge tunic was issued for trial to the troops in Egypt. It looked much cooler than the garment it replaced, and it would certainly stand the wear and tear of a campaign far better. The appearance of most of the British coats was very bad. They were stained with perspiration, spotted with dirt and grease, and were altogether far from creditable, although the marks were an unavoidable sequence of hard work and rough campaigning. They were in marked contrast with the "khakhi" dress of the Indian Contingent, a drab color, with which the cotton drilling used in the hot season in India is dyed. Absolutely, of course, one was as clean as the other, but relatively the khakhi looked fresh and neat, while the red serge was hopelessly begrimed.

The traditions of an army are not lightly to be neglected. England's soldiers in any other color but the immemorial scarlet can hardly be conceived, but a suitable attire for active service in hot climates was greatly needed by them when in Egypt. Such an attire could easily be found in the color and material which have stood the test of Indian campaigning.

THE DESTRUCTION OF EGYPTIAN AMMUNITION.

9. The experience at Alexandria after the bombardment, when all ammunition found in the Egyptian magazines was destroyed, was repeated at Tel-el-Kebir on a similarly large scale.

As Arabi's army had disappeared, and, practically, the whole of Lower Egypt was in the hands of the British, and, furthermore, as the latter were acting in the name of the Khedive to re-establish his authority, there was certainly no necessity for this measure. Its object is not evident.

MILITARY BARRACKS AT ABBASIEH.

10. The military establishment at Abbasieh is on the edge of the desert to the north and east of Cairo, and was intended for a school of instruction. The barracks are large and well planned in all respects, are provided with ample wash-rooms, &c. A mortar battery and some siege guns were mounted on the desert side. Accommodation was available here for about 5,000 men.

The condition of these barracks when the Egyptians marched out was filthy beyond words. Sleeping apartments and corridors had been used as latrines, and the walls were infested with vermin.

EGYPTIAN FIELD PIECES.

11. The field guns employed by the Egyptians were of three types: 9 and 8^{cm} Krupp steel B. L. R., and Lahitte 9^{cm} M. L. R. howitzers of bronze. Lettering these types A, B, and C, the following is the return of artillery captured during the campaign on the Ismailia and Tel-el-Kebir line:

Date.	Place.	Type.	No.
Aug. 25	Tel-el-Mahuta	A	6
Sept. 9	Kassassin	B	2
9	......do.........	A	1
9	......do.........	C	1
13	Tel-el-Kebir	A	42
13	......do.........	B	10
13	......do.........	C	7

The principal particulars of these guns are given in the next table:

Type.	Number of grooves.	Width in centimeters.		Weight in kilograms.	Length of gun in meters.	Charge in pounds.	Weight of shell in pounds.	Height of wheels in meters.		Height of axis of trunnions.	Track of wheels.	Weight of canister.
		Lands.	Grooves.					Gun.	Limber.			
						Lb. oz.	Lb. oz.					Lbs.
A	16	7	1.4	395	2.02	1 8	14 10	1.56	1.24	1.60	1.65	11
B	12	7	1.1	269	1.93	1 0	9 14	1.56	1.24	.99	1.65	7
C	6	2.2	2.5	...... {	1.32 / .95 }	0 11	8 6	{ 1.20 / .98 }	1.20	{ .84 / .66 }	{ 1.40 / .87 }	......

NON-COMMISSIONED OFFICERS.

12. The writer of this report was impressed by the intelligence displayed by the non-commissioned officers whom he observed, as well as by the very large share they seemed to have in the business routine of the companies.

THE RESERVES.

13. He was also very especially impressed by the physique and good bearing of the men of the reserves, of whom no less than 11,030 out of

1,650 responded to the call. Of the balance, the absence of 135 could be satisfactorily accounted for. About 1,500 joined various regiments and 15,000 still remained at home. As the first real test of the new army system, this result is certainly encouraging. This new system has for its object the passing of a large number of men annually through the active line in order that a numerous and well-trained reserve may be formed. It is in this way that England purposes building up a large regular force ready for mobilization, trusting to the militia and volunteers for effective supplement.

OFFICERS.

14. This report would be incomplete without mention of the character of the British officers as a body.

The most indifferent observer could not fail to notice on their part a desire to be in the midst of the work, whether campaigning or fighting; a cheerful manner under even the most trying circumstances; and a commendable spirit of good-fellowship. Their great object was to secure the opportunity of distinction and to profit by it when secured. If fortunate in this respect, the troubles and hardships incident to their life were as nothing. The Commander-in-Chief was supported by a set of officers who only required permission to go ahead and do their duty— the execution followed at once, and was marked by intelligence, zeal, and perseverance.

It is impossible not to attribute this *morale* to the fact that their *promotion is always by selection, captains retiring at forty years of age, majors at forty-five, &c.* This is not the place to discuss the general question of how the flow of advancement should be regulated, but none the less is it a duty to record the conviction that the plan adopted in the British army (while not free from abuse or gross favoritism) produced, in the body of officers who controlled and carried out the operations in Egypt, *a corps of young, active, zealous, and capable men*, of whom no service, however high its standard, need be ashamed.

THE PRACTICE OF MENTIONING JUNIORS IN DISPATCHES.

15. To this circumstance is due one of the most marked features of all the official reports, whether naval or military.

Every officer's record is based mainly on the commendation he receives from his superiors as officially expressed. The practice is an inherent part of correspondence relating to deputed work, and is unsparingly resorted to when the case seems to warrant it. *The sense of duty well done may be all an officer has a right to expect, but until human nature changes entirely, even the most conscientious person will not fail to find a stimulus to still greater exertions in the field or more prolonged and earnest labors in the cabinet in the thought that his efforts, if successful, will be-*

come part of the annals of the service to which he devoted his life without reserve.

BALLOONS WERE NOT USED.

16. When the character of the country over which General Wolseley marched to Tel-el-Kebir is considered, the failure to employ balloons for the purpose of lookout and reconnaissance is explicable only on the assumption that the means were not on hand in England. The flatness and barrenness of the desert made it absolutely impossible to approach unobserved from a very moderate elevation. It would seem as though captive balloons would have been among the first provisions for the campaign, as they certainly would have been among the most useful.

LONG SERVICE VERSUS SHORT SERVICE.

17. The principal technical issue of the war in Egypt was the merits of the short-service system, a bone of contention even to-day in the British army.

Whether long-service (twenty-one years) men would have done better is a question attended with all the difficulty which is proverbially involved in the proving of a negative. They might have been hardier, more seasoned, indeed the evidence drawn from the record of the marines is clear on this point (the younger men furnished more than their quota of invalids), but that they would have behaved with more steadiness on the march and more coolness in the fight cannot be shown. No system can be satisfactory which does not provide for a leaven of old soldiers. It takes time to teach the recruit that the enemy feels exactly as uncomfortably as he feels himself, and the best master is a comrade in ranks to whom fighting is no new matter, and who stands to his work because it is his duty and his habit to do so.

The present tendency of army reform is towards a happy combination of the old and the new systems, retaining such features of the one as will yield a supply of capable non-commissioned officers and a nucleus of hardened campaigners, and of the other as will continue the process of swelling the reserves by annual increments of trained men, ready to return when wanted to fill their old battalions up to the war strength.

Given a few years for the results of the method to manifest themselves, it is not to be doubted that the British infantry will be counted, as of old, most formidable, and its presence on a European battle-field as a potent factor in the result.

THE CAMPAIGN AS A WHOLE.

18. While the enemy encountered in Egypt was not of a nature to develop the highest qualities of the British soldier, still, as a fairly adequate trial of the scheme which has been in operation for the last decade, the campaign, although full of lessons in detail, must be regarded also as abounding in promise for the future.

UNIFORMS AND EQUIPMENT TOO ELABORATE.

19. One great danger threatens the organization as a whole in the tendency to increase the equipment beyond the needs of actual work. *Thorough preparation for fighting should be the first care of those in authority.* Subordinate only to that is the reduction of the outfit to a least possible amount. It seems ill-advised, to say no more, to adhere in times of peace to uniforms, trappings, and paraphernalia generally *which are unhesitatingly discarded when war breaks out.* Of the armies of all the larger European powers, that of England is unquestionably most open to this criticism. It may, however, be safely predicted that this objection will not hold much longer, so determined are the persons responsible for the well-being of the army to render it as efficient as is possible. Much opposition will be met, for a more conservative body than English army officers cannot be found, but prejudice and opposition will hardly prevail in the face of the real necessities of the case, now completely understood.

THE CHARACTER OF THE EGYPTIANS.

20. From the time Alexandria was first occupied until the war was ended the Egyptians may be said to have invariably wasted their opportunities. At hardly any time was Alexandria even reasonably secure. Ramleh could have been turned by a night advance, and the city taken, for the garrison was weak to imprudence.

The neglect to seize or block the Suez Canal is almost incredible. That Arabi should have been guided by the interested counsels of M. de Lesseps is but a further proof of his utter incapacity.

Every phase of the campaign was marked by stupidity on the part of the Egyptian commanders, while cowardice on that of the rank and file was shockingly frequent. The British expeditionary force, with certain reservations already specified, did its work well, but no one can believe that the nature of this work was a real measure of the ability of England's soldiers.

FINAL RECOMMENDATIONS.

21. The extensive employment and valuable services of seamen on shore during the campaign are not features peculiar to the British navy alone.

In our service, parties of blue-jackets and marines are frequently landed in various parts of the world for police duty in cases of emergency, panic, or distress, and in times of general peace their performances make up the real active history of the Navy. These parties are not organized alike, *while their equipment, ranging over the whole field of individual taste,* is in marked contrast with the uniformity observed in certain foreign services.

This report cannot find a better ending than in the urgent recommendation *to abolish so-called "battalions" from our ships of war,* and substitute in their stead *homogeneous "landing parties,"* capable of self-supporting and sustained action in the field at some little distance from the base, and of indefinite combination at will into efficient naval brigades.

The details of such a scheme must be worked out by *a central authority*, and their observance be *insisted* upon as a better criterion than the now popular and *(con rispetto) burlesque dress-parade.*

War Series, No. III.

INFORMATION FROM ABROAD.

REPORT

OF THE

SH NAVAL AND MILITARY OPERATIONS

IN

EGYPT,

1882.

Part II......PLATES.

Part I—TEXT.
Part II—PLATES.

PLATE 2.

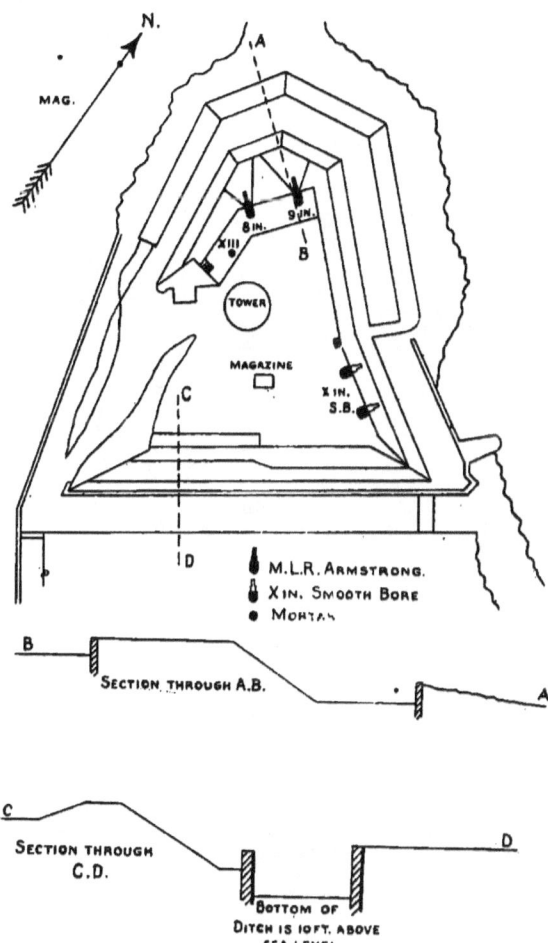

FORT SILSILEH.

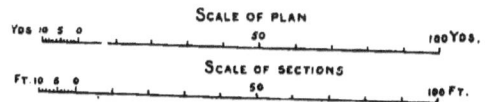

PLATE 3

FORT PHAROS, AS SEEN FROM THE CAUSEWAY LEADING TO IT FROM THE CITY.

PLATE 4.

FORT PHAROS. NORTH-WEST FACE. THE PRINCIPAL ONE ENGAGED
SHOWING THE EFFECT OF THE BRITISH SHELL.

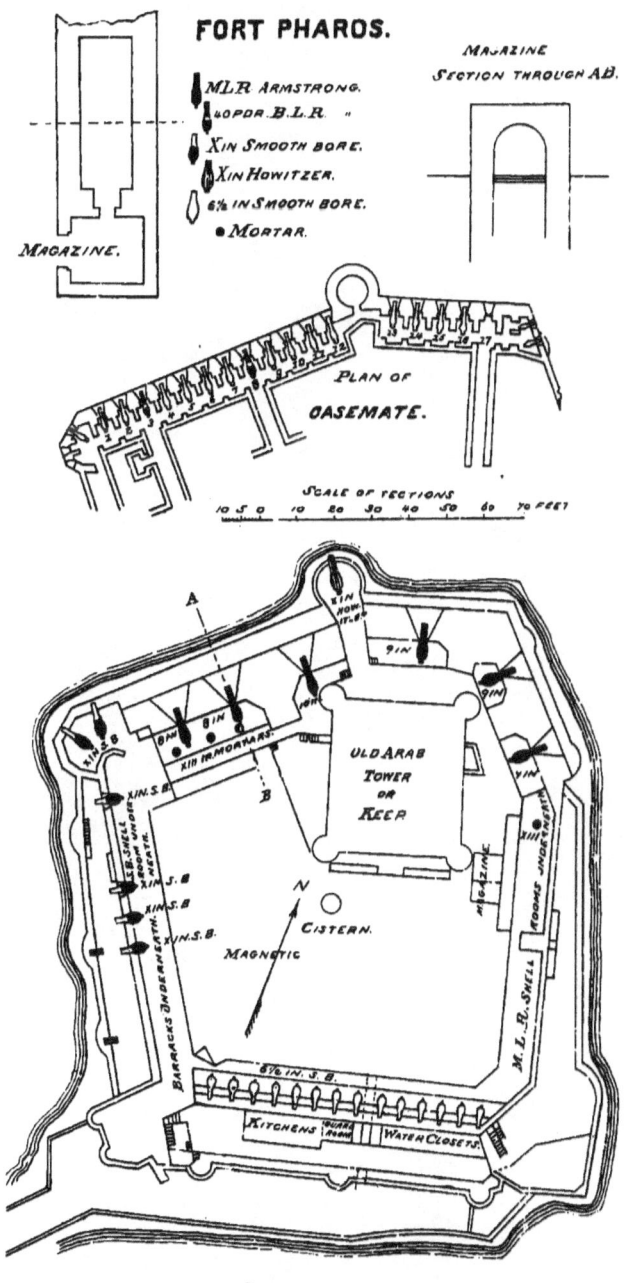

PLATE 6.

FORT PHAROS.

Fig. 44.

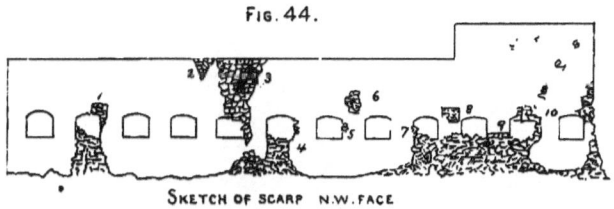

Sketch of scarp N.W. face

Fig. 45.

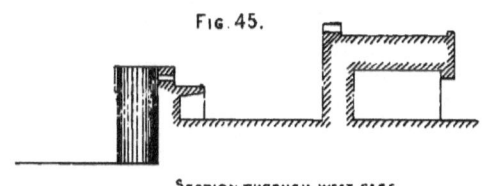

Section through west face

Fig. 46.

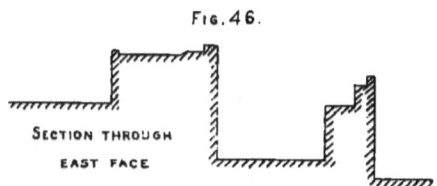

Section through east face

Fig. 47. Fig. 48.

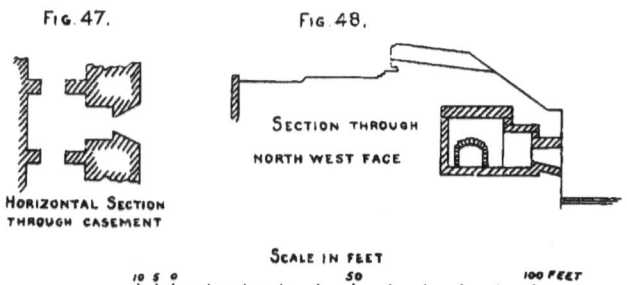

Horizontal Section through casement

Section through north west face

Scale in feet

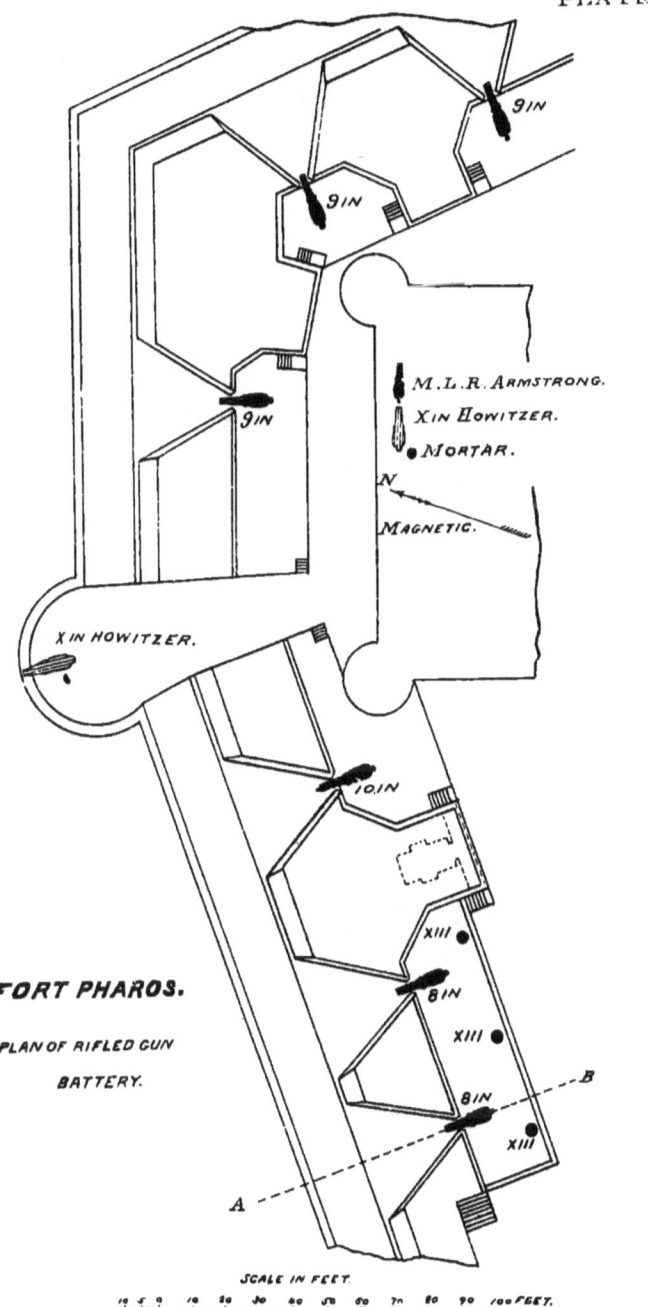

PLATE 8

UPPER BATTERY OF FORT PHAROS.
8 IN. M. L. R. GUNS IN FOREGROUND. DISTANT VIEW OF FORT ADA.

PLATE 9

FORT PHAROS. 8 IN. GUN BATTERY.
CONDITION OF WEST FACE OF KEEP AFTER BOMBARDMENT

PLATE 10.

FORT PHAROS. SOUTH-WEST ANGLE OF KEEP.

PLATE II

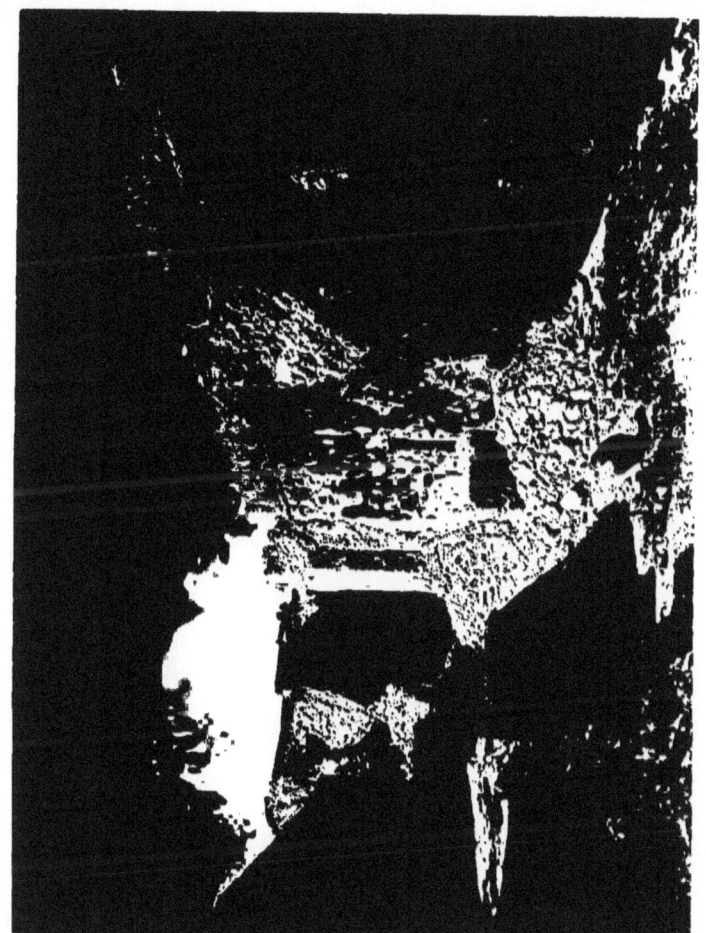

INNER SCARP, WESTERN FACE OF FORT PHAROS
IN THE FOREGROUND IS ONE OF THE INFLEXIBLE'S BATTERING SHELLS. (PALLISER CHILLED).

PLATE 12.

FORT PHAROS. WESTERN FACE, INSIDE VIEW.
IN THE MIDDLE DISTANCE IS A WORK KNOWN AS ADA LUNETTE.
IN THE BACKGROUND IS THE CITY OF ALEXANDRIA.

PLATE 13.

FORT PHAROS. 10 IN. M. L. R. DISABLED

THIS GUN, A 12-POUNDER, WAS BOWLED OFF ITS CARRIAGE. IT FELL, THROUGH THE ROOF OF THE KITCHEN ADJOINING AND STUCK MUZZLE DOWN, IN THE DEBRIS

PLATE 15.

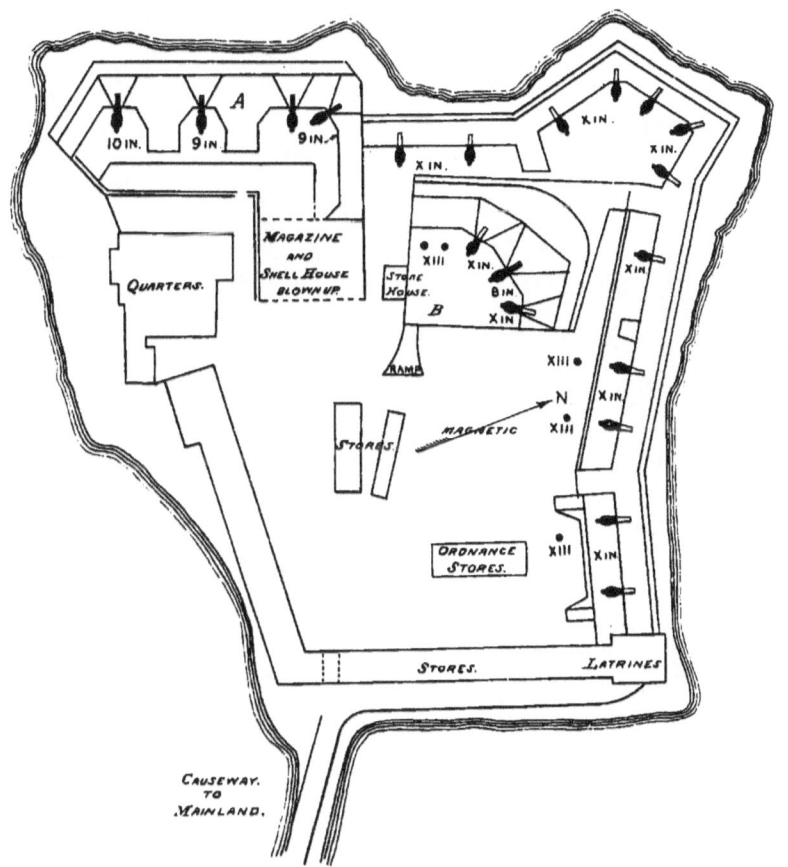

FORT ADA.

- Armstrong M.L.R.
- X Inch Smooth Bore.
- Mortar.

PLATE 16.

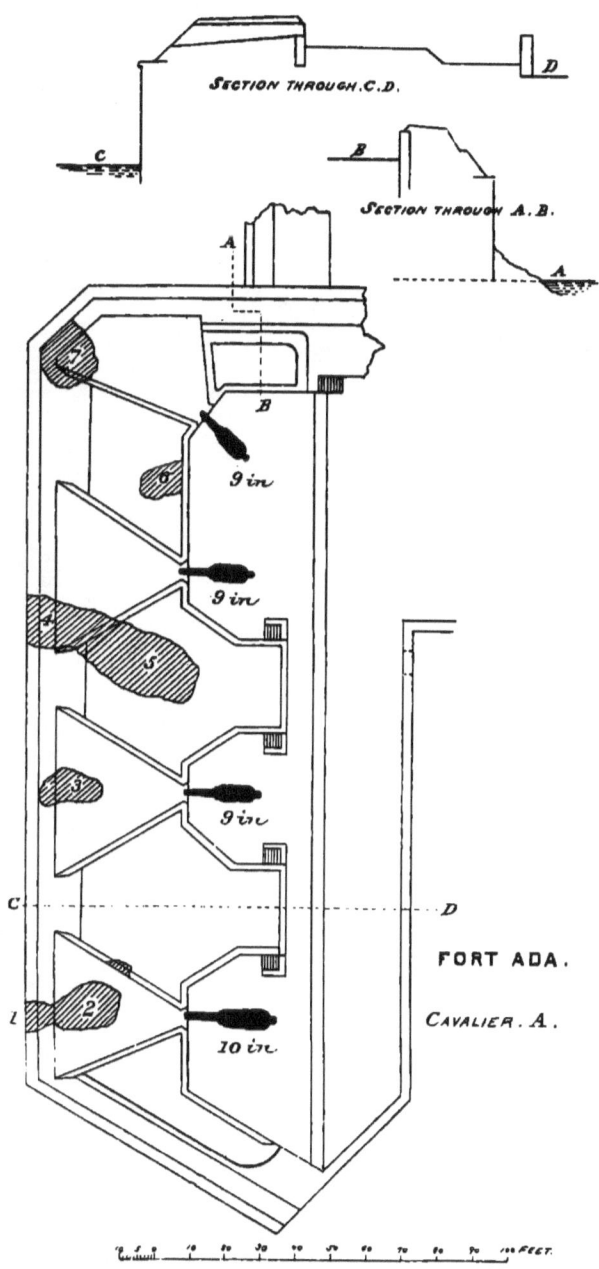

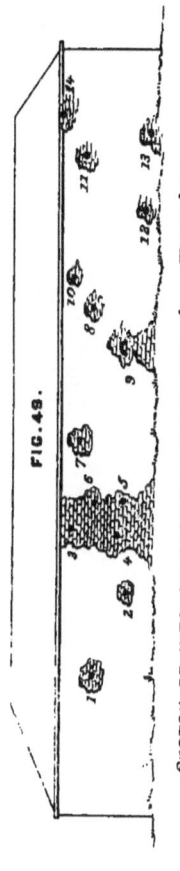

FIG. 49.

SKETCH OF HITS ON SCARP OF CAVALIER. A. FORT ADA.

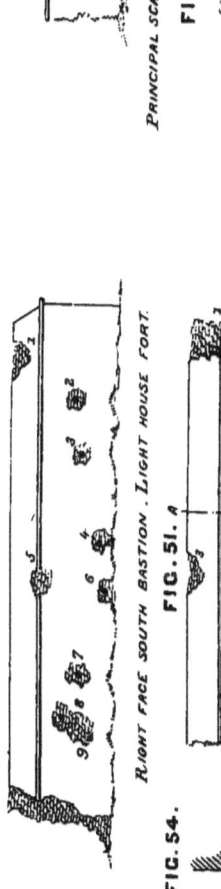

FIG. 50.

RIGHT FACE SOUTH BASTION. LIGHT HOUSE FORT.

FIG. 51.

SECTION THROUGH LEFT FACE. NORTH BASTION. LIGHT HOUSE FORT. A.B.

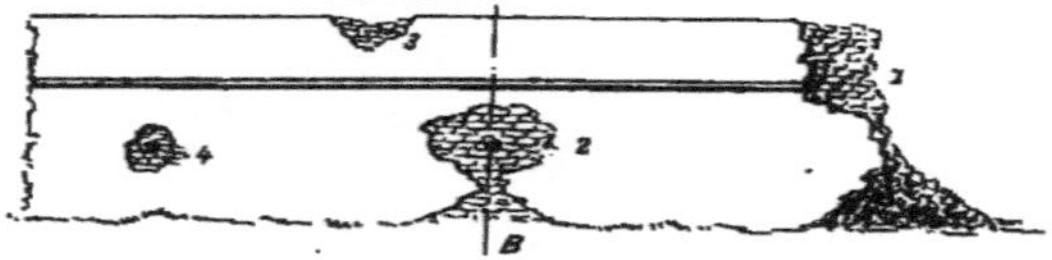

FIG. 52.

PRINCIPAL SCAR IN CURTAIN OF LIGHT HOUSE FORT.

FIG. 53.

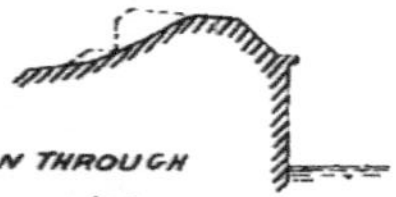

SECTION THROUGH BREACH IN PARAPET OF CURTAIN OF LIGHT HOUSE FORT.

FIG. 54.

PLATE 18.

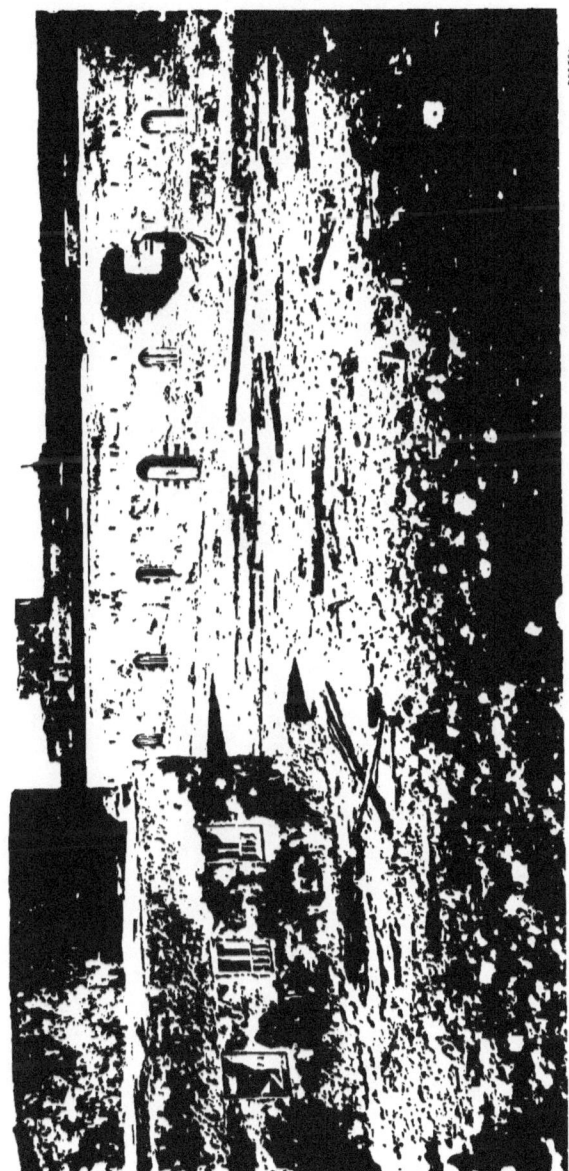

INTERIOR OF FORT ADA.

EXPLODED MAGAZINE AT ADA.

PLATE 20

FORT ADA, THE DISMANTLED GUNS.

PLATE 21.

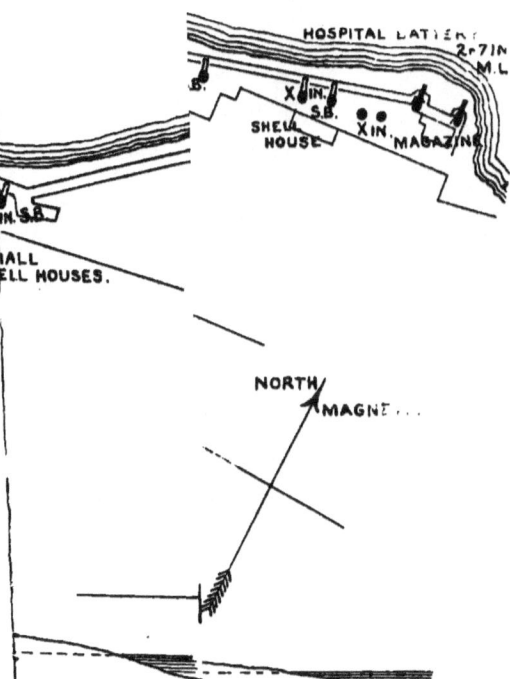

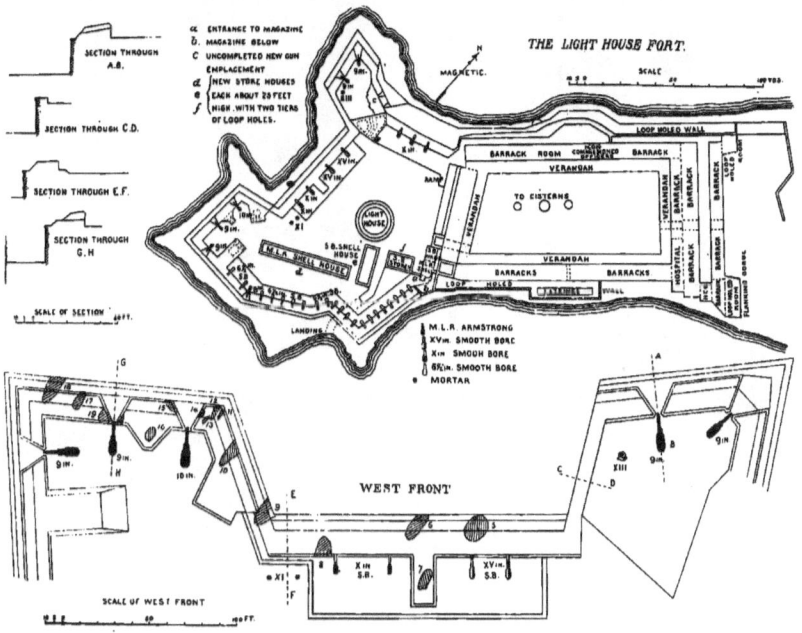

PLATE 22.

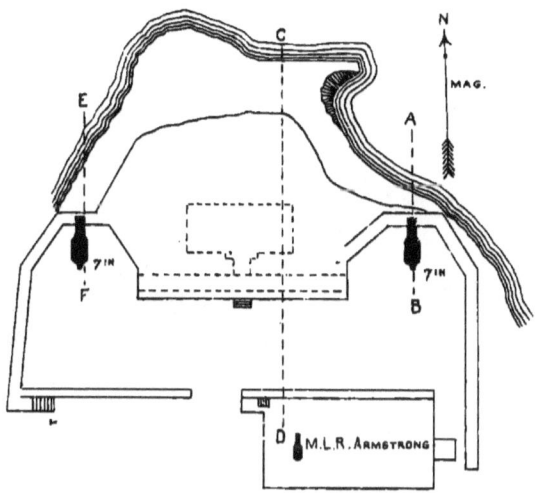

THE HOSPITAL BATTERY.

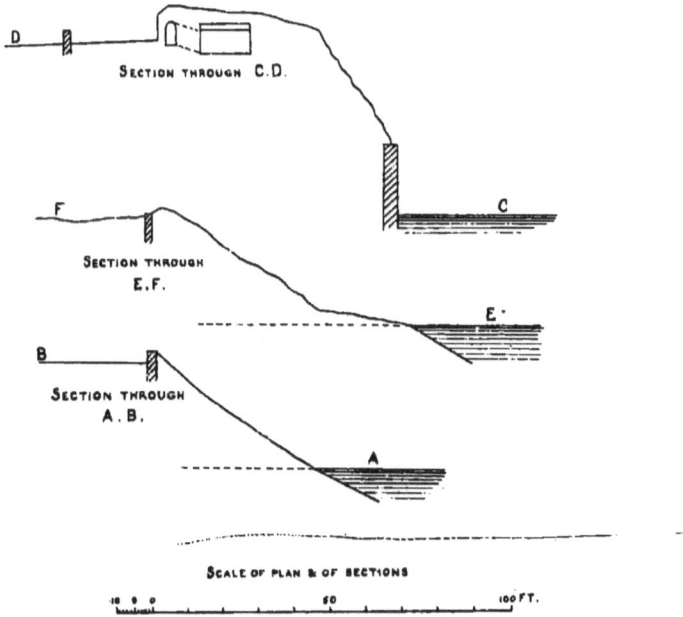

PLATE 23.

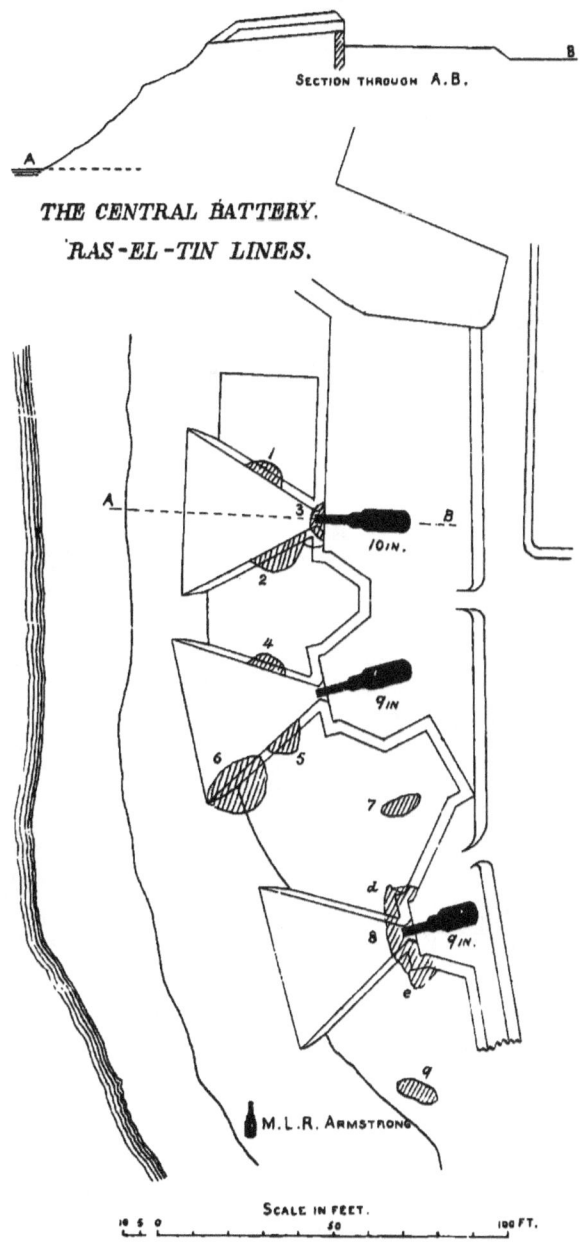

PLATE 24.

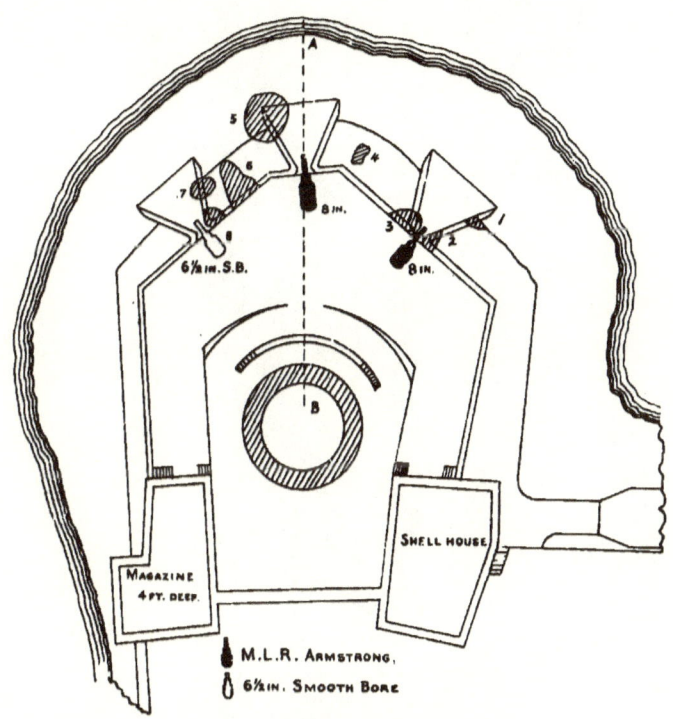

THE TOWER BATTERY.
RAS-EL-TIN LINES.

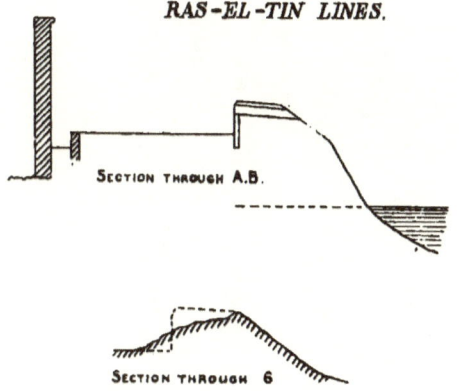

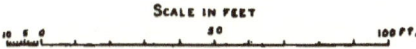

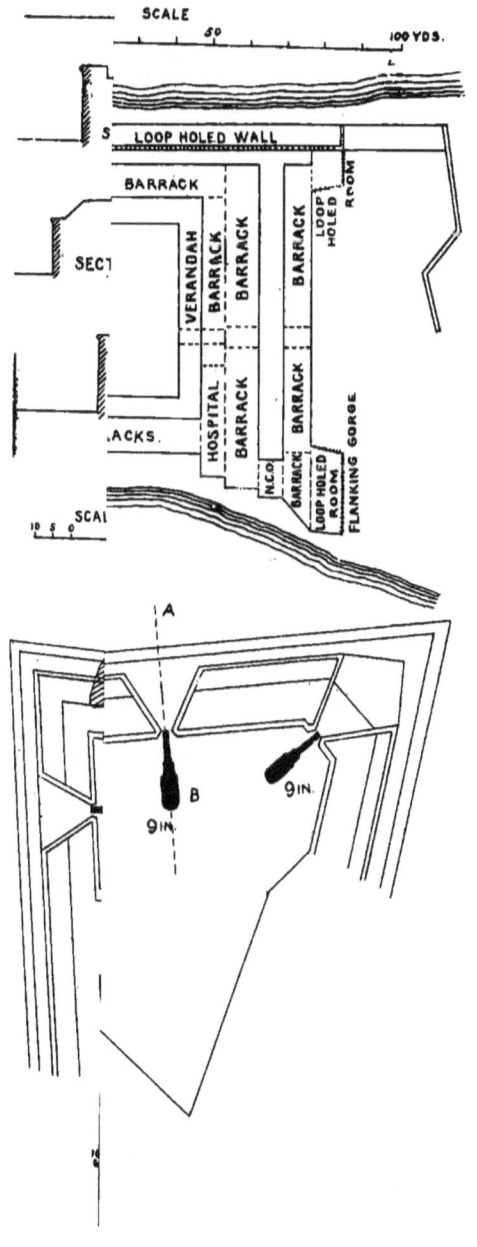

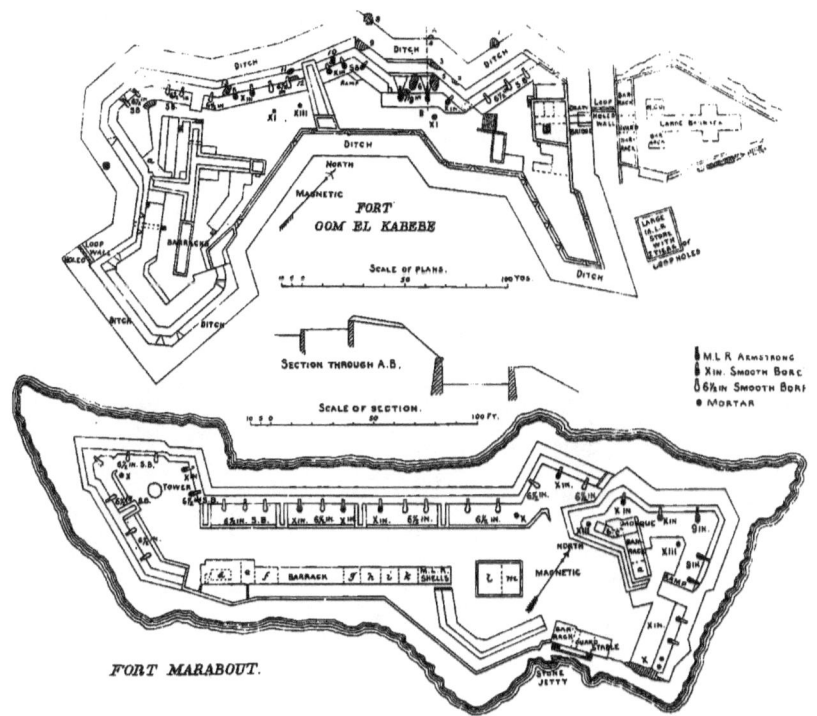

PLATE 26.

INTERIOR VIEW OF NORTHERN BASTION OF THE LIGHT HOUSE FORT.

PLATE 28

PLATE 29.

INTERIOR OF LIGHT HOUSE FORT.

PLATE 30.

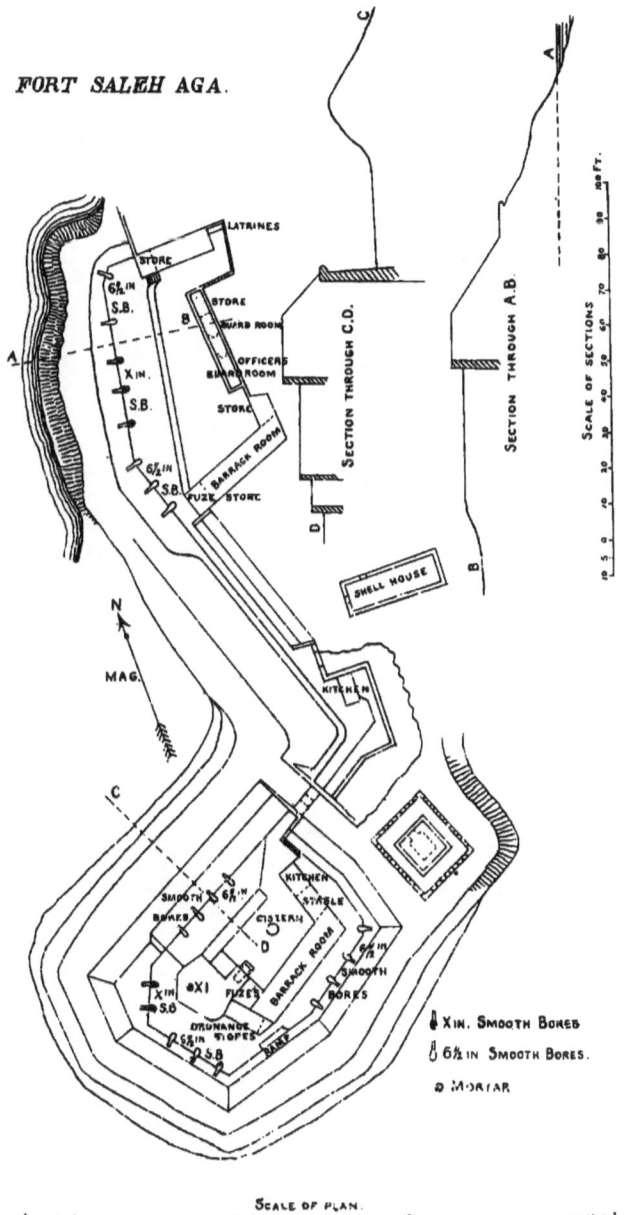

RIFLED GUN BATTERY, FORT OOM-EL-FARADJE.

DISTANT VIEW INSIDE HARBOUR OF BATUM. THE WHITE BUILDING ON THE LEFT IS THE KASTETIN PALACE.

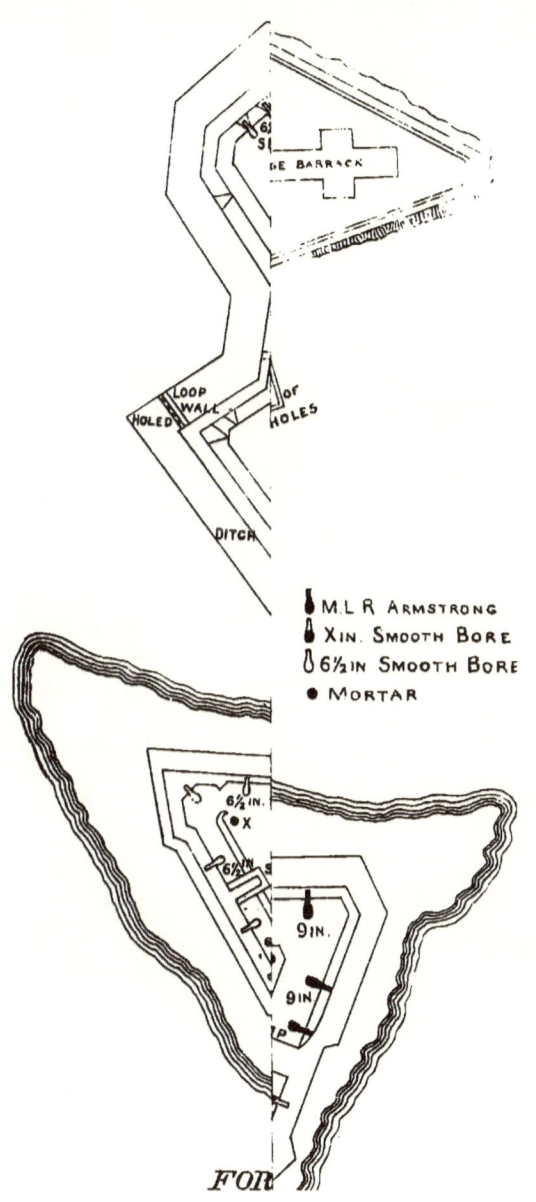

PLATE 36.

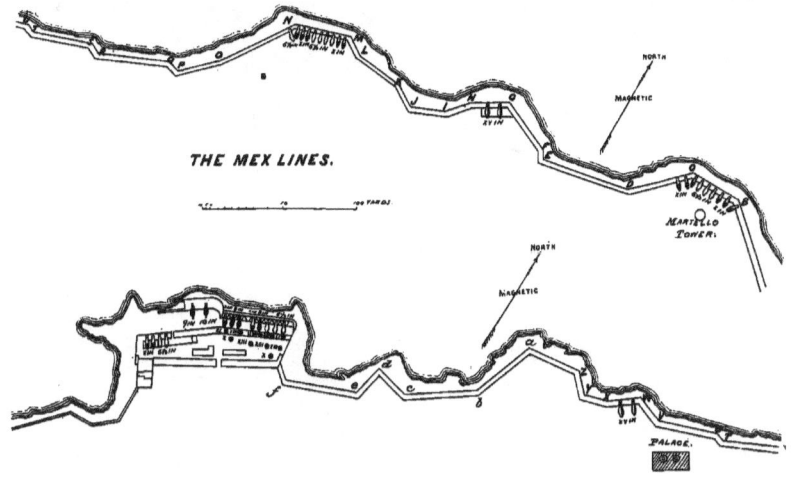

THE MEX LINES.

PLATE 33

INTERIOR OF OOM-EL-KABEBE, LOOKING WEST.

PLATE 34.

WESTERN COURT OF OOM-EL-KABEBE.
IN THE FOREGROUND IS THE BREECH PORTION OF A G 1·2 IN. S. B.

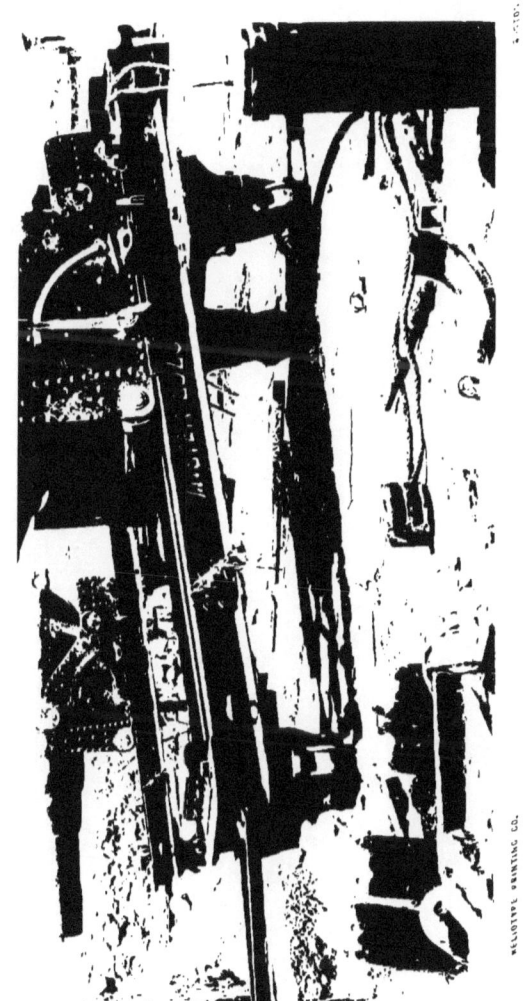

THE RIFLED GUNS IN OOM-EL-KABEBE.

PLATE 36.

NORTH

MAGNETIC

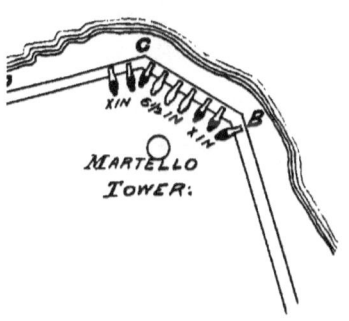

MARTELLO TOWER.

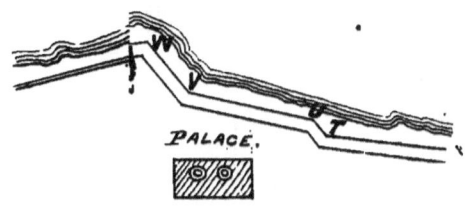

PALACE.

Armstrong.
Smooth Bore.
Smooth Bore.
Smooth Bore.
9R.

THE POSITION AND DEFENSIVE WORKS AT

RAMLEH.

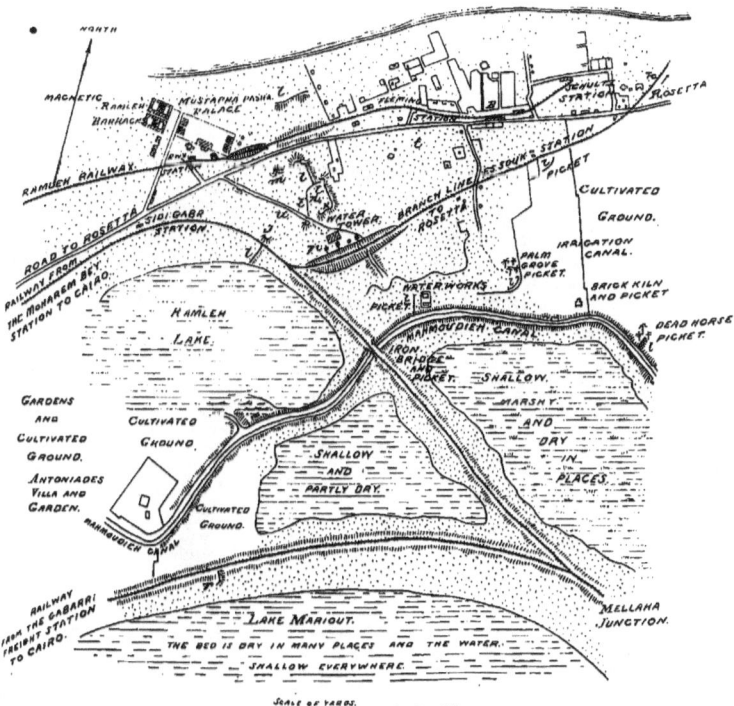

PLATE 37.

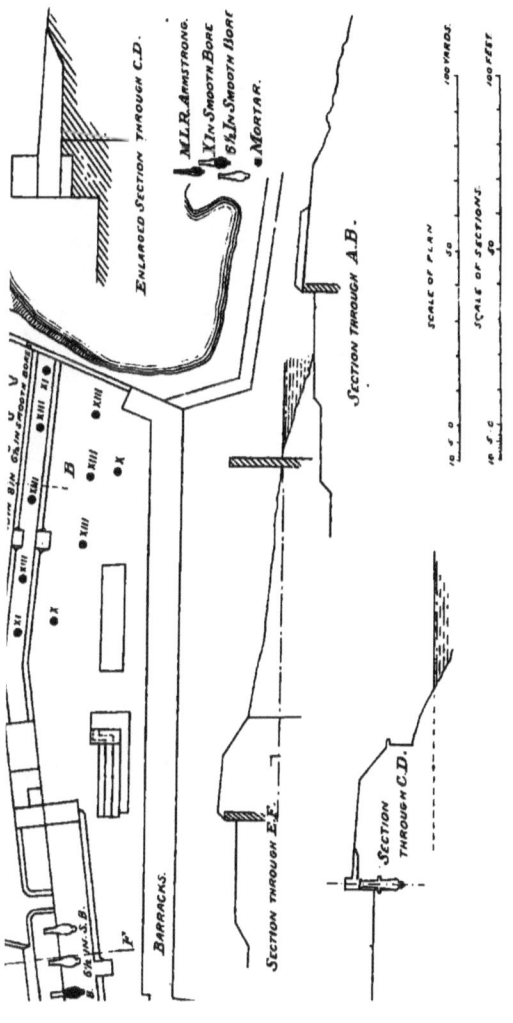

PLATE 88.

WESTERN LOWER BATTERY OF FORT MEX.
THE GUNS WERE WRECKED WITH GUN COTTON.

INTERIOR OF FORT MEX, LOOKING WEST.

PLATE 40.

INTERIOR OF FORT MEX LOOKING EAST.

PLATE 41.

EASTERN BATTERY OF MEX. LOOKING WEST

FORT NEX. 9 IN. M. L. R. WRECKED BY GUN COTTON

PLATE 13

INTERIOR OF WESTERN LOWER BATTERY OF MEN

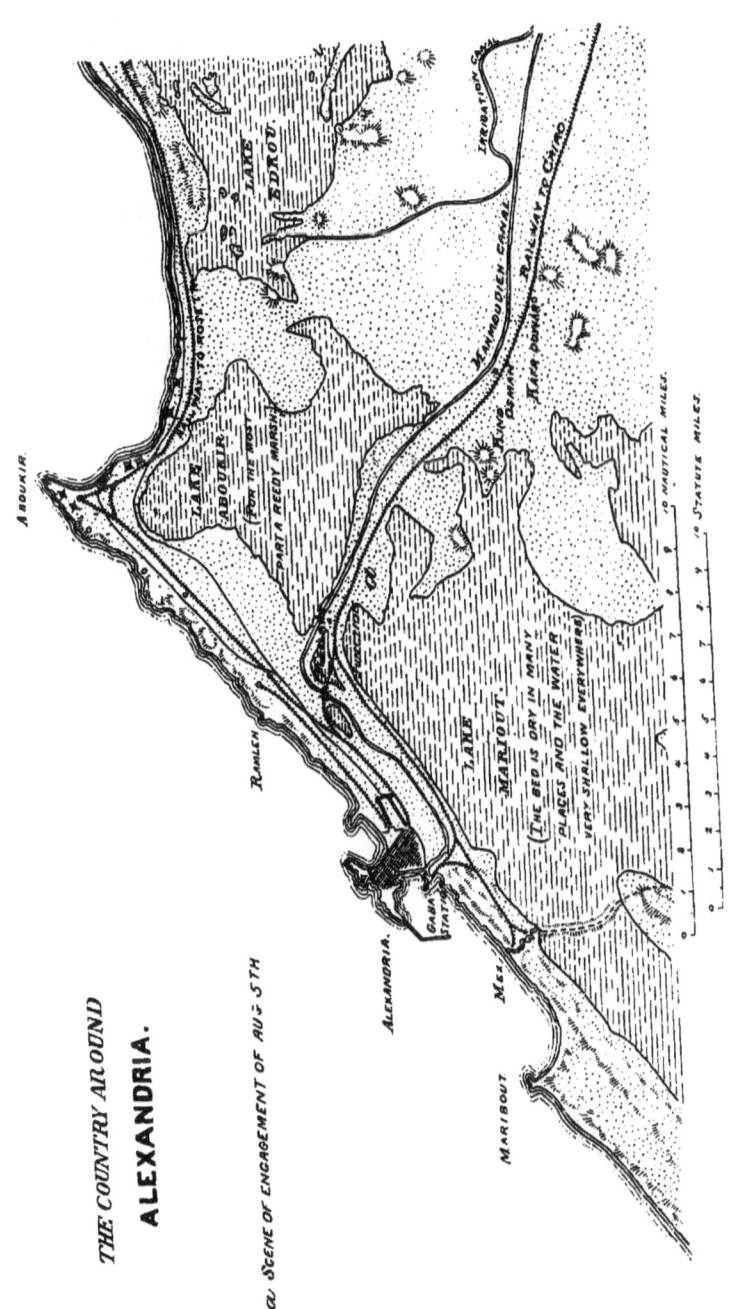

MAGN*E*

RAMLEH

ROAD TO
RAILWAY FROM
THE MOHAREM
STATION TO C

GARDENS
AND
CULTIVATE*
GROUND.

ANTONIA
VILLA AN*
GARDEN.

RAILWAY
FROM THE GABA*
FREIGHT STATI*
TO CAIRO.

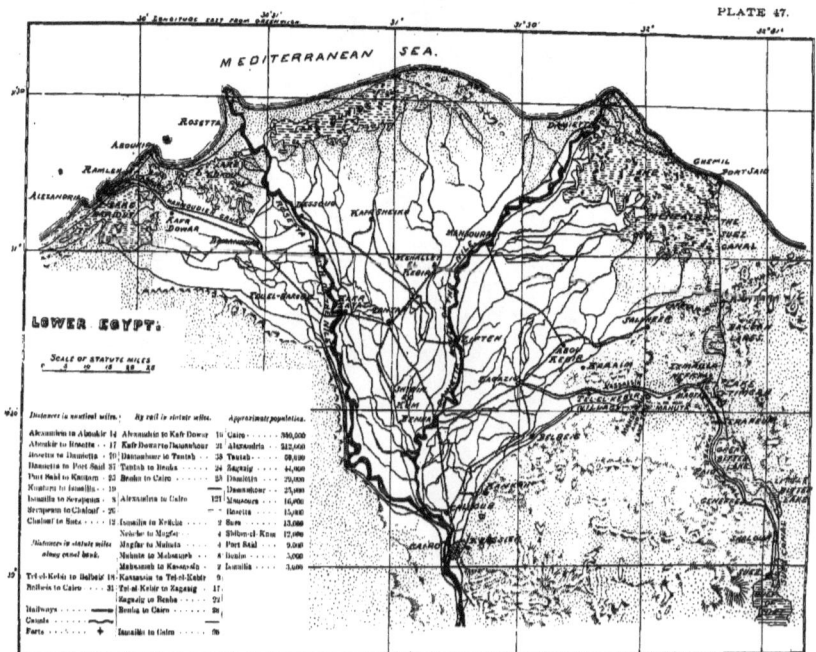

PLATE 47.

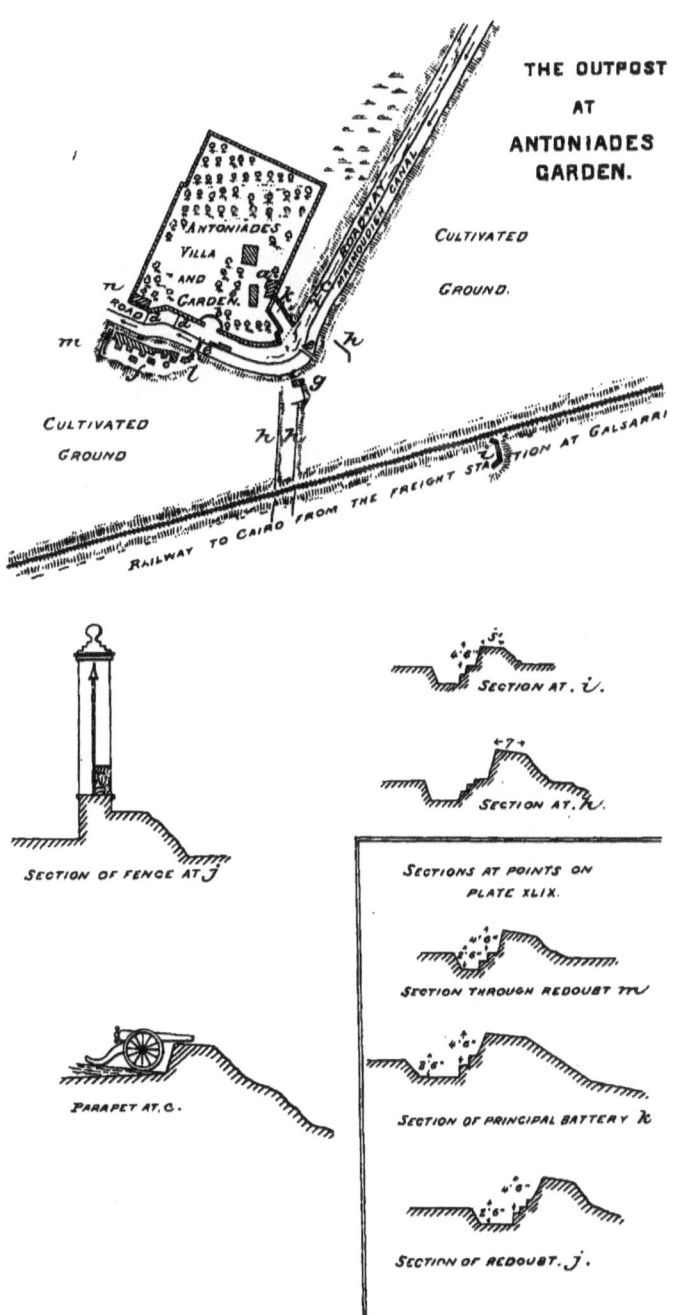

PLATE 47.

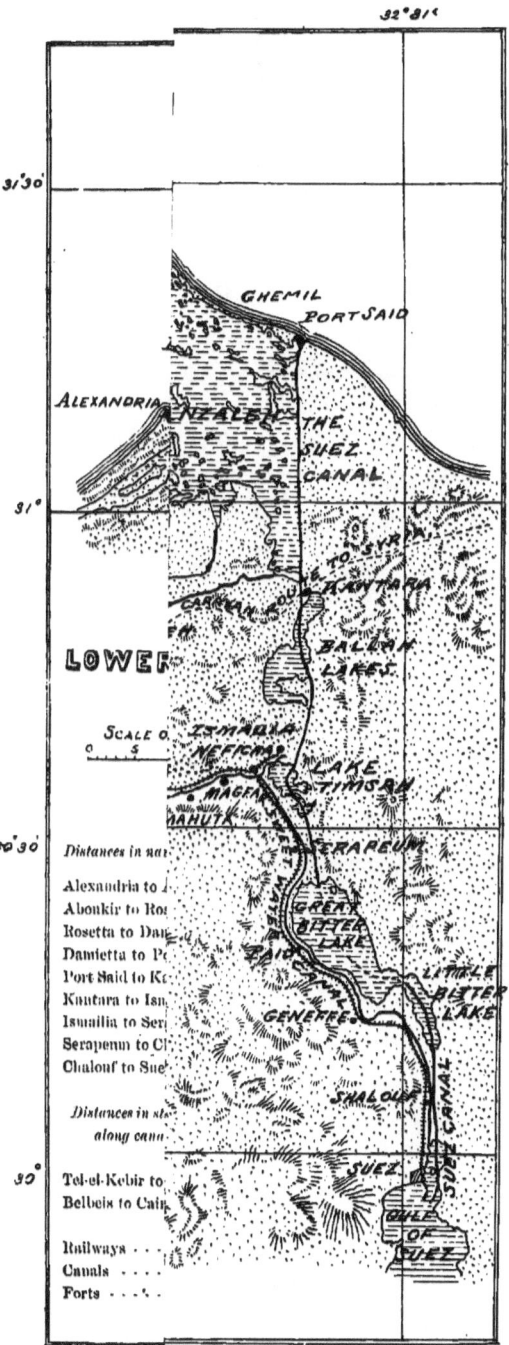

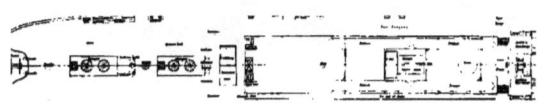

PLATE 48.

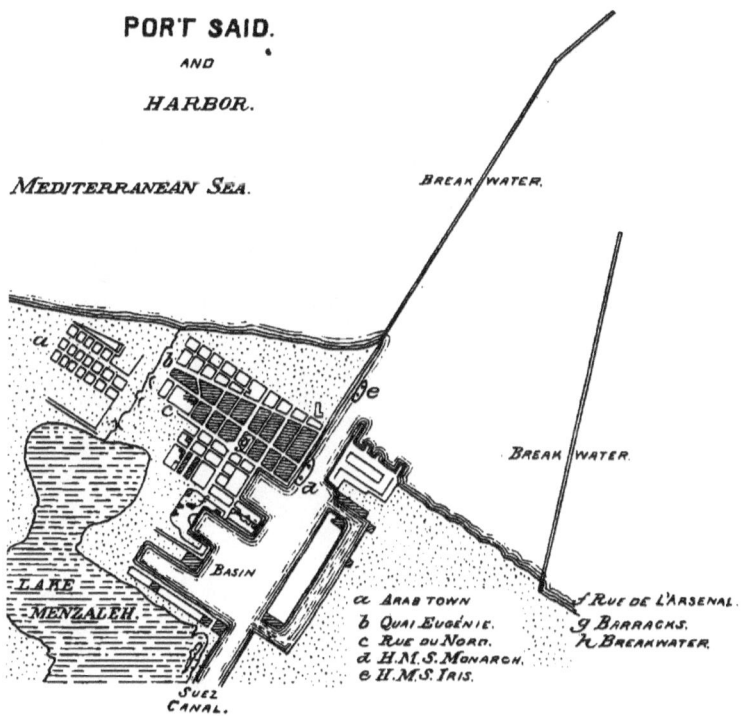

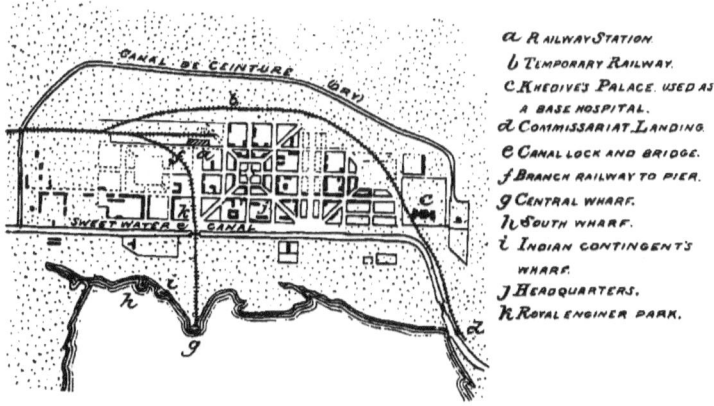

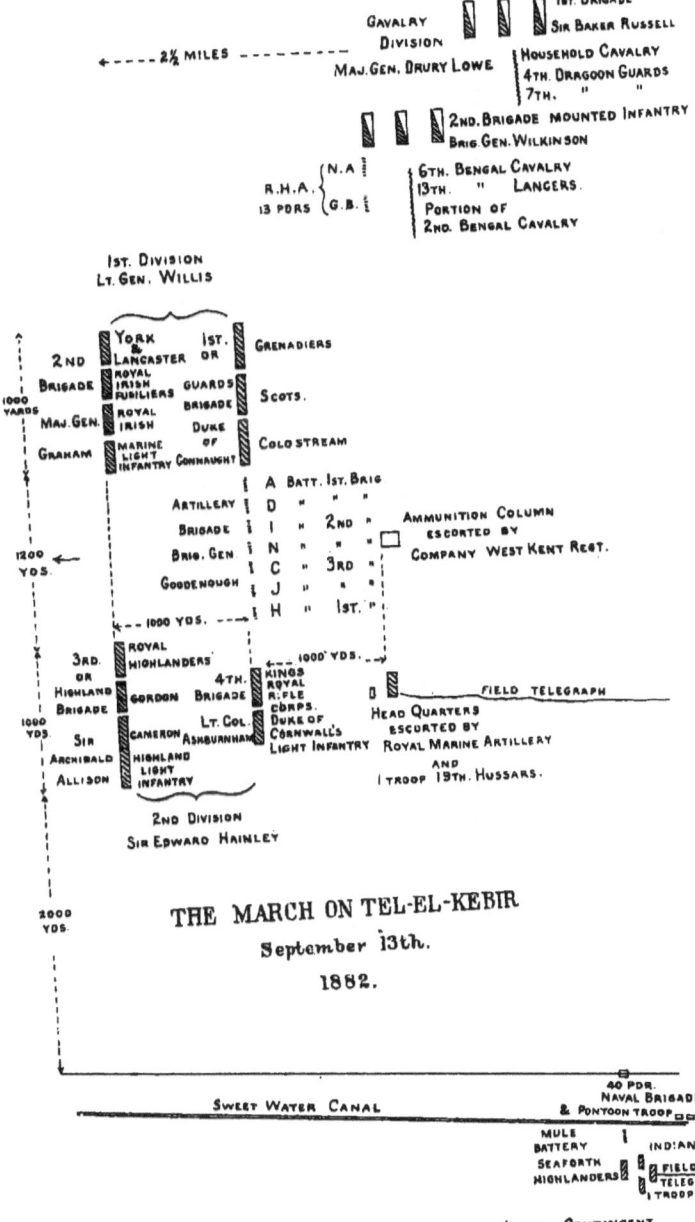

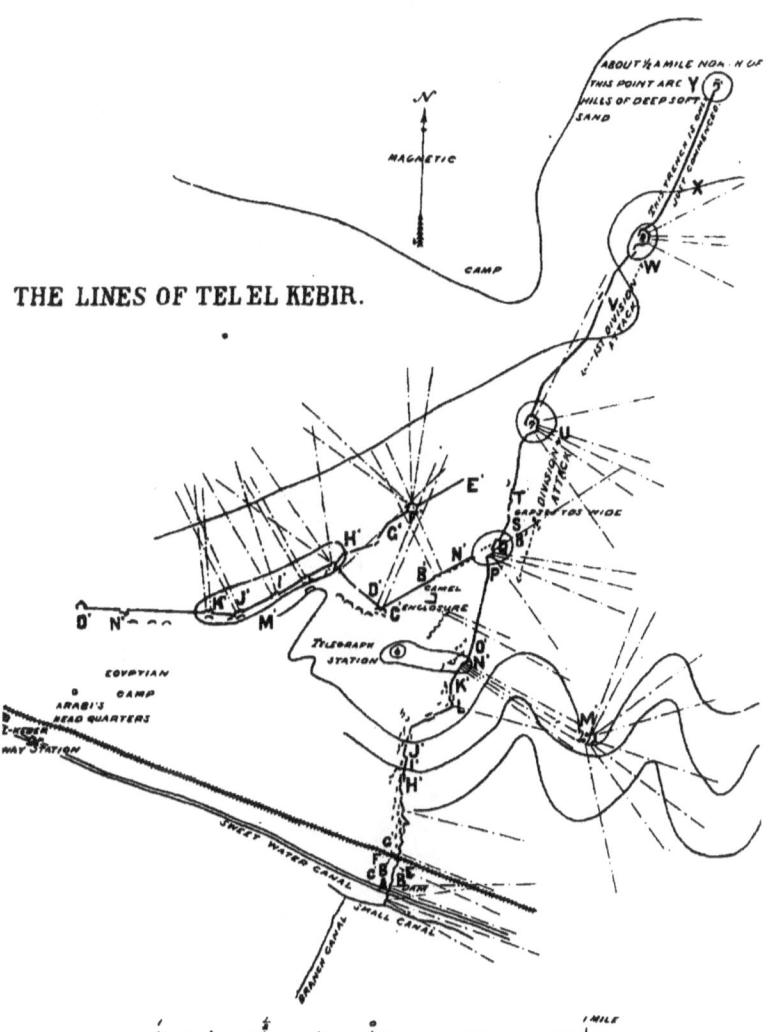

PLATE 51.

PLATE 52.

INTERIOR OF REDOUBT IN TEL-EL-KEBIR LINES.

IN THE TRENCHES AT TEL-EL-KEBIR

PLATE 54.

TEL-EL-KEBIR. THE REDOUBTS ON THE CANAL BANKS.

PLATE 55.

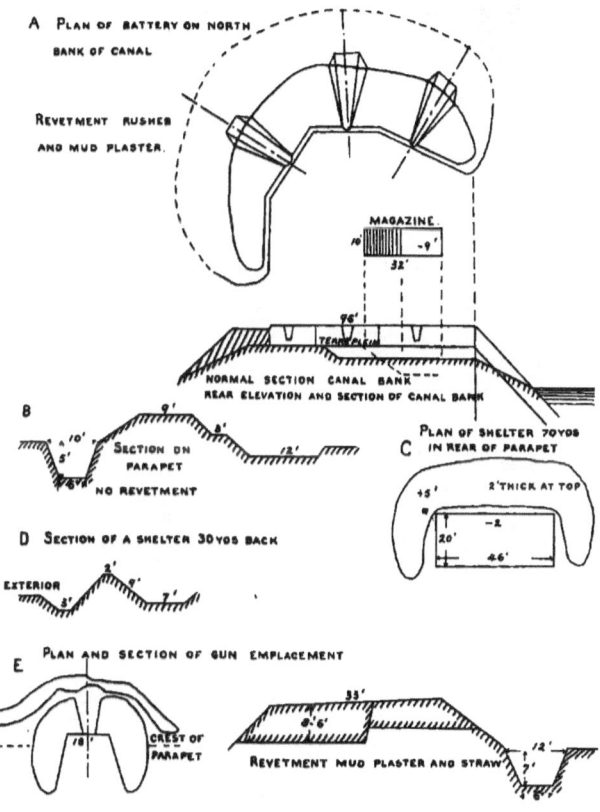

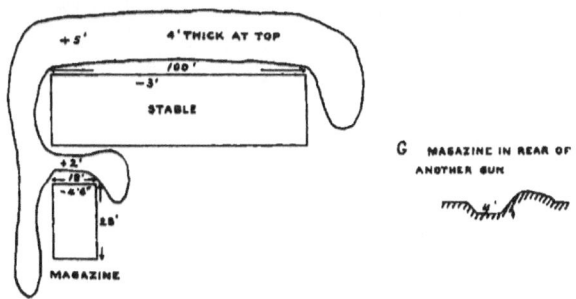

PLATE 56.

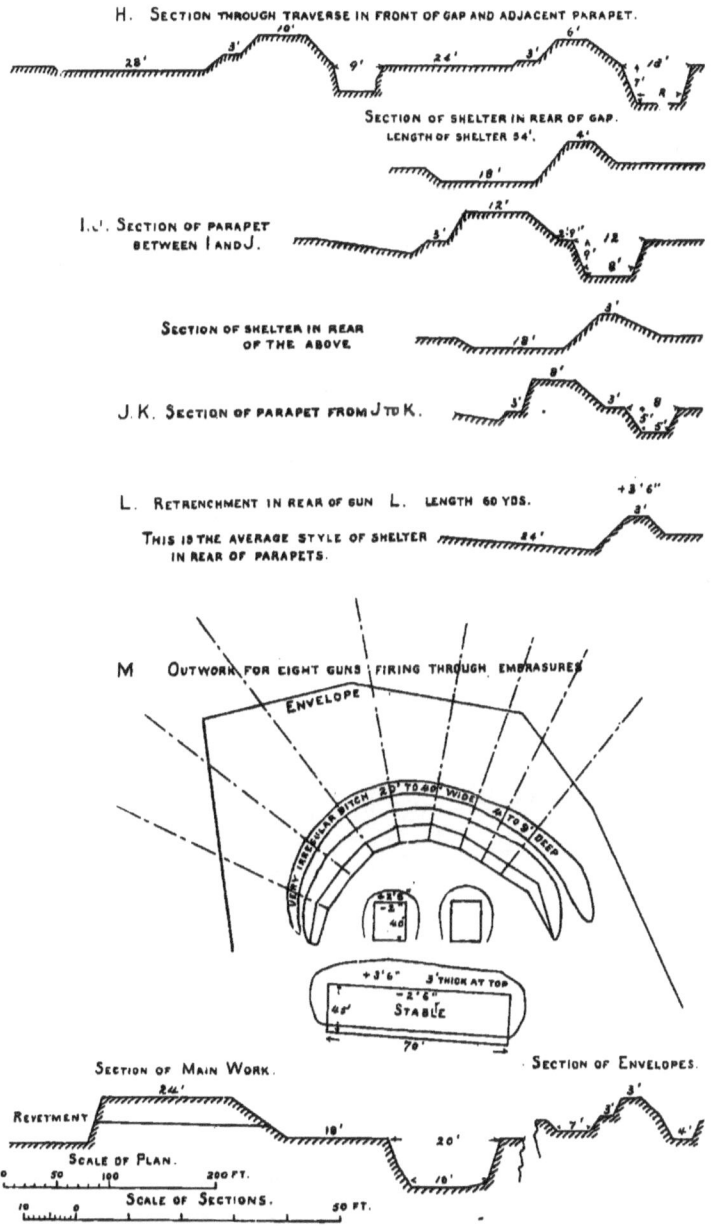

PLATE 57.

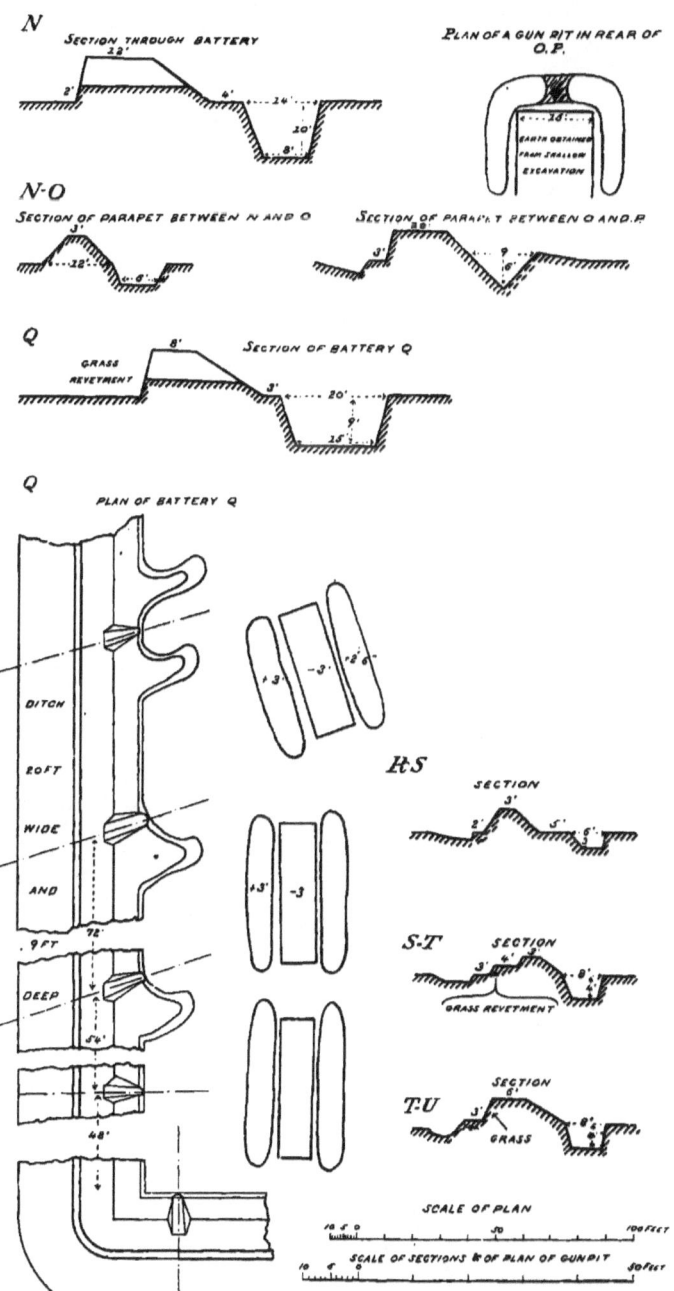

PLATE 58.

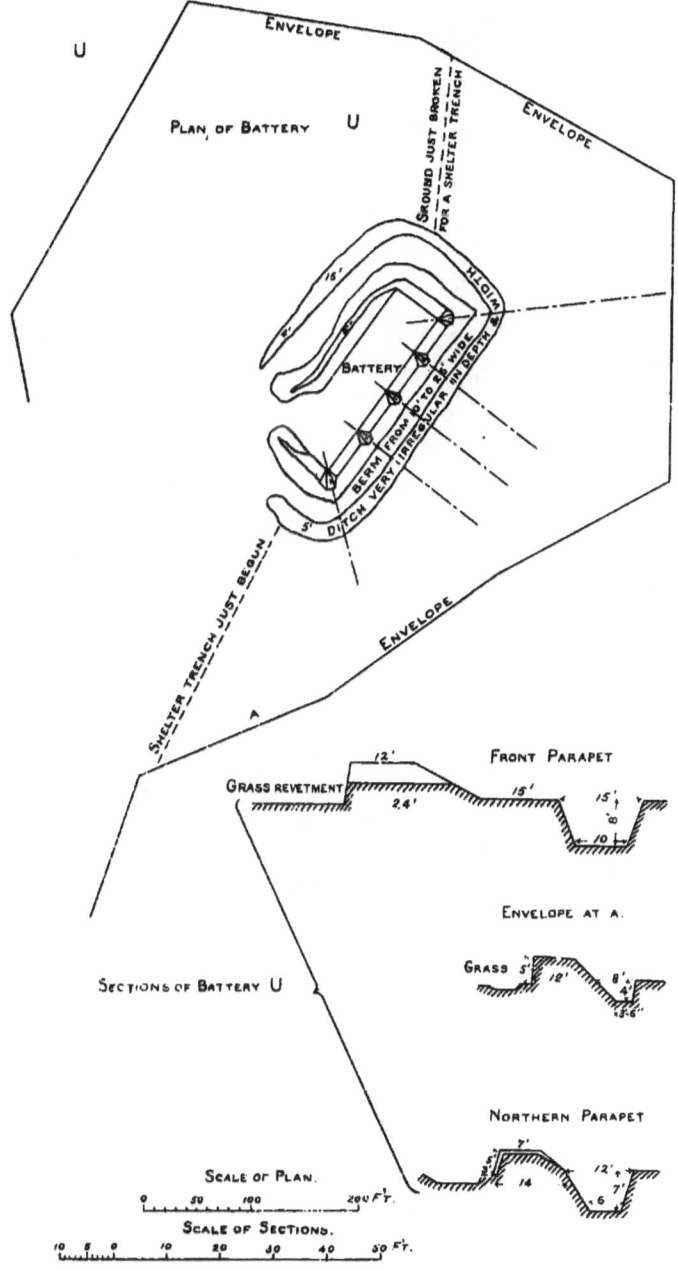

PLATE 59.

V Section at V. Scale 1/240

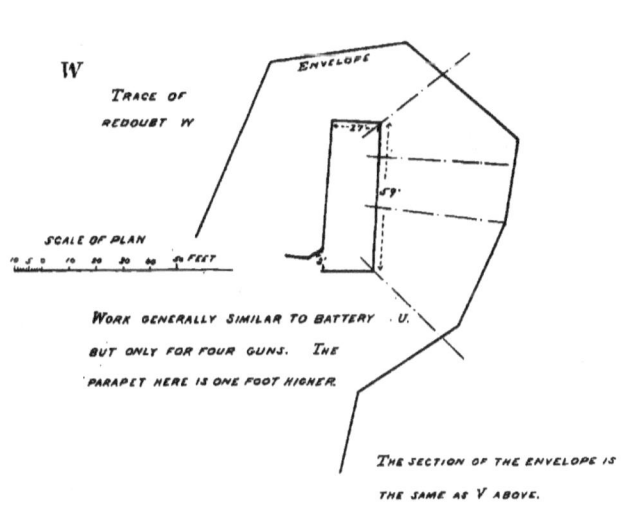

W Trace of Redoubt W

Scale of Plan

Work generally similar to battery U. but only for four guns. The parapet here is one foot higher.

The section of the envelope is the same as V above.

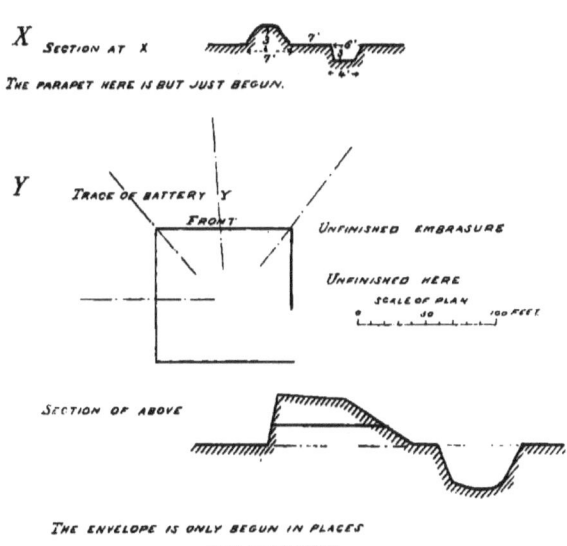

X Section at X

The parapet here is but just begun.

Y Trace of Battery Y
Front
Unfinished embrasure
Unfinished here
Scale of Plan

Section of above

The envelope is only begun in places.
Scale of Sections

PLATE 60.

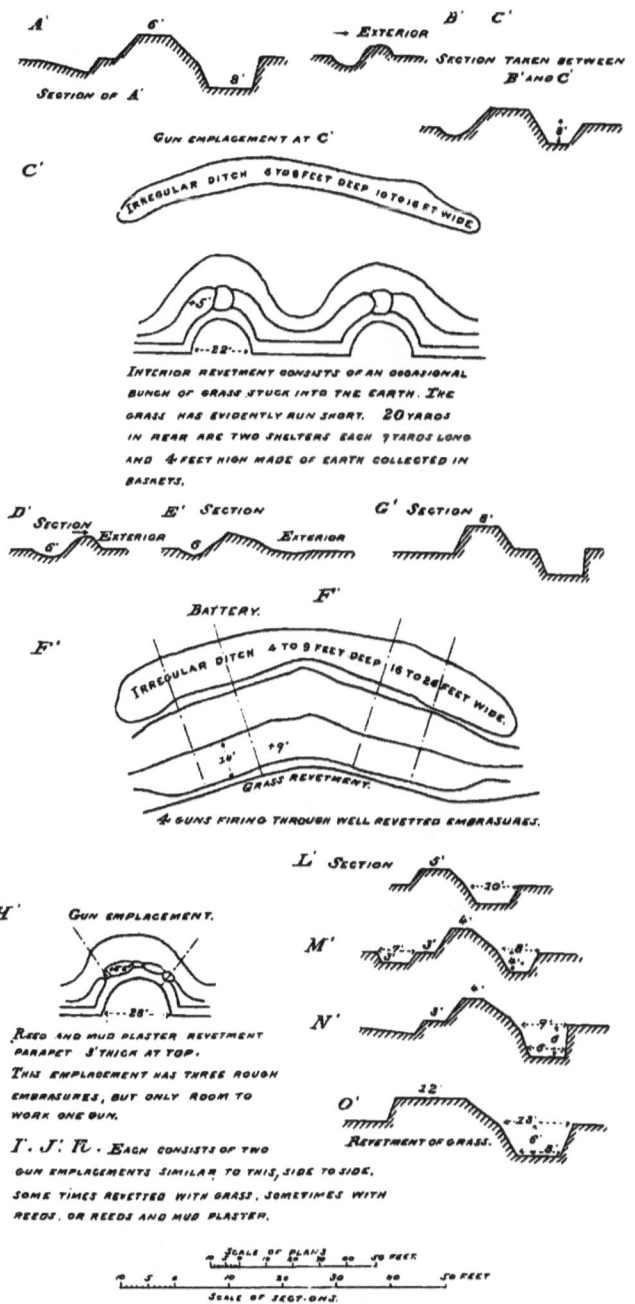

www.ingramcontent.com/pod-product-compliance
Lightning Source LLC
Chambersburg PA
CBHW051854300426
44117CB00006B/396